Complete
Hairdressing
Science

O.F.G. KILGOUR BSc, MIBiol, MSCS

AND

MARGUERITE McGARRY BSc

Complete Hairdressing Science

Heinemann: London

William Heinemann Ltd
10 Upper Grosvenor Street, London W1X 9PA

LONDON   MELBOURNE
JOHANNESBURG   AUCKLAND

First published 1984
Reprinted 1986

ISBN 0 434 91058 9

Printed in Great Britain by Billings, Worcester

To my wife Barbara for her continual encouragement over all the years this book has been in publication.

O.F.G.K.

I wish to dedicate my section of the book to the memory of my parents to whom I owe so much.

M.M.

Contents

Acknowledgements   xi

Section 1   The Salon and Services   1

1   Salon Premises   3
    1.1   Salon structure   3
    1.2   Protection   4
    1.3   Science   5
    1.4   Chemistry   5
    1.5   Physics   6
    1.6   Questions   7
    1.7   Multiple choice questions   8

2   Salon Water   9
    2.1   Water cycle   9
    2.2   Water sources   9
    2.3   Water treatment   10
    2.4   Salon cold water system   10
    2.5   Protection   11
    2.6   Water usage   11
    2.7   Physics   11
    2.8   Chemistry   14
    2.9   Questions   16
    2.10 Multiple choice questions   16

3   Salon Energy   17
    3.1   Energy   17
    3.2   Solar energy   17
    3.3   Human body energy   18
    3.4   Salon fuels   18
    3.5   Salon gas system   18
    3.6   Releasing chemical energy   20
    3.7   Chemistry   20
    3.8   Physics   23
    3.9   Questions   23
    3.10 Multiple choice questions   24

4   Salon Electricity   25
    4.1   Sources   25
    4.2   Electrical terms   26
    4.3   Distribution of electricity   27
    4.4   The salon electrical installation   27
    4.5   Electrical power and cost   28
    4.6   Salon circuits   29
    4.7   Circuit safety   30
    4.8   Electrical switches   33
    4.9   Physics   33
    4.10 Chemistry   33
    4.11 Questions   34
    4.12 Multiple choice questions   35

5   Salon Heating   36
     5.1   Heat sources in the salon   36
     5.2   Salon heating requirements   36
     5.3   Salon heat transfer   37
     5.4   Salon direct heaters   37
     5.5   Central heating   38
     5.6   Salon heating controls   40
     5.7   Salon heat insulation   40
     5.8   Salon sound insulation   41
     5.9   Physics   41
     5.10 Questions   44
     5.11 Multiple choice questions   44

6   Salon Environment   46
     6.1   Salon conditions   46
     6.2   Air condition: purity   47
     6.3   Air condition: warmth   48
     6.4   Air condition: water or humidity   48
     6.5   Air condition: movement of air   50
     6.6   Fire causes   51
     6.7   Salon lighting   53
     6.8   Chemistry   56
     6.9   Physics   58
     6.10 Questions   59
     6.11 Multiple choice questions   60

7   Salon Cleaning   61
     7.1   Need for salon cleaning   61
     7.2   Nature of salon soils   61
     7.3   Salon water hardness   62
     7.4   Salon hot water   64
     7.5   Salon cleaning materials   66
     7.6   Salon surface cleaning   69
     7.7   Salon cleaning methods and
           equipment   69
     7.8   Salon waste disposal   70
     7.9   Physics   71
     7.10 Chemistry   71
     7.11 Questions   73
     7.12 Multiple choice questions   73

Section Two   Hairdressing Processes

8   Hair Removal   77
     8.1   Equipment   77
     8.2   Electrical epilation   78
     8.3   Chemical preparations   79

     8.4   Physics   80
     8.5   Chemistry   84
     8.6   Chemical composition of hair   85
     8.7   Questions   88
     8.8   Multiple choice questions   88

9   Hair Cleaning   89
     9.1   Nature of soils   89
     9.2   Cleaning equipment   90
     9.3   Hair cleaning preparations   90
     9.4   Hair washing preparations (or
           shampoos)   91
     9.5   Hair rinsing preparations   93
     9.6   Hair condition   95
     9.7   Physics   95
     9.8   Chemistry   97
     9.9   Questions   100
     9.10 Multiple choice questions   100

10   Hair Setting   102
     10.1   Natural hair form   102
     10.2   Keratin macromolecule bonds   102
     10.3   Setting terms   103
     10.4   Cohesive hair set   104
     10.5   Temporary hair set   105
     10.6   Hot permanent hair set   106
     10.7   Cold permanent hair set   108
     10.8   Physics   111
     10.9   Chemistry   112
     10.10 Questions   114
     10.11 Multiple choice questions   114

11   Hair Colouring   115
     11.1   Natural hair colour   115
     11.2   Chemistry of hydrogen
            peroxide   116
     11.3   Hair bleaching preparations   119
     11.4   Pigments and dyes   121
     11.5   Pigments   121
     11.6   Hair dyes   122
     11.7   Physics   124
     11.8   Chemistry   127
     11.9   Questions   128
     11.10 Multiple choice questions   129

12   Hair Drying and Dressing   130
     12.1   Conditions needed for drying   130
     12.2   Hair-drying equipment   131

12.3   Salon socket outlets   133
12.4   Appliance plugs   133
12.5   Appliances flexes   134
12.6   Earthing of a salon appliance 135
12.7   Electric shock   137
12.8   Summary of electrical
       precautions   137
12.9   Dressing preparations   137
12.10 Chemistry   139
12.11 Physics   139
12.12 Questions   141
12.13 Multiple choice questions   141

13 Treatments   143
    13.1   Radiant energy   143
    13.2   Infra-red ray treatments 143
    13.3   Ultra-violet treatment   146
    13.4   Massage treatment   148
    13.5   High frequency treatment 149
    13.6   Steam vapour and ozone
           treatment   151
    13.7   Vacuum treatment   151
    13.8   Faradic treatment   152
    13.9   Galvanic treatment   152
    13.10 Nail manicure preparations 152
    13.11 Chemistry   154
    13.12 Perfumes   155
    13.13 Questions   158
    13.14 Multiple choice questions 158

Section Three   The Hair, Head and Body

Introduction   159

14 The Head   161
    14.1   The anatomy of the head   161
    14.2   Bones of the cranium   161
    14.3   Bones of the face   162
    14.4   Muscles of the head and face 162
    14.5   Muscles of the neck   163
    14.6   Nerves of the face   163
    14.7   The blood vessels of the head
           and face   164
    14.8   Questions   165
    14.9   Multiple choice questions 165

15 The Digestive System and Nutrition 166
    15.1   Introduction: body organization 166

15.2   Food   167
15.3   Classes of food nutrients   167
15.4   Digestion   169
15.5   Enzymes   170
15.6   Absorption   171
15.7   Defaecation   172
15.8   Importance of a balanced diet 172
15.9   The excretory system   172
15.10 Excretory organs   172
15.11 Questions   174
15.12 Multiple choice questions   174

16 The Respiratory System and Energy 175
    16.1   Respiration   175
    16.2   Breathing organs and respiratory
           passages   175
    16.3   Mechanism of breathing   176
    16.4   Control of breathing   177
    16.5   External and internal
           respiration   177
    16.6   The circulatory system, blood
           and transport   178
    16.7   Blood groups   179
    16.8   Blood diseases   180
    16.9   The heart   181
    16.10 Circulation   182
    16.11 Blood vessels   182
    16.12 The lymphatic system   183
    16.13 Questions   184
    16.14 Multiple choice questions 184

17 Body Control   185
    17.1   Introduction   185
    17.2   The nervous system and
           movement   185
    17.3   Nervous tissue   185
    17.4   The central nervous system 186
    17.5   The peripheral nervous system 186
    17.6   Reflex action   188
    17.7   The automatic nervous system 189
    17.8   The endocrine system and
           behaviour   189
    17.9   The reproductive system   189
    17.10 Questions   191
    17.11 Multiple choice questions 191

18 The Skin and Hair   192
    18.1 Nourishment of the skin   192
    18.2 Skin structure   192
    18.3 Hair growth cycle   194
    18.4 Factors affecting hair growth and
          health   194
    18.5 Temperature control by the
          skin   195
    18.6 Questions   196
    18.7 Multiple choice questions   197

**Section Four   Diseases, Hygiene, First Aid
                  and Safety**

19 Disorders of the Skin and Hair   201
    19.1 Pathogens and non-pathogens   201
    19.2 Recognition of skin disorders   203
    19.3 Fungal infections   203
    19.4 Bacterial infections   203
    19.5 Viral infections   204
    19.6 Parasitic infestations   204
    19.7 Systematic and glandular
          disorders — non-infectious   205
    19.8 Hereditary conditions   206
    19.9 Disorders caused by contact
          with irritant substances   206
    19.10 Disorders due to harsh
          treatment   206
    19.11 Effects of the weather   206
    19.12 Ageing of the skin   207
    19.13 Questions   207
    19.14 Multiple choice questions   207

20 Personal Hygiene   209
    20.1 Care of skin — hair   209
    20.2 Care of hands and finger nails   210

20.3 Care of the feet   210
20.4 Balanced diet   211
20.5 Care of mouth and teeth   211
20.6 Suitable clothing   212
20.7 Mental health   213
20.8 Smoking   213
20.9 Drinking   213
20.10 Posture and deportment   214
20.11 The skeletal system   214
20.12 The muscular system   216
20.13 Physical fitness and the benefits
      of exercise   218
20.14 Questions   218
20.15 Multiple choice questions   218

21 Salon Hygiene   219
    21.1 Sterilization   219
    21.2 Salon surfaces and dust   221
    21.3 Tools and equipment   221
    21.4 Washbasins, drains and traps   222
    21.5 Ventilation and heating in
          the salon   222
    21.6 Questions   223
    21.7 Multiple choice questions   223

22 Safety in the Salon   225
    22.1 Health and Safety at Work Act
          1974   225
    22.2 First aid   226
    22.3 First-aid kit in the salon   229
    22.4 Accident prevention   229
    22.5 Fire precautions   230
    22.6 Questions   231
    22.7 Multiple choice questions   231

Indices   233

Acknowledgements

It is my pleasure to express sincere thanks to Mrs V.C.Stirling for her faultless work in preparing the typescript, and also to former colleagues and friends who gave kind help in the earlier editions.

I wish to record my appreciation to individuals and organizations, particularly to Dr M.L.Ryder. A.R.C.Animal Breeding Research Organisation, and the Unilever Research Lab-

I express my sincere gratitude to the staff of William Heinemann for help, guidance and continued confidence in the success of this completely revised edition.

My thanks to Dr E.B.White, BSc, PhD for reading the revised material and offering helpful suggestions: Mrs M.Upfield, SRN, for her valuable comments and suggestions on the First Aid Section: Dr M.Wynn, MB, ChB for her help regarding diseases and their treatment: Mrs J.Foster for typing the manuscript: The Kingston-upon-Hull Fire Fighting Service for their advice on Fire Precautions.

Section One
The Salon and Services

1 Salon Premises

1.1   SALON STRUCTURE

Building materials used in salon construction are water, sand, clay, lime, wood plastics, and different *metals*, iron, copper, aluminium and chromium.

Foundations are made of concrete (cement, sand and small stones) poured into wide trenches. The broad foundations support the building and prevent it sinking into the sub-soil.

Walls separate the salon interior from the external environment, and are built of *porous* bricks or blocks of clay, stone or concrete. A *non-porous* damp-proof course (DPC) made of waterproof materials is laid over a layer of bricks near to the foundations. This prevents water, rising from the wet subsoil, reaching the upper layers of brickwork in the wall.

Outer salon walls are built with double *skins* usually with a *cavity* between the outer skin of bricks and the inner skin of building blocks. Inner surfaces are covered with wall plaster.

Doors and windows are fitted into frames, with a *lintel* beam above which supports the upper layers of walls. A groove or *throating* is found in or near the lintel of doors and windows, and also in the sloping window *sill*, to allow rainwater to fall away from the wall.

Ground floors of a modern salon are *solid* with a damp-proof course laid over concrete, and broken stone hard core layers. Tiles and floor-covering materials finish the floor surface.

Ceilings are made of plaster boards pinned to the ceiling joists.

Roofs are constructed with wooden *rafters* meeting in a *ridge* board; these frames are fixed to the outer wall tops. Roofing *felt* is fixed to the rafters by narrow *battens* on to which are hooked or nailed down the roof tiles or slates.

Suspended floors are found in upper rooms, and may be the ground floors of old buildings. They consist of *floor boards* nailed to *joists*; beneath the floor is a space through which *air* must pass freely from *ventilator bricks;* these are seen on the outer walls outside the building.

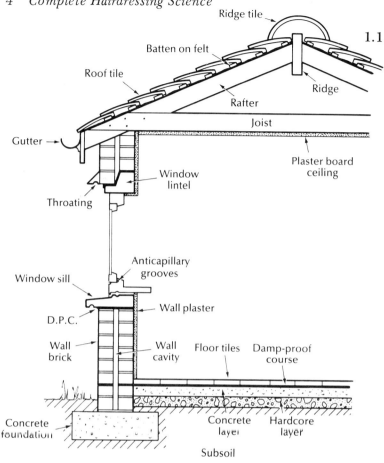

1.1   Structure of a salon building

1.2   PROTECTION

A salon provides protection from the *external environment*.

(*a*) *Shelter* from wind, rain, heat and cold. A salon should provide a pleasant, comfortable and clean environment, by having a suitable heating and ventilation system (*see* Section 6.2).

(*b*) *Damp*. The roof tiles, gutters, door and window sill, and lintel throatings lead water *away* from the building walls. Rainwater can *soak* into the wall to cause damp and coldness. Rainwater drains into the *rainwater pipes* from the roof gutters and into a *gully*, covered by a grid, and then into a *drain* or *soakaway* (*see* Figure 7.4).

The main causes of damp in a salon are the following:

1 *Penetrating damp* from damaged roof, cracked walls, blocked gutters, and rainwater pipes.
2 *Rising damp* due to a broken or faulty DPC, or soil above the DPC level.
3 *Burst* pipes or overflowing cisterns and tanks.
4 *Condensation damp* (*see* Section 6.4).

Damp can cause damage to interior decor, coldness, and affect health of salon occupants. It is also a source of danger and electric shock when using electrical appliances in damp areas.

(*c*) *Accidents* may occur in a salon through tripping, or slipping on stairways and floor surfaces.

(*d*) *Salon maintenance* is necessary to protect the building from timber rot, and metal corrosion, by frequent painting and damp prevention by efficient ventilation (Section 6.5).

(*e*) *Salon security*, against break-ins by thieves is achieved by fitting security locks, bolts, chains and alarm systems. *Insurance* companies will provide *cover* for damage to salon premises arising from *certain* causes, for example *storm* causing roof damage, and the bursting of water pipes.

1.3 SCIENCE

Matter is anything that occupies space and has mass or weight. Everything in the salon is matter which can be found in one of three different *physical states*.

Solid matter has a definite shape, for example a building brick or human hair. *Liquid* matter takes on the shape of the container, for example water or perming lotion. *Gaseous* matter can fill a container of any size, for example, air or mains natural gas.

1.4 CHEMISTRY

Chemistry is the science or knowledge concerning the *composition* of matter. All substances found in the salon and human body are either chemical *elements* or chemical *compounds*, as pure *single* substances or *mixtures*.

Chemical elements are the simplest forms of matter which cannot be split into simpler substances by chemical means. There are approximately 100 different chemical elements on earth. Some elements are *metals* which are mainly solids (exception, mercury) and are good conductors of heat and electricity in addition they have a metallic *lustre*. Other elements are *non-metals* in the form of solid (sulphur), gas (oxygen) or liquid (bromine).

Symbols are used to represent one *atom* (*see* Section 4.9) of an element; this is either one or two letters, the first letter is always a capital and the second letter is a small letter.

Chemical compounds are substances formed

Metals		Non-metals	
Name	Chemical Symbols	Name	Chemical Symbols
Aluminium	Al	Boron	B
Antimony	Sb	Bromine	Br
Calcium	Ca	Carbon	C
Copper	Cu	Chlorine	Cl
Iron	Fe	Fluorine	F
Lead	Pb	Hydrogen	H
Magnesium	Mg	Iodine	I
Mercury	Hg	Neon	Ne
Potassium	K	Nitrogen	N
Selenium	Se	Oxygen	O
Silver	Ag	Phosphorus	P
Sodium	Na	Silicon	Si
Tin	Sn	Sulphur	S

Table 1.1   List of chemical elements

by the chemical union of two or more different chemical elements. For example, water is a chemical compound, composed of hydrogen and oxygen *combined* together chemically. Water, like most chemical compounds, does not resemble the elements from which it is made.

There are more than a *million*, or 1 000 000, *different* chemical compounds; up to 100 different chemical compounds are encountered in hairdressing *preparations*.

Organic and inorganic chemical compounds

All chemical compounds are either *organic* or *inorganic* compounds.

Organic compounds are the compounds which contain *carbon*, and come from living things, for example, sugars from green plants, and edible oils from peanuts and whales.

Inorganic compounds originate from non-living materials, such as rocks and minerals, for example, iron compounds in iron ore, silicon compounds in sand.

Table 1.2 summarizes important differences between organic and inorganic compounds.

	Organic Chemical Compounds	*Inorganic Chemical Compounds*
Examples	Coconut oil, citric acid, paraffin wax.	Sodium chloride (salt), magnesium carbonate, zinc oxide.
Sources	Plants and animals	Rocks, minerals and ores.
Composition	Always contain CARBON.	Carbon only present in *carbonates* and a few other compounds.
Effect of heat	Melt easily and can *char* or blacken showing presence of carbon.	Melt with difficulty at high temperatures. Do not char.
Chemical names	End mainly in: —ANE, —ENE, —OL, —ONE, —IC, —OIC, —OATE.	End mainly in: —IDE, —ATE or ITE. Can have prefix PER— and THIO—.

Table 1.2   Summary of differences between organic and inorganic chemical compounds

Synthesis is the chemical process of formation of chemical compounds from chemical elements or simpler chemical compounds. Most chemical compounds in hairdressing preparations are made synthetically.

Analysis is the chemical process of breaking down a chemical compound into its component *elements*. Human hair is a complex chemical compound having the following analysis: carbon, 50%; oxygen, 20%; sulphur, 5%; nitrogen, 18%; hydrogen, 7%; all these elements are combined together *chemically*.

Mixtures can consist of two or more substances of elements or compounds, present in *differing* amounts, and can be separated by simple physical methods. Most hairdressing and cosmetic *preparations* are mixtures of two or more compounds.

Chemists separate mixtures or purify substances by the processes of *filtration* (Section 2.8) and *distillation* (Sections 2.7 and 13.12).

Formula

The smallest part of a compound or element that can exist on its own is called a *molecule*. For example, the oxygen molecule is composed of two oxygen atoms, the water molecule of two hydrogen and one oxygen atoms. The composition of molecules of different substances can be shown by a *formula*: the formula for oxygen is O_2, and water has the formula H_2O.

Some organic compounds, including human hair, have very large molecules composed of hundreds of atoms, and are called *macromolecules*.

1.5   PHYSICS

Physics is the science or knowledge concerning the behaviour of matter and *energy*.

Measurements

Physics is very much concerned with *measurement* of matter and energy.

Length. The unit of length is the *metre*, various multiples and submultiples are used, each of which has a separate symbol.

```
1 kilometre(km)   = 1000 metres
1 metre(m)        =  100 centimetres
1 centimetre(cm)  =   10 millimetres(mm)
1 millimetre(mm)  = 1000 micrometres(μm)
```

Rulers marked in centimetres and millimetres give measurement of length to the nearest millimetre.

Calipers are used when rulers cannot be used, and are accurate to the nearest tenth of a millimetre.

Micrometers, screw-gauge instruments, are for very small measurements and use a *vernier* scale and measure to one hundredth of a millimetre, or to 10 micrometres (μm).

Area

The area of a *surface* is measured in units of metres *multiplied* by metres:

i.e. 1m × 1m = 1m² or one *square* metre,

or in units of square centimetres, cm², or square millimetres, mm². Adult human bodies have a surface area of between 1.4 and 1.8 square metres.

Mass

Mass is the *quantity* of matter in a body; the unit of mass is called the *kilogramme*. The mass of a body will be the same in all parts of the earth, but the *weight* of a body is affected by the pull of gravity, and will vary slightly in different parts of the earth. For *general* purposes, weight and mass have the same value.

1 kilogramme(kg) = 1000 grammes(g)
1 gramme(g) = 1000 milligrammes(mg)
1 milligramme(mg) = 1000 microgrammes(μg)

Spring balances measure mass to the nearest gramme.
Direct reading balances are accurate to one-tenth of a gramme and are suitable for general purposes weighing, in the making of various hairdressing preparations. Substances can be weighed directly on to a previously weighed piece of paper covering the balance pan, or into a previously weighed beaker.

Pressure
Pressure is the force or weight acting on a unit area.

$$\text{Pressure} = \frac{\text{Force (weight)}}{\text{Area}}$$

The pressure exerted by a building brick on the ground depends on the area of brick face in contact with the ground. The large face area exerts a *low* pressure, the small face area exerts a *high* pressure.

Pressure is measured in small units called pascals (Pa), and larger units, kilopascals (kPa).

1000 pascals = 1 kilopascal (kPa)

Solids, such as the weight of the salon structure, will exert a pressure on the foundations (Section 1.1). Similarly the weight of the body pressing on the fingers will exert a pressure transmitted through the area of the finger tips in contact with the scalp, in *scalp massage*.
Fluids, or substances which can *flow*, include liquids and gases, all of which can exert pressure. The pressure exerted by water and air are described in Sections 2.7 and 3.8.

Capillarity

Capillarity is the rising of liquids in narrow tubes or pores, caused by surface tension forces (*see* Section 9.7). If glass capillary tubes of different diameters (bores) are supported in a dish of coloured water, the capillary rise will be greatest in the narrow bore tubes.
Capillary action causes water to rise through the tiny capillary spaces in porous bricks, causing *rising damp*, and the soaking up of water by a *towel* or blotting paper.
Note: If capillary tubes are inserted into liquid mercury, the mercury level *falls* inside the tube, it does not rise by capillarity as for other liquids.

1.6 QUESTIONS

1 Explain what is meant by rising damp.
Describe an experiment showing how it can occur.
What method is used to prevent this dampness in a salon building?

2 What is meant by pressure?
Describe how the weight of a salon building is supported.

3 Explain the terms chemical element, and chemical compound.
Which of the following are chemical compounds: water, sulphur, soap, iron, lead, and hydrogen peroxide?

4 Explain the main differences between organic and inorganic compounds.
Which of the following are organic compounds: ethanol, magnesium sulphate, lead nitrate, ethanoic acid, sulphuric acid, methane?

5 Explain how the circumference of the head is measured.
What instrument is used?
Also explain how the diameter of a human hair can be measured.

6. What part of the body is measured in (*a*) centimetres; (*b*) micrometres; (*c*) kilogrammes; (*d*) milligrammes?

1.7   MULTIPLE CHOICE QUESTIONS

1 One of the following is a liquid at room temperature:
(*a*) sulphur
(*b*) carbon
(*c*) mercury
(*d*) copper.

2 The diameter of an average human scalp hair is between:
(*a*) 0.0025 to 0.01 cm
(*b*) 0.025 to 0.1 cm
(*c*) 0.25 to 1.0 cm
(*d*) 2.5 to 10.0 cm

3 The total area of skin on the human body is about:
(*a*) 1.5 to 2.0 sq mm
(*b*) 1.5 to 2.0 sq cm
(*c*) 1.5 to 2.0 sq dm
(*d*) 1.5 to 2.0 sq m.

4 One of the following is an important non-metal component element of hair:
(*a*) aluminium
(*b*) sodium
(*c*) nitrogen
(*d*) nickel.

5 Which of the following represents one atom of the substance:
(*a*) CuO
(*b*) Cu
(*c*) H_2O
(*d*) O_2 ?

6 Which one of the following will have the largest molecule compared to the others:
(*a*) hydrogen peroxide
(*b*) glucose
(*c*) oxygen
(*d*) keratin?

2 Salon Water

2.1 WATER CYCLE

The amount of water on earth is *constant*, it is continuously circulated by the *water cycle* by means of the sun which changes its physical state from liquid to vapour by *evaporation*. The vapour is changed to *liquid*, rain or dew, by *condensation*; it can also be *solidified* into snow and ice (Figure 2.1).

All living plants and animals need a supply of water.

1 *Photosynthesis* is a process of *food* manufacture in green plants which uses water as one raw material.
2 *Transpiration* is a process of water *vapour* loss and circulation through leafy green plants. Water is drawn in by roots to evaporate from the plant surface.
3 *Respiration* (*see* Section 16.1) in plants and animal produces water *vapour* as a by-product.
4 *Sweating* (*see* Section 18.5) which occurs in man and mammals produces *liquid* water as the main component of sweat.
5 *Combustion* (Section 6.8) or the burning of

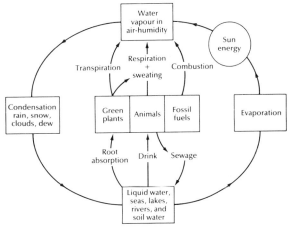

2.1 The water cycle

fuels produces water *vapour* as a by product.
6 *Excretion* produces watery *urine*.

2.2 WATER SOURCES

The human body is almost 70 per cent water, and requires a supply of water either as a *drink* or as a component of *food*. It is a *legal* requirement in the U.K. that a salon must have a clean supply of *drinking water*.

The water supply to a salon is provided by *Area Water Authorities* who take the water from the following sources:

(*a*) *Surface water* is rainwater that collects in upland *reservoirs*, *rivers*, *lakes*, or house rainwater *butts*.

(*b*) *Groundwater* is rainwater that has passed through *porous* soil and rock, to collect on an underground *non-porous* layer of clay or rock. Large underground water wells are emptied by *boreholes* and pumps, smaller wells are emptied by pumps. *Artesian wells* empty themselves by a gushing action controlled by valves. Small springs continually discharge underground water.

(*c*) *Recycled water* is previously 'used' water taken from a river and purified. The water has been used by towns higher up the river, and its *effluent* carefully treated before discharging as clean water into the river again.

(*d*) *Seawater* can be *desalinated* or *distilled* in Middle-Eastern and Arabian countries.

2.3   WATER TREATMENT

Rainwater collected in clear air is the purest form of *natural* water; other natural waters may contain *suspended* or *dissolved* impurities.

Dissolved impurities are added as the rainwater flows over or through certain rocks, mainly limestone. Seawater contains approximately 2.5 per cent dissolved *salts* of sodium, potassium, calcium and magnesium.

Water can be *polluted* by *inorganic* salts; lead, nickel, ammonia, nitrates, and sulphates from agricultural fertilisers, and chemical factory wastes. *Organic* chemicals such as detergents and disinfectants, cause water pollution.

1 *Storage and sedimentation* in large reservoirs allows *suspended* impurities, e.g. clay, silt and mud to settle. Sunlight and air also purify the stored water.
2 *Filtration* is a means of removing fine suspended particles by passing the water through filter beds of graded stone. The water is purified biologically and chemically in certain water works.
3 *Sterilisation* is the process of destroying harmful micro-organisms, by means of chlorine gas, a powerful disinfectant. The water may be *aerated* prior to chlorination.
4 *Fluoridation* is the addition of *fluoride* salts, which may be present naturally in some water. These salts are needed for teeth and bone formation.

2.4   SALON COLD WATER SYSTEM

Water flows into the Water Authority's *water main* pipe from reservoirs and water towers under very high *pressure* (*see* Section 1.5). A water *supply pipe* leaves the water main to reach an outdoor *stop tap*, from this a *service pipe* runs into the salon premises, to be controlled by an indoor *stop tap*. When this tap is turned off, all the salon water supply is stopped.

A water *meter* may be located before the indoor stop tap.

A pipe runs to one tap from the service pipe to provide *drinking water*, other pipes may directly supply the wash basins and water closet.

A *rising main* pipe can supply a *cold water cistern* in the roof space; this cistern in turn can supply the hot water system (*see* Section 7.4), wash-hand-basins, and w.cs. Since water is stored in the cistern it can become *unfit* to drink, through dust contamination, or from houseflies, and even from mice, rats or birds which can enter the roof space.

A *cistern ball valve* automatically allows the storage cistern to fill up with water as it is used within the salon. A similar ball valve is found in a w.c. cistern. The floating *ball* moves the connecting *arm*, causing the slide valve to open or close the open end of the water pipe. In the event of the valve becoming faulty, water will escape by the *overflow* to discharge outside the salon.

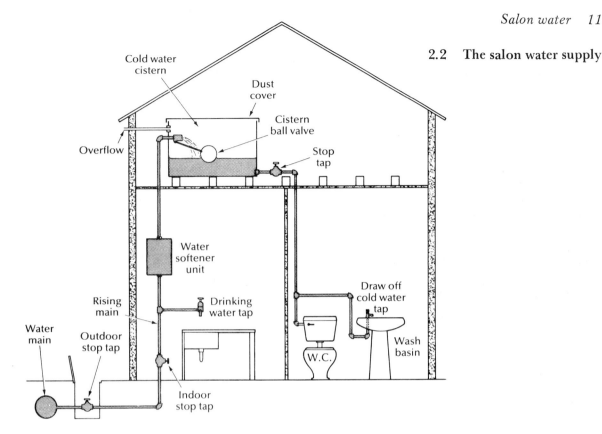

Draw-off Taps

Draw-off taps are always fitted to the *end* of a water pipe, and have openings to empty water into washing basins. The usual type of draw-off tap in a salon is called a *pillar tap*. This tap has a shield or cover which can be unscrewed to give access inside. Inside the tap is a *washer* of fibre, rubber, or leather, connected to a metal *jumper*. When the tap is closed the washer closes the opening of the *washer seating*, and holds back the water.

Water will drip from a closed tap if the washer is *worn*; it will escape past the *spindle* if the *gland nut* is slack.

2.5   PROTECTION

When water *freezes*, its volume *increases* by nearly 10 per cent; this causes an increase in pressure sufficient to split the metal pipe or push a pipe joint apart. Bursts will only be seen when the water melts or *thaws*. In the event of a burst pipe turn off the nearest *stop tap*.

Cold water pipes should be protected from cold air and draughts by means of *insulation*, such as expanded polystyrene, glass fibre, or rag strips. Frozen pipes without splits can be thawed with a hair dryer.

2.6   WATER USAGE

The average *total* amount of water used by each person each day is about 220 litres (the consumption is shown in Table 2.1). Most of this, namely 95 per cent, is used in some *cleaning* process.

2.7   PHYSICS

Volume

Volume is the amount of *space* occupied by matter; solid, liquid or gas.

Purpose	Amount
W.C. flushing	66*l* (30%) at 8–12*l* to flush the pan
Personal washing	55*l* (25%) (40*l* is HOT WATER) (A mains shower uses 20*l*, an instantaneous water heater shower 2*l*.)
Washing machines	33*l* (15%)
Cleaning premises	28*l* (13%)
Dishwashing	20*l* (9%)
Food preparation	8*l* (4%)
Car wash and gardening	6*l* (3%)
Drinking water	2*l* (1%)

Table 2.1   Total amount of water used, per person, per day

Volume is measured in *litres* (*l*) and in millilitres (ml).

1 litre (*l*) = 1000 millilitres (ml).

An alternative to the millilitre is called the *cubic centimetre* (cm³).

$$1000 \ cm^3 \ = \ 1000 \ ml$$

Measuring liquid volumes

Volumes of liquids can be measured by four different kinds of apparatus; *measuring cylinders* are most commonly used and are fairly accurate, whilst less commonly used but more

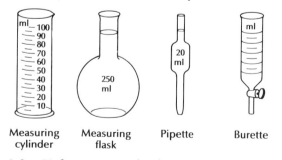

Measuring cylinder   Measuring flask   Pipette   Burette

2.3   **Volume measuring instruments**

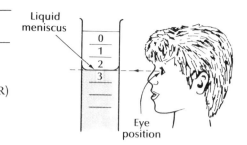

Liquid meniscus   Eye position

2.4   Reading the level of liquid in a measuring instrument

accurate apparatus includes *measuring flasks*, *pipettes* and *burettes*.

When reading the *level* of liquid in a measuring apparatus, hold the apparatus at eye level and read the lower line of the curved liquid surface or meniscus. (The meniscus of *mercury* is inverted.)

Gas volumes are measured using graduated gas jars or tubes, similar to inverted measuring cylinders.

Solid volumes can be measured by lowering the solid to be completely immersed in water of a *displacement vessel* and carefully measuring the *volume* of water it displaces into a measuring cylinder.

Water pressure

The pressure in water *increases* with *depth*, or *height*. This is shown using the tall can with side outlets at various depths. Water spurts out with the greatest pressure from the *lowest* jet, and least pressure from the uppermost jet.

The *vertical* distance between the level of water in the can and the position of the outlet spout is the *head of water*. The demonstration shows that pressure acts in *all* directions, *vertically* as well as horizontally (Figure 2.5).

The greater the head of water the greater the pressure; this is achieved by obtaining water from upland water reservoirs, water towers, or salon water storage cisterns. Water from a drinking water tap will have a much *greater* pressure, than water from the storage cistern to washing basin taps.

High pressure water jets are used under warm water in *water pressure massage*.

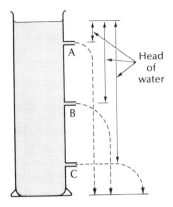

2.5 **To show pressure in water increases with depth**

Matter change of physical state

Substances can *change* their physical state by adding *heat* to them in *heating*, or withdrawing heat from them in *cooling*.

Water can exist in the solid, liquid and gas states, as shown as follows (the names of the different *physical changes* are given):

Solidification	Condensation
Solid ◄——— Liquid ◄——— Gas
(Ice) ———► (Water) —·—► (Steam)
Melting or Fusion	Boiling or Evaporation

Melting or Fusion is the change of state from a crystalline solid to a liquid and takes place at a *definite* temperature called the *melting point*. Ice melts at 0°C. Non-crystalline substances such as waxes in lipsticks and solid brilliantines have *no* definite melting point.

Solidification is the change of state from a liquid into a crystalline solid at a definite temperature, the *freezing point*. Crystalline substances generally *increase* sharply in volume when the liquid freezes; this is seen when water forms ice causing burst pipes. Non-crystalline substances such as waxes in lipsticks and solid brilliantines *decrease* in volume on solidification.

During *wax depilation* and *wax bath treatments* the molten wax gives up its heat to the skin as the wax solidifies, this heat is called *latent heat*.

Boiling is the change from a liquid to a *vapour* or gas, the change taking place *throughout* the body of liquid at a definite temperature, the *boiling point*. Water boils in the *salon steamer* at 100°C.

Certain substances, e.g. salt, sodium chloride, can *lower* the melting point of ice and increase the boiling point of water above the normal 100°C.

Pressure changes can also affect the boiling point of water as follows:

(*a*) *Lowering the air pressure* (*see* Section 3.8) will cause water to boil at temperatures *lower* than the normal 100°C.

(*b*) *Increasing the air pressure* causes the water to boil at temperatures *higher* than normal, above 100°C.

The pressure cooker, steam *sterilizers* and *autoclaves* (Sections 21.1 and 9.2), use the higher boiling point of water, 110°C – 130°C for quicker cooking and complete microbe destruction.

Volatile liquids	Non-volatile liquids
Evaporate rapidly and easily below or at room temperature	Evaporate with some difficulty, or not at all, at room temperature
Water	Almond oil
Ammonium hydroxide	Peanut oil
Ethanol (methylated spirits)	Castor oil
Ethanoic acid (acetic acid)	Coconul oil
Propanone (acetone)	Propanetriol (glycerine)
Propanol (propyl alcohol)	Lanolin
Methylbutyl ethanoate (amyl acetate)	Liquid paraffin
Lavender oil	Olive oil
Rose oil	Sulphuric acid
Witch hazel	
Tetrachloro-ethane	
Petrol	

Table 2.2 **Comparison of volatile and non-volatile liquids**

Evaporation is the change from a liquid to a *vapour* and occurs from the liquid *surface* at almost *any* temperature. Latent heat is needed to evaporate a liquid.

Protection

Some volatile organic liquids used in the salon produce *toxic* vapour when inhaled and highly *flammable* vapour liable to cause fire or explode. Bottle *labels* will indicate if this is so. Use volatile solvents in *well-ventilated* places and never smoke whilst using them, or allow *naked flames* to burn near.

Condensation is the change of *vapour* into *liquid*. Condensation *dampness* is seen as damp patches on cold walls, or *steaming* of windows and mirrors.

Distillation is a method of the *separation* of different liquids or the separation of *dissolved* substances from *mixtures*. It involves *evaporation* by boiling followed by *condensation* of the vapour as a condensed liquid called a pure *distillate*.

The volatile liquid vapour is usually condensed by a water-cooled condenser.

Distilled water is pure and free from any impurities such as dissolved air and salts. It is used for salon steamers, and in preparing pure cosmetics and hairdressing preparations.

Steam distillation is the method of separating *volatile* essential oils from plant material (*see* Section 13.12) by means of the apparatus shown in Figure 2.6.

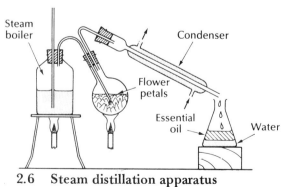

2.6   **Steam distillation apparatus**

2.8   CHEMISTRY

Water is a chemical compound of hydrogen and oxygen, called *hydrogen oxide*, chemical formula H_2O.

Distilled water is tasteless and without any smell, whilst *drinking* water may have a certain taste due to dissolved substances, salts and air.

Water of Crystallization is the water which forms certain *hydrated* crystalline substances. For example, *blue* copper sulphate crystals are hydrated due to water of crystallization. When strongly heated in a test tube the water of crystallization is driven off as steam, leaving *white anhydrous* powdery copper sulphate.

$$Blue \xrightarrow{\text{Heat}} White$$

hydrated copper   *anhydrous + Steam*
sulphate crystals   *copper sulphate*

A Test for Water involves adding white anhydrous copper sulphate powder to a *wet* substance; if it turns blue the wetness is due to water.

Hygroscopic substances have the power of absorbing water vapour from the air. Hair, paper, sodium chloride (salt), sodium hydroxide (caustic soda), anhydrous calcium chloride and propanetriol (glycerine) are all hygroscopic substances.

Efflorescent substances *lose* their water of crystallization when exposed to air, the clear transparent crystals of sodium carbonate (washing soda) and sodium sulphate (Glaubers salts) become white *powdery* substances on exposure to room air.

Protection

Bottle Caps and Stoppers should always be *replaced*, since a hairdressing preparation may have hygroscopic or efflorescent components, and on prolonged exposure to air, the preparation may be damaged, making it useless.

Solutions

When substances are added to water they may slowly disappear or *dissolve* in the water to form a clear transparent *solution*. The substance which dissolves, for example sugar, is called the *solute*, and the liquid which it dissolves in, water, called the solvent.

Solute   + solvent = solution
Sugar + solvent   = sugar solution.

Water is a solvent for most ionic *inorganic* compounds which form *ions* in the solution.
Organic solvents are of *many* different kinds, for example ethanol (methylated spirits) dissolves mainly *organic* substances, to form *molecules* in the solution.

Solubility of a solute is the amount in grammes which will dissolve in 100 grammes of a solvent. Many different ionic inorganic substances are very *soluble* in water; for example sodium chloride (salt), copper sulphate and sodium sulphate. They do not dissolve or are *insoluble* in organic solvents, ethanol (methylated spirits) and petrol.

Similarly many *organic* substances are *insoluble* in water, for example, paraffin wax, lanolin and olive oil. But these substances are *soluble* in organic solvents.

Generally a *warm* solvent will dissolve more solute than a *cold* solvent. *Saturated solu-*

Solution	Example
1 Gases dissolved in liquids	Air in water. Ammonia in water. Methanal (formaldehyde) in water. Chlorine in water.
2 Liquids dissolved in liquids	Ethanol (methylated spirits) in water. Propanetriol (glycerine) in water. Lavender oil in ethanol (methylated spirits)
3 Solids dissolved in liquids	Sodium chloride (salt) in water. Citric acid in water. Shellac in ethanol (methylated spirits). Celluloid in propanone (acetone).

Table 2.3 Examples of solutions

tions are solutions which contain as much solute as can be dissolved at a certain *temperature* of solvent. Gases are *less* soluble in warm solvents.
Concentrated solutions contain large amounts of solute, and can become saturated when no more solute dissolves.
Dilute solutions contain small amounts of solute.
Filtration is an important technique for *separating* insoluble substances from soluble substances. The insoluble substance may be

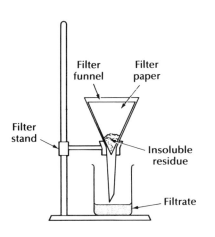

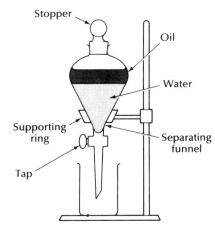

2.7   **Filtration and separation apparatus**

suspended in the solvent, and may also settle as a *sediment*, with a *clear* solution above it.

The solution and its suspension are poured or *decanted* into a folded *filter paper* held in a *filter funnel* supported in a *filter stand*. The insoluble *residue* remains on the filter paper, whilst the clear solution collects as a *filtrate* in a container beneath the funnel.

Immiscible Liquids are those liquids which are unable to mix together or dissolve in each other, for example liquid paraffin and water, hexane and water, or petrol and water.

Immiscible liquids are separated using *separating funnels* fitted with taps and stoppers. This technique is used to remove water from organic solvents used for wig cleaning (Figure 2.7).

2.9   QUESTIONS

1 Explain the terms solute, solvent, solution and soluble.
  Give one named example of these terms in hairdressing practice.
2 Describe techniques used for separating (*a*) talcum powder accidentally added to ethanol (methylated spirits); and (*b*) water present in wig cleaning solvent.
3 Draw and label a diagram showing the cold water supply in a salon. Indicate the correct location of the following: supply pipe, cold water storage cistern, drinking water tap, stop tap and ball valve.
  Explain the term head of water.
4 The following is a recipe for a lotion:

Citric acid	25
Water distilled	75
Propanetriol (glycerine)	20
Magnesium carbonate	5

  Describe (*a*) the physical state; (*b*) the units and method of measurement; (*c*) the solubility of each ingredient.
  What is distilled water?
  Why is it used instead of tap water?
5 Describe the procedure to deal with (*a*) a burst cold water pipe; (*b*) a dripping tap.

6 Why should the stopper or cap be replaced on a bottle of solvent, or one containing certain chemicals?

2.10   MULTIPLE CHOICE QUESTIONS

1 During the water cycle, water passes from the lakes and rivers into the air by a process of:
  (*a*) transpiration
  (*b*) condensation
  (*c*) evaporation
  (*d*) precipitation.
2 The main water supply is usually sterilized by:
  (*a*) fluoridation
  (*b*) chlorination
  (*c*) ion exchange
  (*d*) sand filtration.
3 To which of the following parts of a sink water tap is a washer fitted?
  (*a*) cover
  (*b*) spindle
  (*c*) jumper
  (*d*) seating.
4 The salon washbasin empties straight into the:
  (*a*) soil pipe
  (*b*) gutter
  (*c*) gulley
  (*d*) stack pipe.
5 In order to examine and clean out the blockage for a washbasin that will not empty, one of the following is removed:
  (*a*) inspection chamber cover
  (*b*) gulley trap grid
  (*c*) cleaning eye cap
  (*d*) washbasin plug.
6 A mixture of oil of lavender and water can be separated by:
  (*a*) sublimation
  (*b*) steam distillation
  (*c*) filtration
  (*d*) chromatography.

3 Salon Energy

3.1 ENERGY

Energy is *essential* in a salon, it is the means to do *work*, and is usually associated with *movement*. Energy is available in different forms, namely *chemical, heat, electrical, atomic* and *radiant* energy light and radio.

Table 3.1 summarizes the uses of energy in a salon.

Use	Energy source
Human body activity and movement	Energy providing food
Equipment: Dryers, waving machines, lighting vacuum cleaner, spin dryer	Electricity
Hot water	Electricity, gas, solid fuel and sunshine
Space heating	Electricity, gas, solid fuel, sunshine, also human body heat.

Table 3.1 Uses of energy in the salon

The Salon energy balance

Table 3.2 summarizes the ways in which a salon gains and loses its energy. Note that the gain is approximately *equal* to the loss, indicating a *flow* of energy *through* the salon.

3.2 SOLAR ENERGY

1 **Sunlight** is the source of all energy for *life* on earth. Sunlight is a form of *radiant energy* which can be trapped by green plants, and used to make food, mainly *carbohydrates*, from water and carbon dioxide. This process of food manufacture is called *photosynthesis*, and is also the source of *oxygen* on earth.

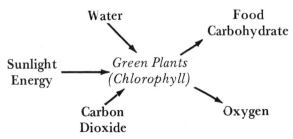

Salon energy gains (%)			Salon energy losses (%)			
Sunshine, passes through windows and heats walls	—	16	*Through*	walls	40	
				roof	30	
				windows	25	— 82
				floor	5	
Occupants, give off body heat	—	5				
Hot *water* and pipes give off heat	—	12	*Ventilation*, open doors, windows, draughts		—	10
Appliances and lights	—	7				
			Hot water down the drains		—	8
Space heating system	—	60				
Total		100		Total		100

Dampness requires *latent heat* to evaporate — variable percentage

Table 3.2   Salon energy balance

2 **Energy Flows** from the sun into green plants which *produce* food (carbohydrates, lipids, proteins) and oxygen; these products are used or *consumed* by animals and human beings.

In this way the solar energy is changed into different *forms*, partly as *heat* and partly as *chemical* energy in food. The solar energy is *changed* and never destroyed, and ends up by flowing back to *outer space* around the earth.

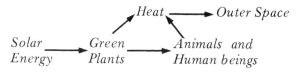

3 **Solar Energy** of sunshine provides 10 to 25% of the energy to *heat* a salon depending on the season. Water can be heated by *solar panels* made up of *copper pipes* laid against a black solar heat absorbing background, located on a rooftop.

4 **Heat Pumps** are the means of recirculating *heat* which *drains* from plants, animals and buildings into soil and water, apart from that which *radiates* and is lost into outer space. Heat pumps are 'reverse refrigerators' drawing heat *from* soil and water and thus making them cold and giving up this heat

by *radiators* inside the salon. The *pump* is driven by electricity, the heat *output* is 2½ times the electrical energy *input*.

3.3   HUMAN BODY ENERGY

Human body energy comes from food such as *glucose* by *respiration* which gives energy as body *heat* (60 per cent) and in the form of *chemical* energy (40 per cent) as a chemical compound called *adenosine triphosphate* or ATP; this causes muscles to contract and is seen as body *movement*.

3.4   SALON FUELS

Fuels which can be used in a salon are: *solid* fuel, coal, coke and certain smokeless fuels; *liquid* fuels, paraffin and light fuel oil; *gaseous* fuels, bottled gas, and main natural gas. These fuels are called *fossil fuels* and have formed from the remains of plants and animals.

Table 3.3 summarizes the main components of fossil fuels, storage and care in use.

3.5   SALON GAS SYSTEM

The *gas main* pipe connects to the salon by a gas *service pipe*. A gas *control cock* is located next to the gas *meter*; this cock turns off all

Fuel	Composition	Storage	Care in use
Solid fuels Coal Coke Smokeless Fuel	All contain carbon 82–95% 90% 90%	Large store needed	Dusty. Flues must be swept often. Fireguards needed for open fires.
Liquid fuel Paraffin and Light Oil (Petrol)	Contain hydrocarbons	Storage tanks needed	Fire control valve needed. Attention to burners. Oil spills are dangerous.
Gaseous Fuel Bottled Gas	Hydrocarbon *propane* and *butane*	Storage needed	Leaks can cause *suffocation*.
Natural Mains Gas	Mainly *methane* hydrocarbon 90%	No storage needed	Explosions if ignited.

Table 3.3 Fuels, composition, storage and care

gas to the salon and its position should be known in the event of gas *leakage*.

Installation *pipes* take gas to different *points* in the salon, each gas point is controlled by *gas taps*. These may have *drop down* controls, *removable* gas-tap keys, or be directly connected to the appliance.

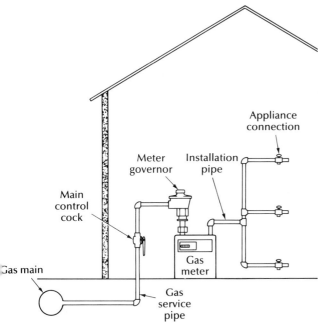

3.1   Salon gas supply

Protection

1 **Leakage** of gas can cause fire and explosion. Inhalation causes *suffocation*.
2 In the event of a *gas leak*:
    (*a*) **Open** all doors and windows.
    (*b*) **Extinguish** naked flames – *no* smoking.
    (*c*) Turn off all gas Taps.
    (*d*) If leak continues – **Turn off Main Control Cock** and contact **Gas Authority**.

Proper *ventilation* is required for all gas appliances, with correct unblocked *flues*, and *guards* to open gas fires.

Gas costs

The *meter* measures the amount of gas used in a salon in cubic *metres* (or feet), on direct reading cyclometers, giving the reading in numbers. The *volume* of gas used is changed into *therms* by multiplication by the gas *energy value*

$$\text{Gas volume} \times \begin{array}{c}\text{Energy}\\\text{value per}\\\text{cubic metre}\end{array} = \text{Therm}$$

The therm is then charged at a certain rate (1984: 34 pence/therm).

3.6   RELEASING CHEMICAL ENERGY

Foods and fossil fuels have *molecules* held together by *bonds*; when *new* bonds are formed chemical energy is *released*. The *burning* of *carbon* (foods and solid fuels) produces energy since new bonds form to make carbon dioxide:

$$\begin{pmatrix} \text{Carbon} \\ \text{Foods and} \\ \text{fuels} \end{pmatrix} + \text{oxygen} \longrightarrow \begin{matrix} \text{Carbon} \\ \text{dioxide} \end{matrix} + \text{Energy}$$

This is called an **Exothermic** chemical change.

The following are the main energy releasing processes in a salon:

1 *Respiration* (*see* Section 16.1) the release of energy from glucose in the human body cells, with the formation of *carbon dioxide* and *water*.
2 *Combustion*, also called 'burning', a process of combination of *oxygen* with carbon and hydrogen (in fuels and foods) to release energy as *heat* and *light*, and form *carbon dioxide* and *water*. *Controlled* combustion is used in salon *boilers* burning solid, liquid or gaseous fuels.
3 *Explosion* is a very *rapid* process of combustion — it involves gases, and solvent vapours, and can involve finely *powdered* substances. The *energy* released in an explosion can demolish a salon.

3.7   CHEMISTRY

Carbon is a *solid* chemical *element*, and occurs in widely different forms as diamonds, graphite (in pencils), charcoal, soot and lampblack. Lampblack is the substance formed when certain oils burn without sufficient air. It is used to make eye *mascara* by mixing with soft soap or certain waxes.
Hydrogen is a *gas*; a small amount is present in natural gas. It is found in many *compounds*, water, acids and most organic compounds.
Hydrocarbons These are *compounds* of hydrogen and carbon.

$$\begin{matrix} Hydrocarbon \\ Molecules \end{matrix} = \begin{matrix} Many \\ carbon \\ atoms \end{matrix} + \begin{matrix} Many \\ hydrogen \\ atoms \end{matrix}$$

Many different hydrocarbons are present as a *mixture* in *petroleum*.

Table 3.4 gives the names of the important

Hydrocarbon name	Physical state	Salon use
PETROLEUM GASES Methane, Ethane, Propane, Butane or Alkanes	Colourless gases	1 Natural mains gas 2 Bottled gas 3 Raw material for soapless detergent making.
Hexane	Volatile liquid boiling point 68–70°C	Solvent wig cleaning. (Replaces carbon tetrachloride.)
Paraffin (Kerosene)	Liquid	Liquid fuel.
Liquid Paraffin (Medicinal white paraffin)	Oil liquid	Skin lubricant, liquid brilliantines and and cosmetic creams
Soft Paraffin (Petroleum jelly)	White to yellow greasy solid	Cosmetic creams, solid brilliantines, lipstick.
Hard Paraffin Wax	Waxy white solid	Cosmetic creams, wax depilatories

Table 3.4   Hydrocarbon used in the salon.

hydrocarbons, their physical state and uses in the salon.

Terpenes are hydrocarbon compounds often found as mixtures in *essential oils* produced by certain plants. Essential oil of lemon and orange contains *limonene*, whilst turpentine from pine resin contains the terpene *pinene*. All are volatile liquids with pleasant smells and are extracted from plant petals, leaves, stems and fruits by *steam distillation* (*see* Section 13.12).

Chlorofluoro—Hydrocarbons are compounds of chlorine and fluorine with hydrocarbons such as *ethane*. *Trichloro-fluoro-methane* is one example of these compounds used as aerosol spray *propellent* and in fire extinguishers.

Carbon tetrachloride is a volatile liquid which produces a *poisonous* gas in contact with hot surfaces; it should only be used in well-ventilated areas away from naked flames. A preferable solvent is *tetrachloro-ethane* or *hexane*.

Carbohydrates are organic compounds containing carbon, hydrogen and *oxygen*, and are the components of sugars and starches. Natural *gums* such as *tragacanth*, *karaya* and *agar*, extracted from various plants, consist of mixtures of carbohydrates, and are components of *setting* lotions.

Lipids are compounds of carbon, hydrogen and oxygen, and form the plant and animal oils and fats.

Apart from their use in foods, lipids are important raw materials for cosmetic, soap, and soapless detergent manufacture. Lipids are *esters* being made up of two main components, namely propanetriol (glycerine) and different *fatty carboxylic acids*.

Lipid =
    Propanetriol + Fatty carboxylic acid
    (glycerine)

Coconut Oil =
    Propanetriol + Dodecanoic acid
    (glycerine)   (Lauric acid)

Beef Fat =
    Propanetriol + Octadecanoic acid
    (glycerine)   (Stearic acid)

Olive Oil =
    Propanetriol + Octadec-9-Enoic acid
    (glycerine)   (Oleic acid)

Waxes are obtained from plant and animal sources as shown in Table 3.6. They consist of carbon, hydrogen and oxygen, and have *two* main components.

Waxes =
    Carboxylic Acids + Fatty alcohols

Spermaceti Wax =
    Hexadecanoic acid + Hexadecanol
    (Palmitic acid)   (Cetyl Alcohol)

Plant lipids	Animal lipids
Mainly *liquid* oils at room temperature	Mainly *solid* fats at room temperature
Peanut oil, almond oil, olive oil, castor oil, sunflower oil	Lard — pork fat, suet — beef fat, tallow — mutton fat
Coconut oil and cocoa butter are *solid* fats	Fish lipids are liquid oils

Table 3.5　Comparison of pland and animal lipids

Plant waxes	Animal waxes	
Carnauba and *Candililla* from certain plant leaves	*Lanolin*	— sheep wool wax
	Beeswax	— honeycomb wax
	Spermaceti	— whale wax
	Sebum	— human skin secretion

Table 3.6　Comparison of plant and animal waxes

	Lipids (+ waxes)	Hydrocarbons	Carbohydrates
EXAMPLES	Olive oil, lard, beeswax	Liquid paraffin, soft paraffin, paraffin wax, and terpenes	Glucose, cane sugar, starch
CHEMICAL ELEMENTS	Carbon, hydrogen, and oxygen	Hydrogen and carbon	Carbon, hydrogen and oxygen
COMPOSITION	Fatty Lipid = carboxylic acid + propanetriol (glycerine)	Hydrocarbons Alk*anes*, methane to hexane essential oils — terpenes	Units of glucose
PHYSICAL STATE	Liquid — oil Solid — fat + wax Non-volatile	Gases, volatile liquids and non-volatile solids	All solids
EDIBILITY	Edible	Non-edible (mainly harmful). Essential oils — flavours.	Edible
USES	Soaps, soapless detergents, cosmetics, foodstuff	Brilliantines and cosmetics Perfumes/flavours — essential oils	Gums — setting lotions, foodstuff
SOLUBILITY	Soluble in organic Insoluble in water.	Soluble in organic solvents. Insoluble in water.	Some soluble in water. Remainder insoluble in solvents.

Table 3.7   Comparison of hydrocarbons, lipids and carbohydrates

Beeswax =
   Hexadecanoic acid + Tetradecanol
   (Palmitic acid)   (Myricyl alcohol)

Lanette wax is a prepared wax, used in formulation of cosmetic creams.

Lanette Wax =
   Octadecanol   +   Hexadecanol
   (Stearyl alcohol)   (Cetyl alcohol)

Lanolin is a complex mixture of fatty carboxylic acids, fatty alcohols *cholesterol* and lipids. Sebum has a similar composition.

Chemicals from wood

Wood is mainly the carbohydrate *cellulose used for making rayons*. When *distilled* it produces several important chemicals:

(*a*) *charcoal* or carbon.
(*b*) *methanol* (methyl alcohol) to make methylated spirits; a salon and perfume solvent.
(*c*) *propanone* (acetone) a solvent for nail lacquer.
(*d*) *ethanoic acid* (acetic acid), a component of vinegar hair rinse.

Chemicals from coal

Coal, when distilled, produces a number of chemicals of which the following are of importance in hairdressing:
(*a*) *coke* or carbon solid fuel.
(*b*) *ammonia* for cold wave lotion making and as a catalyst for hydrogen peroxide bleaching.
(*c*) *hydrocarbons*, benzene, toluenes and

naphthalene for making soapless detergents and 'coal tar' and diamine dyes.

(d) *phenol* (carbolic acid) for making disinfectants, dyes and plastics.

3.8 PHYSICS

Measuring energy

All forms of energy are measured in units called Joules (J) by instruments called *calorimeters*.

1 kilojoule (kJ) = 1000 joules (J)
1 megajoule (MJ)= 1000 kilojoules (kJ) = 1 000 000 joules (J)

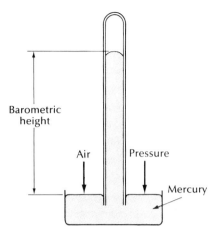

3.3   **Simple mercury barometer**

The chemical energy in fossil fuels and foods is measured in kilojoules (kJ) and megajoules (MJ) (*see* Section 15.2). Figure 3.2 shows the *energy value* of 1 kilogramme of different substances.

1 cubic metre of natural gas =   34 MJ
1 'unit' of electricity   =   3.6 MJ

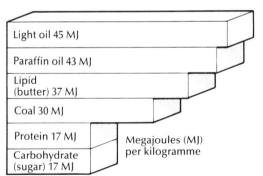

3.2   **Energy value of 1 kg of different substances**

Gas pressure

Air forms a layer up to 150 metres high around the earth. This blanket of air has *weight* and causes *air pressure* (*see* Section 1.5).

Air pressure can be shown by filling a glass tumbler to the brim with water and gently pressing a sheet of paper over the open end. The tumbler is inverted and the water is held in the tumbler by the air pressure which is *greater* than the 'head of water' pressure.

Barometers are used to measure air pressure. *Mercury* barometers are glass tubes completely filled with liquid mercury, the pressure is measured as a *barometric height* in millimetres (mm) of mercury, average air pressure being 760 mm of mercury; this is equal to 101 *kilopascals* (kPa) (Figure 3.3).

Aneroid barometers record the air pressure directly by change in shape of a small box from which air has been removed.

A *gas manometer* is an instrument, or gauge for measuring the gas *pressure* of a salon natural gas supply. The U-shaped tube is water filled and connected to a gas tap. The gas pressure is measured in millimetres as the *difference* in height between the two water levels. In order that gas flows *out* of the open gas tap it must have a pressure *greater* than that of the surrounding air. Therefore the gas pressure equals air pressure *plus* the height of water in the manometer gauge.

3.9   QUESTIONS

1 Explain the term *energy*.
  For what purposes is energy needed in a salon?
2 Describe the supply of one form of fossil fuel to a salon, and the precautions necessary in its use.
  How is energy released from the fuel?
3 Explain the terms hydrocarbon and carbohydrates.
  Give named examples of each and their use in the salon.
4 Give examples and uses in the salon of named examples of:
  (*a*) lipid oils;
  (*b*) mineral oils;
  (*c*) essential oils;
  (*d*) tar oils.
5 Briefly explain the chemical difference between the following and their salon uses:
  (*a*) lard;
  (*b*) soft paraffin;
  (*c*) beeswax;
  (*d*) karaya gum.
6 What are the sources and salon uses of:
  (*a*) ammonia;
  (*b*) methanol (methyl alcohol);
  (*c*) ethanoic acid (acetic acid);
  (*d*) liquid paraffin;
  (*e*) lanolin.

3.10   MULTIPLE CHOICE QUESTIONS

1 Which one of the following is a member of the class of chemical compounds called lipids?
  (*a*) soft paraffin
  (*b*) petrol
  (*c*) coconut oil
  (*d*) oil of cloves.

2 The name given to the grease extracted from sheep wool is:
  (*a*) sebum
  (*b*) lanolin
  (*c*) cholesterol
  (*d*) lard.
3 Herbs and spices are components of beauty preparations and they mainly provide:
  (*a*) hormones
  (*b*) vitamins
  (*c*) colouring material
  (*d*) essential oils.
4 When a container full of water with a sheet of paper placed across the mouth of the container is inverted the water does not escape because of:
  (*a*) water pressure
  (*b*) air pressure
  (*c*) surface tension
  (*d*) solid pressure.
5 Which of the following does *not* require oxygen to release its heat energy?
  (*a*) solid fuel
  (*b*) natural gas
  (*c*) fuel oil
  (*d*) electricity.
6 In a salon gas supply which of the following is the correct arrangement for the flow of gas after the service pipe enters the salon from the gas main?
  (*a*) meter—meter governor—main control cock-boiler
  (*b*) main control cock—meter—meter governor—boiler
  (*c*) meter governor—main control cock—meter—boiler
  (*d*) main control cock—meter governor—meter—boiler.

4 Salon Electricity

4.1 SOURCES

Electricity is the *main* source of energy in hairdressing salons, *natural gas* second main source.

Electric *current* is the *flow* of electricity in a *conductor*, such as a copper wire, and is produced by the following energy *changes*:

(*a*) *Chemical energy into electrical energy.* Chemical action in *dry cells* or dry batteries. As the chemicals are used up less electricity is made and the cells are discarded. It is a useful *portable* and *compact* source of electric current.

(*b*) *Electrical energy into chemical energy.* Electric current is *stored* in acid accumulators, as chemical energy. *Discharging* produces electric current, whilst *charging* refills the acid accumulator. This is a useful *store* or standby supply for emergency use, when main electricity is not available.

(*c*) *Mechanical energy into electrical energy.* The *dynamo* or electric generator produces electric current by *turning* a coil of insulated wire, the *armature*, between the

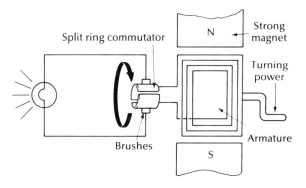

4.1   Direct current generator

poles of strong magnets, or *electromagnets*. The electric current is collected from the *commutator* by spring mounted graphite carbon brushes (Figure 4.1).

The mechanical *turning power* for the armature is provided as follows:

1 *Engine* power, from engines driven by petrol, gas or oil.
2 *Wind* power from windmills.
3 *Water* power from water with a 'head of pressure' from reservoirs, called *hydroelectric* power.

4 *Steam* to turn turbine wheels, the steam is generated from coal, oil or atomic heat sources.

4.2   ELECTRICAL TERMS

Direct current, d.c., is obtained from dry batteries, acid accumulators, and direct current dynamo generators. This current flows always in the *same* direction.

Alternating current, a.c., is obtained from alternating current generators or *alternators* using a special commutator.

The flow of electricity reaches a *peak* in one direction, decreases, to *reverse* this flow and reach a peak in the opposite direction. This forms one *cycle*.

Main electricity in the U.K. repeats this cycle 50 times in *one second*, and is said to have a *frequency* of 50 Hertz; the Hertz (Hz) is the unit of frequency (*see* Section 13.5).

Note: Alternating current can be changed into *direct* current by means of a *rectifier*.

Voltage is the *electrical pressure* measured in units called *volts* (V) by means of a *voltmeter*.

In order that electricity can *flow* there must be a pump to supply *electrons* (*see* Section 4.9). Generators, batteries and accumulators all provide the necessary electrons and *voltage*.

Small voltages of *millivolts* (mV) activate muscles in the human body.

Safety

High voltages can be *fatal*, *low* voltages, e.g. about 6 V and less, as from dry batteries, are harmless.

Table 4.1 summarizes voltages of different electricity sources.

Note: Always check the operating voltage for an electrical appliance by looking at the appliance *label*, and nameplate on the supply *meter*, or socket *outlet*.

Amperage is the rate of *flow* of electric current, measured in units called *amperes* (A)

Source	Voltage
One dry cell	1.5 V d.c.
Batteries of more than one dry cell	3 to 12 V d.c.
Car accumulators	6 – 12 V d.c.
Continental and American countries mains supply	110 – 120 V a.c.
Main supply, U.K.	240 V a.c.

Table 4.1   Voltages of different electricity services

by means of an *ammeter*. *One* ampere is six million, million, million electrons flowing per second!! An electric shaver may take *one* ampere, a hairdryer *five* amperes, a water heater *13* amperes.

In certain hairdressing treatments, d.c. currents are measured in *milliamperes*, mA

Resistance is a measure of the *ease* with which a current flows through a wire. All *metals* allow electric current to flow easily and are electrical *conductors*, many organic materials, plastics, wood, and porcelain *resist* the flow of electric current and are called electrical *insulators*.

The *resistance* also depends on the *size* of the wire, *thick* copper wire has a lower resistance than *thin* narrow copper wire (*see* Section 5.9). The *length* of wire also affects resistance, *short* wires have *lower* resistance compared to *long* wires. Resistance is measured in units called *ohms* (Ω).

Different metals have different resistance values; silver, aluminium and copper are of *low* resistance, whilst iron, tungsten and the alloy nichrome have a *high* resistance.

Ohms Law shows the *relationship* between *voltage*, *current* and resistance as follows:

Volts	=	Amperes × ohms
Amperes	=	Volts ÷ ohms
Ohms	=	Volts ÷ amperes

Ohms Law and its application seldom enter into hairdressing calculations.

The following shows how the *resistance* of an appliance is calculated.

Example: A hairdryer takes 6 amperes at 240 volts. Its resistance will be found from:

Ohms = Volts ÷ amperes.

$$\text{Resistance of hairdryer} = \frac{240 \text{ V}}{6 \text{ A}}$$

$$= 40 \text{ ohms.}$$

4.3   DISTRIBUTION OF ELECTRICITY

The salon electricity is brought from the *generating station* by way of a *step-up* transformer which changes the main voltage from 11 000 V to 132 000 V. A *grid* network of overhead cables supported on pylons brings the electricity to *step-down* transformers which change the voltage from 132 000 V to 240 V.

Transformers are devices for changing the voltage of *alternating* current, a.c. Bathroom shaver socket outlets for 110 and 240 V have a transformer in them.

4.4   THE SALON ELECTRICAL INSTALLATION (Figure 4.4)

An electric *circuit* is the flow of electric current from the *positive* terminal to a *negative* terminal, and its *complete* path through conductors and appliances (Figure 4.3).

A circuit will have its components shown by *symbols* (Figure 4.2), and will include a *switch*, to break or complete the circuit. The switch is *before* the appliance.

(*a*) The *main supply* cable enters the salon as two thick *insulated* wires, one with a red cover is the live line or positive (+) feed conductor, the other with a *black* cover is the *neutral* return or negative (−) conductor.

(*b*) The main supply enters a *sealed* electricity board *main fuse*; this can only be opened by the electricity board staff.

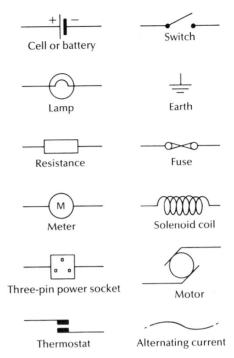

4.2   Electrical circuit symbols

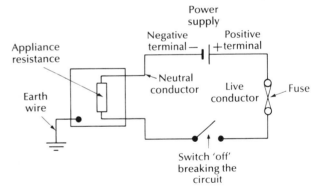

4.3   A simple electrical circuit

(*c*) A *time switch* may be located before the *meter* with its cyclometer dial. The nameplate on the meter shows the main voltage and frequency.

(*d*) The consumer's unit consists of a *main switch* and set of *fuses* or *circuit breakers* (*see* Section 4.7).

(*e*) *Cables* lead from the consumer's unit to the different salon circuits. These cables are hidden from view beneath floorboards or

4.4   The salon electrical circuit

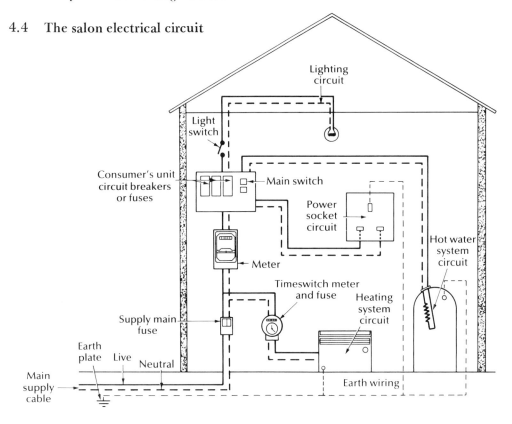

above ceilings and may be surrounded by metal protective *conduit* pipes.

The cables have thick grey coloured plastic outer covering, and the conductors have *red* (live), *black* (neutral) and *green* (earth) plastic insulation. All the conducting wires are of *thick* copper. The *earth wire* and its purpose is described in Section 12.6.

4.5   ELECTRIC POWER AND COST

Power is measured in units called *watts* (W), and is equal to one joule (J) for *one* second (*see* Section 3.8).

$$\text{Watt} = 1 \text{ Joule per second}$$
$$1 \text{ kilowatt (kW)} = 1000 \text{ watts (W)}$$

The electric *meter* is a *joule* measuring meter or joule-meter. The electric meter records *UNITS* of electricity used in a salon.

$$1 \text{ 'UNIT'} = 3.6 \text{ Megajoules.}$$
Since 1 watt per
$$\text{second} = 1 \text{ joule,}$$
$$1 \text{ watt for one } hour = 3.6 \text{ Kilojoules}$$
1000 watts or a kilowatt for one hour
$$= 3.6 \text{ Megajoules.}$$

Therefore the electricity board unit is:

one kilowatt per hour (kWh) = 3.6 MJ.

A kilowatt hour, or 3.6 MJ, or one UNIT of electricity in 1984 costs about 5 pence in the U.K.

Loading or appliance wattage

The loading or wattage of an electric cable or appliance is calculated from the following:

$$\text{Watts} = \text{Volts} \times \text{Amperes}$$

The voltage in a salon in the U.K. will always be 240 V, but the amperage will differ in cables and appliances; this can be measured by ammeters.

Example: A salon hair-dryer takes 2 amperes at the mains voltage of 240 V. Its wattage or loading will be calculated as follows:

$$W = A \times V$$

Wattage or loading = $2 \times 240 = 480$ watts

Table 4.2 gives the wattage/loading of some salon appliances. The *nameplate* fixed to the appliance usually shows its *wattage*.

Units consumed by appliances

Since 1000 watts for *one* hour = one UNIT, the units used by an appliance in one hour is calculated as follows:

Wattage ÷ 1000 = UNITS used in one hour.

A shower on high heat setting is rated 7 kW. Therefore units used in one hour =

$$\frac{7000}{1000} = 7 \text{ units.}$$

Cost is therefore 7 × rate per unit.

Appliance	Wattage/loading
Dryshaver	8 W
Hair clippers	20 W
Towel rail, heated	150 W
Vacuum cleaner	250 W
Floor polisher	250 W
Hand hair-dryer	500 W
Salon dryer	800 – 1000 W
Steamer	800 W
One bar electric fire	1 kW
Two bar electric fire	2 kW
Sink water heater	2 kW
Washing machine	3 kW
Tumbler dryer	3 kW
Shower hand set	4, 5 to 7 kW

Table 4.2   Wattage-loading values of different electrical appliances

4.6   SALON CIRCUITS

There may be three or four main circuits in a *modern* electric installation:

(*a*) *Lighting* circuits to carry current to all electric lights.

(*b*) *Power* circuit to socket for plug connection for salon appliances by means of a *ring* circuit.

(*c*) *Fixed appliance* circuit direct to space heaters, water heaters, storage and under-floor heaters.

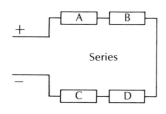

4.5   Series arranged circuits

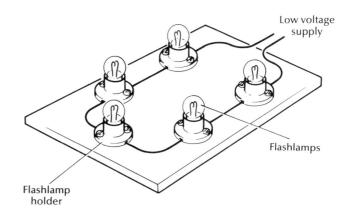

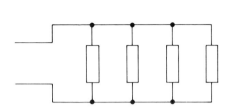

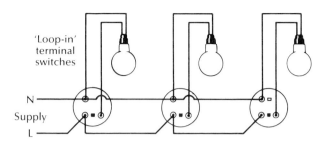

'Loop-in' terminal switches

N — Supply

L

4.6   Parallel arranged circuits

Series circuit arrangement consists of appliances or resistances arranged one after the other. This arrangement is used for short window *display* lighting, similar to Christmas tree lighting (Figure 4.5).

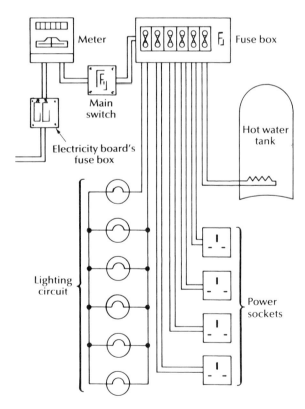

Meter

Fuse box

Main switch

Electricity board's fuse box

Hot water tank

Lighting circuit

Power sockets

4.7   Old-type distributive circuit

Parallel circuit arrangement is the normal arrangement in salon power circuits, and lighting circuits. This ladder-like arrangement of a parallel circuit is shown in Figure 4.6. The failure of one outlet does not affect the other outlets; each can be operated *independently*. The *switches* are always placed in the *live* side or feed wires.

The modern *ring main* power circuit (Figure 4.4) has the following features:
1 *One* cable supplies all outlet sockets, *both* ends of the cable connect *one* point in the main consumer's supply unit. Economical in wiring.
2 All socket outlets are of a *standard* size and pattern and take a standard plug.

Former and now obsolete *distributive* circuits (Figure 4.7) had the following features:
1 One cable to each and every outlet socket. Expensive in wiring. All cable ends terminate at separate points in the consumer's unit.
2 Socket outlets were of different size and required different sized plugs.

4.7   CIRCUIT SAFETY

(*a*) *Short circuits* (Figure 4.8) occur when bare live and neutral wire conductors touch. This happens when insulation perishes as in old *rubber* insulated cables, or when the insulation dries and cracks. Old distributive circuits had rubber insulated cable which tends to perish after ten to twenty years. These, therefore, must be replaced by longer-lasting plastic *polythene* insulated cable. Short circuits also occur in *faulty appliances*.

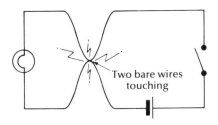

4.8   Short circuit

(*b*) *Overloading* of cables occurs when *excess* current passes through them. Cables are available in different sizes to carry 5, 10, 15, 20, 30 and 40 amperes. If the cable carried a higher amperage than it can stand it will *overheat* (*see* Section 5.9), the insulation will *melt* and nearby wood and other flammable house building materials will catch *fire*.

Overloading occurs by connecting too many heavily *rated* or loaded appliances to *one* socket by means of an *adaptor*. ONE APPLIANCE TO EACH SOCKET, otherwise

fit more sockets. Adaptors are unsafe and cause overloading of cables (Figure 4.9).

Fuses (Figure 4.10)

The *fuse* is intentionally the *weakest* part of an electric circuit; it is usually a thin piece of fuse wire which *melts* at a certain amperage, 2, 5, 10, 13, 15 or 30 amperes (*see* Section 5.9). The fuse wire is held in a rewirable *fuse holder*, or inside a disposable *cartridge fuse*. This is fitted into the *live* or lead conductor in a circuit.

Both kinds of fuse can be found in the consumer's unit fuse box, whilst cartridge fuses are found in the appliance *plug* or *inside* certain appliances.

Correct fuses prevent fire and overloading

The correct fuse *size* for U.K. circuits and appliances is calculated from the following:

$$\text{Wattage} \div 250 = \text{U.K. Fuse Size}$$

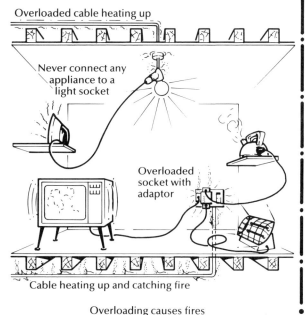

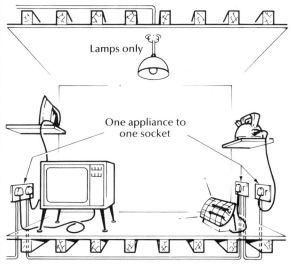

Overloading causes fires

4.9   Overloading causes fire

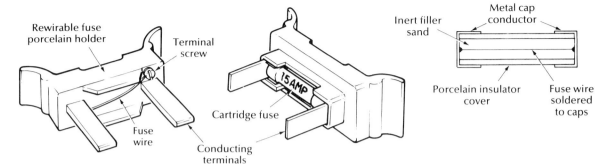

4.10   Fuses

If an electric kettle is rated 3 kW its correct plug fuse size is as follows:

$$3000 \div 250 = \text{U.K. Fuse Size}$$

Therefore a 13 ampere cartridge fuse is fitted in the plug.

Cable loading
Similarly if the kettle is to be connected to a certain socket outlet, that outlet must have a cable able to carry *over* 13 amperes, or a 20 ampere cable is fitted. A 5 or 10 ampere cable would rapidly overheat.

Outlet overloading
If *three*, 3 kW electric kettles are connected by an adaptor to a socket, the total wattage is 9 kW. Therefore the cable *loading* is

$$\frac{9000}{250} = 36 \text{ amperes}$$

Since the socket cable is only 20 ampere the cable will be overloaded and overheated.

Circuit Breakers

Instead of rewirable and cartridge fuses, the consumer's units can contain *circuit breakers* which automatically switch themselves off if a circuit is overloaded or if an appliance is faulty. The circuit breakers can be *switches* or

push buttons, and are available in 5, 10, 15, 20, 30 and 45 ampere sizes.

Current is restored by *resetting* the miniature circuit breaker switch or push button.

Rewiring a fuse

1 Switch off the consumer unit *main switch*.
2 *Blown* fuses have broken or melted fuse wire.
3 Replace the wire with one of the correct *amperage*.
4 Wind the new wire *clockwise* around the retaining screw of the fuse holder.
5 Run the wire across to the other retaining screw, do not stretch it.
6 Replace the fuse holder in the consumer unit.
7 Switch on the consumer unit main switch.

Replacing and testing cartridge fuses

1 Switch off main switch in consumer's unit.
2 Remove each cartridge and test with the circuit shown in Figure 4.11.

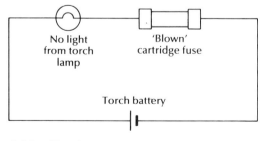

4.11   Testing a fuse

3 A faulty cartridge fuse will not light up the lamp.
4 Push the new cartridge fuse of correct amperage into the fuse holder.
5 Switch on the consumer unit main switch.

Fuse Sizes

Lighting circuit fuse	*5 ampere*
One socket outlet	*15 ampere*
Immersion heater circuit	*30 ampere*
Ring main power circuit	*30 ampere*

4.8 ELECTRICAL SWITCHES

Switches are the means of breaking and completing a circuit and are always fitted to the *live* supply conductor.
Safety. Never operate a switch with WET HANDS! (*see* Section 22.4). *Pull-cord switches* fitted to the ceiling **must** control outlets near to wash basins and water taps. *No* socket outlets are allowed near *water* basins and taps.

Telephones operate by electricity supplied by the telephone authority, they are *not* connected in any way to the salon supply.

4.9 PHYSICS

Atoms

All chemical elements are made up from *atoms*, these are made up of three basic particles:
(*a*) *electrons* or tiny particles of electricity with a *negative* charge;
(*b*) *protons* are larger particles of electricity with a *positive* charge;
(*c*) *neutrons* are large neutral particles.
The atom is *neutral* because it has *equal* numbers of electrons and protons.

Electric current

Electric pressure or voltage will cause *electrons* to flow along a metal conductor. Electrons enter at the *positive* or live end of the wire and leave at the *negative* end or return.

4.10 CHEMISTRY

Molecule bonds

Atoms are joined together by *links* or *bonds* to form the *structures* of chemical compounds. There are different links or bonds.
(*a*) **Ionic** links/bonds are found in crystalline salts, for example, sodium chloride and other inorganic salts. These substances are *solids* and do not *melt* easily, and will usually *dissolve* in water. They conduct electricity when melted or in solutions of water, and are called *electrolytes.* (*See* Sections 7.5 and 10.2.)
(*b*) **Metallic** links/bonds are found only in *metals*, the atoms are bound together by electrons; these electrons make metals good *conductors* of electricity and *heat*.
(*c*) **Covalent** links/bonds are found in most organic compounds, which are usually insoluble in water, but dissolve in certain organic *solvents*. They do not conduct electricity and are called *non-electrolytes*. Strong covalent bonds form between the *carbon* atoms of all organic compounds.
(*d*) **Hydrogen** links/bonds are *very weak* bonds between *molecules* (groups of atoms) and between hydrogen and oxygen atoms in many organic compounds which have large molecules or *macromolecules*; these include hair and certain plastics (*see* Section 10.2).
Macromolecules do not conduct electricity and are electrical *insulators*, e.g. polythene; they are only *soluble* in certain solvents.

Polymers

Polymers are organic compounds with *macromolecules* made up from *many* smaller unit molecules, *monomers*, by a process called *polymerization*. The polymer macromolecules can resemble a long *chain*, or coiled spring, or be a *tangled* web. The compounds often have names beginning with *poly-*.

Natural polymers	Synthetic polymers	
	PLASTICS:	
	POLYETHENE (POLYETHYLENE)	– plastic sheets and bags
POLYSACCHARIDES:	POLYPROPENE (POLYPROPYLENE)	– plastic bowls, wig fibre
CELLULOSE – cotton, linen and rayons	POLYVINYL CHLORIDE	– cable insulation and wigs
STARCHES – in foods	POLYSTYRENE	– packing and tiles
GLYCOGEN – in foods	POLIVINYL ACETATE and POLYVINYL PYRROLIDONE	– hair lacquer
	POLYAMIDES	– nylons, in clothing, wigs
PROTEINS – POLYPEPTIDES		
KERATIN – in hair and wool	POLYACRYLONITRILES	– 'Acrilan', 'Orlon' – clothing, textile fibre
FIBROIN – silk	Also	
Different proteins in foods	MODACRYLICS	– 'Dynel', 'Kanekalon', 'Teklan' – wig fibres
	POLYESTERS	– 'Terylene', 'Dacron'
	POLYURETHANE	– Stretch stockings, swimsuits, foundation garments
		– 'Lycra', 'Spanzelle'

Table 4.3   Natural and synthetic polymers

Polymers can be either *natural* or man-made, *synthetic, as* shown in Table 4.3.

Polymer structure

Monomer	+	*Monomer*	+	*Monomer*	=	*Polymer*
Amino acid	+	*Amino acid*	+	*Amino acid*	=	*Protein*
Glucose	+	*Glucose*	+	*Glucose*	=	*Cellulose (Polysaccharide)*
Ethene	+	*Ethene*	+	*Ethene*	=	*Polyethene Plastic polymer*

Many thousands of monomer units go to make a macromolecule *polymer*.

Thermoplastic Polymers
Many polymer plastics, e.g. polythene, can be *softened* on warming and *hardened* by cooling. In this way plastic bowls and containers are moulded into shapes, and wig fibres *waved*.

Thermosetting Polymers
These include urea-formaldehyde (carbamide-methanal), phenol-formaldehyde, and melamine-formaldehyde plastics, called 'Bakelite', 'Formica', Wareite', etc., used in electric switch and socket covers, plugs, and electrical appliance covers and telephones. They cannot be reshaped by heating, since they char and blister, they are also *brittle* and crack on impact.

Dimethyl hydantoin methanal (formaldehyde) is a thermosetting resin used in hair lacquer setting lotions.

4.11   QUESTIONS

1 Briefly describe each of the following and its purpose:
 (*a*) dynamo generator;
 (*b*) transformer;
 (*c*) rectifier;
 (*d*) electrical conductor.
2 What is the purpose of an electrical insulator?
 How can a cable be *overloaded* and *short circuited*?
3 What are the main devices in a salon circuit to prevent *fire* arising in salon cables and wiring?
4 Explain the terms: (*a*) *voltage;* (*b*) *amperage;* (*c*) *frequency,* with respect to a salon circuit.
5 If a 'unit' of electricity costs 6 p, calculate the cost of electricity in a salon in which all appliances, heating and lights consume a total of 70 kilowatt hours.
 What is the relationship between watts, amperes and volts?
6 What devices can break or complete an electric circuit?
 Where are they located in the circuit?
 If an electric socket outlet is near water taps, how is the current from it controlled?
7 Which chemical compounds conduct electricity?
 What types of bonds/links are between the atoms?
8 What types of bonds or links are found in macromolecules?
 Give examples of important natural and synthetic *polymers* found in hairdressing.
 Why are certain synthetic polymers used for appliance and cable insulation?

4.12   MULTIPLE CHOICE QUESTIONS

1 Which of the following is a natural vegetable fibre?
 (*a*) hair
 (*b*) linen
 (*c*) polyamide—nylon
 (*d*) polyester—Terylene.
2 Which of the following synthetic plastic resins is thermoplastic?
 (*a*) polyethene (polythene)
 (*b*) phenol methanal (formaldehyde)
 (*c*) melamine methanal (formaldehyde)
 (*d*) carbamide methanal (urea formaldehyde).
3 Atoms of chemical elements are made up of equal numbers of:
 (*a*) electrons and protons
 (*b*) ions and protons
 (*c*) neutrons and electrons
 (*d*) electrons and ions.
4 The rate of flow of electric current is measured in units called:
 (*a*) amperes
 (*b*) watts
 (*c*) ohms
 (*d*) volts.
5 An appliance is rated at 500 W and is connected to a plug top. What size fuse is needed to fit in the plug top if the main supply is 240 V?
 (*a*) 3 A
 (*b*) 5 A
 (*c*) 10 A
 (*d*) 13 A.
6 What is the frequency of mains electricity in a salon?
 (*a*) 13 A
 (*b*) 240 V
 (*c*) 50 Hz
 (*d*) 2 kW.

5 Salon Heating

5.1 HEAT SOURCES IN THE SALON

The main sources of heat in a salon are: sun-shine, occupants, hot water, appliances and lights, and the space heating systems, sum-marized in Table 3.2 The *amount* of energy from each source will vary throughout the *seasons* of the year. There will be less *free* solar heating in winter and more in summer. On a sunny day in winter, a salon can obtain 6 kWh (equal to *three* 2 bar electric fires used for one hour) as *free* heat to heat the building.

5.2 SALON HEATING REQUIREMENTS

The *total* yearly or daily requirement of energy for a salon for **all** purposes is measured in *kilowatt-hours* (kWh) (*see* Section 4.5).

The amount of energy used for *space heating* a salon is about 60 per cent of the *total* energy requirements. The remaining 40 per cent is used for appliances, water heating and ventilation.

Table 5.1 summarizes the *total* energy need, and energy needed for *space heating* of different sized salon rooms and premises.

Room or premises	Annual total energy needs (kWh)	Annual space heating energy (KwH)	Daily needs and equivalent in two bar electric fires
Small room (3m x 2.5 m)	2 000	1 200	3 kWh or 1½ electric fires
Large room (5.5 m x 4.5 m)	6 000	3 600	10 kWh or 5 electric fires
Small salon premises (3 to 4 rooms)	10 000	6 000	16 kWh or 8 electric fires
Large salon premises (6 to 10 rooms)	30 000	18 000	50 kWh or 25 electric fires

Table 5.1   Energy needs for salon heating

Legal requirements

(*a*) It is a *legal requirement* in the U.K. that the salon heating system must be free from *fumes*.

(*b*) The *minimum temperature* of 16°C must be attained in one hour.

(*c*) *Room thermometers* must be conspicuous and show the room temperature.

5.3 SALON HEAT TRANSFER

Heat energy reaches the occupants in a salon from *heat sources* by three methods (Figure 5.1):

(*a*) *Radiation* is heat energy in the form of heat rays called *infra-red rays*. It does not require matter to carry it and it can travel through empty space or a *vacuum*. Infra-red rays are *reflected* by polished surfaces.

(*b*) *Convection* is the carriage of heat by fluid particles of water or air. Hot air and water *rises*, whilst cold air and water *falls*, producing heat movement in *convection currents*.

(*c*) *Conduction* is the vibration of particles in heated solids, liquids and gases. The *electrons* in *metals* move between the atoms and pass from the warmer to the cooler regions. Most metals are good *heat conductors*, non-metals, glass and plastic are poor heat conductors. Air is the poorest conductor of heat.

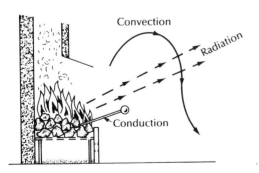

5.1   Methods of heat transfer

5.4   SALON DIRECT HEATERS
[See also Section 21.5]

Two main methods are used in the salon: *direct heaters* for local heating by *portable* or *fixed* fires and heaters, or *central heating* from one system.

Heater efficiency

This is measured as a *percentage* to show how much *useful heat* is given out from the *fuel*, gas, solid fuel, oil or the *electricity* consumed by the heater.

For example, *all* (100 per cent) of the electricity used by an electric fire is changed into useful heat, therefore its efficiency is 100 per cent. Only 30 per cent of the coal chemical energy burning in an open grate is useful heat, the remaining 70 per cent is lost in various ways, mainly up the chimney and heating the fireplace and chimney.

Solid fuel direct heaters

Fixed solid fuel direct heaters include the *open fire* in a grate, heater efficiency 30 per cent, and the solid fuel *closed fire* or stove providing a heater efficiency of 60 — 70 per cent. Both heaters transfer heat by radiation and convection, and require a flue.

Safety:
1 Fit guards where there are children.
2 Sweep flues regularly.
3 Provide a good air supply.

Paraffin oil direct heaters

Portable flueless heaters with paraffin oil burning from a *wick*, heater efficiency 95 per cent, the heat being transferred mainly by convection.
Safety:
1 Refill them out of doors.
2 Keep out of the way of draughts, people curtains and furnishings.

3 Never refill when alight.
4 Never carry them about alight.

Gas direct heaters

(*a*) *Portable* bottled gas heaters, have a heater efficiency of almost 100 per cent, they are flueless and provide heat by convection and radiation.

(*b*) *Fixed* natural gas heaters can be of the *convector* type, with an efficiency of 70 per cent; or the combined *radiant convector* with an efficiency between 50 — 70 per cent.

Small convector heaters do not require a flue, whilst large convector and radiant/convector heaters require a chimney flue, or a *balanced flue* (Figure 5.2) which heats the incoming outside air to supply the burners. Balanced flues are fitted to gas-fired central heating boilers.

Safety :
1 Guards should be on all radiant fires.
2 Flues should be regularly checked for *blockages*.
3 Supply plenty of *air* to heater.

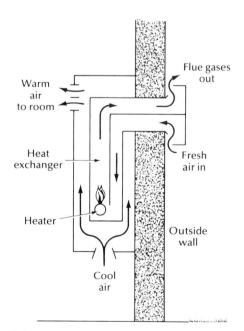

Warm air to room

Heat exchanger

Heater

Flue gases out

Fresh air in

Outside wall

Cool air

5.2   **A balanced flue convector heater**

Electric direct heaters

Heat is produced when an electric current flows through a *heater element*.

(*a*) *Convector heaters* draw *air* over the heater element either by convection or *forced convection* from a fan. A rapid way of heating up a room.
Safety: Do not cover or drape clothes over convector heaters.

(*b*) *Radiant heaters* are *high* heat sources, with the element as a bar with a *reflector* backing. The element is enclosed in a *silica* tube in medium heat sources.
Safety: Guards should be fitted to all radiant heaters.

Low heat sources have the element between panels or metal tubes as in wall heaters, or can be embedded in the wall or floor as in under the floor heating.

(*c*) *Storage heaters* use off-peak power and have the element embedded in concrete blocks. The heater efficiency is 90 per cent, and the heat is released by natural convection or forced convection by means of an electric fan.

5.5   CENTRAL HEATING

Heat from a fuel or electricity is used either to heat *water* in a boiler, or to heat *air* (Figure 5.3).

Hot-water central heating (Figure 5.4)

(*a*) Water in the *boiler* is heated *primarily* by gas, oil, solid fuel, which has a heater efficiency of 65 per cent, compared to 100 per cent for electrical boiler heating.

(*b*) A small *feedtank* provides water for the boiler, steam from the boiler escapes by an *expansion pipe* into the feed tank.

(*c*) Narrow pipes circulate the hot water to *radiators* or *convectors* in the salon by natural *convection*.

(*d*) A small pump returns the *same* water back to the boiler for reheating.

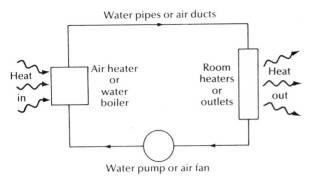

Water pipes or air ducts

Heat in → Air heater or water boiler → Room heaters or outlets → Heat out

Water pump or air fan

5.3 Simple central heating systems

Note: Hot water is *not* drawn from the boiler for taps — this is made by a *hot-water system* (*see* Section 7.4) using the central heating system or by *direct* heating.

Safety:

1 Do not tamper with controls.
2 Keep all materials away from the boiler.

Warm-air central heating

This can be with or without *air conditioning* (*see* Section 6.5).

(*a*) Cold air is heated by gas, oil or electricity in an *interchanger*.

(*b*) Warm air then passes through *ducts* to enter the salon rooms at *floor* level.

(*c*) Returned air is *purified*, filtered, moistened and warmed, or cooled depending on the *season*. Used air is extracted from the room at ceiling level.

A central heating system can have a *secondary* heat source from solar panels (Section 3.2), heat pumps (Section 3.2) and by allowing *waste* hot water in *drains* to heat water circulating in heat exchanger pipes back to the salon boiler (*see* Section 7.8).

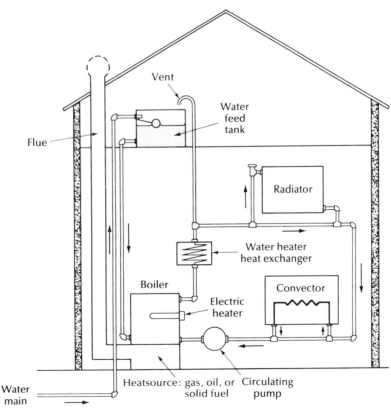

5.4 **Salon central heating system**

5.6   SALON HEATING CONTROLS

Salon room *temperatures* should be 21°C (70°F) for *full heating* or 13–18°C (55–64°F) for *background* heating during working time. Passageways and stores should be 16–18°C (61–64°F) for *full* heating or 10–12°C (50–54°F) for background heating.

Temperatures of rooms can be controlled *manually* by turning them off and on as a person *senses* excessive heat or cold, or it can be done *automatically* as follows:

(*a*) *Time controls* are clockwork timers which switch on *direct* or *central* heating systems at set times of the day.

(*b*) *Thermostats* are devices which provide a steady temperature in a room, boiler, or an appliance.

Bimetal thermostats may be fitted *outside* the salon to turn on the heating system as the outside temperature falls. Similar thermostats are found in many salon appliances.

Thermostatic valves are fluid filled and control radiators and convectors in the heating system.

5.7   SALON HEAT INSULATION

Salon heat loss (Figure 5.5)

Living human bodies generate their heat by *metabolism* (*see* Section 16.1), a salon building must be *warmed* by the methods previously described, otherwise it loses its heat. The methods of heat loss for human bodies and salon buildings are similar, *conduction, convection, radiation* and *evaporation* of water, sweat or dampness.

Clothing

Clothing is made from various natural and synthetic *polymer fibres* (Section 4.10), which are spun into *yarns* and woven or knitted into various *clothing materials*. Woven and knitted materials have numerous meshes to trap air in *air spaces* which are excellent

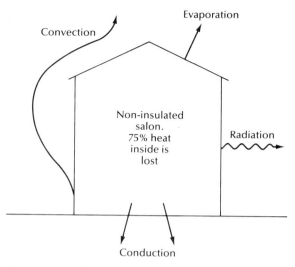

5.5   Salon heat loss

insulators of heat. The polymer fibres are also *poor* conductors of heat.

A human body *must* lose heat amounting to about 2 kilowatt hours or 7 MJ daily, otherwise it would become overheated and suffer *heatstroke*. *Loose fitting*, woven or knitted clothing material allows this heat and perspiration loss.

Salon insulation and heat loss

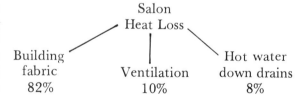

(*a*) *Hot water* to the drain can have its heat recovered by reheating incoming cold water in a *heat exchanger*.

(*b*) *Ventilation* heat losses are difficult to recover unless air conditioning systems are installed (Section 6.3). Open doors and *draughts* cause much heat loss. Fitting *self-closing* doors reduces heat losses.

(*c*) *Fabric* or heat loss through salon structure is as follows (*see* also Table 3.2):

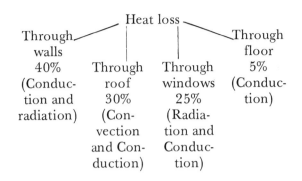

Through walls 40% (Conduction and radiation)

Through roof 30% (Convection and Conduction)

Through windows 25% (Radiation and Conduction)

Through floor 5% (Conduction)

Reducing heat losses

(*a*)   **Draught excluders** overcome heat loss through poorly fitting windows and doors.

(*b*) **Walls** in modern salon premises are *cavity walls* (Section 1.1), the air space between the two skins acts as a heat insulator. The cavity space can be filled with *foamed* polymer or mineral wool, this reduces heat loss through the wall by 75 per cent.

Walls can be insulated by means of expanded polystyrene foam *veneer* (5mm thickness), applied to the inner wall surface. This helps to overcome condensation dampness.

(*c*) **Roof** insulation includes aluminium *foil*, and loose *granules* of mineral wool, and *blankets* of glass fibre, or mineral wool, laid between the ceiling joists.

(*d*) **Window** insulation is achieved by *double glazing*, with two panes of glass and a dry sealed *air* space between the panes. Single panes can be insulated with a second sheet of glass or plastic fixed by various means. Lined *curtains* and window *shutters* are additional methods.

(*e*) **Floors** can be covered in underlay and carpet, and solid floors are insulated with foam polymer when they are laid down. Suspended floors (Section 1.1) can be insulated beneath the boards with aluminium foil or mineral and glass wool blanket.

(*f*) **Lagging** is the means of insulating cistern tanks and water pipes with expanded polystyrene, glass fibre wool blanket, or loosely wrapped rags. This is important to prevent *freezing* of water in the water system. Some cold water pipes are fixed to *warm* walls in a salon.

Hot water *storage cylinders* are fitted with a *jacket* of insulating material.

5.8   SALON SOUND INSULATION

Sound or *noise* is a form of energy, which can be *prevented* from entering the salon by the *same* methods as for salon heat insulation given in Section 5.7.

The following are additional methods of sound insulation: *hoods* and *cowls* fitted to ventilators and chimneys, outer doors with double skins and a sound insulating *lobby* between these insulated doors.

5.9   PHYSICS

Effect of heat on matter

(*a*)   **Solids** *expand* on heating and *contract* on cooling. This can be shown by a bar and gauge experiment. Molecules vibrate *rapidly* and cause an increase in volume when heat is applied to them.

Different substances expand by different amounts when heated together. The *alloy* invar shows very small expansion compared to brass. A *bimetal strip* is made from invar and brass sandwiched together.

The *thermostat* (Section 5.6) contains a bimetal strip which *bends* on heating.

(*b*) **Fluids** *Different* liquids expanded by *different* amounts when heated equally, for example ethanol (ethyl alcohol) expands more than water or mercury, they also expand *more* than solids.

Hot water will *float* on cold water because of its increase in volume over cold water.

Thermostatic valves contain organic liquids which readily expand on heating.

Different gases on heating all expand by the *same* amount.

Temperature

Temperature means the *relative* hotness and coldness of a body compared to melting ice or boiling water. Temperature is therefore a *number* on some chosen *scale*, shown on *thermometers*.

Thermometers *do not* measure heat. Heat is measured in joules by the *calorimeter* (Section 3.8).

(*a*) **Celsius**, Symbol °C, temperature scale is divided into 100 degrees between 0°C, melting ice, and 100°C boiling water.

(*b*) **Fahrenheit**, Symbol °F, temperature scale is now almost obsolete and is divided into 180°, as shown in Figure 5.6.

To change from °C to °F
   Multiply °C by 1.8 and add 32.
   Example: 59°C to °F
   59 × 1.8 = 106.2 + 32 = 138.2°C

To change from °F to °C
   Subtract 32° from °F, and multiply by 0.556
   Example: 70°F to °C
   70 − 32 = 38 × 0.556 = 21.12°C.

Thermometers are of various types summarized as shown in Table 5.2.

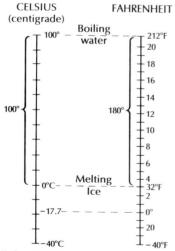

5.6   **Temperature scales**

Thermometer	Use and range
1 LABORATORY mercury in glass	Available in a wide range of temperatures, and in Celsius and Fahrenheit scales
2 ROOM mercury or spirit in glass	Mounted on a wooden or plastic scale indicating room temperature 18–21°C
3 BIMETAL invar/brass	Contain a bimetal coil or rod, connected to a travelling pointer. Measures a wide range of temperatures from 10° to 300°C on various appliances.
4 HOT WATER mercury in glass	Measures water temperature for hair washing and bathing. Hot 43°C, warm 39°C, tepid 32°C, atemperate 27°C, cool 21°C, cold 10°C
5 CLINICAL mercury in glass	Measures human body temperature with a range of 35–45°C. Normal body temperature 36.9°C (Figure 5.7)
6 MAXIMUM and MINIMUM, spirit in glass	For *recording* the *highest* and *lowest* temperatures in a room over a period. It is reset by a small magnet.

Table 5.2   Types of thermometers

Heat transmission

The following experiments are used to demonstrate heat transmission

Conduction
(*a*) The thermal *conductivities* of different *solid* substances are demonstrated using a metal tank of hot water into which are inserted wax coated *rods* of glass, wood, iron,

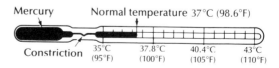

5.7   **Clinical thermometer**

copper and a plastic, e.g. Perspex. The wax melts over *different* distances indicating the different thermal conductivities.

(*b*) The poor thermal conductivity of *water* is shown by sinking a lump of ice in a boiling tube with wire gauze around it as a sinker in water. The water can be made to *boil* above whilst the ice remains solid beneath (Figure 5.8).

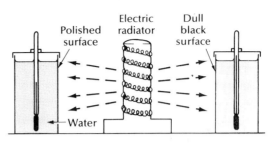

5.9   Heat radiation experiment

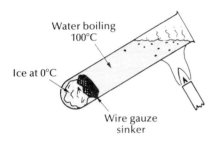

5.8   Water is a poor heat conductor

Insulation
The heat insulating properties of different materials depend mainly on the amount of *air* with its very poor heat conductivity, trapped amongst heat insulating solid materials.

Several small metal containers are wrapped with different heat insulation materials, and each container supported on a cork tile, and boiling water poured into each container. Cork stoppers with thermometers are inserted into each container and the rate of *cooling* or heat loss observed. The best heat insulator shows the least heat loss.

Radiation
Radiated heat is produced by all warm bodies and consists of *infra-red* or *electromagnetic waves* (*see* Section 13.1), these can be *reflected* or *absorbed* on striking a body.

(*a*) *Dull* and *black* surfaces are *good* heat radiators and absorbers, but *poor* reflectors.

(*b*) *Smooth* and *bright* surfaces are *poor* heat radiators and absorbers, but *good* reflectors.

Radiation and its relationship to surfaces can be demonstrated using a bright polished

can and a dull black can each full of water, placed at an equal distance from a heat source as in Figure 5.9. The temperature rise in each container is carefully noted.

Convection
During convection heat is carried from one point to another by *movement* of molecules of liquid or gas.

The convection *current* in water can be demonstrated using the apparatus which resembles a simple hot water central heating

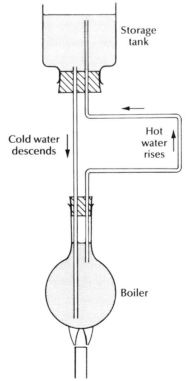

5.10   Heat convection in water

system (Figure 5.10). Coloured water is placed in the upper storage container.

Heating effect of electric current
(*see* also Sections 4.2 and 4.7)

When an electric current flows through a conductor, some of the energy is changed into *heat energy*. The *amount* of heat produced depends on the following:

1 *Material* of the conductor, whether it is copper with a low *resistivity* or if it is an alloy, e.g. *nichrome* nickel/chromium or a metal element, *tungsten*, with a high resistivity. *Resistivity* is the resistance of similar-sized cubes of the material at $0°C$.

2 *Dimensions* of the conductor. *Short* and *thick* conductors, have a lower resistance than *long* and *thin* conductors of the same material.

3 *Current flowing*. As the amperage and voltage *increase* the temperature of the conductor will also increase.

The heating effect is of importance in space heating appliances (Section 5.4), fuses (Section 4.7), lighting (Section 6.7), and various salon hairdressing appliances (Section 12.2).

5.10   QUESTIONS

1 Briefly describe the main ways in which heat travels from a *named* type of salon direct heater.

2 What are the main ways in which heat is lost in a salon?
Describe methods to overcome this heat loss.

3 What are *heat* conductors, radiators and convectors?

4 Describe a simple hot-water central heating system.
How is the heat production *controlled* in this system?

5 Explain how an electric current produces heat.
What is the importance of the conductor material, size, and current amperage?

6 Describe one flueless heating appliance and one appliance requiring a flue, which use a fossil fuel.
Indicate their approximate heating efficiency.

7 What means are used to determine human body temperature, room temperature and water temperature?
Convert the following Fahrenheit temperature $140°F$ to the corresponding temperature on the Celsius scale.

5.11   MULTIPLE CHOICE QUESTIONS

1 Which of the following devices serves to maintain a steady temperature at a specific heat setting in a salon dryer?
(*a*) cartridge fuse
(*b*) three heat switch
(*c*) bimetal thermostat
(*d*) earth wire.

2 Which of the following is an insulator or nonconductor of heat?
(*a*) invar steel
(*b*) nichrome
(*c*) rubber
(*d*) brass.

3 Which of the following flueless room heaters will *not* add to the humidity of the room air?
(*a*) radiant electric fire
(*b*) natural gas fire
(*c*) solid fuel fire
(*d*) paraffin oil fire.

4 Which two of the following are the main means by which heat leaves a salon storage heater?
(i) diffusion
(ii) conduction
(iii) radiation
(iv) convection
(v) reflection
(vi) evaporation
(*a*) (i), (ii)
(*b*) (iii), (iv)
(*c*) (v), (vi)
(*d*) (iv), (v).

5 In a gas central heating system, the gas used is charged for by the:
(a) litre
(b) kilogram
(c) therm
(d) kilowatt hour

6 Which of the following devices would regulate the room temperature in a gas central heating system?
(a) gas governor
(b) time switch
(c) air thermostat
(d) boiler thermostat.

6 Salon Environment

6.1 SALON CONDITIONS
[*See* also Section 21.5]

The salon *environment* is made up of the *external surroundings* in which the hair-dresser *works* and in which the client expects *physical comfort*.

The salon *internal environment* can be affected by the climate, weather and season. In addition it is affected by *activities* taking place in the salon, movement of people, washing, drying, processing and salon heating.

The main *environmental conditions* in the salon are summarized as follows:

A *comfortable* salon environment will provide certain environmental conditions *acceptable* to the human body. The human body is able to maintain steady *internal environment* conditions by wearing suitable *clothing* and various mechanisms which include a body temperature *thermostat* located in the brain. *Extreme* external conditions of heat and cold, fumes, lighting and humidity will cause *discomfort* to the body, and also affect body *efficiency*, *temperament*, *personality* and *behaviour*.

Table 6.1 summarizes the environmental conditions which provide comfort and discomfort in a salon.

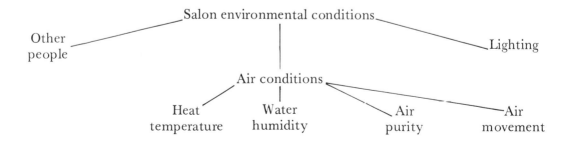

Environment condition	Comfort	Discomfort
Space	Roomy and spacious with ample space between occupants and equipment	Overcrowded and cramped for space. Leading to *accidents*.
Lighting	Subdued, restful, with even lighting of dark passages and areas	Glaring or dim light, leading to *accidents*
Air conditions		
(a) Temperature	Temperate and mild	Overheated or cold
(b) Humidity	Stimulating	Moist and sticky. Dry and arid.
(c) Purity	Odourless, dust free and fresh	Odorous, dusty, and stale
(d) Movement	Draught free	Draughty.

Table 6.1   Effect of salon conditions on body comfort

Activity	Salon environmental effect				
	Temperature	Moisture	Harmful Gases	Odours	Dust and microbes
Body functions: respiration, sweating and movement	✓	✓	✓	✓	✓
Space heating by: fossil fuel, gas, oil, solid fuel	✓	✓	✓	✓	Ash
Electric heaters	✓	—	—	—	—
Smoking	—	✓	✓	✓	✓
Washing	✓	✓	—	✓	–
Drying	✓	✓	—	✓	✓
Hairdressing processes	✓	✓	✓	✓	✓

Table 6.2   Summary of salon pollutants' sources

Activities affecting the salon environment are summarized in Table 6.2 and as follows.

6.2   AIR CONDITION: PURITY

Pure air is a mixture of 20% *oxygen*, and 80% *nitrogen*, with 0.03% carbon dioxide, and *variable* amounts of water vapour (*see* Section 6.4).

The different harmful impurities or *pollutants* of salon air are summarized in Table 6.3.

Legal requirement
In the U.K. it is a *legal requirement* that there is effective ventilation and the air is free from *fumes* from the *heating* system.

Salon air impurity or pollutant	Source
Micro-organisms (*see* Section 19.1)	From coughing, sneezing, spitting, breathing, and body functions. Cause various *diseases*.
Dust and dirt and other *solids*	Dry soil, soot, hair spray lacquer, skin scales, hair cuttings, fibres and fluff from towels and dryers. Can cause skin and lung *infection*.
Odours	*Body odours* arise from micro-organism activity on *unwashed* skin, and lack of personal hygiene (Section 20). Fossil fuel and tobacco *smoke and tars*. *Hairdressing preparations* particularly cold waving, depilatory and solvents, can cause *lung* disease.
Carbon dioxide CO_2	*Respiration* by-product (Section 16.1). *Fuel* combustion by-product. Should not exceed *0.5%* by volume, when it becomes harmful and causes *suffocation*.
Carbon monoxide CO	*Tobacco smoking*, and fossil fuels burning with *insufficient* air. Highly *poisonous*.
Sulphur dioxide SO_2	By-product in burning coal and oil fuels (not formed from bottled or natural gas). Causes bronchitis and *lung* disorders.
Ash	Product of burning coal, solid fuel and tobacco. May cause *lung* disorders.

Table 6.3   Harmful pollutants of salon air

Air purification methods

1 Efficient *chimneys* and *flues* which take away the products of combustion of fuels will reduce salon air pollution.
2 *Air changing* by removal and replacement of stale air by various ventilation methods (*see* Section 6.5).
3 *Salon cleaning* to reduce airborne dust and dirt.
4 *Air disinfection* by means of micro-organism destroying agents.
   (*a*) aerosol *disinfectant* sprays containing various bactericidal chemicals, for example, QACs, *cationic detergents* (Section 7.5);
   (*b*) *ultraviolet* radiation mainly from sunlight or from ultraviolet ray air purifiers;
   (*c*) *ozone* is a gas somewhat similar to oxygen, and can be used to purify air by ozone apparatus; it reforms oxygen in addition to being a bactericide.
5 *Air filtration* is part of an air conditioning system (Section 6.6).
6 *Photosynthesis* produces oxygen as a by-product; green flowering potted plants can help in salon air purification.

Aerosol *deodorants* blanket or *mask* unpleasant odours with a pleasant odour. They are *not* air purifiers or fresheners. Cold wave perming lotions require *masking* with a perfume.

6.3   AIR CONDITION : WARMTH

The temperature or *warmth* of salon air is related directly to salon heating methods (Chapter 5), which aims to provide an *acceptable* temperature for the human body.
   (*a*) Salon *operatives* expending energy during their work require an environmental temperature of $13° - 17°C$.
   (*b*) Salon *clients* who are *relaxing* in the salon, require an environmental temperature of $20°C - 23°C$.
   In the circumstances in order to satisfy the *client*, the salon *operatives* can be lightly clothed to overcome body overheating.

6.4   AIR CONDITION: WATER OR HUMIDITY

Sources: Water is a volatile liquid which

enters the air by *evaporation* or *boiling* Section 2.7) and by the processes occuring in the *water cycle* (Section 2.1). In the *hair-dressing* salon the additional sources will include water vapour from: hair-dryers, shampooing, steaming, processing, together with the respiration and perspiration of the occupants.

Humidity is a measure of the *amount* of water vapour in the air. In a day between 7 to 14 litres of water is vapourized in a salon; one person produces approximately *one* litre daily as water vapour from *sweating* and from the *lungs*.

Effect of humidity

(a) *Excessive* humidity affects the rate of evaporation of sweat and in turn the body is not effectively *cooled* down, the skin feels clammy and uncomfortable.

(b) *Low humidity* affects loss of water from the respiratory *membranes* lining the lungs, their dryness can lead to respiratory *infections*.

Humidifiers

Solid fuels, gas and oil all produce water vapour as a combustion product. Electric direct heaters do not add combustion products to air and consequently *dehydrate* or dry the air and reduce its humidity. Water vapour producing *humidifiers* are fitted to electric direct heaters and into warm air central heating systems (*see* Section 6.6).

Hygroscopic materials

Hygroscopic materials (Section 2.8) include hair, wool and cotton. Wool and cotton furnishings and curtains will help to *control* humidity in a salon and thus reduce humidity. Synthetic polymers, for instance, plastics used in furnishings will not have this beneficial effect because they are *non-hygroscopic* materials.

Normal humidity of air

The *normal relative* humidity of air or the *humidity comfort* levels are between 50 and 70 per cent. *Below* 50 per cent it is *dry* and over 70 per cent *wet*, neither of which contribute to *humidity comfort*.

Condensation

Warm air holds more water than cold air. As the air temperature falls the air will reach *saturation* point and liquid water or *dew* begins to form. This will occur on cold *surfaces* of walls, ceilings, windows and floors.

If the air *relative humidity* exceeds 70 per cent for prolonged periods *condensation damp* will occur causing the growth of *moulds*.

Preventon of condensation dampness (Figure 6.1)

The following methods are used:
1 *Ventilation* or air movement (Section 6.5)
2 *Wall insulation* (Section 5.7).
3 Window double glazing (Section 5.7), tubular or strip heater installation. Condensation drip grooves can be fitted to *drain* the condensate away.

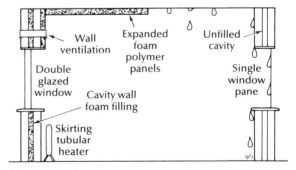

6.1   **Condensation damp prevention**

Salon dampness

Dampness in salons can be due to several causes:

1 *Condensation* damp.
2 *Hygroscopic* damp due to hygroscopic salt impurities in wall plaster.
3 *Rising or capillary damp* (Section 1.2).
4 *Penetrating damp* (Section 1.2).
5 *Burst pipes* or overflowing cisterns (Section 2.5).

6.5   AIR CONDITION: MOVEMENT OF AIR

Ventilation is the process of *movement* and *circulation* of air. It is a *legal requirement* in U.K. salons that the ventilation system is *effective*.
1 **Wind** is a *large* scale movement of air, caused by convection (Section 5.3). Air moves from a region of *high* air pressure to one of *low* air pressure (Section 3.8).
2 **Natural draughts** are small scale movements of air *within* a salon caused by air being (*a*) *drawn* through a room by *combustion* and *respiration* or oxygen use in the room; (*b*) *forced* into a room by outside *wind pressure*.
3 **Forced draughts** are movements of air within a salon caused by (*a*) *extraction* or *suction* of air by means of extractor fans; (*b*) *insertion* or *blowing* of air into a room by blowers.

Effect of air movement

Moving air in a ventilated room has the following effects:
(*a*) *Stale air*, odours and gases are removed and replaced by fresh odourless air.
(*b*) *Moisture* is removed from around the body surface, and other wet surfaces by allowing evaporation or *drying* (Section 12.1). Humidity of the air is reduced *if* replaced by less humid air.
(*c*) *Airborne* micro-organisms (anaerobes) are destroyed by oxygen in fresh air.
(*d*) *Heat* is *removed* which is an *advantage* in the summer season, but a heat loss disadvantage in the winter season.

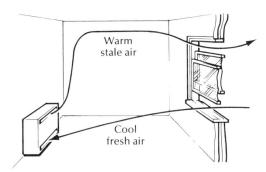

6.2   Room ventilation

Ventilation is important for the air space under *suspended floors* and in *roof* spaces, to prevent damp and growth of mould leading to *wet* and *dry rot*.

Methods of ventilation

1 **Windows and doors**, allow *free* entry of air. An open window can result in 10—20 room *air changes* per hour (Figure 6.2).
2 **Chimneys and flues** with fuel burning appliances will draw air through wall ventilators, and floor ventilators, by natural draught. Additional draught can come from poor fitting doors, windows and cracks in floorboards (Section 5.7). Room air changes by this method are between 5 – 7 times an hour.
3 **Extractor fans** are electrical *motors* turning fans at various speeds, which can extract air at various rates between 10 – 20 times an hours depending on the motor *wattage* and room *volume*. Extractor fans are fitted either into the outer wall or window of a salon, and require ventilator *inlet*.
4 **Combined ventilation** (Figure 6.3) **and Heating System** Warm **air heating** can be with or without air treatment when this is known as the *air-conditioning* system, and includes a *blower* fan to force *conditioned air*, that is air which has been *purified, humidified* and *warmed or cooled*, through ducts into salon rooms. The conditioned air *inlet* is at *floor* level and the stale *used* air *extractor* is at ceiling level.

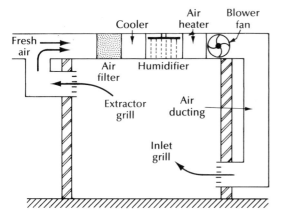

6.3   Air conditioning system

(*a*) Air is purified by *filtration*, ultraviolet *radiation*, and by *ozone*.

(*b*) Control of humidity is by a *humidostat*, and air temperature by a *thermostat*.

(*c*) *Refrigerators* cool the air, whilst *heat pumps* or other heat sources warm the air.

Features of a good ventilation/heating system

1 **Silent** air movement, no outside noise.
2 **Odourless** air.
3 **Purified**, dust, dirt and microbe free air.
4 **Comfortable humidity**, 50 − 70 per cent.
5 **Comfortable warmth**, 18 − 22°C.
6 **Air movement**, draught free, for a fresh feel to the circulating air.
7 **Continuous air change**.

6.6   FIRE CAUSES
[*see* also Section 22.5]

Three conditions are needed to make a fire:

Heat + Fuel + Oxygen = Fire

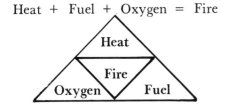

Heat can be provided by:

(*a*) Direct salon *heaters* and central *heating systems*, and hot water pipes.

(*b*) Sunlight.

(*c*) *Naked flames*: matches, lighters, open fires, cigarettes.

(*d*) *Sparks*, from defective electrical switches, lights, appliances.

(*e*) *Overloaded* electric cables and flexes (Section 4.7).

(*f*) *Bacteria* (anaerobes) multiplying in rubbish and refuse in dark unventilated places.

Fuel

This includes *combustible* materials that will burn or undergo combustion.

1 *Fuels*, any hydrocarbon, wood, oil, petrol, flammable *solvents*, bottled gases. These should be stored *outside* the salon.
2 Flammable materials, most plastic polymer furnishings, furniture, polystyrene tiles, gloss paints. Towels and clothing materials. Wigs and postiche. Rubbish, waste paper, cardboard, hair cuttings and empty plastic containers.
3 *Human bodies* burn.

Oxygen

1 *Air*, particularly *moving* air.
2 *Oxygen* from gas cylinders.
3 *Oxygen rich* chemical compounds including: hydrogen peroxide, perborates, chlorates (weedkillers), nitrates (fertilisers), persulphates, bromates, all of which are called *oxidising agents*. These chemicals must be stored *apart* and away from flammable materials.

Fire precautions and prevention
[*see* also Section 22.5]

It is a *legal requirement* in the U.K. that salons must have *fire precautions*, fire *extinguishers and appliances*, *fire exits* such as stairs, ladders and/or ropes of a certain required standard laid down by local *Fire Authorities*.

Every salon should have a *fire drill* procedure.

Electrical precautions

1 **Wiring and flex** should not be damaged or perished.
2 **Overloading** of cables and flexes should not occur (Section 4.7).
3 **Main switch** position must be known (Section 4.4), and turned *off* in the event of fire.
4 **Wall socket** switches must be turned off and plugs disconnected from socket at night and when not in use.

Storage

1 **Flammable** solvents and materials must be kept in a *cool* store away from heat. Bottles must be on *ground level* to prevent accidents from bottles breaking in falling off shelves.
2 **Fire supporting** or **Oxygen rich** materials should be kept in a metal cupboard away from flammable materials.
3 **Materials**, curtains, towels, etc. should not be draped over or on salon radiators, convectors or direct heaters. Asbestos and glass fibre are the only flame-proof *non-flammable* materials. Other materials have varying resistance to burning or *flammability*.
4 **Cigarettes.** Ample ashtrays must be available and their contents diposed separately from sweepings and flammable rubbish *outside* the salon.

Fire Extinguishing

This is the work of the Fire Brigade — call them in **any** *event immediately.*

In the *meantime*, fires can be extinguished by: (*a*) *fuel starvation*, (*b*) *fire cooling*, (*c*) *fire*

Good Resistance to burning	Low flammability	High flammability
Modacrylic	Flame retardant treated cotton, rayon, acetate	Acetate, acrylics, cotton, linen, rayons, triacetate, and their blends
Polyvinyl-chloride (PVC)	Nylons	
'Nomex' nylon	Polyesters	

Table 6.4   Fibre flammability

smothering by means of fire extinguisher appliances.

Fire starvation
(*a*) Turn **off main gas tap, or oil fuel tap.**

(*b*) *Remove* flammable materials, furniture, clothing, and above all **people** from near the fire.

Fire cooling methods
(*a*) Turn off heat source — electricity at **main switch.**

(*b*) Spray *water* on fires that are *not* due to oil (oil floats on water) or due to *live* electricity.

Fire smothering methods
(*a*) **Close** doors and windows.

(*b*) **Blanket** a fire with rugs, mats, dry sand, soil or asbestos *fire blankets*.

(*c*) **Foam** fire extinguishers release foam to smother fires caused by *oils*.

(*d*) **Carbon dioxide** *gas* extinguishers and sodium bicarbonate dry *powder* extinguishers release a blanket of dense carbon dioxide gas which extinguishes electrical and other fires (Figure 6.4).

(*e*) **Soda/acid** extinguishers release carbon dioxide gas by the action of sulphuric acid on a solution of sodium bicarbonate. The gas CO_2 and water serve to blanket and cool the fire (Figure 6.4).

(*f*) **Chloro-fluoro Hydrocarbon** or *vapour-*

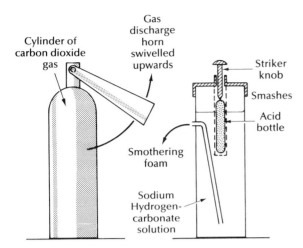

6.4   Carbon dioxide and soda-acid fire extinguishers

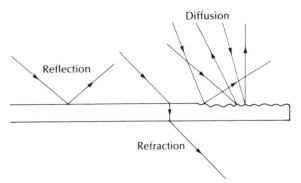

6.5   Reflection, refraction and diffusion of light rays

izing liquid extinguishers contain organic compounds (Section 3.7) which form a dense blanket of *vapour* to suffocate a fire caused by electricity.

(*Some* aerosols contain similar substances as propellants, but other aerosols contain flammable *butane*. Store all kinds of aerosols away from heat.)

Fire alarms operate by either *bimetal* strips or expansible *fluid* heat detectors, or by *smoke* detectors, which set off alarms in a bell circuit powered by *dry* batteries and *not* by mains electricity.

6.7   SALON LIGHTING

It is a *legal requirement* in the U.K. that salons, passageways and stairways are well *illuminated*.

Nature of light

Light is a form of *energy*, produced from several sources. It travels in the form of waves or *rays*, similar to radiant heat energy (Section 5.3). Light rays travel in *straight lines* from a light source *point*, seen when a beam of sunlight streams through an opening in the curtains of a darkened room.

When a ray of light strikes a substance, three things can happen to it according to the *material* and nature of its surface (Figure 6.5).

(*a*) *Reflection* occurs from a smooth polished surface, when the light rays are returned according to the laws of reflection (Section 6.9).

(*b*) *Refraction* occurs when light rays penetrate into and through a material, the light is *bent* at the surface of the materials.

Transparent materials permit the passage of all light, allowing objects to be seen through it, e.g. clear glass in windows and lenses, and certain polymer plastics. *Opaque* material does not permit passage of light rays, for example wood, metals, and certain polymer plastics. *Translucent material*: some light is allowed to pass through the material but objects cannot be seen clearly, e.g. frosted glass, translucent paper and polymer plastics, and human hair.

(*c*) *Diffusion of light* rays occurs when they are *scattered* in different directions by *rough* irregular *matt* surfaces.

Salon daylighting

The interior of a salon is illuminated by either *daylighting* or *artificial* lighting. Sunlight out of doors is fifty times as strong as light inside near a salon window. The sun is a powerful source of light energy, which enters the salon interior by wall *windows* or roof *skylights*, the glass of which must be kept *clean* to allow complete refraction and prevent light loss by diffusion.

Different types of glass apart from *clear glass* can be used with effect in salon windows and skylights, and doors.

Wired glass is a means of *security*, and holds glass together when broken, and prevents fire spreading. *Toughened glass* is for display windows and doors. *Prismatic glass* refracts light into overshadowed rooms. *Textured and patterned glass* diffuses strong sunlight.

Salon position

In the U.K. the sun rises in the *east* in the morning, and during most of the day the sun shines from the *south*, to set in the west in the evening.

Windows and rooms facing south will be the most brightly daylighted rooms, whilst those facing north will have poor daylighting.

Greenhouse effect

Salon windows which face south allow sun rays (light and infra-red) to refract through the window glass into the room. In the room the sun rays are *reflected* from walls, ceilings and windows; this results in *overheating* of the room, in a similar way to a greenhouse. The greenhouse effect can be overcome by fitting curtains, blinds or shutters to the windows, or applying a transparent heat reflecting *film* to the window inner surface.

Artificial lighting

Artificial lighting can be from gas and oil *lamps*, which produce light as a product of *combustion*. Both methods are sources of salon *emergency* lighting.

Electric lighting to supplement or replace daylighting is by means of the electricity in the lighting circuit (Section 4.6), with *separate* circuits on each salon floor.

Filament lamp lighting is by means of filament lamps which contain an extremely thin *tungsten* wire filament, of a very high resistance. This tungsten wire becomes *white* hot when the current flows (Section 5.9). The electrical energy is converted into mainly *light* energy in addition to *heat* energy (Figure 6.6).

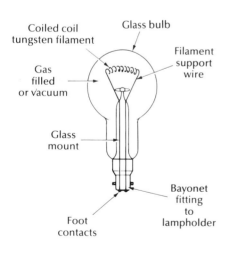

Filament lamp

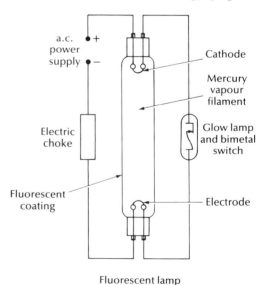

Fluorescent lamp

6.6   Filament and fluorescent tube lamps

To prevent the filament from *burning away*, the filament lamp is either filled with an inert gas – *gas-filled*, or is completely empty – *vacuum* lamps. The filament can be of a *single coil* or a *coiled coil* type, the latter gives off more light that a single coil lamp.

Lamp wattage

The degree of brightness of a lamp is indicated by its *wattage*. This is marked on the lamp, together with its operating mains *voltage*.

High wattage, 150 or 100 W indicates high light intensity. Medium wattage includes 80 and 60 W, whilst low wattage lamps down to 5 W are very dim night-lights.

Lamp lighting costs

To find the number of *hours* lighting for *one unit* of electricity divide 1000 by the lamp wattage.

Example: a 60 W lamp can be used for
$$1000 \div 60 = 16.6 \text{ hours.}$$
The average lamp *life* is 800 – 1000 hours.

Reflector or infra-red ray lamps are similar to filament lamps but have an internal silvered reflector surface, which concentrates the light and heat in 'spot' lighting.

Fluorescent lamps (Figure 6.6)

These are tubes of glass coated internally with a *fluorescent* powder. The electric current passes through the tube as electrons conducted by *mercury vapour* which fills the tube. Invisible *ultraviolet* rays are produced which change into white *visible* light on contact with the fluorescent powder. Most of the electrical energy is converted into light, and very *little* heat energy is produced.

Features
1 Longer life (5000 hours) and twice as much light as filament lamps.
2 Less heat and less expensive to run than filament lamps.
3 Type of light produced can be varied to include *warm* white, and *natural* white; this can affect colour matching (Section 11.7).
4 Fluorescent lamps are available in different lengths from 150 mm (4 W) to 2440 mm (125 W). 10 W are needed to illuminate each *square metre* of floor area.

Lamp holders

Lamps are connected to *lighting points* which can be *electrified tracks* suitable for spot lighting and for clipping on several light fittings and reflector lamps; or *lampholders* connected to ceiling *roses*, for *one* light fitting.

Lampholders support filament and certain fluorescent lamps, by means of their bayonet fittings, the lampholder connects with the ceiling rose by an *earthed* flex.

Modern lampholders, including those made of metal, are earthed as in Section 12.6.

Wiring a lampholder (Figure 6.7)
1 Switch *off* the main switch at the meter.
2 Unscrew the lampholder *cover* and thread the flex through the cover.

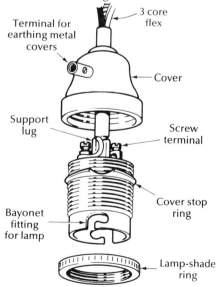

Terminal for earthing metal covers

3 core flex

Cover

Support lug

Screw terminal

Bayonet fitting for lamp

Cover stop ring

Lamp-shade ring

6.7 Lampholder connections

3 Insert the bared wire ends of the 3 core flex as follows: *brown* and *blue* into the screw terminals, hook them under the small lugs to take the weight of the lamp and its fitting. Connect the *green/yellow* earth to the screw terminal in the cover.

4 Reassemble the cover.

Light fittings

Lampholders may have a *shade* connected by the *shade ring*. The type of shade, which is fitted, depends partly on the type of filament lamp used.

Clear glass filament lamps produce a bright intense light source, and are fitted into closed lamp shades.

Care! A lamp stronger than 60 W can cause melting of plastic lamp shades. *Opal, pearl and silica* lamps give a softer, *diffused* light suitable for fitting in *open* type lamp shades.

Glare

A dazzling bright intense salon illumination can cause *discomfort* to the occupants through light *glare*. The causes of glare in a salon are:

(*a*) *Light sources* which are unshaded, e.g.

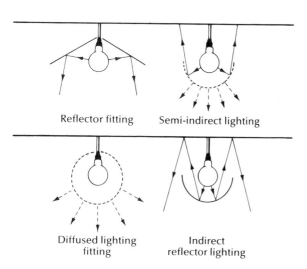

Reflector fitting   Semi-indirect lighting

Diffused lighting   Indirect
fitting   reflector lighting

6.8   Salon light fittings

fluorescent lamps or clear glass filament and reflector lamps (Figure 6.8).

(*b*) *Surfaces* which are smooth and high *reflecting*, mirrors, windows, gloss painted walls, ceilings, polished and chrome furniture and fittings.

Glare can be overcome or prevented by the following methods:

(*a*) Fit *diffuser* shades to light sources, in the form of translucent shades which completely surround the lamp source to provide *diffused lighting*; or *partly* surrounds the light source to give *semi-indirect lighting*. Indirect *reflectors* can cause light to be reflected from background walls or ceilings.

(*b*) *Walls and ceilings* should be finished in pale warm colours, with *matt* non-reflecting finish.

(*c*) *Spot and reflector lighting* should be restricted to illuminate displays, or small areas where fine work is undertaken.

(*d*) *Even illumination* without areas of shadow or dark coloured surfaces; this involves careful placing of salon mirrors.

6.8   CHEMISTRY

Air is a mixture

Air can be changed into *liquid air* and then *distilled* to separate the oxygen from nitrogen, this method of separation shows air is a *mixture* of gases.

Air composition

The composition of air is approximately 80 per cent *inert* nitrogen and 20 per cent oxygen. This can be shown by sprinkling *iron* filings inside a long graduated tube, and inverting the tube of *air* in a jar of water. Rusting of iron uses up oxygen from the air and the level rises by one-fifth or 20 per cent by volume.

Nitrogen gas is inert and takes no part in rusting, combustion, respiration or in any chemical change occurring in air.

Oxides

Oxygen when pure is colourless, odourless and a tasteless *gas*.

Almost all chemical elements combine with oxygen to form chemical compounds called *oxides*; this process is also called *oxidation*.

Oxidation

Element + Oxygen ⟶ Element oxide.

Oxides can be classified like this.

Acidic Oxides
These are oxides of *non-metals*.

Non-metal + Oxygen = Acid oxide.

They dissolve in water to produce *acids*.

Acid oxide + Water = Acid,

most of which turn neutral litmus indicator *red*.

Examples are:
(a) Carbon + Oxygen = Carbon dioxide

Carbon dioxide + Water = Carbonic acid

(b) Sulphur + Oxygen = Sulphur dioxide

Sulphur dioxide + Water = Sulphurous acid

Basic oxides
These are oxides of metals.

Some basic oxides dissolve in water to form soluble bases of *alkalis* which turn neutral litmus indicator *blue*.

Metal oxide + Water Alkali or Soluble base.

Examples are:
(a) Calcium + Oxygen = Calcium oxide

Calcium oxide + Water = Calcium hydroxide

(b) Magnesium + Oxygen = Magnesium oxide

Magnesium oxide + Water = Magnesium hydroxide

Neutral oxides
These are oxides which are neither acidic nor basic, but *neutral*.

Examples are:
Carbon + Oxygen = Carbon monoxide (highly poisonous)

Hydrogen + Oxygen = Water

Other oxides include the *peroxides*.

Process	Air gas			
	Oxygen	Carbon dioxide	Sulphur dioxide	Water vapour
Combustion	Necessary	Formed from carbon and carbon compounds	Formed from sulphur and sulphur compounds	Formed from hydrogen and hydrogen compounds
Rusting	Necessary	Helps but not necessary	Not involved	Necessary
Respiration	Necessary	Formed	Not involved (harmful to lungs)	Formed
Bleaching and cold waving	Necessary	Not involved	Can bleach	Necessary

Table 6.5   Chemical processes and the air components involved

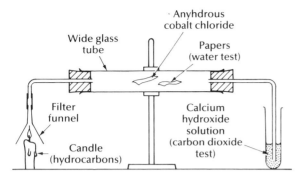

6.9   Testing the combustion products of a burning candle

Products of combustion

The main products of *combustion* are carbon dioxide, water and sometimes sulphur dioxide.

A burning candle of wax hydrocarbon is placed under a funnel as shown in Figure 6.9. The water vapour produced causes either blue anhydrous cobalt chloride paper to turn *pink*, or anhydrous copper sulphate from white to *blue*. The carbon dioxide turns the clear calcium hydroxide (lime-water) cloudy.

When a small amount of sulphur burns in a gas jar of air and the gas formed is mixed with water containing pink potassium permanganate, the pink colour is *bleached* by sulphur dioxide gas.

Carbon dioxide

Carbon dioxide does not support combustion or allow respiration to occur. This can be shown by placing a mixture of tartaric *acid* and sodium hydrogen carbonate powders in a beaker, together with a lighted candle. When water is slowly poured on to the powder mixture it releases a *foam* of carbon dioxide gas which extinguishes the candle flame.

6.9   PHYSICS

Diffusion is a process which occurs in liquids and gases, and involves the *movement* or transport of *molecules* from gas or liquid, from a region of high strength or concentration to a region of low concentration. This is the way in which odours and water vapour spread in *still air*.

Humidity measurement

$$\text{Relative humidity} = \frac{\text{Actual amount of water in air}}{\text{Maximum amount the air could hold at the } same \text{ temperature}}$$

Relative humidity is expressed as a percentage, for example, if the relative humidity is 50 per cent at 20°C, it means the air *can* hold another 50 per cent water vapour to become completely *saturated* at 20°C.

Hygrometers are instruments to measure relative humidity directly, and depend on the change in the *length* of *hair* or *paper* due to their hygroscopic property (Section 2.8).

Figure 6.10 shows a *hair hygrometer*. In moist air the hairs *lengthen*, and in dry air they *shorten*; this change is recorded as *magnified movement* via pulleys and a spring controlled pointer.

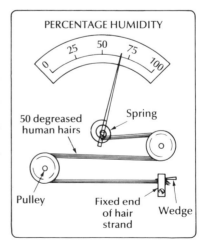

6.10   Hair hygrometer

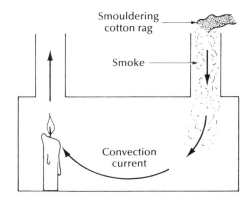

6.11 Heat convection in air

Gas convection

Convection *currents* in gases can be shown using the apparatus in Figure 6.11. *Cold* smoky air from the smouldering cloth is drawn down the chimney to replace the *hot* air which rises from above the candle.
Safety: When there is a fire outbreak and the room fills with smoke, the hot poisonous smoke *rises* to the ceiling, and any air entering the rooms will be cold and at *floor* level. Consequently one should *crawl* along the floor instead of standing upright in leaving.

Law of reflection of light

The law of light reflection, which also applies to heat ray reflection states that the *angle* formed by the *incident* ray is *equal* to the angle formed by the *reflected* ray as shown in Figure 6.12.

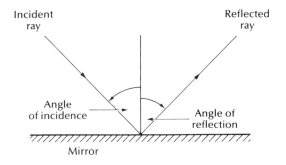

6.12 Law of light reflection

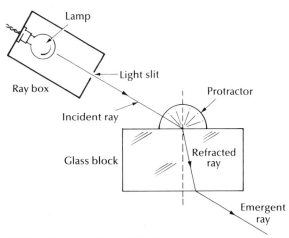

6.13 Refraction of light

This can be demonstrated by means of a flat or plane *mirror* and a *ray* box source of light rays. The ray box can produce a single narrow light beam which can be made to reflect from the mirror, angles being measured with a *protractor*.
Refraction of the light ray can be shown using a glass block as in Figure 6.13.

6.10 QUESTIONS

1 Describe the importance of *space* in obtaining a pleasant salon environment.
2 What are the *four* main factors in providing comfortable air conditions in a salon.
3 Describe the three main conditions for a fire to occur in a salon. Outline the methods of fire extinguishing whilst waiting for the fire brigade to arrive.
4 What are the main causes of discomfort arising from poor salon lighting, and how are they overcome?
5 Explain the following terms: (*a*) diffusion of air; (*b*) diffusion of light; (*c*) relative humidity; (*d*) reflection of light.
6 Briefly describe the sources of light in a salon.
Describe the light fittings used in direct and indirect salon illumination.
When is light refracted?

6.11   MULTIPLE CHOICE QUESTIONS

1 The approximate composition of air is:
 (*a*) 50% oxygen, 50% nitrogen
 (*b*) 80% oxygen, 20% nitrogen
 (*c*) 20% oxygen, 80% nitrogen
 (*d*) 90% oxygen, 10% nitrogen
2 Oxygen is essential for one of the salon processes to take place:
 (*a*) shampooing
 (*b*) steaming
 (*c*) bleaching
 (*d*) conditioning.
3 The filament wire in an electric filament lamp is made of:
 (*a*) nichrome
 (*b*) invar
 (*c*) tungsten
 (*d*) copper.

4 The light producing part of the fluorescent tube lamp is excited by the action of:
 (*a*) electrons
 (*b*) ultra-violet rays
 (*c*) infra-red rays
 (*d*) X-rays.
5 Hydrogen peroxide is a hazardous material in the event of fires since it:
 (*a*) provides exothermal heat
 (*b*) is a flammable liquid
 (*c*) provides oxygen
 (*d*) provides hydrogen
6 The hazard involved when using vaporizing liquid extinguishers in confined poorly ventilated spaces is the:
 (*a*) tendency for the extinguisher to explode
 (*b*) heated vapours are harmful if inhaled
 (*c*) floor becomes greasy and slippery
 (*d*) danger of electrocution.

7 Salon Cleaning

7.1 NEED FOR SALON CLEANING

Salon *cleaning* is an important *regular daily* process of removing soils and *waste* from the *environment* within the salon.

---Salon cleaning---

Soil removal from surfaces	Soil removal from materials	Salon waste removal	Human waste removal
Walls, floors mirrors, furniture and appliances	Towels, gowns, curtains and carpets	Hair cuttings, solutions, cotton wool, packaging	Faeces and urine

It is a *legal requirement* in the U.K. that a salon should be *clean*, particularly the floors, windows and skylights, and that *washing* facilities should be provided, together with facilities for storage of protective and outdoor clothing.

7.2 NATURE OF SALON SOILS

Salon *soils* are either *solid* or *greasy*, and are summarized as follows:

(*a*) **Dust** is the solid, small particle-soiling material, such as dry garden soil, soot, ash from solid fuels and cigarettes, which enter the salon from *outside* traffic of nearby industry. Dust produced inside the salon, includes: human skin scale dandruff, *fibres* of hair, and fluff from clothing, towels and furnishings, and talcum *powders*.

Unless removed, this dust can provide a food source for *fleas*, *bugs* and *house mites*, which breed in dust-filled floor and furniture crevices.

Dust clings to surfaces by the force of attraction of static electricity (*see* Section 7.9). This can be demonstrated by rubbing a dry plastic comb or ballpoint pen on the sleeve and holding over dry fragments of paper or cereal bran, when the *electrostatic* attraction picks up the fragments (Figure 7.1).

(*b*) *Chemical deposits and/stains* include *rust* on iron, green *verdigris* on copper or burnt

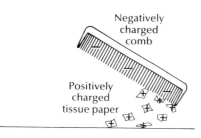

Negatively charged comb

Positively charged tissue paper

7.1   Electrostatic attraction

deposits on heating irons. *Stains* are chemical substances seen as tide marks of scum on wash basins, from various hairdressing processes, shampooing, and colouring. These cling by either *chemical bonding* to the surface (Section 4.10) or by *adsorption*.

The chemical *stain* can be demonstrated by adding a pinch of Methyl Violet 2B dye powder to warm water in a glass container. Leave the mixed coloured solution to stand, then empty completely.

Leave the container to dry and note the coloured stain within; this clings by *adsorption*.

Add a small amount of ethanol (methylated spirits) to the container and swirl it around inside. Note how the stain is rapidly removed by *solvent* action.

(*c*) *Grease* soils include lipid, hydrocarbon and waxy deposits from the skin *sebum*, or greasy *cosmetics* and hair *preparations*. Greasy soils cling to surfaces by a force of attraction called *adhesion*, an attraction which exists between molecules of *different* substances.

Most surfaces are grease attracting and in turn the grease attracts *dust* soil particles.

Greasy soils are invisible and can be disclosed on *glass* or metalware by dusting with a *mixture* of three parts powdered cornflour, three parts white china clay, and one part gum Acacia powder. When the excess powder is blown away, the grease marks are revealed by the dust clinging to the invisible greasy soil.

Ceramic or *china* and *earthenware* materials can disclose their invisible greasy soils by dusting with a *mixture* of seven parts black lampblack (carbon) powder, two parts graphite (carbon) and one part gum Acacia powder. The soils are revealed by blowing away the excess powder.

(*d*) *Micro-organisms*, bacteria, fungi are *living* organisms found soiling the different salon surfaces, and are invisible to the naked eye (*see* Section 19.1).

7.3   SALON WATER HARDNESS

Water which lathers easily with a *small* amount of soap, (the lather lasting for at least five minutes), is called *soft water*. Hard water requires a *considerable* amount of soap to form a *lasting* lather and also produces a sticky *scum* or *curd*, forming a tide-mark in wash basins.

Cause of hardness

Almost 65 per cent of salons in the U.K. have hard water, whilst soft water is received by salons mainly in Scotland, Wales and Northern Ireland.

Section 2.2 describes how natural water is collected. During this process it *dissolves* certain water-soluble salts. The amount is measured in *parts per million* (ppm). The very soft waters have a hardness of 0 to 50 ppm, moderately hard water 150–220 ppm, and very hard water over 500 ppm.

There are two types of water hardness *differing* in the salts dissolved in the water.

Temporary hardness

This is caused by *hydrogen carbonates* of calcium and magnesium; these form as rain-water containing carbon dioxide percolates through *limestone* — calcium carbonate rock (Section 7.10).

When temporary hard water is heated to above 60°C, the water is softened and the hardness removed. This happens by the breakdown of the hydrogen carbonates into *insoluble* carbonates and carbon dioxide gas.

This *chemical change* is shown as follows:

$$\begin{array}{c}\text{Calcium or magnesium}\\\text{Hydrogen carbonate}\\\text{(soluble salts)}\end{array} \xrightarrow{\text{(heat)}} \begin{array}{c}\text{Calcium or}\\\text{magnesium}\\\text{carbonate}\\\text{(insoluble}\\\text{salt)}\end{array} + \begin{array}{c}\text{Carbon}\\\text{dioxide}\\\text{gas}\end{array} + \text{Water}$$

Note: *Water* is a product of the chemical change, the amount being very small.

Calcium and magnesium *carbonates* are white powdery substances, which form *fur* or *scale* inside kettles and could also collect inside *boilers*.

Permanent hardness

If water remains hard *after* heating, the cause is due to soluble salts or *sulphates* of calcium and magnesium, which are unaffected by heat.

Total water hardness

Temporary — *Permanent*

Due to hydrogen carbonates of calcium or magnesium — *Due to sulphates of calcium or magnesium*

Table 7.1 summarizes the disadvantages and advantages of hard water.

Removal of hardness

(*a*) **Main water softeners** are connected to the water *service pipe*, by-passing the drinking water tap which receives *untreated* water.

Disadvantages	Advantages
1 Curd or scum formation clings to skin and material surfaces	1 A pleasant taste
2 Causes excessive use of soap	2 Dissolved calcium, magnesium and fluoride salts are beneficial to teeth and bone formation
3 Fur or scale blocks pipes, and causes overheating and fuel waste in boilers	
4 Fur or scale is removed by expensive removal processes	

Table 7.1 Disadvantages and advantages of hard water

The water softeners contain a plastic polymer resin which is a supply of *sodium ions* packed into a column or tower. The hard water passes through the *ion-exchange* resin and is softened by *exchanging* calcium/magnesium ions for sodium. See (A) below. In time all the sodium ions are drawn from the resin and must be replaced. This is done by flushing sodium chloride (salt) solution through the tower. See (B) below.

(*A*)

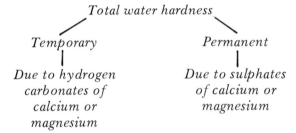

$$\begin{array}{c}\text{Sodium ions}\\\text{resin}\end{array} + \begin{array}{c}\text{Calcium or}\\\text{magnesium}\\\text{ions}\end{array} \longrightarrow \begin{array}{c}\text{Calcium or}\\\text{magnesium}\\\text{ions}\\\text{resin}\end{array} + \begin{array}{c}\text{Sodium}\\\text{ions}\\\text{in soft}\\\text{water}\end{array}$$

(*B*)

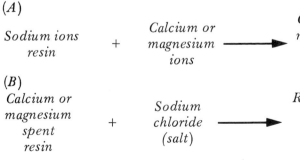

$$\begin{array}{c}\text{Calcium or}\\\text{magnesium}\\\text{spent}\\\text{resin}\end{array} + \begin{array}{c}\text{Sodium}\\\text{chloride}\\\text{(salt)}\end{array} \longrightarrow \begin{array}{c}\text{Regenerated}\\\text{sodium}\\\text{ions}\\\text{resin}\end{array} + \begin{array}{c}\text{Calcium}\\\text{magnesium}\\\text{chloride}\\\text{to waste}\end{array}$$

Small portable *water deionizers* are used to provide softened water in laboratories. In this process the carbonate and sulphate salts are changed by the *ion exchange* resin into *acids*, which in turn are removed by another ion exchange resin to form ion-free *pure water*, suitable for cosmetic preparations.

(*b*) **Chemical water softeners** are those chemical compounds which are added *directly* to hard water, instead of fitting a softener into the service pipe.

1 *Sodium carbonate* or washing soda, or *sodium sesquicarbonate*, the main component of bath salts, removes both temporary and permanent hardness by *exchanging* carbonate for sulphate and hydrogen carbonate.

Similar changes occur with ammonia (ammonium hydroxide), and sodium borate or borax.

2 *Sodium hexametaphosphate* is a soluble salt which softens water without forming any *insoluble* deposit, as in the case of sodium carbonate. In addition it does not form a scum or curd with soap.

Chemical water softeners are important components of many different salon *cleaning preparations* (Section 7.5).

7.4   SALON HOT WATER (Figure 7.2)

Hot and cold water are important as one of the *main* salon cleaning materials. Hot water is produced either instantly by *instantaneous*

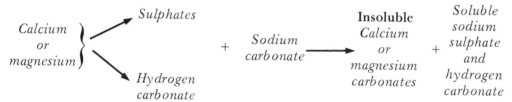

7.2   Salon hot-water system

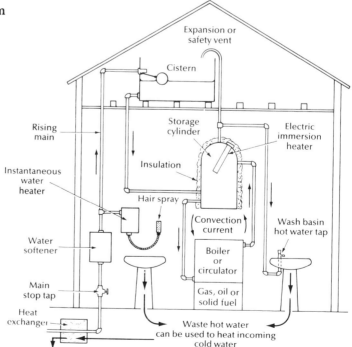

water heaters, or heated by different methods and stored in tanks or *storage* water cylinders.

Instantaneous water heaters

In their simplest form these consist of a special water carrying pipe heated by gas or oil, or a small boiler heated by electricity.

The instantaneous water heater is located *close* to wash basins, sinks or showers.

1 *Small* amounts of hot water *immediately* available.
2 Only the amount of water *used* is heated.
3 No heat is *lost* in long length of hot water piping or storage cylinders.
4 *Lagging* and extensive *pipes* are not required.
5 The electrical heater is *small* and compact and wall mounted.
6 Independent of *space heating* system.

Storage water heating

Hot water is stored in large copper *cylinders*

holding up to 125 litres. The water in the cylinder can be heated *directly* by an electric *immersion heater*.

Alternatively hot water is circulated by *convection* currents from a gas, oil or solid fuel heated *boiler*. In all cases the cold water supply is from a water storage cistern.

The *central heating* system heats water in the storage cylinder through a *heat exchanger* or coil of copper pipes inside the cylinder. The coil is supplied with hot water from the central heating system *boiler*.

1 *Large* amounts of water are available.
2 Unused water is *stored* until required.
3 Considerable heat lost *between* boiler and cylinder, and in piping system.
4 *Lagging* is needed for cylinders.
5 The system occupies considerable *space*.
6 Heat required in *summer*, when central heating system is shut down.

Salon wash basins

Salon wash basins and sinks consist of a

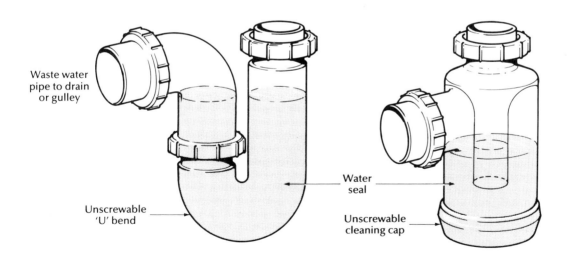

Waste water pipe to drain or gulley

Unscrewable 'U' bend

Water seal

Unscrewable cleaning cap

7.3   Wash-basin taps

container provided with hot and cold pillar taps (Section 2.4), and a *waste outlet*, which may have a *strainer*, into which the basin *plug* fits. The waste outlet connects to a U-shaped *trap* fitted with a *cleansing eye*. Water automatically fills the trap to form the *water seal* when the basin is emptied; it prevents entry of *odours* from the *drains* (Figure 7.3).

The *overflow* allows water to escape into the trap in the event of the basin accidentally overfilling.

A *waste pipe* connects the basin to the soil and waste *stack*. A *bottle trap* which is easily unscrewed, is an alternative basin trap fitting.

Clearing a blocked basin

1 First use a rubber *sink plunger* pressing it downwards over the basin outlet, *block* the basin overflow with a cloth.
2 If the plunger does not clear the blockage, place a bucket beneath trap. Undo the *cleansing eye*, or *bottle trap*, and allow water to fall into the bucket. Insert a length of springy curtain wire to move any obstruction beyond the trap neck. Replace the cleaning eye and *wash out* the bottle trap.

7.5   SALON CLEANING MATERIALS

The process of cleansing salon surfaces, or removing *soils*, requires the use of different *cleaning materials*. Detergents are chemical compounds which remove soils, the detergents being used as *solutes*, dissolved in *water*. Detergents are also called *surface active agents* or surfactants; they *detach* the soil from a surface, which is then dispersed or dissolved in the *water*.

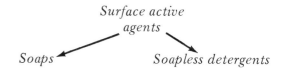

Soaps

Soaps are the oldest known surfactants made from edible *lipids* (Section 3.7). The fatty carboxylic acids are combined with *alkalis* (Section 6.8), such as potassium and sodium hydroxide. Tallow, coconut and palm oils are the main lipids for soap making or *saponification*.

Propanetriol (glycerine) is an important by-product of saponification.

Hard waters produce the *insoluble* scum with soaps.

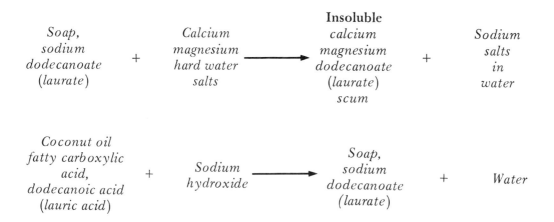

Ions

Soaps, like many other chemical compounds with *ionic bonds* in their molecules (Section 4.10), form *ions* which have either a *positive* or *cation* or *negative anion* electrical charge. An ion being an electrically charged *atom* or *group* of atoms.

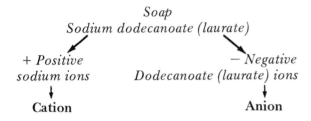

Soap
Sodium dodecanoate (laurate)

+ *Positive*   − *Negative*
sodium ions   *Dodecanoate (laurate) ions*

Cation   **Anion**

The sodium ion or *cation* is very small compared to the dodecanoate (laurate) ion or *cation* which is a *long chain or tail* of 13 carbon atoms, the negative charge being in the *head*.

Since soaps form large *anions* they are also called *anionic detergents*.

Soapless detergents

There are now *many different* kinds of soapless detergents and they are classified into *three* main groups, depending on the *charge* in the *head* of the largest ion.

An important feature of soapless detergents is that they *do not* form an insoluble scum with hard water.

1 *Anionic detergents*

These have a *negative* charge in the *head* connected to a long chain of carbon atoms in the *tail* of the anion.

Anionic detergents include *soaps*, and the following:

(*a*) *Sulphonated lipid oils*, oils such as olive, castor or coconut oil treated with sulphuric acid.

$$\begin{matrix} Lipid \\ oil \end{matrix} + Sulphuric\ acid \rightarrow \begin{matrix} Sulphonated \\ lipid\ oils \end{matrix}$$

Turkey red oil is made from castor oil.

(*b*) *Fatty alcohol sulphates* are made by changing the fatty *acids* of lipids into fatty *alcohols*. Dodecanol (lauryl alcohol) comes from coconut oil. The alcohols are then changed to fatty alcohol sulphates with sulphuric acid.

$$\begin{matrix} Dodecanol \\ (lauryl\ alcohol) \end{matrix} + \begin{matrix} Sulphuric \\ acid \end{matrix} \rightarrow \begin{matrix} Dodecanyl\ hydrogen \\ sulphate\ (lauryl \\ hydrogen\ sulphate) \end{matrix}$$

From this *starter* compound several useful surfactants are produced by different combinations with other chemical substances.

(*c*) *Hydrocarbon sulphonates.* Since lipid oils, coconut and olive are more valuable in foodstuffs, anionic detergents are made from petroleum *hydrocarbons* or *alkanes*, and can include benzene, naphthalene (Section 3.7) combined with sulphuric acid. These are collectively called *alkyl aryl sulphonates*.

$$\begin{matrix} Alkane\ Hydrocarbons \\ (Benzene,\ Naphthalene) \end{matrix} + \begin{matrix} Sulphuric \\ acid \end{matrix} \rightarrow \begin{matrix} Alkyl\ aryl \\ sulphonates \end{matrix}$$

Anionic detergent	Physical form
Dodecanyl (lauryl) sodium sulphate	Paste, powder or needles
Dodecanyl (lauryl) ammonium sulphate	Liquid or paste
Triethanolamine dodecanyl (lauryl) sulphate	A thin, or viscous liquid
Monoethanolamine dodecanyl (lauryl) sulphate	Liquid, or different viscosities
Dodecanyl (lauryl) magnesium sulphate	Liquid

Table 7.2 Physical forms of main anionic detergents

Alkyl aryl sulphonates are available as liquids, pastes and powders, and are the main components of *washing* powders and liquids (Table 7.2).

2 *Cationic detergents*

This group of detergents have a *positive* charge in the head connected to a long chain of carbon atoms in the tail of the cation.

Most cationic detergents are compounds called *quaternary ammonium* compounds, or called QACs for short. One example is *cetyl trimethyl ammonium chloride*.

Apart from being surfactants, they are also *antibacterial, fabric softeners* and hair *conditioners*. They are not normally used in salon cleaning preparations as detergents.

3 *Non-ionic detergents*

This group of detergents has a *neutral* group in the head connected to a long chain of carbon atoms in the tail.

Non-ionic detergents are complex compounds called *ethoxylates* combined with fatty alcohols, fatty acids, or amines. One named example is *cetyl alcohol ethoxylate*. They are liquids or waxy solids. They are mainly used in *mixtures* of detergents with

Soaps	Soapless detergents
Insoluble scum formed with hard water	No scum formed, calcium and magnesium salts of detergents are all *soluble*
Alkaline and can affect the skin	Mainly *neutral* and generally harmless to the skin
Cannot be used in *acid* solutions	Can be used in *acid* solutions, e.g. toilet bowl cleaners, acid shampoos
Moderate disinfecting and antiseptic property	QACs — cationic detergents are powerful disinfectants and antiseptics
Prepared mainly from *lipids* and *alkali* sodium hydroxide	Prepared partly from lipids, or hydrocarbons and *acid* sulphuric acid
Will not lather or with sodium chloride (salt) or seawater	Mix with sodium chloride — causing thickening of solution

Table 7.3   Comparison of soaps and soapless detergents

cationic detergents QACs, and in *low foaming* washing powders. The soaps and soapless detergents are compared in Table 7.3.

Salon Cleaning Material	Component							
	Anionic Detergent (%)	Cationic Detergent (%)	Non-ionic Detergent (%)	Abrasive Powders (%)	Acid (%)	Naphtha Solvents (%)	Sawdust (%)	Water (%)
Washing Powder	20	—	5	—	—	—	—	—
Washing-up liquid	40	—	2	—	—	—	—	To 100
Disinfectant	—	2	1	—	—	—	—	To 100
Basin and tile cleaner	—	5	5	75	—	—	—	15
Floor dewaxer	—	5	5	—	—	90	—	—
Toilet bowl cleaner	1	2	—	—	15	—	—	To 100
Floor sweeping compound	3	2	—	—	—	—	80	15

Table 7.4   Summary of composition of some salon cleaning materials

Other salon cleaning materials

1 *Abrasives*
These are paste or powder preparations in which the *abrasive* material is powdered brick, pumice, china clay, fine sand or emery powder, or powdered forms of *silica*. They are used mixed with *detergents* in various scouring preparations.

2 *Solvents* (Section 2.8)
Organic *solvents* include the following useful for removing greasy soils and various chemical stains:

Ethanol (methylated spirits) for certain dyes, shellac, ballpoint ink.

Naphtha solvent for dewaxing, and degreasing surfaces.

Propanol (propyl alcohol) an alternative solvent to ethanol (methylated spirits).

3 *Emulsifying agents* (Section 9.7)
Emulsifiers, such as *triethanolamine* serve as components of polishes which *emulsify* or change the greasy soils into easily removed creamy *emulsions*.

4 *Disinfectants*
These can be various *bactericidal* chemical compounds including *phenols* (carbolic acid), *cresols* (creosote oil), *methanal* (formaldehyde), and also cationic detergents QACs, mixed with non-ionic detergents. *Soaps* are also added components as in 'Lysol'.

5 *Sweeping compounds*
These are moistened mixtures of sand, sawdust mixed with QACs cationic detergents, or phenols and cresols. They absorb moisture and dust, partly by capillarity (Section 1.5).

Safety: Cleaning compounds are mainly *flammable* and should be stored as for Section 6.6. Table 7.4 lists the main components of salon cleaning materials.

Material	Affected by
Synthetic polymers:	
Polypropylene	Cabinets; affected by hot solvents, abrasives and bleach
Polyethylene	Buckets; affected by petrol, benzene, abrasives and melts at 110–115°C
Acrylic	Lampshades, wash basins; affected by propanone (acetone) ethanol, turpentine, abrasives, softens at 100°C
Polyvinyl chloride	Floor tiles, salon upholstery; affected by propanone (acetone), benzene, bleach, abrasives, softens at 80°C
Polyurethane	Foams in furniture; affected by solvents, and flammable
Thermosetting resins	Melamine, table tops; affected by strong acids and alkalis, abrasives. Unaffected by solvents and detergents
Painted surfaces	Affected by strong alkali, sodium carbonate, heat causes blistering, turpentine. Moulds grow in humid condition, removed by household bleach
Polished wood	Affected by most organic solvents and heat
Glass	Unaffected by solvents or detergents. Use *mild* abrasives
Ceramics	Porcelain, earthenware wash basins and w.c. pans; unaffected by solvents, household bleach, acids, or abrasives

Table 7.5 Substances affecting salon surface materials

7.6 SALON SURFACE CLEANING

The salon *fabric*, walls, windows, ceilings, doors and floors, together with salon *furnishings*, furniture and *fittings* all have different surfaces, made with different *materials* and *finishes*.

Table 7.5 lists the substances or conditions which affect salon surface materials.

7.7   SALON CLEANING METHODS AND EQUIPMENT

The various cleaning materials and preparations are *applied* and *removed* from salon surfaces either by *hand* or *machinery*. Table 7.6 summarizes the methods, materials and equipment used.

7.8   SALON WASTE DISPOSAL

(*a*)   **Water closets** or W.C.s are either *wash-down* or *siphonic* pans, using 8–12 litres of water to flush the pan, from a cistern called a *water-waste preventer*. The cistern is supplied with water by way of a *ball valve* (Section 2.5). Water leaves the cistern by a *piston* which raises water up a *siphon pipe*. W.C. pans always contain a *water seal*, similar to the wash basin (Section 7.4).

Drainage (Figure 7.4)

Pipes carrying water-borne *waste* from a salon are either *waste water* pipes from wash basins, or *soil pipes* carrying faeces and urine.

In a modern salon both waste water and soil pipes connect with a single *stack pipe*, the upper part goes to roof level as a *ventilator* and its open end is covered with a wire cage. The lower end of the stack pipe connects with an underground *drain* pipe.

Waste from rainwater pipes and *sometimes* from wash basins can collect in a *gully* fitted with a grid which leads by a *water seal* to an underground drain pipe.

Inspection chambers with heavy rectangular iron lids give access to the *open pipes* and *rodding eyes* for purposes of removing blockages. There are usually *two* inspection chambers linked together. Drain pipe from the inspection chamber then empties into the public *sewer* pipe.

(*b*)   **Incinerators** are essential for com-

Cleaning Method	Materials	Equipment
WASHING Soaking Rinsing Detergent Rinsing	Various detergents and fabric conditioners	Washing machines
HOSING Water pressure removes soils	Some detergents	Main cold or hot water through hose or spray head
SWEEPING	Dry or wet sweeping mistures	Brooms and brushes
POLISHING	Polishes, seals, dewaxing pre-parations	Cloths, polishing machines, wet or dry polishing
VACUUM By suction or blowing	Powder shampoo for carpeting	Vacuum cleaners. Blowing suitable for electrical appliance cleaning
ELECTRICAL FITTINGS TURN OFF MAIN ELECTRICITY	Detergents	Moist cloths, vacuum cleaner, blowers

Table 7.6   Equipment and substances used in salon cleansing methods

bustion of sanitary towels which frequently cause drain blockage otherwise. The inspection chamber overflows with foul water when a drain is blocked. The obstruction is removed by *rodding*, using a plunger and long rods.

(*c*)   **Sink waste disposal units** are electrically driven motor units which *cut up* and *grind* waste to a paste-like waste which is flushed into the drainage system.

Sewage systems *dilute*, and *treat* foul waste water. Soaps and soapless detergents cause *foaming* in sewage; this is overcome partly by micro-organisms *feeding* on the soaps and certain soft or *biodegradable* detergents. Certain *hard* or *non-biodegradable* anionic detergents may cause foaming which cannot be removed by micro-organisms. Most

7.4 Salon waste disposal and drainage system

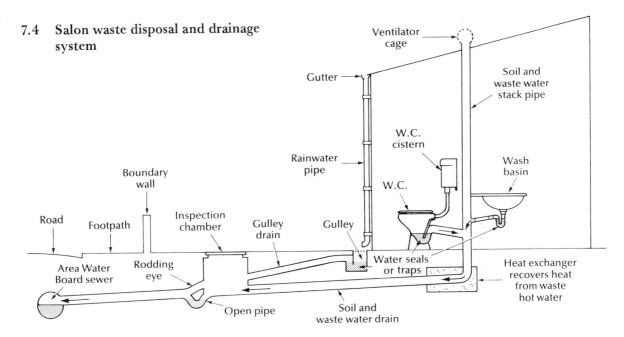

salon detergents are soft *biodegradable* detergents.

(*d*) **Rubbish disposal**: salon rubbish or *refuse* includes *hair cuttings, packaging, paper*, sweeper and vacuum *dust*. These are collected from room bins and wastepaper baskets and placed in an outside dustbin with lid, or waste sack.

Care is needed in disposal of cigarette ashtrays. An outside *incinerator* can be used to dispose of combustible waste.

7.9 PHYSICS

Electrostatics

Materials can be charged by *friction* or rubbing two surfaces together. This occurs in brushing, combing, dusting or polishing.

If *electrons* (Section 4.9) are removed from a material it will have a surplus of protons and become *positively charged*. The surface which *gains* the electrons will become *negatively* charged.

Positive charges are obtained by rubbing glass or cellulose acetate (rayons) with *silk*.

Negative charges are obtained by rubbing ebonite and certain plastics with fur.

Electrical *insulators* are substances which collect charges on their *surfaces*, they do not move *through* the material. Electrical conductors allow the charge to pass *through* them; the charges *drain* away to the *earth* (*see* Section 12.6). Hair and human skin and most surfaces are *negatively charged. Anionic detergents* have a *negatively* charged head, whilst *cationic detergents* have a *positively* charged head.

(*a*) *Like* charges *repel* each other, positive repels positive, and negative repels negative. Fold a rectangle of polythene and rub it vigorously, the two halves have the *same* charge and repel each other.

(*b*) *Unlike* charges *attract* each other, positive attracts negative and negative attracts positive charges. This is seen when hair is drawn towards a brush or comb. Dust is attracted to rubbed surfaces.

Cationic detergents will be attracted towards *negatively* charged skin and hair or salon surfaces. These detergents are also called *antistatic* substances.

7.10   CHEMISTRY

Carbon dioxide, CO_2

Carbon dioxide is an important product of *respiration*. There is 130 times more CO_2 in the air breathed out from the lung than in room air.

Calcium hydroxide

This is a clear solution of *alkali* much weaker than sodium hydroxide.

Blow or breathe out air through a glass tube into calcium hydroxide solution and note the formation of cloudiness, continue blowing and note how the cloudiness disappears. The *chemical reaction* given below takes place between CO_2 and calcium hydroxide.

These chemical changes show how *temporary* hard water is formed from limestone (calcium carbonate) and rainwater containing CO_2.

Sulphur

Sulphur is the chemical element which forms many important *compounds*. *Sulphides* are compounds with metals, for example *copper sulphide*, or compounds with non-metals, for example *hydrogen sulphide* (poisonous — bad eggs).

Sulphuric acid, H_2SO_4

This is a very strong corrosive acid; when added to water in a thin stream it causes the solution to become hot. It must be handled with utmost care *wearing* protective overalls, gloves and eye goggles.

Soap making

1 Dissolve a pellet of potassium hydroxide in 150 cm^3 of water. Handle with care — wear gloves and eye goggles.
2 Add 15 g of octadecanoic acid (stearic acid) to the solution and heat to 60°C with stirring.
3 Remove the heat and stir until cool.
4 Note the soapy touch of the soap and test its lathering property.

Curd formation

1 Prepare temporary hard water by blowing into limewater until it is *clear*. Add a pinch of magnesium and sodium sulphate crystals, stir to dissolve and thus make it *permanently* hard water.
2 Test this water with soap solution, and different soapless detergents and observe if curd is formed.

Soapless detergents can be prepared according to the Unilever Laboratory Experiment Number 2 'Preparation of sodium alkylbenzene sulphonate'. This must be done strictly under *supervision*.

Unilever Laboratory Experiment No 1 'Preparation of soap' is available from Unilever Education Section, Unilever House, Blackfriars, London EC4P 4BQ.

| *Carbon dioxide* | + | *Calcium hydroxide* | $\longrightarrow$ | **Insoluble** *calcium carbonate* | + | *Water* |

| *Insoluble calcium carbonate* | + | *Carbon dioxide* | + | *Water* | $\longrightarrow$ | **Soluble** *calcium hydrogen carbonate* |

Ammonia

This is a gas, NH_3: It dissolves in water to form ammonium hydroxide, NH_4OH. It should be handled with great care. *NEVER* smell it, wear protective gloves and eye goggles when handling it.

Amines

These are organic compounds related to ammonia, and include *triethanol-amine*, used in many *anionic* detergents and by itself as an *emulsifier*.

Quaternary ammonium compounds, QACs, are important *cationic* detergents.

7.11 QUESTIONS

1 What substances cause hardness of water? Describe methods of softening water by (*a*) adding chemicals; (*b*) by main water softening appliances.
2 Describe what is meant by a soap, and soapless detergent.
   What are the main differences between soapless detergents and soaps?
3 What is an *ion*?
   Explain the terms cationic, anionic and non-ionic with reference to *detergents*.
4 Describe the composition of some important salon cleaning materials.
   Indicate which surfaces are *not* suitable for certain cleaning agents.
5 Explain the purpose of a water seal with reference to wash basins and water closets.
   What cleaning agents are used for these salon fittings?
6 Describe the methods of producing hot water in a salon by instantaneous and storage water heaters.
   Compare their advantages and disadvantages.
7 Write brief notes on (*a*) distilled water; (*b*) deionized water; (*c*) chemically softened water; (*d*) temporary hard water.

7.12 MULTIPLE CHOICE QUESTIONS

1 One of the following causes hardness of water and is removed by boiling the water:
   (*a*) sodium hydrogen carbonate (bicarbonate).
   (*b*) calcium hydrogen carbonate (bicarbonate).
   (*c*) sodium chloride
   (*d*) calcium sulphate.
2 Which of the following are the raw materials for the manufacture of soapless detergents?
   (*a*) plant and animal waxes
   (*b*) petroleum hydrocarbons
   (*c*) resins
   (*d*) essential oils.
3 The typical salon water softener apparatus which acts by ion exchange consists essentially of a substance providing one of the following ions:
   (*a*) calcium
   (*b*) magnesium
   (*c*) sodium
   (*d*) potassium.
4 Hair attracts positively charged surfactant molecules. These molecules are called:
   (*a*) anionic
   (*b*) cationic
   (*c*) amphoteric
   (*d*) nonionic.
5 Heat passes from the heat exchanger or calorifier to heat the cold water mainly by:
   (*a*) conduction
   (*b*) convection
   (*c*) radiation
   (*d*) diffusion.
6 A fire broke out in a pile of salon refuse heaped in a dark corner under a stairway. Since the salon had been closed over a holiday period, the cause of the fire could have been:
   (*a*) friction
   (*b*) bacteria
   (*c*) sunlight
   (*d*) ethanol.

Section Two
Hairdressing Processes

8 Hair Removal

8.1   EQUIPMENT

1 **Forceps** or tweezers are instruments for tightly holding and withdrawing a single hair from its follicle by *traction*. Forceps are simple *machines* by means of which a force or *effort* is used to overcome the almost *equal* force holding the hair in the follicle called the *load* (Figure 8.1).

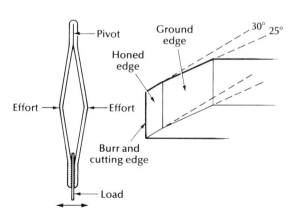

8.1   Forceps and razor cutting edge

2 **Razors** are single *blade-like* instruments with a *cutting edge* formed from a *ground* edge and a *honed* edge (Figure 8.1).

The ground edge is formed at an angle of 25° on a *grind-stone*, the honed edge is *honed* at an angle of 30° on an *oilstone*. A *burr* builds up on the cutting edge which is slowly removed by thinning it away by gently rubbing the blade both sides on a fine oilstone.

A razor sharp cutting edge will cut a hanging piece of wallpaper with ease. The cutting edge is renewed frequently on a leather *strop*.

Open razors and razor blades may have a *single* ground edge on one side, or may be *double* ground on both sides. The ground edge may be either *plane* or flat, or *concave* or hollow ground.

The razor is another simple machine in which the hair stubble provides a resistance or *load*. The *effort* being the force transmitted through the fingers holding the razor instrument. This is almost *equal* to the force produced by the load. A greater *pressure* will be transmitted along the small *surface* area of the razor edge, a blunted cutting edge will transmit a *lower* pressure.

Lubrication with mineral oil is essential when honing a razor's cutting edge. Lubrication is required when the razor is in use for shaving and hair cutting, this is provided by the soap lather or alternative *preshave* lubricant. Lubrication overcomes *friction* forces between surfaces in contact, namely the hair *cuticle* surface and the razor's cutting edge.

3 **Scissors** are cutting instruments with two blades each with cutting edges and also honed and ground surfaces. Scissors are simple machines with the two blades *pivoted*, allowing their cutting edges to slide over each other. The hair provides the *load* or resistance to the *effort* transmitted through the scissors from the fingers (Figure 8.2).

Scissors in which the handles are *longer* than the blades will provide a *greater* shearing or cutting force than short-handled scissors. Long-handled scissors have a greater *mechanical advantage* by allowing a *small* effort to overcome a *larger* load.

Scissors require the same *maintenance* care as open razors in frequent *honing* of the cutting edge. Less frequent *grinding* may be required when blades are seriously damaged or worn.

4 **Hair clippers** have cutting heads, consisting of *two slotted* blades with cutting edges which slide over each other by a scissor-like manual action, or electrically driven vibrator action. Hair enters a slot and is cut by the shearing force. The effort is either provided as body or electrical energy.

5 **Shavers** have different shaving *systems*, rotary, micro-slot or foil. In all cases a cutting, edged blade moves against a stationary barrier plate with holes to allow entry of hair stubble through small slots or circular holes. The effort to operate the shaver is provided by electrical energy. Shavers operate on either 120 or 240 V. A preshave *lubricant* assists the shaving process and prolongs the blade sharpness.

Protection

Electric trimmers and shavers are *double insulated*, symbol ▣ and have a double casing to protect the user from electric shock. A *two core* flex supplies the appliance with electricity and is connected to a *two pin* plug. It is without an earth wire or earth system (*see* Section 12.6).

6 **Shaving mirrors** are necessary to provide a *magnified* image of a small area of the face when the mirror is *near* to the face. This type of mirror has an *inwardly* curved surface or is *concave*. The make-up mirror is identical.

8.2   ELECTRICAL EPILATION

Two methods are used in *epilation* or removal of hair by a process to include its papilla or root.

Electrolytic epilation (Figure 8.3)

This is the process by which *chemical decomposition* occurs by the passage of electricity through a solution of *ions* (Section 7.5).

Electrodes are used to conduct the electricity, the *anode* being the positive (+) terminal, and the *cathode* the negative (−) terminal connected to a source of low voltage *direct current* (d.c.) of a battery or from a rectifier. The negative cathode forms *alkali* which

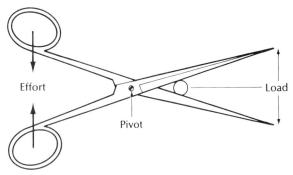

8:2   Scissor arrangement of load and effort

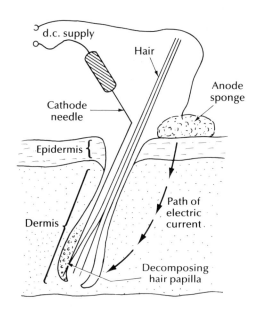

8.3   Electrolytic hair removal

liquefies tissues and hair. The positive anode forms *acids* which can cause tissues to *coagulate*. *Note*: it is the *products* of electrolysis which cause decomposition of hair and not the current.

The alkali-producing cathode is inserted as a platinum/iridium or stainless steel needle into the hair follicle base. A powerful lens and good illumination is needed to assist in this process.

The anode or *indifferent* electrode is a saline (sodium chloride solution) soaked pad placed on the skin surface. A direct current of 1 to 3 *milliamperes* is passed for 1–3 seconds, the current being controlled by a foot-switch. When bubbles of gas, *hydrogen*, are seen to emerge from the follicle, the hair is removed by forceps traction.

Diathermy epilation

(*See* Section 13.5). This method of hair removal involves destroying the hair root or papilla by *heat*.

Heat is generated at the tip of an *active electrode* by means of a *short wave* or medium frequency *alternating current* (a.c.) produced by a special oscillator valve in the *diathermy machine*. The frequency is between 500 000 and 3 million Hertz, or ten thousand to 60 thousand times the frequency of mains electricity (50 Hz).

An *indifferent* electrode is applied to the skin surface, whilst the *active* electrode is inserted into the hair follicle, using a lens and good illumination. Current control for fractions of a second is by means of a foot-switch.

Hair is withdrawn from the follicle by traction. No gas bubbles or foaming occurs, and far more hairs can be removed by this method as compared to electrolysis – 100 to 200 in a 30 minute session.

8.3   CHEMICAL PREPARATIONS

Depilatories are various substances which remove hair in *part*, the root or papilla remains intact allowing further hair *regrowth*.

Wax depilatories

These are mixtures of paraffin wax, beeswax and/or turpentine resin, melted together with a small amount of turpentine. The *low* melting point wax mixture is warmed and applied to the skin and allowed to solidify. The solidified wax is pulled away withdrawing hairs by traction.

Abrasive depilatories

These are pumice stone blocks or emery boards or gloves which remove hair by abrasion at skin surface level; a lubricant mixture of soap and water lather is used to reduce friction.

Chemical depilatories

Sodium hydroxide (caustic soda) is a means of dissolving hair and is sometimes used to remove hair blockages in salon waste water pipes.

Sulphides are compounds of different elements and sulphur and include barium sulphide, sodium sulphide. These are mixed with zinc oxide and starch to form a smooth paste, applied to the skin and allowed to remain 2–4 minutes. Sulphides can cause skin burns and are poisonous if swallowed.

Thiolethanoates (*Thioglycollates*) of ammonia and calcium are alternative components of hair-removing preparations (Sections 10.7 and 10.9).

Keratolytic substances are chemical reagents able to remove keratin, the main component of hair, finger-nails and the thin tough outer horner layer of skin (Section 18.2). Keratolytic agents remove skin scales and dandruff. They include *acids*, salicylic, benzoic, lactic, citric, malic acids, and *sulphide* of selenium.

A simple *dandruff lotion* consists of 0.5 per cent salicylic acid keratolytic, 9 per cent almond oil, and 90 per cent toilet spirit with added perfume.

Pre-shaver lotion

This consists of a non-greasy *lubricant* with good spreading properties and includes the following *esters*, iso-propyl hexadecanoate (iso-propyl palmitate), or iso-propyl tetra-decanoate (iso-propyl myristate), 1 per cent of which is dissolved in 99 per cent toilet spirit to which a perfume is added.

Shaving soaps

These soaps are mixtures of *soap* detergents and *lubricants* similar to those used in pre-shaver lotions, whilst shaving *creams* have a similar composition to a cream shampoo (Section 9.3) and also contain lubricants.

They assist in wet razor shaving by the following action:

1 Water causes the hair fibres to *swell* and *stiffen*, water entering by *hygroscopic*

action; the increase in thickness is about 15 per cent of its *dry* thickness.
2 Lubricants and soaps allow the blade to *glide* smoothly over the skin.
3 Stiff *lather* helps to maintain the hairs in an erect position.
4 Evaporation of the foam is reduced by lubricant additives.

After-shave lotions

These lotions have a similar composition to toilet waters, friction and Cologne lotions (*see* Section 13.12). They consist of about 4 per cent perfume essence in a mixture of water and toilet spirit (industrial methylated spirits). Small quantities, usually less than 1 per cent of different substances, may be added: *menthol* (cooling effect), propanetriol (glycerine), moisturizing effect. The total effect of the after-shave lotion is to cool by evaporation, and act as an *astringent* causing the tightening of the skin by surface contraction, and closes the skin *pores*.

8.4   PHYSICS

Elasticity of hair (Figure 8.4)

Elasticity is that physical property that enables the hair fibre to change in length when a pulling or stretching force is applied to it, as in *traction*, and to *recover* its original length when the stretching force is removed.

If the *elastic limit* is exceeded, it will *lose* its elasticity due to a breakage in the *molecule structure*. When the elastic limit is *exceeded*, the hair will continue to increase in length and will *break* at the *break point*.

The percentage elongation and breaking force required to break hair is demonstrated using the apparatus in Figure 8.4.

$$\text{The percentage elongation} = \frac{\text{Stretched length} - \text{Original length}}{\text{Original length}} \times 100.$$

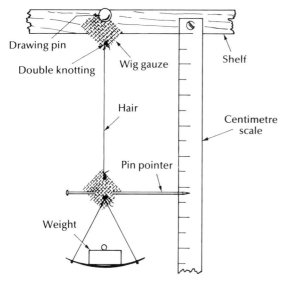

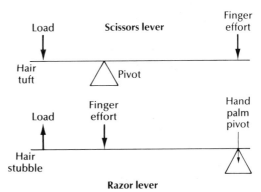

8.4 Elasticity of hair

For example a 'dry' hair at room humidity stretches from the original length 22 cm to 29 cm, and breaks at a force of 60 grammes force. Its percentage elongation is

$$\frac{29 - 22}{22} \times 100 = 32 \text{ per cent.}$$

Factors affecting the elasticity of hair
1 'Dry' hair has a *low* elasticity.
2 Wet hair has a greater elasticity than dry hair. Hair *saturated* with water has a percentage elongation of 50 per cent. Water acts as an 'internal lubricant' to the hair molecule.
3 *Steamed* hair is exceedingly elastic with percentage elongations from 100 to 175 per cent.
4 *Chemical compounds* which affect the chemical composition of hair also affect its elasticity.

Supercontraction of hair

If hair is stretched by 50 per cent and then *kept stretched* in steam, or cold dilute sodium hydroxide solution, or phenol (carbolic acid) solution, for a certain time, when it is *released* the hair will shorten slowly until it is almost

8.5 Levers in scissors and open razors

30 per cent *less* than its original length. This is called *supercontraction*. *See* Unilever Laboratory Experiment No 7 'Supercontraction of Hair'.

Levers (Figure 8.5)

A *lever* is the simplest machine consisting of a rigid *bar* turning about a *pivot*. A force, the *effort*, is applied to one part and this overcomes the force of the *load* at another point. The scissors and open razor are examples of the lever principle.

Electrolysis

Electrolytes are those substances which conduct electricity when they are dissolved in water. They include acids, alkalis and salts which are composed of *ions*.

The *chemical decomposition* or splitting up of an electrolyte when a current of electricity passes through the solution is called *electrolysis*.

Sodium chloride (common salt) is an important component of human body *tissue fluid*. Electrolysis of sodium chloride occurs in water as follows:

	Sodium	Chloride
Sodium chloride →	cations AND + ions	anions − ions

	Hydrogen	Hydroxide
Water →	cations AND + ions	anions − ions

When the current is passing, the following occurs:

(*a*) *Sodium* cations and *hydrogen* anions with + charge move to negative electrode or cathode and form *sodium hydroxide* and hydrogen gas bubbles. The alkali changes neutral litmus blue.

(*b*) *Chloride* anion and *hydroxide* anion with – charge move to the positive electrode or anode and form *hydrochloric* acid and *hypochlorous* acid, a component of domestic hypochlorite bleach. Both acids change neutral litmus indicator *red*.

Mirrors

Mirrors are highly polished plates of glass with a back coating of a *reflecting* layer of silver metal, or an alloy of tin and mercury; a further protective coating or red lead paint covers the outermost surface. Some mirrors are made from sheets of highly polished stainless steel but are liable to scratched surfaces.

Mirror cleaning lotion can be prepared by mixing 5 g of magnesium carbonate (abrasive) with 40 cm³ isopropanol (solvent) and 55 cm³ of water (solvent). A trace of colour and perfume essence can be added.

Percentage composition

This is a means to show the composition or make-up of a mixture. It indicates the number of parts in one hundred of each component.

Percentage is calculated as follows:

$$\frac{\text{Amount of component}}{\text{Total amount of } all \text{ components}} \times 100 = \quad \%$$

Image formation in a plane or flat mirror (Figures 8.6 and 8.7)

An *object* such as a lighted torch lamp will give out *light rays* which travel as straight lines towards the mirror surface. The rays are reflected according to the *law of reflection* (Section 6.9). *The reflected rays* enter the human eye where an *image* of the object will be seen.

(*a*) The image is positioned at an *equal distance* behind the mirror as the object is in front.

(*b*) The image is *equal in size* to the object.

(*c*) The image is *laterally inverted*, the object's right side becomes the image's left side (Figure 8.8).

Salon wall mirrors can be used for the following purposes:

(*a*) *Salon decor* to reflect displays of hair dressing preparations.

(*b*) *Reflect light* in parts of the salon with poor natural lighting.

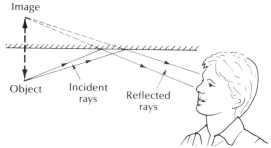

8.7   Formation of an image in a flat or plane mirror

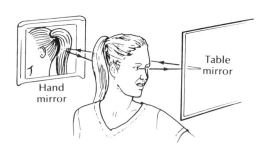

8.6   Reflection in a plane hand mirror

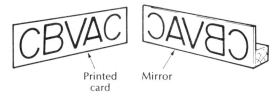

8.8   Lateral inversion

(*c*) Increase the *apparent* size of a room and give an added dimension of apparent spaciousness.

(*d*) *Security* mirrors to observe areas which are not staffed such as stores, entrances, and areas where clients need occasional attention as at dryers. *Two-way* mirrors allow salon supervision from staff rooms.

Curved mirrors

Curved mirrors are either (*a*) *concave* or magnifying mirrors or (*b*) *convex* or diminished image mirrors.

Concave mirrors will give a *magnified* image of an object provided it is *close* to the mirror. Light rays from the object are reflected at the concave mirror surface to form an *enlarged* image behind the mirror as shown in Figure 8.9.

Convex mirrors give a small or diminished image of objects at a *distance* from the mirror surface. The image seen is a *wide angle* view of a large area. This type of mirror is usually a *security* mirror for a general allover view of the salon (Figure 8.10).

Magnifier lens

Light rays can be *refracted* or bent when they pass from air through glass. If the glass is a triangular prism in sectional view, the light rays can be refracted as shown. A *convex lens*

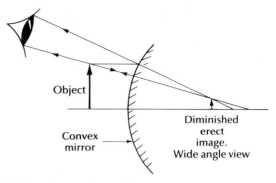

8.10 Formation of an image in a convex mirror

can be compared in sectional shape to *two* glass triangular prisms which bend or refract light rays from an object as in Figure 8.11.

A convex lens or converging lens forms an *enlarged* image of an object as shown in Figure 8.12.

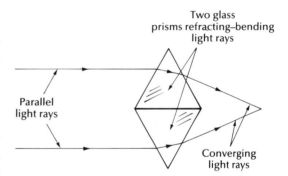

8.11 To show refraction of light by two glass prisms

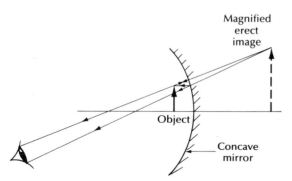

8.9 Formation of an image in a concave or magnifying mirror

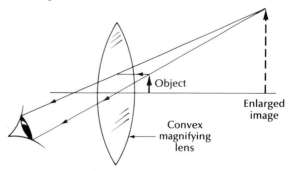

8.12 Formation of an image by means of a magnifying lens

8.5   CHEMISTRY

Hair fibre structure

Hair is a natural *fibre* formed by cells of a living human being; other natural fibres include wool, cotton, and silk. *Man-made* fibres are not made as products of living cells, they include the synthetics, nylons, and modacrylic fibres.

A *fibre* is a solid material with a length much *greater* than its width, with varying degrees of *fineness*; some are *coarse* (eyelashes), others are very *fine* (downy hair). Most fibres are *flexible* and *elastic*. Natural fibres are *hygroscopic*, whilst most man-made fibres have little, if any, hygroscopic property.

Man-made fibres
Man-made fibres used in clothing, furnishings and wigs, are produced by fibre *spinning* methods involving the passage in *liquid* form of the polymer, either melted or dissolved in a solvent, through many tiny holes in a *spinneret*.

The man-made fibre generally has a *smooth surface*, is usually *transparent*, but can be opaque and artificially coloured. The fibre may be straight or *crimped* with artificial waves. Most are *circular* in cross-section and of variable or *uniform* thickness.

Physical structure of human hair (Figure 8.13)

The *physical* structure of human hair has been studied by means of the *light microscope* with magnifications up to 1000 times, and by means of the *electron microscope* with magnifications up to 500 000 times. Photographs taken with light microscopes are called *photomicrographs* and those from electron microscopes are called *electron micrographs*.

Light microscopes show the human hair fibre to be composed of *three* main regions or layers.

(*a*) *Cuticle region* consisting of *several* (7 – 11) layers of overlapping flattened cells or *scales*, the free edge being towards the hair tip. The cuticle surface has a *characteristic scale pattern* which distinguishes human hair from wool and other mammal fibres. The scales overlap like tiles on a roof and give the hair fibre *smoothness* from root to tip and *roughness* from tip to root. The cuticle scale is composed of outer *epicuticle*, middle *exocuticle*, and inner layer or *endocuticle*.

(*b*) *Cortex region* forms the main internal structure and consists of *many cortex cells*, embedded in a non-cellular *matrix*, which appear to have a *spindle* or cigar shape. Inside the cortex cells the *remains* of a cell *nucleus* may be found. Two regions may be distinguished called the *orthocortex* and *paracortex*, using dyeing techniques.

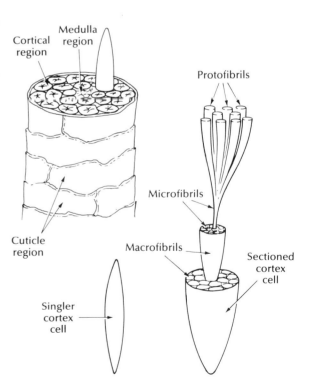

8.13   **The fine structure of hair (from an adaptation after Dr M. L. Ryder, 'Hair', *Studies in Biology* No. 41, Institute of Biology, 1973)**

(*c*) *Medulla region*. This may be present in *coarse thick* hairs which are called medullated hairs. It is absent from *fine thin* hair which is called non-medullated hair. The medulla is a soft spongy honeycomb of *cells* and *air spaces* and appears black when seen through the light microscope since the air is opaque to light rays which cannot pass through it.

Electron microscopes show the cortex cells to be composed of *macrofibrils*; these in turn consist of *microfibrils* and finally *protofibrils*.

Nothing further is seen with the electron microscope beyond the protofibril which resembles a *three* stranded *rope*.

8.6 CHEMICAL COMPOSITION OF HAIR

Hair chemical elements

The chemical elements which combine together to form the complex compound of *keratin* are listed in Table 8.1, together with their average percentage.

The *analysis* of human hair to indicate the chemical elements present is conducted as follows on finely chopped hair which has been oven *dried* at 110°C.

Element		Percentage
Carbon	C	50
Oxygen	O	20
Nitrogen	N	18
Hydrogen	H	7
Sulphur	S	4
Other elements including phosphorus	P	1

Table 8.1   Percentage composition of hair keratin

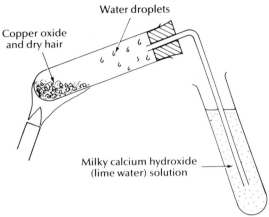

8.14   Testing for carbon and hydrogen in hair

1 **Carbon and hydrogen** are indicated by mixing the *dry* hair with *dry* copper II oxide and heating the mixture in the apparatus shown in Figure 8.14.

Copper II oxide is an *oxidizing agent* which oxidizes the carbon and hydrogen in hair to carbon dioxide and water respectively.

Hair carbon   +   oxygen from copper II oxide → carbon dioxide

Hair hydrogen +   oxygen   →   water

Water is seen as condensed droplets of liquid which collect in the test tube's cooler regions near the stopper. It may be tested with white anhydrous copper sulphate. *Carbon dioxide* turns the clear calcium hydroxide (lime water) cloudy.

2 **Nitrogen and sulphur** are tested for mixing dry hair with dry *soda lime*, a strong alkali, and heating the mixture in the apparatus shown in Figure 8.15.

Sulphur in hair is *reduced* by adding hydrogen to form unpleasant smelling *hydrogen sulphide* gas which turns moist lead ethanoate (lead acetate) test paper *black*.

Nitrogen in hair is reduced by hydrogen to form *ammonia* gas which causes moist red litmus paper to turn *blue*, or yellow turmeric paper a brown colour.

There is no suitable simple chemical method to indicate the presence of oxygen in hair.

Hair, the polypeptide protein

Hair or the chemical compound *keratin* can be broken down into its component units called *amino acids* by a process called hydrolysis, to produce hair *protein hydrolysate*.

Hair is a natural polymer or *protein polypeptide* composed of monomer units or amino acids.

$$\begin{array}{c} Protein \\ Polypeptide \\ Hair \end{array} \xrightarrow{\textbf{Hydrolysis}} Amino\ Acids$$

Amino acids contain an *amine* group and a *carboxylic acid* group.

Hair keratin is composed of *eighteen different* amino acids listed as follows, together with their percentage. The names of amino acids usually end in *-ine*, but a few end in *acid* (Table 8.2).

The *macromolecule* of keratin consists of a *main chain* or polypeptide chain composed of the eighteen different amino acids present in varying numbers throughout the polypeptide chain.

$$\begin{array}{c} Keratin \\ polypeptide \\ chain \end{array} = Valine\ +\ Threonine\ +\ Cystine\ +\ Leucine\ +\ \begin{array}{c} Other \\ Amino \\ acids \end{array}$$

Peptide links or bonds

These join the different amino acid units together in the long polypeptide chain. The *peptide* link forms between amine and carboxylic acid groups.

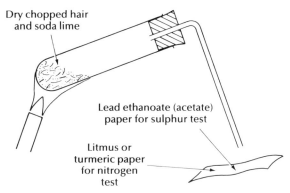

8.15   Testing for nitrogen and sulphur in hair

Amino acid name	Percentage by weight
Alanine	4
Arginine	9
Aspartic acid	7
Cystine (contains sulphur)	11
Glutamic acid	13
Glycine	6
Histidine	1
Isoleucine	3
Leucine	8
Lysine	3
Methionine (contains sulphur)	0.4
Phenylalanine	4
Proline	6
Serine	9
Threonine	6
Tryptophan	0.6
Tyrosine	4
Valine	5

Table 8.2 Amino acid present in hair heratin

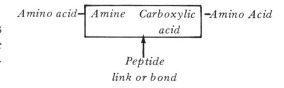

$$\begin{array}{c} Keratin \\ polypeptide \\ chain \end{array} = \begin{array}{c} Amino \\ acid \end{array} \underline{\quad\quad} \begin{array}{c} Amino \\ acid \end{array} \underline{\quad\quad} \begin{array}{c} Amino \\ acid \end{array} \underline{\quad\quad} \begin{array}{c} Amino \\ acid \end{array}$$

Peptide links or bonds

Alpha and beta keratin

X-ray studies showed that the polypeptide chain molecule of keratin was a *coiled spring*; when the keratin molecule was *stretched* it became a *straight* chain.

The *unstretched* form of keratin having a *coiled spring* structure, is called alpha, α (Greek letter A) keratin, and the *stretched* form is called beta, β (Greek letter B) keratin.

α-Keratin ⟷ β-Keratin

Unstretched hair coiled spring   *Stretched hair straight chain*

The *elasticity* of hair fibres is therefore explained by the coiled spring alpha keratin molecule.

Later it will be explained that there are many bonds linked to the main chain, amongst them are the *hydrogen bonds*. The hydrogen bonds are attracted *electrostatically*; these bonds are *weaker* than other keratin molecule

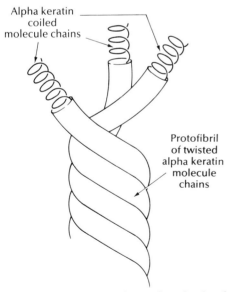

8.16 **Alpha–keratin molecules in the protofibril**

Human hair	Man-made fibre
Made by living cells	Chemical synthesis
Natural polymer	Synthetic polymer
Monomer units 18 different amino acids	One monomer unit, usually a hydrocarbon
Hygroscopic	Usually non-hygroscopic
Cellular complex fibre structure	Non-cellular fibre structure
Cuticle surface patterned	Usually a smooth surface
Variable thickness from different hair papillae	Uniform thickness from one spinneret
Different structure from root to tip	Uniform structure, *no* root or tip
Naturally coloured	Colourless — coloured to order
Can be supercontracted	Cannot be supercontracted
Not thermoplastic.	·Mainly thermoplastic
Breakdown with strong heat	Are heat moulded
Chemically active with different reagents	Less chemical active
Easy to dye	Difficult to dye

Table 8.3   Comparison of hair and man-made fibres

bonds and help to give hair its elasticity. They are *broken* by moist steam and can reform in new positions causing *supercontraction* of hair (Section 8.4).

Protofibrils in the hair cortex consist of *three* alpha-keratin chain molecules twisted together like three strands in a rope (Figure 8.16).

Summary of hair structure

Chemical elements: C H O N S P
- Monomer units: 18 different *AMINO ACIDS*
- Polymer = Polypeptide protein α-KERATIN chain molecule
- Protofibrils = Three α-*KERATIN* chain molecules
- Microfibrils = Eleven protofibrils
- Macrofibrils = Many microfibrils
- Cortex cell = Many macrofibrils
- Hair fibre = Many cortex cells

8.7 QUESTIONS

1 Briefly describe the physical structure of human hair as disclosed by the light and electron microscope.
2 Explain the chemical structure of hair with reference to the following terms: chemical elements, amino acids, polypeptide main chain, alpha and beta keratin.
3 Explain what is meant by *elasticity* of hair. What factors affect the elasticity of hair? Which links or bonds are broken when hair is overstretched?
4 Describe methods of hair removal. Which method prevents hair growing again?
5 Write short notes on each of the following: (a) double insulation; (b) grinding and honing; (c) lubrication in shaving: (d) after-shave lotion.

8.8 MULTIPLE CHOICE QUESTIONS

1 Which of the following would indicate the percentage chemical composition of human hair?

	Carbon	Hydrogen	Oxygen	Nitrogen	Sulphur
(a)	51	13	35	—	—
(b)	47	7	16	28	—
(c)	26	5	34	—	34
(d)	51	7	19	18	5

2 Which of the following treated hairs will show the greatest stretching when a force is applied to them?
(a) dry hair
(b) cold wet hair
(c) warm wet hair
(d) steamed hair.

3. The natural ability of hair to absorb water into itself is called its:
(a) efflorescence
(b) hygroscopicity
(c) deliquescence
(d) impermeability.

4 A fibre seen through the microscope as a cylindrical shape with a surface of over-lapping scales, the edges of which point towards the fibre tip, would be:
(a) polyester
(b) linen
(c) silk
(d) hair.

5 The effect of diathermy in hair removal is to destroy the hair papilla by:
(a) heat
(b) electrocution
(c) chemical action
(d) electrolysis.

6 If the surface of dark coloured hair is oily and the fibre scales are flattened, most of the light falling on the hair will be:
(a) refracted
(b) reflected
(c) diffused
(d) deviated.

9 Hair Cleaning

9.1 NATURE OF SOILS

Soils described in Section 7.2, are of two main kinds.

Solid soil materials, soot and dust, cling to dry hair fibres by very weak attraction forces which exist between molecules of all substances, and by electrostatic attraction. This force can be overcome by *shaking* the hair in air or water or brushing or by hosing when the solid soils are easily removed.

Liquid soil materials, such as oily human sebum cling to the hair surface by the force of attraction or *adhesion*, a force between molecules of *different* substances. Greasy substances have a *strong* force of adhesion between grease or lipid and hair molecules.

Similarly solid soils will cling to liquid soils by the force of adhesion.

The *force of cohesion* is the force of attraction between molecules of *similar* substances. Force of cohesion holds a water drop together, whilst the force of *adhesion* holds water on the hair surface, or on a glass surface (Figure 9.1).

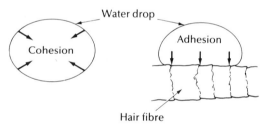

9.1   Water cohesion and adhesion

Cleaning aims to *detach* the soil from the hair surface by breaking down the force of *adhesion* or other attractive forces holding liquid and solid soils to the hair fibre.

Disclosing hair soils

Shine an ultra-violet ray lamp (Section 13.3) on the back of a person's head in a darkened room; the person must wear special protective goggles or spectacles which *absorb* ultra-violet rays.

Caution: Ultra-violet rays can damage the eye surface. The ultra-violet lamp should be held at least a metre away from the head. Ultra-violet rays cause certain substances to *fluoresce* and soils will show *fluorescence* on the hair surface.

9.2   CLEANING EQUIPMENT

Hairdressing tools and equipment in contact with the hair *must* be clean and free from all soils, particularly living soils or *micro-organisms* (*see* Section 19.1). Soiled tools and equipment will *add* soil to hair.

Soiled tools and certain equipment can be cleaned by the methods described in Section 7.7 to produce *non-sterile* surfaces. *Sterile* surfaces, completely free from living micro-organisms, can only be produced by various processes of *sterilization*, which can be *physical* processes using heat or radiation or *chemical* processes using *disinfectants* (*see* also Section 21.3). Before any sterilization process the articles *must have been cleaned*, since many sterilizing agents *cannot penetrate* surfaces covered in solid or liquid soils.

Physical methods of sterilization

Heat
Heat either in a dry oven, or moist heat in an autoclave. The autoclave produces a *higher* boiling point for water boiled under high pressure.

(*a*) 110°C under 150 kilopascals, is suitable for sterilizing, china, glass and metal items.

(*b*) 130°C under 200 kilopascals, is suitable for sterilizing face cloths and towels.

Ultra-violet radiation (see Section 13.3)
Short wave ultra-violet rays are bactericidal and are produced by *mercury vapour* tube lamps, in special cabinets. These rays will not penetrate soiled surfaces coated with solid and liquid soil barriers. All items *must be cleansed* previous to placing in the ultra-violet ray cabinet.

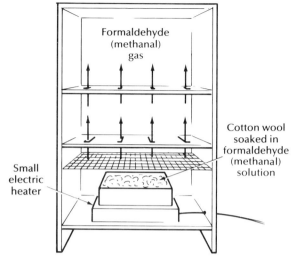

9.2   Methanal (formaldehyde) disinfecting cabinet

Ultra-sonic radiation
Ultra-sound is a very high frequency sound produced by ultrasonic transducers. This sound is not audible to the human ear.

Items, to be sterilized, are placed in a cleansing solution of detergent and exposed to ultrasonic radiation, which *dislodges* all surface soils and also *destroys* all living micro-organisms.

Chemical methods of sterilization (Figure 9.2)

Various chemicals have micro-organism-destroying properties. Methanal (formaldehyde) in a 40 per cent solution of the gas methanal in water is used in salon disinfecting cabinets. When heated the methanal gas escapes from the solution since its *solubility* is reduced with rising temperature. The gas circulates by *convection* and *diffusion* inside the cabinet.

9.3   HAIR CLEANING PREPARATIONS

Hair soils can be removed by different cleaning preparations *with or without* water. The following are the main waterless preparations for hair cleaning.

Solvents

These are liquid organic compounds such as *tetrachloroethane*, and *hexane*, substitutes for the harmful former solvent carbon tetrachloride. They are excellent solvents for the liquid oily sebum, and leave the solid soils in *suspension* which can be removed from the solvent by *filtration*. Solvents are used for cleaning *hair* wigs and postiche. *Synthetic fibre* wigs can be affected by organic solvents — p.v.c. and polythene for example.

Dry powder hair cleansers

These consist of a perfumed mixture of *absorbent* powders such as French chalk, powdered chalk, or starch and Fullers earth. These powders absorb liquid and solid soils from the hair fibre by the force of adhesion.

Talcum powders are dusting powders applied to the skin following shaving or bathing. The perfumed mixture serves to absorb *water* moisture, skin oily *sebum*; it may also have a slight *medicinal* action, and smoothes the skin.

The following is a formula for a typical *dusting powder*.

Caution: In the preparation of any cosmetic to be applied to the skin, all the ingredients must be of a *high* degree of purity. The materials must be of B.P. or B.P.C. *quality*. *Laboratory* quality materials have not been tested for cosmetic use, and could cause injury, and possible skin disorders and infections.

Dusting powder
(*a*) Magnesium octadec-anoate (stearate) B.P. 5 g — this forms in soap scum, and causes the powder to cling to the skin.

(*b*) Light magnesium carbonate B.P. 5 g — absorbent and whitener.

(*c*) French chalk or purified talc 88 g — moisture and grease absorbent.

(*d*) Boric acid or zinc oxide B.P. 2 g — a medicinal component.

Carefully mix the components in a large dry tin container previously washed and scalded with hot water. Add a few drops of perfume and continue to mix by shaking in the sealed tin container.

Spirit Lotion
(also called hair frictions: Section 13.12)

These are a form of solvent hair cleaners consisting mainly of purified toilet spirit, ethanol (60 to 80 per cent) with variable amounts of pure water (40 to 20 per cent). A trace of soap (0.5 per cent) and perfume is added. The cleaning action depends mainly on the grease solvent action of ethanol. After application the lotion is *wiped* from the hair.

Caution: The lotion can harm the eyes and they must be protected during the lotion's application.

9.4   HAIR WASHING PREPARATIONS (or SHAMPOOS)

Hair *washing* or shampooing is a process of cleaning hair or man-made fibre wigs with *detergents* which *act* with *water*.

The hair washing process is essentially a *three* stage process of:
1 Pre-rinse and/or soaking.
2 Wash with detergent and water — usually warm, 40°C, but can be *cold*.
3 Final rinsing with water or different rinses.

Pre-rinsing

This process removes solid soils held by weak attractive *forces*, and also allows the dry hair to swell by water intake by *hygroscopic* properties of hair. When hair absorbs moisture it gives out *heat* by exothermic reaction. This prevents *chilling* of the skin when hair is wet.

The *detergent* component of a shampoo can be either a *soap* or *soapless* detergent.

Soap-type shampoo

This is prepared by dissolving 20 g of green soft soap in 25 cm³ toilet spirit or ethanol, and adding 75 cm³ of water followed by filtration. Perfume is added together with a trace of edible colouring.

Soap-type shampoo is suited only for use in soft water, as insoluble *scum* forms in hard water.

Soapless-type shampoos

The soapless detergent component used is mainly the highly soluble *anionic detergent* Section 7.5). The *non-ionic* detergent is also found in some soapless detergent shampoo mixtures.

Soap can also be present in certain shampoo mixtures. Shampoos are available in different *physical* forms:

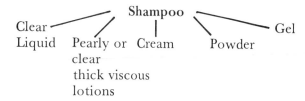

Clear   Shampoo
Liquid   Pearly or Cream   Powder   Gel
         clear
         thick viscous
         lotions

Liquid soapless shampoo

The clear liquid shampoo is a 25 to 40 per cent solution of a liquid anionic soapless detergent dissolved in water. The anionic detergents used are Dodecanyl (lauryl) sulphates. See (A) below.

Lotion soapless shampoo

The viscous 'pearly' lotion shampoo is a 45 per cent solution of liquid anionic soapless detergent together with an *opacifier*, 2 per cent, with detergent properties. See (B) below.

Powder soapless shampoo

This is a solid *mixture* of a finely powdered anionic soapless detergent, 20 per cent, mixed with *alkaline* salts.

20%   80%
Sodium   *Sodium*   *Powder*
dodecanyl   + *sequis-*   =   *soapless*
(lauryl)   *carbonate*   *shampoo*
sulphate   *powder*
powder

Cream shampoo

(*a*)   A *soapless cream shampoo* is an *emulsion* of a *small* amount of lipid oil in a *large* amount of water containing anionic soapless detergent. *Emulsifying waxes* are used to make the emulsion. See (C) below.

Place 40 g of sodium dodecanyl (lauryl) sulphate *paste*, 16 g of emulsifying wax B.P., 5 cm³ almond oil and 40 cm³ of water in a previously cleaned beaker scalded with hot water. Gently heat the mixture over a small flame to 80°C. Remove from heat and blend to a smooth cream, adding perfume as the mixture cools (Figure 9.3).

(*A*)   *Triethanolamine or monoethanolamine or ammonium* } *Dodecanyl (lauryl) sulphate* + *60 – 75% water* = *Liquid soapless shampoo*

(*B*)   *Sodium dodecanyl (lauryl) ether sulphate* + *Opacifier* + *50% Water* = *Pearly lotion shampoo*

(*C*) *Lipid oil* + *Emulsifying wax* + *Sodium dodecanyl (lauryl) sulphate* + *Water* = *Soapless cream shampoo*

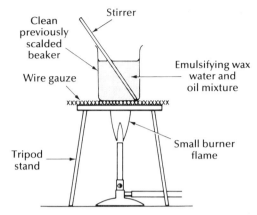

9.3 Apparatus for cream, emulsion preparation

(*b*) A cream shampoo *with* soap is prepared in a similar manner to the soapless cream shampoo, replacing the emulsifying wax and oil with pure soft soap powder. The soap acts as a *thickening* agent. See (D) below.

Place 40 g of sodium dodecanyl (lauryl) sulphate paste, 10 g of pure soap powder, and 60 cm³ of water in a previously cleaned beaker scalded with hot water. Gently heat the mixture with stirring to 80°C, remove from heat and blend to a smooth cream, adding perfume as the mixture cools.

Shampoo additives

A shampoo has the following basic composition:

Shampoo = Detergent + Water + Additives

Additives include a range of substances with different functions, listed as follows. (Additives of doubtful or nil function are not included.)

1 **Perfume,** an essential component of all shampoos (*see* Section 13.12).

2 **Colour,** usually an edible food colouring gives the preparation *visual* appeal.

3 **Opacifiers** are components providing a pearly visual effect; they are partly waxy and detergent in composition. Examples include calcium and zinc octadecanoates (*stearates*).

4 **Emulsifiers** provide creams of oils in water by means of various emulsifying waxes or liquids such a triethanolamine.

5 **Preservatives** are needed in shampoos containing edible lipid oils or soaps which can feed micro-organisms and become rancid. Methanal (formaldehyde) is a typical preservative.

6 **Foam stabilizers** are required to prevent the foam collapsing; they are mainly *non-ionic* ethoxylate detergents.

7 **Thickeners** make liquid and lotion shampoos thick or *viscous* by means of adding sodium chloride or sodium sulphate.

8 **Medicaments.** Simple ingredients of medicated shampoos include camphor, 0.25%, menthol, 0.05%, thymol, 0.5%, and terpineol, 0.4%. These are components of certain essential oils, with antiseptic properties.

Anti-dandruff or keratolytic shampoos contain organic acids, *hydroxybenzene carboxylic acid* (salicylic) and *benzoic* acids, *coal tar* extract, *cade* oil, or *selenium sulphide*. Zinc pyridine thiol N-oxide is effective against dandruff.

Anti-infestive shampoos for fungal infection contain *undecylenic acid*, and head lice infection is treated with gamma benzene hexachloride or malathion *insecticides*.

9.5 HAIR RINSING PREPARATIONS

Following the shampooing or washing process

Sodium dodecanyl (lauryl) sulphate)	+	Soap powder	+	Water	=	Cream shampoo with soap

the hair is rinsed to remove any surface deposits on the hair.

1 *Water rinse* removes all water-soluble detergents and salts, and allows insoluble lipid surface coatings to remain.

2 *Acid rinses* may be liquid or cream preparations containing ethanoic acid (acetic acid), citric, or lactic acids in a 3 per cent concentration in water. The acid component has the following functions:

(*a*) Remove hard water soap *scum* or calcium and magnesium *soaps* which cling to the hair surface.

(*b*) *Neutralize* traces of alkali from soap, shampoo, or after cold perming and bleaching.

(*c*) *Cuticle scales* are flattened and give the hair a smoother easier-to-dress surface.

(*d*) *Overbleached* hair forms a jelly-like surface coating removed by acid rinses.

3 *Alkaline hair rinses* are either liquid or cream preparations containing alkaline borax, sodium hydrogen carbonate, or weak ammonium hydroxide. The functions are as follows:

(*a*) Remove excess grease and *lipid* oils.

(*b*) *Neutralize* acid residues remaining from bleaching with acid stabilized hydrogen peroxide.

(*c*) Cuticle scales are *raised*.

4 *Conditioner rinses* are mainly cream preparations containing *cationic* detergents or QACs; these compounds having a *positive* charge, are held to the fibre by electrostatic attraction between the hair fibre's surface *negative* charge. *Proteins* such as egg white

are components of conditioners and are readily absorbed by damaged hair.

The functions of a conditioner rinse are as follows:

(*a*) Provide a *protective* surface coat.

(*b*) The QACs are *antiseptic* and antidandruff.

(*c*) Hair fibres acquire a *soft texture* or feel, by smoothing down the cuticle scales.

(*d*) Hair *appearance* is improved by a film of gloss.

(*e*) *Lubricant* component helps to make the hair easier to comb. Lanolin is the usual ingredient.

(*f*) *Static electricity* is neutralized and 'hair fly' or 'fly-away', the *repulsion* of hair fibres by each other, prevented.

(*g*) Increase *bulk* by protein absorption. Certain *plastic* polymers have a similar effect.

Acid conditioner cream

This is prepared by mixing 10 g of emulsifying wax B.P. with 2 g citric acid, 2 cm^3 almond oil and 86 cm^3 of pure water, in a previously cleaned and scalded beaker. The mixture is heated to 80°C and withdrawn from the heat and stirred vigorously until cool. Perfume is added as required. See (A) below.

Cationic conditioner cream

In this preparation the cationic detergent *cetrimide* is combined with the emulsifying wax as cetrimide emulsifying wax B.P. Lanolin is the lubricant component. See (B) below.

(*A*)

$$\underset{2\%}{Citric\ acid} + \underset{2\%}{Almond\ oil} + \underset{10\%}{Emulsifying\ wax} + \underset{86\%}{Water} = Acid\ Conditioner\ Cream$$

(Hydroxypropane tricarboxylic acid $=$ citric acid)

(*B*)

$$\underset{3\%}{Lanolin} + \underset{10\%}{Cetrimide\ Emulsifying\ wax} + \underset{87\%}{Water} = Cationic\ Conditioner\ Cream$$

The ingredients are mixed and heated together to 80°C. Withdrawn from heat, they are stirred vigorously until cool. Perfume is added as required.

9.6 HAIR CONDITION

The *physical condition* of hair is a combination of *several* properties which include: appearance (Section 11.1), colour, elasticity, thickness, surface texture, moisture content and porosity.

1 *Texture* is associated with the presence or absence of a *medulla* within the hair fibre, resulting in *coarse* or *fine* hair fibres.
2 *Moisture content* affects the hair fibre thickness; *dry* hair will be lank and *moist* hair will be bulky. The variable *humidity* of air will therefore affect hair condition.
3 *Porosity* of hair is *increased* by all hairdressing treatments, bleaching, perming or exposure to bright sunlight or chlorinated water. These processes damage the hair's *epicuticle* layer. Damage to the epicuticle causes the cuticle scales to project *upwards*, resulting in a *harsh* feel or texture. Proteins are readily absorbed by damaged or over-processed hair.
4 *Sebum* or lipid oils coat the hair surface as a transparent light *reflecting* layer, producing *gloss* or sheen. They also waterproof the hair fibre and *decrease* its porosity.
5 *Static electrical* charges increase on the hair surface through brushing and combing. Neutralization of these excessive negative charges is by means of positively charged quaternary ammonium compounds, QACs.
6 The natural *elasticity* of hair gives it vitality or 'bounce'. Hair damaged by overstretching with excessive traction will *lose* its elasticity since the elastic limit has been exceeded.

Chemically damaged hair when treated with the dye, acridine orange, will show fluorescence when viewed in ultra-violet ray light.

9.7 PHYSICS

Surface tension

If finely powdered sulphur is sprinkled on the surface of water in a clean beaker the powder will show up the 'skin' which appears to cover the water. If a drop of ethanol or a surface active detergent is added, the 'skin' is broken and the powder sinks.

Neighbouring molecules inside the water attract each other by the force of *cohesion*. Molecules of water on the surface are being pulled *inwards* towards the interior of the water. This *inward pull* in liquids, *contracting* the liquid surface, is called *surface tension*.

Surface tension is *seen* when wet hairs cling together and it can be demonstrated in a soap film by attaching two cotton threads to stiff wires.

Surface active detergents and certain other chemical substances, e.g. ethanol will *reduce* the surface tension of water. This occurs by means of the detergent *molecule* having a water-attracting, or *hydrophilic* group, or *head*, and a water-hating or *hydrophobic* group, or a *tail*.

The water-soluble hydrophilic group, or head, will push itself in *between* the water molecules and thus reduce the force of attraction between them and also reduce its surface tension.

The water *droplet* which forms on a *surface*, is made to collapse or spread resulting in the *wetting* of the surface, by the detergent surface action.

Sebum lanolin and *silicone oil* creams form thin films on hair fibres which prevent the wetting of the fibre by water which collects on the surface as droplets easily removed by *shaking* the hair fibres (Section 12.1).

Emulsions

The three physical states of matter, solid,

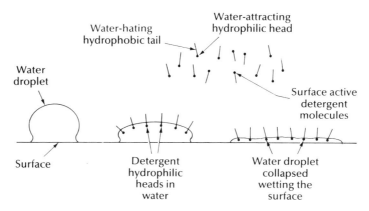

9.4   Wetting action of surface active detergent

liquid and gas, can be found as *mixtures* of each other.

Suspensions are mixtures of an insoluble *solid* in a *liquid*, for example, calamine lotion, and the opacifier in shampoo lotion.

Emulsions are mixtures of one insoluble liquid in another liquid, for example, almond oil in water, as in certain conditioner *creams*. Emulsions have one liquid *dispersed* as tiny *droplets* called the *dispersed phase*, whilst the liquid in which it is dispersed is called the *continuous phase*.

(*a*) A 2 per cent solution of almond oil in 98 per cent water is called an oil *in* water emulsion or O/W emulsion.

(*b*) A 2 per cent solution of water in 98 per cent almond oil is called a water *in* oil emulsion or W/O emulsion.

Emulsion type	Dispersed phase	Continuous phase
Oil in water O/W	Oil	Water
Water in oil W/O	Water	Oil

Stability

A *stable* emulsion will remain a cream and does not settle out into two layers. Opaci-

fiers are present in *stable* suspensions, but calamine lotion is an *unstable* suspension and settles out on standing.

Emulsifiers

These are chemical substances which are added to allow a *stable* emulsion to form between different liquids by *emulsification*.

$$\underset{A}{Liquid} + \underset{B}{Liquid} + Emulsifier = \underset{Emulsion}{Stable}$$

Soapless *detergents* and certain emulsifying *waxes* are emulsifiers for forming oil *in* water emulsions, other emulsifiers are needed for water *in* oil emulsions.

Identification of emulsions

Microscope method
View a smear or drop of emulsion, e.g. milk or butter, on a clean microscope slide. The dispersed phase droplets will be easily seen. Add a drop of water; if the water blends freely the emulsion is an O/W.

Chemical staining
Sprinkle a 50/50 mixture of powdered methylene blue and oil soluble Titan yellow on the emulsion on a clean microscope slide. View

the stained smear with a hand lens or through the microscope.

(*a*) O/W emulsions will show an overall colour of *blue*.

(*b*) W/O emulsions will show an overall colour of *yellow*.

Detergent action (Figures 9.4 and 9.5)

Surface active detergents cleanse soiled hair fibres during the *washing* process as follows:

1 The water surface tension is *lowered* by the surface active detergent allowing the fibres to be wetted. This involves the *hydrophilic* heads of the detergent weakening the intermolecular forces between water molecules.

2 *Anionic detergents* have a negatively charged hydrophilic head. The long tail of hydrocarbons is *lipophilic* or attracted to the oily grease coating the fibre. The *lipophilic* tails of the anionic detergent are inserted into the grease film, the *hydrophilic* heads then draw the film as a droplet of oil into the water.

3 *Negative charges* around the tiny oil droplets *repel* the similar charges of neighbouring soil droplets in the water. In this way they form a stable oil *in* water emulsion.

4 *Agitation* or rubbing helps to dislodge the soil film from the fibre surface, and breaks up *large* soil/oil droplets.

5 *Foaming* of the detergent produces a suspension of air *in* water *foam*: this helps to suspend the dislodged soils.

6 The *natural negative* charge on the fibre surface *repels* any suspended soils returning. Consequently anionic and non-ionic detergents are usual components of shampoo mixtures. Cationic detergents are *not* suitable since they coat the fibre with a positive charge.

Anti-redeposition or suspending agents are used in washing machine powders to prevent redeposition of soils on washed cotton.

9.8 CHEMISTRY

Concentration

Concentration means the *quantity* of a substance in a known quantity of another substance.

Percentage is a way of expressing concentration. For example 2 per cent almond oil solution has a ·concentration of 2 *parts* almond oil in 98 *parts* of water. The *parts* can be measured in equal cupfuls, or in a measure of metric *volume* or *weight*.

Weight for weight concentration, or W/W, indicates the concentration of the almond oil as 2 grammes in 98 grammes of water.

Volume for volume concentration, or V/V, indicates the concentration as 2 cm^3 almond oil in 98 cm^3 of water.

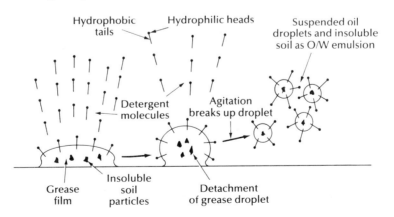

9.5   **Cleansing action of a surface active detergent**

Weight/volume concentration, W/V, indicates the weight 2 grammes almond oil in the volume of water, 98 cm³.

Acids (Table 9.1)

Acids are an important group of chemical compounds, many of which are *sour* tasting, *corrosive*, and which contain *hydrogen* that can be exchanged for a metal.

Coloured *indicators*, such as litmus, change colour with acids. Litmus turns *red* in acid solutions.

Inorganic acids are *strong* acids and completely *ionize* in water — 100 per cent.

Organic acids are *weak* acids and *partly* ionize in water — less than 0.1 per cent; contain carboxylic acid group.

Bases (Table 9.2)

A *base* will react with acids to form a *salt* and *water* by *neutralization*.

Alkalis are bases which dissolve *readily* in water, for example, sodium hydroxide.

Bases and alkalis are *bitter* tasting, *highly corrosive* to skin and hair, and have a *soapy* feel. They turn litmus indicator *blue*.

Neutralization is a chemical reaction between an acid and an alkali to form a salt and water.

$$Acid \ + \ Alkali \ = \ Salt \ + \ Water$$

The examples below are important neutralization reactions related to hairdressing. Most salt names end in -ATE.

pH Scale — Hydrogen ion concentration

Water *ionizes* into *equal* amounts of hydrogen and hydroxyl ions:

$$H_2O \longrightarrow H^+ \ + \ OH^-$$

Water	Hydrogen ion	Hydroxyl ion

Since there are equal amounts of each ion, or their concentrations are equal, the water is *neutral*.

Acids form more *hydrogen* ions than bases which form more *hydroxyl* ions.

Acids   high concentration H^+ ions
Alkalis   high concentration of OH^- ions *or* low concentration of H^+ ions.

pH is a measure of the concentration of hydrogen ions. The symbol, small *p* capital *H*, forms a pH *scale* reading from pH 1 to pH 14.

$$pH \longleftarrow \quad pH \quad \longrightarrow pH$$
$$1 \qquad\qquad 7 \qquad\qquad 14$$

Very strong acid	Neutral pure water	Very strong alkali

pH values can be measured using the *Universal Indicator* which changes colour with pH as shown in Figure 9.6. This indicator shows, by its colour change, the approximate pH of a substance.

Caution: When a strong alkali is used in a cosmetic preparation, the final pH of the mixture must be determined with Universal

(A) Thiolethanoic (thioglycollic) acid + Ammonium hydroxide → Ammonium Thiolethanoate (thioglycollate) (cold wave lotion) + Water

(B) Octadecanoic (stearic) acid + Sodium Hydroxide → Sodium Octadecanoate (stearate) (soap) + Water

(C) Citric acid (acid hair rinse) + Sodium hydoxide (residual soap alkali) → Sodium citrate + Water

Acid	Appearance	Uses
STRONG		
Hydrochloric	Colourless, strong smelling	Making many other chemical compounds
Sulphuric	Oily liquid	Soapless detergent manufacture
Nitric acid	Yellow, strong smelling	Dye manufacture — nitro dyes
WEAK		
Ethanoic (acetic)	Strong smelling — vinegar, sour beer	Hair rinses
Hydroxypropane tricarboxylic (citric) acid	White crystals — lemon juice	Hair rinses and conditioner
Hydroxypropanoic (lactic) acid	Syrupy liquid — sour milk	Hair and skin lotion
Hydroxy benzoic (salicylic) acid	White crystals	Anti-dandruff and keratolytic
Thiolethanoic (thioglycollic) acid	Unpleasant smelling liquid	Cold wave lotion and depilatory
Octadecanoic (stearic) acid	White waxy solid	Hair and cosmetic creams and lotions

Table 9.1   Important acids in hairdressing

Base	Appearance	Uses
Ammonium hydroxide	Strong smelling solution of gas in water	Alkaline hair rinse, cold wave lotion, and in bleaching lotions
Triethanolamine	An oily organic base	Emulsifying agent, soapless detergent manufacture
Monoethanolamine	Similar	Similar
Sodium hydroxide (caustic soda)	White hygroscopic solid	Soap manufacture, and cosmetic cream
Potassium hydroxide (caustic potash)	White hygroscopic solid	Soap manufacture, nail cuticle remover
Calcium hydroxide	Clear liquid	Turns cloudy with carbon dioxide

Table 9.2   Important bases in hairdressing

Salt	Appearance	Uses
Ammonium thiolethanoate (thioglycollate)	Unpleasant smilling liquid	Cold wave lotion, chemical depilatory
Borax — sodium tetraborate	White crystalline solid	Alkaline component of hair rinse and cosmetic creams
Calcium carbonate (chalk)	White powder	Talcum powder
Magnesium carbonate	White powder	Talcum powder, bleaching paste
Zinc carbonate (calamine)	White powder	Talcum powder and calamine lotion
Copper sulphate	Blue crystals	Sulphide dyes
Cadmium sulphate	White crystals	Sulphide dyes
Cobalt sulphate	Red crystals	Sulphide dyes

Table 9.3   Important salts in hairdressing

pH	Application, or effect on hair
0 – 4	Hardens the hair — no general application
4 – 6	WEAKLY ACIDIC — acid hair rinse and conditioner. Skin surface pH
7	NEUTRAL water, soapless detergent
8 – 9	WEAKLY ALKALINE — soaps, and cold wave perming lotions
10 – 14	STRONG ALKALINE — chemical depilatory, dissolves hair at high pH 14

Table 9.4   Some important hairdressing pH values

Acid ←———— Neutral ————→ Alkali

pH Hydrogen ion concentration	1,2,3	4	5	6	7	8	9	10	11,12,13,14
Universal indicator colour	Red	PINK	ORANGE	YELLOW	GREEN	GREEN	BLUE	BLUE	VIOLET	Violet

9.6   Colour changes at different pH with universal indicator

Indicator test paper, to make certain the pH is near neutral, pH 7.

Cream shampoo with soap

Weigh out 50 g of sodium dodecanyl (lauryl) sulphate *paste*, add 7 g of octadecanoic (stearic) acid, and 1 g of sodium hydroxide (**Care — Corrosive**). Mix with 50 cm³ of pure water. Heat the mixture to 70° – 80°C,

remove from heat and stir vigorously until cool. Transfer a portion of the mixture on to Universal Indicator paper to determine the pH. If at all alkaline, add more stearic acid and reheat and cool until pH is almost 7.

9.9   QUESTIONS

1 What are *emulsions* and *suspensions?*
Give examples of each and their uses in hairdressing.
2 Describe the main components of a soap and non-soap shampoo.
List the main additives together with their functions in a cream soapless detergent shampoo.
3 Explain the term *surface tension*.
Describe how an anionic soapless detergent removes solid and liquid soil from a hair fibre.
4 Write short notes on each of the following:
(*a*) neutralization; (*b*) pH; (*c*) acid; (*d*) salt.
5 Describe the method of use and composition of hair cleaning preparations other than of soaps and soapless detergents.
6 Write a descriptive essay on what is meant by *hair* condition.
7 Describe the process of cleaning and sterilising a metal comb.

9.10   MULTIPLE CHOICE QUESTIONS

1 Which of the following quantities are needed to make a litre of 5 per cent 2-hydroxy-propane-tricarboxylic (citric) acid solution?
(*a*) 5 g acid 995 cm³ water
(*b*) 50 g acid 950 cm³ water
(*c*) 5 g acid 95 cm³ water
(*d*) 50 g acid 99.5 cm³ water.

Sodium dodecanyl (lauryl) sulphate + Octadecanoic acid (stearic acid) + Sodium hydroxide —— Neutralization ——→ Sodium octadecanoate (stearate) soap + Sodium dodecanyl (lauryl) + Water

Soap cream shampoo

2 Which of the following indicates an acid pH or acidity?
  (a) pH 10
  (b) pH 8
  (c) pH 7
  (d) pH 4.
3 Ethanoic (acetic) acid and sodium hydroxide react together to form a salt called:
  (a) ammonium ethanoate (acetate)
  (b) ethyl ethanoate (acetate)
  (c) ammonium sulphate
  (d) sodium ethanoate (acetate).
4 One of the following additives to a medicated shampoo is the medicament:
  (a) methanal (formaldehyde)
  (b) thymol
  (c) ammonium chloride
  (d) lanolin.

5 In the following recipe for a cosmetic preparation which component is the disperse phase?
  (a) water 93%
  (b) almond oil 5%
  (c) emulsifier 2%
  (d) benzene carboxylic (benzoic) acid 0.05%.
6 The clinging of wet hairs together shows one of the following:
  (a) static electricity
  (b) friction forces
  (c) surface tension
  (d) hygroscopic attraction.

10 Hair Setting

10.1 NATURAL HAIR FORM

The form of naturally *straight* or *curly* hair may be caused by *two* mechanisms controlled by *genes*. Curly hair is *dominant* or *inherited* over straight hair.

(*a*) *Follicle shape*: a *straight* follicle will form a straight hair fibre, whilst a twisted or spiral shaped follicle will form a curly or *crimped* hair fibre.

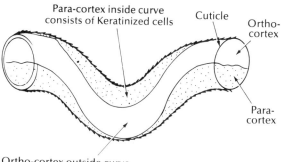

Para-cortex inside curve consists of Keratinized cells

Cuticle

Ortho-cortex

Para-cortex

Ortho-cortex outside curve consists of keratinzing cells

10.1 Keratinization and formation of hair wave (From an adaptation after Dr M.L.Ryder, 'Hair', *Studies in Biology*, No.41, Institute of Biology, 1973.)

(*b*) *Keratinization* is the process during which the hair fibre cells *harden* with keratin and die off. Close to the root the hair fibre is *soft* and *unkeratinized*.

Straight hairs have hardened cells all *around* the fibre and inwards from the cuticle. Curly or crimped wool fibres show keratinization or hardening of cells to *one side* of the fibre called the *paracortex*, whilst the *orthocortex* keratinizes at a later stage. This area takes up dyes better than the paracortex (*see* Section 8.5) (Figure 10.1).

The hardened keratinized cells are on the *inside* or concave part of the fibre, whilst the *soft keratinizing* cells are on the *outside* or convex part of the fibre, thus producing a wave or crimped *form*.

10.2 KERATIN MACROMOLECULE BONDS

The large macromolecule of *keratin* is a *polypeptide* composed of a long *chain* of amino acid *units*. This large molecule needs at least *four* different kinds of bonds to hold thousands of component atoms of C, H, O, P, S and N together.

The coiled spring-like polypeptide chains of the keratin molecule described in Section 8.6 have bonds *within* the polypeptide chains and other bonds *between* polypeptide chains — called *cross links* (Figure 10.2).

1 **Peptide bonds** are within the polypeptide chain, between the amino acid units. They are *very strong* covalent bonds, and form the 'backbone' of the molecule. They are only broken by *strong* alkali.

2 **Hydrogen bonds** are thought to join the spirals or coils of the coiled chain together. They form between neighbouring hydrogen atoms and oxygen atoms in adjacent spirals. There are a great number of hydrogen bonds in keratin, and they are *weak* bonds easily broken by hot water, and make wet hair very elastic, and *decrease* the fibre *strength* (Section 4.10).

3 **Van der Waals forces** are forces of attraction between the neighbouring atoms in adjacent spirals of the polypeptide chain coil. They are *very weak* forces, easily overcome by stretching the fibre.

4 **Ionic bonds**, also called **Salt links**, form as cross linkages between neighbouring *chains*, like rungs between ladder stiles. They form from amino groups $-NH_2$ and carboxylic acid $-COOH$ groups of the amino acids. These fairly strong bonds are broken by acids, and alkalis. Carboxylic acid $-COOH$ groups have a *negative* charge, whilst the amino $-NH_2$ groups have a positive charge. Since there is an *excess* of carboxylic acid groups in the amino acids of keratin, the net result is that hair keratin is *negatively charged*. This negative charge *attracts* the cationic detergents or QACs which have a *positive* charge.

5 **Disulphide bonds** composed of covalent bonds between *two* sulphur atoms, are cross linkages formed by the sulphur containing *cystine* amino acids. They are strong bonds broken only by certain chemical

Bond	Strength	Broken by
VAN DER WAALS FORCES (force of attraction between adjacent atoms in keratin coil	Very weak	Stretching
Hydrogen bonds (electrostatic attraction between neighbouring *hydrogen* and *oxygen* atoms)	Weak	Phenol solution or moist steam
Peptide bonds between adjacent amino acid units in polypeptide chain	Very strong	Strong alkali — chemical depilatories
CROSS LINKAGES *Ionic bond/Salt links* formed between amino and carboxylic acid groups in *opposite* chains	Fairly strong	Acid or alkali
Disulphide covalent bond between *cystine* sulphur atoms in opposite chains	Strong	Cold wave reducing agents and boiling water

Table 10.1   Bonds in the hair keratin molecule

reagents used in cold waving or by boiling water.

Table 10.1 summarizes the main bonds present in keratin.

10.3   SETTING TERMS

Set is a term used to describe the *change in form* or *length* of a natural or synthetic man-made *fibre* following a certain *treatment*.

Heat set is the process of setting a fibre in a new form. Man-made synthetic fibres are *thermoplastic* and some can be set in waves, as in wigs, by means of heat. A selected *optimum* temperature is required to prevent complete *melting* of the fibre.

Human hair when heated above 127°C is degraded or denatured and undergoes *irreversible* damage, with *singeing* at higher temperatures.

Hair set: Human hair can be set by three

10.2   Keratin molecule bonds

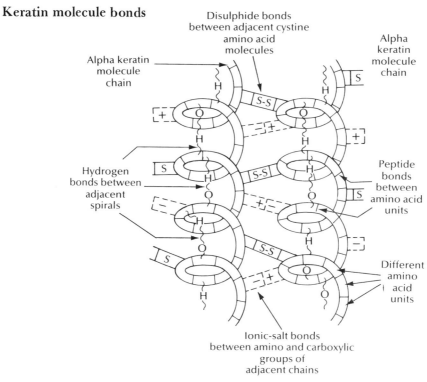

main methods related to the *persistence* of the *set in water*

(*a*) *Cohesive* set will disappear in cold water.

(*b*) *Temporary set* persists in cold water but disappears in boiling or hot water.

(*c*) *Permanent set* persists in both cold and boiling or hot waters.

Human hair set can be either a *bend set* in which the hair fibre is *waved* or curled in a bent stretched condition; or *length set* when *straightened* from a curly or bent condition into a *straight* stretched condition.

10.4   COHESIVE HAIR SET

This method involves *wetting hair* with cold water to increase its water content when its elasticity *increases*. If the wet hair is now stretched and *dried* around a roller, and *kept* dry, it will remain in its new form. The drying can be by blow dryers or evaporation at room temperature into air of *low* humidity. Once

the *cohesively* set hair is wetted with water it recovers its original unstretched length rapidly.

Cohesive set can be demonstrated as follows:

(*a*) Collect several long human hairs together into a bundle knotted at each end. Measure the length between the knots.

(*b*) Thoroughly soak the hair bundle in a shampoo solution.

(*c*) Support the bundle at one end and stretch it with a 100 g weight at the other end.

(*d*) Dry the supported hair bundle with a hair dryer, measure its length.

(*e*) Soak the stretched and dried bundle in the shampoo solution, and measure its length after soaking. The stretched hair will now have recovered its original length.

Setting lotions

Setting lotions are solutions of a *fixative* which serves to coat the hair fibre surface and cement neighbouring fibres together, with a *flexible* deposit which preserves a cohesive set, and forms a *barrier* to *prevent water* loss or entry to and from the fibre. The humidity of the air will affect the cohesive set; *damp* air will destroy the set and *dry* air will maintain the set.

(*a*) *Dressing preparations* (*see* Section 12.9) which contain an *oily* component such as lanolin or liquid paraffin which are present in brilliantines, hair creams, control creams and conditioners, will coat the hair fibre with an oily *seal* or water-resistant *barrier*.

(*b*) *Gum setting lotions* consist of 1 per cent solutions of either gum tragacanth or karaya in a mixture of ethanol and water. The gum is dissolved in about 15 cm^3 of toilet spirit to which perfume is added. The mixture is then slowly stirred into 95 cm^3 of pure water. Methanal is used as a preservative to prevent *mould* growth in storage. Gums form a *stiff* coating to the hair fibre.

(*c*) *Plastic setting lotions* are either used as *solutions* directly on to the hair or *sprays* from aerosols containing chloro-fluoro-hydrocarbon propellants. They consist of a polymer plastic *resin*, dissolved in ethanol *solvent*; additives include plasticizers which make the resin film on the hair *flexible* (Figure 10.3).

The following resins are used in 5 per cent concentration in ethanol; polyvinyl acetate, polyvinyl pyrollidone and dimethyl hydantoin methanal (formaldehyde) resins. The main *plasticizers* used are propanetriol (glycerine), isopropyl tetradecanoate (isopropyl myristate), dimethyl phthalate, and triacetin.

Water-repellent agents called *silicones*, compounds of silicon, repel moisture from entering the fibre and destroying the cohesive set.

Shellac setting lotions are now no longer used, since the shellac deposit was difficult to remove by ordinary washing.

10.5 TEMPORARY HAIR SET

A temporary set is produced by treating *stretched* hair with cold dilute alkali, e.g.

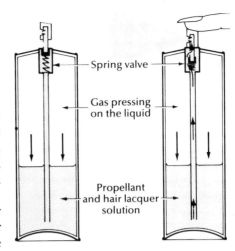

Spring valve

Gas pressing on the liquid

Propellant and hair lacquer solution

10.3   Aerosol spray

ammonium hydroxide, or borax, and water that is *not* too hot, for *long* periods of time.

The temporary nature is seen when the set hair is treated with cold water when it contracts by a *small* amount. If treated with hot water or an alkali rinse it recovers its original length and the set is lost.

Theory

A temporary set differs from the cohesive set by the *breakdown* of certain bonds mainly the *hydrogen bonds*, which is followed by the *formation* of new hydrogen bonds in *new* positions between the polypeptide chain coils. These new bonds are fairly *unstable* and break down on treatment with hot water or dilute alkali.

Equipment

Heated crimping iron
This is an iron *rod* with an iron hair *clamp* to form a tong. The iron is heated in a crimping iron heater (Figure 10.4), or the iron may be heated directly by a butane gas flame or by the heating effect of an electrical current, as in curling tongs or styling wands.

Some electrically heated tongs and styling

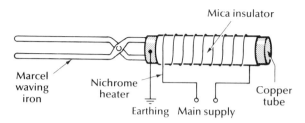

10.4   Marcel iron heater element

brushes have a *steam generator*, to provide steam.

Heated roller or styling brush (Figure 10.5)
This is an electrically heated iron *rod* on to which a *cylindrical* roller or a *brush* is fitted as a sleeve. The roller or brush has a light or low density *metal core* and a *plastic casing* with a heat sensitive indicator.

The iron rod is heated from a heating element controlled by a thermostat; there is *no* direct electrical contract between the element and the rod. Heating is by conduction.

Safety

Electrically heated crimping irons, styling wands or brushes, and the equipment for heating rollers must be used with care.
1 *Water* spilt on the handle or equipment

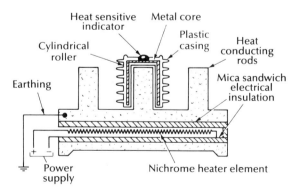

10.5   Roller heater equipment

must be wiped off before switching on the appliance.
2 *Insulation* of the equipment must meet the safety regulations for electrical equipment.
3 *Earthing* (Section 12.6) of the appliance must meet the safety regulations.
4 *Overheating* must not occur since it will cause damage to hair by irreversible *degradation* and unfolding of hair keratin molecules.

Preparations used in connection with temporary hair set include dilute solutions of weakly *alkaline*, 1 per cent borax, hair *moisturizers* to provide water. Cationic QAC conditioner solutions are also used.

10.6   HOT PERMANENT HAIR SET

If the *temporary* hair set treatment is continued for much *longer* times and at higher temperatures near to *boiling* water, the temporary set passes into a *hot permanent* set. This hair set is *permanent* in that it is unaffected by washing in hot or cold water.

Theory

Breakdown of bonds - relaxation
Boiling water attacks *hydrogen* bonds, *ionic* salt bonds, and the cystine *disulphide* bonds in *stretched* hair keratin.

This process of breakdown of bonds in *stretched* hair keratin is called *relaxation*.

Re-formation of bonds
Strong or *stable* bonds form in *new* positions in the polypeptide chain as the temperature continues to remain *high* for a *longer* period of time. The *new* stable bonds form at positions formerly held between the two sulphur atoms of the disulphide bond of *custine*, or between groups of atoms of different amino acids, *lysine* and *alanine*.

The new re-formed bonds are either:
(a) *monosulphide* bonds composed of *one* sulphur atom, -S-, called a *lanthionine* cross link; or

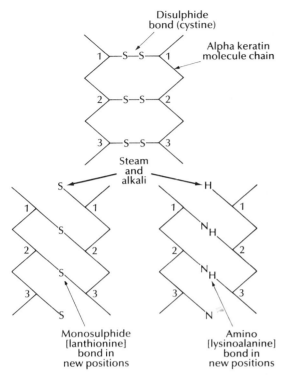

10.6 Hot permanent hair set

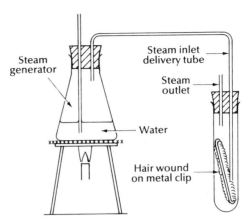

10.7 Experiment to show hot permanent hair set

drying, and removing from the hair clip. The hair can then be washed in a hot shampoo solution, rinsed and dried and the curl or wave permanence examined.

Equipment

The following equipment aims to provide the necessary *high* temperature and steam required for the process.

1 *Steam processing* formerly involved leading steam direct from a boiler by tubes connected to the hair wound on formers, the hair being soaked in *alkaline* lotions of varying composition.

2 *Heat processing* is by hot metal clips, heated by conduction on the hot metal rods or *heater bars* of electrically heated hot permanent waving machines. The hot metal clips are of low density *aluminium* metal, which are clipped on to the hair on its roller surrounded by a protective aluminium foil. The hair being soaked in the alkaline hot permanent waving lotion. The insulating rubber pads protect the scalp from burns (Figure 10.8).

Direct electrical heating by way of electrical heaters attached to the hair on rollers, is an obsolete process, discontinued due to the discomfort caused by the weight of

(*b*) *amino* bonds composed of one nitrogen and one hydrogen atom, -NH-, called a *lysinoalanine* cross link since it forms between amino acids *lysine* and *alanine* (Figure 10.6).

The chemical change which occurs in new bond formation is called *hydrolysis*, or chemical decomposition of hair keratin by boiling water. The *by-products* include unpleasant smelling *hydrogen sulphide* gas, or *sulphide* salts of sodium.

Hot permanent waving of hair can be demonstrated by passing steam from a generator into a test tube containing a switch of hair *tightly* rolled around a *metal* clip roller, in a solution of one per cent borax. Steam enters the solution and causes it to *boil*. The *longer* the treatment is continued, the more permanent the set will become (Figure 10.7).

The permanence of the set can be determined after rinsing the hair in *cold* water,

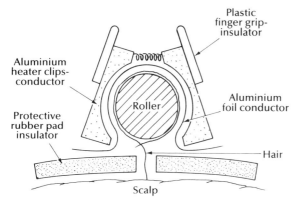

10.8   Hot permanent waving clip

equipment attached to the head and difficulty of heat control.
3 *Exothermic chemical pads* or sachets consist
of a mixture of calcium oxide and potassium permanganate together with a *reagent*
of water and an organic substance which
react together when the reagent moistens
the mixture in the sachet. Considerable
heat is generated *exothermally*, by:
   (a) the conversion of calcium oxide into
calcium hydroxide:

$$\begin{matrix} Calcium \\ oxide \end{matrix} + \ Water \ \rightarrow \begin{matrix} Calcium \\ hydroxide \end{matrix} + \ HEAT$$

   (b) *oxidation* of organic reagent by potassium permanganate.
   The sachet has a waterproof, heat conducting metal foil backing and a porous
upper surface which allows penetration of
the liquid reagent.

Preparations

The solutions used *initially* consisted of
mainly *water* and alkali such as borax, dilute
sodium carbonate, or ammonium hydroxide.
   Later solutions included various chemical
compounds with *reducing* properties, namely
sodium and potassium *sulphite* and *metabi-
sulphites* — the fore-runner of cold wave
lotions.

10.7   COLD PERMANENT HAIR SET

This is a permanent hair set achieved by
chemical change at low temperature or room
temperature. The hair set is permanent in cold
and hot water.

Theory

The process of cold permanent set involves
relaxation or breakdown of cross linkage
bonds of hair keratin in the stretched condition.

Breakdown of bonds
Chemical *reducing agents*, or substances able
to add hydrogen, break down the *disulphide*
bonds in *stretched* hair keratin; at the same
time the *hydrogen* and *ionic* salt bonds are
also broken down.
   The *reducing agents* are sodium sulphide,
sodium hydrogen sulphite, ethanolamine
sulphite, and ammonium *thiolethanoate* (thioglycollate). The reducing agents attack the
cystine disulphide bonds by adding hydrogen
to form *thiol* or -HS groups found in the
amino acid *cysteine*. Once the chemical process
of reduction is started the disulphide bonds
break by an 'unzipping' mechanism like the
opening of a zip fastener.

Re-formation of bonds (Figure 10.9)
This is a process which involves *oxidation*
using a mild oxidizing agent which can add on
oxygen and remove the hydrogen from the
thiol group -SH, and thus re-form the *disulphide* -S-S- bond in a *new* position in the
stretched keratin molecule. The mild oxidizing
agents used are *oxygen-rich* substances such
as oxygen from the *air*, or from chemical
compounds *hydrogen peroxide*, *sodium perborate* and formerly *sodium bromate*.
   During oxidation the *majority* of disulphide
bonds are re-formed, but a number remain
broken and are responsible for the inevitable
chemical damage caused by frequent use of
cold waving lotion. In time the chemically

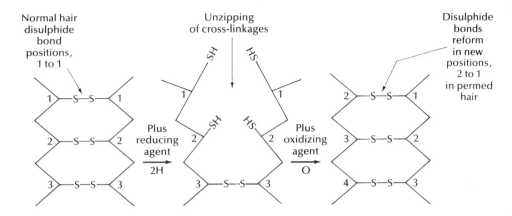

10.9   Cold permanent hair set

damaged hair is replaced by undamaged new hair growth.

Factors affecting the process

Temperature
Since this is a chemical reaction called *reduction*, the *rate* or speed at which it takes place will be increased with *temperature rise*. The rate is *doubled* when the temperature is raised from 15°C to 25°C; this *optimum temperature* can be attained by using normal *body heat* and surrounding the scalp in a heat-insulating plastic thermal or perm *cap*. Alternatively the steamer (Figure 10.10) or infra-red *accelerator* lamp can be used to accelerate the process (*see* Section 13.2).

State of reactants
The reducing lotion is a *liquid*, whilst the hair keratin molecule is a *solid*. The rate of reaction will be *slow*, a quicker reaction would occur if both *reactants* were liquids. The reducing lotion must pass into the hair fibre by *diffusion*, a slow process assisted by ammonia which raises the fibre cuticle scales and allows rapid penetration into the cortex.

Greasy soils and silicone-water repellent barriers must be removed by prior shampooing before applying the reducing lotion.

Concentration
The hydrogen ion concentration or pH must be *alkaline* between pH 7 and 9.5, whilst the concentration of reducing agent need only be about 7 per cent.

Preparations

Cold wave reducing lotions
This lotion consists of the *reducing agent* in the form of the salt ammonium thiolethanoate (thioglycollate) made by mixing 7 per cent thiolethanoic acid (thioglycollic acid) with 3.5 per cent ammonia to a final pH value of between pH 9.3 to 9.6

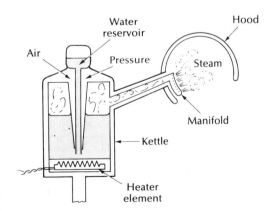

10.10   Salon steamer

The solution is prepared as an *emulsion* with a *non-ionic* emulsifying wax to the extent of 30 per cent in water up to 60 per cent of the total mixture. The emulsion serves to *coat* the hair and allow penetration by diffusion of the reducing agent.

Since the thiolethanoic (thioglycollic) acid has an unpleasant odour, it is usually *masked* with a perfume.

Precautions in use
1 *Iron salts* form purple to red stains with thiolethanoates (thioglycollates), and the lotion must not come into contact with the metal in any equipment, or hair treated with any iron preparation. Containers must be of glass or chemical resistant plastic.
2 *Skin* and finger nails consist of *keratin* and will also be attacked by the reducing lotion. The hands should be protected by wearing rubber gloves. Keep the lotion away from the eyes, face and mouth.
3 *Alkali* and thiolethanoates (thioglycollates) can cause inflammation of scalp cuts and abrasions. Soft paraffin is a useful protective for minor cuts and abrasions.

Cold wave oxidizing lotions
(*a*)   A *powder mixture* can be prepared consisting of 90 per cent *sodium perborate*, the oxidizing agent, mixed with a 2 per cent *anionic* detergent sodium dodecanyl (lauryl) sulphate powder, as a *wetting agent* and 8 per cent citric acid to *neutralize* any remaining alkali from the reducing lotion. The powder is used as a 2 per cent solution in water.

(*b*) *Emulsion preparations* consist of 10 per cent sodium perborate as the *oxidizer*, with 10 per cent of a non-ionic *emulsifying wax* as the emulsifier in 80 per cent water. The emulsion aids the application of the lotion to the hair. The mixture is used without dilution.

Emulsion preparations for mixing with hydrogen peroxide as the oxidizer prior to use, consist of 10 per cent non-ionic emulsifying wax and 2 per cent ammonia to neutralize the hydrogen peroxide stabilizer.

(*c*) *Air* is 20 per cent oxygen and is a *slow* means of oxidizing chemically reduced hair keratin. Former hot permanent hair set processes using *sulphite* and *hydrogen sulphite* reagents caused some *reduction* of disulphide bonds. Oxidation was by means of air after the perming process.

Hydrogen and ionic salt bond re-formation

Rinsing of hair following oxidation with a 30 per cent solution of *magnesium sulphate* salt is considered to assist in the re-formation of hydrogen and ionic salt linkages.

Hair straighteners

Naturally wavy or curly hair is *straightened* by the same process as for cold permanent hair set. The *relaxation* is by means of ammonium thiolethanoate (thioglycollate) at a pH 10 either as an emulsion in a non-ionic base, or as a lotion. The oxidizing agent is similar to those preparations of sodium perborate or hydrogen peroxide previously described.

Neutralizers

These are components as *acids* of the oxidizing mixture to *neutralize* the cold wave reducing lotion *alkali* by *neutralization* but since this process is *secondary* to the main purpose of oxidation the term 'neutralizing' is incorrect for a process that is mainly *oxidation*.

Cold permanent hair set can be demonstrated by preparing a 7 per cent solution of thiolethanoic (thioglycollic) acid in water and adding strong *0.880* ammonia solution from a previously filled burette.
Care: do not inhale. Add a few drops of Universal Indicator solution and *slowly* add the ammonia solution with stirring until the colour is *light blue*, pH 9.

Roll a switch of straight hair tightly on a metal clip roller and immerse in the prepared thioglycollate solution for 30 minutes. Rinse the hair thoroughly in cold water, then immerse in a 10 volume strength solution of hydrogen peroxide for 20 minutes. Wash the test curl in water, dry with a hair dryer and comb it out.

Examine the wave formed in the hair. Test its *permanence* with hot shampoo solution.

Repeat the experiment and omit the use of hydrogen peroxide, allow the hair to *oxidize* in air. Compare the *permanence* of the wave formed with theprevious test curl.

Table 10.2 summarizes and compares the main methods of hair set.

10.8   PHYSICS

Density is defined as weight or *mass* in kilogrammes divided by volume in cubic metres.

$$Density = \frac{Mass}{volume}$$

It is the means of comparing heaviness or lightness of different substances, by measuring the mass of *equal* volumes.

Densities of some common substances

Iron	7.9 kg/m³
Aluminium	2.6 kg/m³
Propanetriol (glycerine)	1.26 kg/m³
Water	1.0 kg/m³
Ethanol	0.8 kg/m³
Petrol-hexane	0.64 kg/m³

Iron values: Iron 7.9 kg/m^3, Aluminium 2.6 kg/m^3, Propanetriol (glycerine) 1.26 kg/m^3, Water 1.0 kg/m^3, Ethanol 0.8 kg/m^3, Petrol-hexane 0.64 kg/m^3

From the above it will be seen that iron heater clips would be *three* times heavier than *equal* sized aluminium heater clips.

Similarly the substances with a density *less* than 1.0 kg/m^3, the density of water, will float on its surface — for example, most oils float on water. Similarly *hot* water has a density *less* than cold water and floats above the cold water.

Conditions and reagents	Cohesive set	Temporary set	Permanent	
			Hot set	Cold set
Permanence	Disappears in cold water	Persists in cold water. Disappears in hot water	Persists in hot water	Persists in hot water
Reagent	Cold water	Warm moist steam	Boiling water and alkali	Thioglycollate/sulphite reducing agent followed by oxidation
Bonds involved	1 Van der Waals forces Molecular lubrication by water	1 Van der Waals forces 2 Hydrogen bonds	1 Van der Waals forces 2 Hydrogen bonds 3 Ionic salt bonds 4 Disulphide bonds	1 Van der Waals forces 2 Hydrogen bonds 3 Ionic salt bonds 4 Disulphide bonds
Change involved	Physical	Physical	Physical and chemical — hydrolysis	Physical and chemical — reduction and oxidation
Amino acids involved	None	None	Cystine also lysine and alanine	Mainly cystine
Links rebuilt	Within chain in new positions	Within chain in new positions	Ditto and between chains as lanthionine and lysinoalanine links	Ditto and between chains as re-formed disulphide bonds

Table 10.2   Summary of the main chemical and physical changes in hair set

Relative Density	% NH₃, (Ammonia)
0.880	35
0.900	28
0.930	19
0.960	10
0.990	2

Table 10.3   Relative density of ammonium hydroxide solutions at 16°C

Substances with a density *greater* than that of water will *sink* in water — for example propanetriol (glycerine) will form a layer beneath water before mixing.

Relative density (R.D.). This was formerly called specific gravity; it is the mass or weight of a substance *divided* by the mass of an *equal* volume of water.

$$\text{Relative density (R.D.)} = \frac{\textit{Mass or weight of substance}}{\textit{Mass or weight of an equal volume of water}}$$

It is an indication of the number of *times* a substance is *heavier* or *lighter* than an equal volume of water.

A *hydrometer* (Figure 10.11) is an instrument for determining directly the relative density of different *solutions*. It consists of a weighed *bulb* and a *stem* marked with the relative density scale. The hydrometer can be a rapid way of determining *concentration* of solutions. For example the relative densities of different strength solutions of ammonium hydroxide are given in Table 10.3.

From Table 10.3 it will be seen that ammonium hydroxide solutions of R.D. 0.880 is the strongest available at 35 per cent. It is sometimes called 'eight eighty ammonia' and must be handled with care and **caution.**

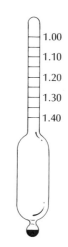

10.11   The hydrometer

Ethanol (methylated spirits) is sold at different relative densities, corresponding to different percentage concentrations.

90 per cent ethanol	0.83 kg/m³
95 per cent ethanol	0.81 kg/m³
100 per cent ethanol or	
absolute ethanol	0.790 kg/m³

The density of ethanol is rapidly determined by means of the hydrometer.

10.9   CHEMISTRY

Hydrogen

Hydrogen, H₂, is a gas which can be made by adding *dilute* HCl, hydrochloric acid (**care — corrosive acid**) to zinc, Zn, metal. This chemical reaction proceeds quite rapidly and bubbles of hydrogen gas are seen to be produced.

Zinc	+	*Hydrochloric acid*	⟶	*Hydrogen*	+	*Zinc chloride salt*
Zn		2HCl		H₂		ZnCl₂

Most strong acids can have their hydrogen replaced by *metals* to form *salts*.

Hydrogen is a gas of very *low density* and a sample can be collected in a test tube. When a lighted taper is put into the test tube of hydrogen gas it burns with a squeaky pop and *water* is the product.

Hydrogen + *Oxygen of air* → *Water*

Reduction

Reduction is a chemical reaction of *three* main kinds in which a substance can:

(a) lose oxygen
(b) gain hydrogen
(c) gain *electrons*.

The *reducing agent* can be *hydrogen* gas, or certain *reducing compounds* which have *reducing properties*; such compounds include the thiolethanoates (*thioglycollates*), or *methanal* (formaldehyde), which can either *remove* oxygen or *add* on hydrogen to another compound. Glucose and vitamin C ascorbic acid are also examples of reducing agents.

1 The *reducing property of methanal* (formaldehyde) is shown as follows:

Thoroughly clean a glass test tube and dissolve a crystal of *silver nitrate* (**care — caustic** burns skin) in distilled or deionized water, add dilute ammonia solution *drop* by *drop* until the cloudiness formed *just* disappears.

Add a little methanal (formaldehyde) and warm the mixture in a water bath to the temperature of boiling water. Note the formation of a *silver mirror*. Methanal *reduces* the silver oxide by *removing* its oxygen leaving pure silver metal. This is the method of silvering *mirrors*. See *A* below.

2 Lipid *oils* can be *reduced or hydrogenated* by passing *hydrogen gas* into the liquid oil, e.g. olive oil, a special *catalyst* is used to speed up the chemical reaction. The reduced or hydrogenated lipid *oils* are changed into *solid* lipid fats. Oleic fatty acid is a *liquid* and it becomes *solid* stearic fatty acid. See *B* below.

See the Unilever Laboratory Experiment Number 3 'The hydrogenation of soft oils'.

The *reduction* of keratin *disulphide* bonds by ammonia thiolethanoate (thioglycollate) does not show any *visible* products, such as are *seen* in the formation of the silver mirror, and the hardening of liquid oils.

The *fact* that disulphide bonds in keratin *are* reduced by hydrogen is difficult to accept by students who often expect to *see* some kind of change.

Reduction and the action of reducing agents is always *opposite* to oxidation and *oxidizing agents*.

| Reducing agents | *Act Against* ⟷ | Oxidizing agents |

Rates of chemical reactions

Many chemical reactions are very *fast*, for example the formation of the silver mirror occurs quite rapidly; these fast reactions usually involve *inorganic* chemical substances.

Organic substances, including hair keratin, react very *slowly*, and hair waving, bleaching or colouring requires fairly long processing or *reaction times*.

Chemical reactions are speeded up by the following conditions:

1 *Temperature.* An increase of temperature

(A) *Silver oxide* + *Hydrogen from methanal (formaldehyde)* ⟶ *Silver metal* + *Water*

(B) *Liquid (oleic) acid Octadec-9-enoic acid* + *Hydrogen* ⟶ *Solid (stearic) acid Octadecanoic acid*

through $10°C$ *doubles* the rate of chemical reaction. Consequently steamers and infrared heat are used as process accelerators.

2 *Concentration*, the more concentrated the reactants are the faster will be the rate of reaction. This applies in certain hairdressing processes such as bleaching or colouring.

3 *Solutions* of reactants work faster than solid reactants; for example *powdered* forms of oxidizing mixtures would take a long time to react compared to the solutions of oxidizing agents.

4 *Catalysts*; these are substances which speed up chemical reactions and are described in the bleaching process (Section 11.3). They are also important as biological catalysts or enzymes (Section 15.5).

10.10   QUESTIONS

1 Describe how a cohesive hair set is formed. What preparations are used to prolong this type of hair set?

2 What bonds are broken and re-formed in a temporary hair set;
What reagents bring about this set?
Describe how a temporary hair set can become a permanent set.

3 Describe the theory, equipment and reagents used in a hot permanent hair set.
Name the bonds which are broken and the types of bonds which are re-formed.

4 Give an account of theory and reagents used in a cold permanent hair set.
Describe how the term neutralization is incorrectly used in this process of hair set.

5 Explain how natural straight and curly hair forms.
What chemical processes are used to straighten naturally curly hair?

6 If hair is treated with concentrated sodium hydroxide of pH 14, what will occur and which bonds of the keratin molecule are destroyed?

10.11   MULTIPLE CHOICE QUESTIONS

1 Arginine, serine and glycine are components of hair and are classed as:
(*a*) alkanoic (fatty acids)
(*b*) amino acids
(*c*) monosaccharides
(*d*) hydrocarbons.

2 The component units of proteins are linked together in the chain through one of the following main linkages:
(*a*) disulphide bonds
(*b*) peptide bonds
(*c*) hydrogen bonds
(*d*) salt links.

3 Which of the following bonds in the hair molecule is attacked by the first stage cold waving chemical reagent?
(*a*) peptide
(*b*) salt
(*c*) hydrogen
(*d*) disulphide.

4 Which of the following substances would be unsuitable as the reagent used in the second stage of hardening the softened hair in cold waving?
(*a*) sodium dodecanyl (lauryl) sulphate
(*b*) hydrogen peroxide
(*c*) sodium peroxoborate (III) (perborate)
(*d*) sodium bromate (V).

5 During water waving or finger waving which of the bonds present in the hair molecule is most easily broken or stretched?
(*a*) peptide bonds
(*b*) disulphide bonds
(*c*) hydrogen bonds
(*d*) salt links.

6 Which of the following is the conditioner used in hair sprays?
(*a*) polyvinyl ethanoate (acetate)
(*b*) ethanol (ethyl alcohol)
(*c*) lanolin
(*d*) dimethyl benzene dicarboxylate (phthalate).

11 Hair Colouring

11.1 NATURAL HAIR COLOUR

Natural hair colour is due to the *insoluble* pigment *melanin* seen as tiny egg-shaped *granules* by means of the light microscope. The melanin pigment is found mainly in the hair *cortex*, but can also be found in the cuticle and medulla region (*see* Section 8.5).

There are *two* forms of melanin; normal or *eumelanin*, brown to black in colour, and *pheomelanin*, yellow to red in colour.

Hair appearance

The *outward visible* characteristics of hair are due to *shades* of colour seen through the *transparent* cuticle. The degrees of shading depend on the following factors concerning the melanin granules.

(*a*) *Granule size*, small granules are seen in the *fair*, and large granules in the *dark* shades.

(*b*) *Granule distribution*, more granules are found in the fully keratinized paracortex than in the orthocortex which has been recently keratinized or hardened. This *uneven* distribution produces attractive shade *tones* along the fibre.

Light rays falling on the hair surface will produce visible effects as follows:

1 *Reflection* on the smooth lipid coated cuticle will produce *bright* points or highlights, sheen or gloss.

2 *Diffusion* or scattering of the light rays by the cuticle edges will show *texture* in an attractive lustre.

3 *Refraction* of light rays will show the melanin pigment which *absorbs* the light and discloses specific colours. The nature of the light whether *sunlight* or *artificial* light will affect the resulting shade of colour (*see* Figure 6.6).

Melanin formation

Melanin granules are formed in special pigment forming *cells* close to the hair papilla called *melanocytes*; the pigment is present within the hair fibre before it emerges from the follicle.

The amino acid *tyrosine* (*see* Table 8.2) is

the raw material for melanin formation, which is *oxidized* by oxygen, using a biological catalyst or enzyme called *tyrosinase*, to form *melanogen*.

$$\begin{array}{ccc} & \text{Oxygen} \\ & \text{Oxidation} \\ \textit{Tyrosine} & \xrightarrow{\hspace{2cm}} & \textit{Melanogen} \\ \textit{amino acid} & & \textit{(dihydroxy-} \\ & \text{Enzyme} & \textit{indole)} \\ & \text{tyrosinase} \end{array}$$

The melanogen then *polymerizes*, joining with other melanogen units, to form a *protein-like* substance, melanin.

$$\begin{array}{ccc} \textit{Melanogen} & \xrightarrow{\text{Oxygenation}} & \textit{Melanin} \\ \textit{(dihydroxy-} & \text{and} & \textit{(Protein-like} \\ \textit{indole)} & \text{polymerisation} & \textit{substance)} \end{array}$$

The melanin is *insoluble* in water, acids, or organic solvents.

Albinism is the complete absence of melanin in the hair and skin. The hair is *white*, due to the lack of the enzyme *tyrosinase* which makes melanin. This is a *hereditary* condition. Grey or white hair or *canities*, is the turning of normal coloured hair to white or grey, a process due to defective tyrosinase formation before the hair is hardened or keratinized.

White-forelock or *leucotrichia* is absence of pigment formation in a specific *area* of the scalp; it is a *dominant* inherited condition. (*See* Section 19.8.)

11.2   CHEMISTRY OF HYDROGEN PEROXIDE

Hydrogen peroxide, chemical formula H_2O_2,

is an important chemical reagent used in several hairdressing processes as a source of *oxygen* in the form of an *oxidizing agent*. Although air contains 20 per cent oxygen it is not a *controllable* source for hairdressing processes.

Preparation of hydrogen peroxide

(*a*)   A weak solution can be made by adding *barium peroxide* (**poisonous**) to dilute sulphuric acid (**corrosive**) until the mixture shows a slight acid reaction to neutral litmus paper. The solution is filtered. *See* (A) below.

(*b*) *Large scale manufacture* involves a chemical reaction of oxidation of compounds called *quinols* into *quinones*. This chemical reaction is important since *quinones* called *anthraquinones* are important *dyes*.

Air (20 per cent oxygen) is blown through *anthraquinol* dissolved in an organic solvent, hydrogen peroxide and the *yellow* dye *anthraquinone* is formed. *See* (B) below.

Pure hydrogen peroxide with a 100 per cent composition is a colourless syrupy liquid, which is explosive if heated or in contact with powered materials.

Chemical test for hydrogen peroxide

Ordinary dilute hydrogen peroxide *solutions* resemble water in having a colourless appearance. When added to a solution of potassium iodide treated with dilute sulphuric acid a brown colour forms due to *iodine* released by the hydrogen peroxide. This turns blue—black when starch solution is added.

(*A*)

Barium peroxide + *Dilute sulphuric acid* → *Hydrogen peroxide* + *Insoluble barium sulphate*

(*B*)

Anthraquinol   +   *Oxygen* ⟶ *Hydrogen peroxide*   +   *Anthraquinone*

Chemical properties

1 Decomposition

Dilute hydrogen peroxide solution is *decomposed* into *oxygen* gas and *water* by different methods (*see* Figure 11.1).

$$\begin{array}{ccc} \text{Hydrogen} \\ \text{peroxide} \end{array} \longrightarrow \text{Water} \quad + \quad \text{Oxygen gas}$$

$$2H_2O_2 \longrightarrow 2H_2O \qquad O_2$$

(*a*) *Alkalis* such as *ammonium hydroxide*, or salts *ammonium carbonate, sodium ethanoate* (sodium acetate), which form alkali on ionization, *rapidly* decompose hydrogen peroxide. These reagents are added during various hairdressing processes and act as *catalysts* to speed up the reaction.

(*b*) *Heat* from any source, sunlight or heating appliances, makes it essential to store hydrogen peroxide in dark brown *light-proof* bottles, or opaque plastic containers, in cool dark *storage*. There is usually an *air space* over the liquid to allow oxygen to accumulate and prevent bursting of the container. At all times store hydrogen peroxide away from *flammable* materials.

(*c*) *Dust* and *finely powdered* substances such as *manganese dioxide* cause rapid decomposition. Stoppers should be replaced immediately to prevent entry of airborne *dust*.

Add a pinch of manganese dioxide to a little hydrogen peroxide solution and place a *glowing* wooden taper in the gas evolved. Oxygen will *relight* the taper and cause it to burn *brighter* than in air, to form *oxides*.

Stabilizers

Different chemical substances including *acids*, sulphuric, phosphoric, or hydroxybenzoic acid (salicylic) are added in *small* amounts (0.5 to 2 per cent), other substances such as ethanol (ethyl alcohol), or propanetriol (glycerine) are also used. These slow down the decomposition of hydrogen peroxide whilst in storage. The addition of *alkali neutralizes* the acid stabilizer.

2 Reduction

Since hydrogen peroxide H_2O_2, contains *hydrogen*, it can act as a *reducing agent* in certain chemical reactions, particularly in *alkaline* solutions, pH 9–15.

Add a crystal of silver nitrate (**care – corrosive**) to distilled or deionized water in a test tube, and then add dilute sodium hydroxide (**care – caustic**) a little at a time to form *brown* coloured silver oxide. Add hydrogen peroxide solution and the brown silver oxide is *reduced* to *black* silver metal.

$$\begin{array}{c} \text{Silver} \\ \text{oxide} \end{array} + \begin{array}{c} \text{Hydrogen} \\ \text{peroxide} \end{array} \rightarrow \text{Silver} + \text{Oxygen} + \text{Water}$$

3 Oxidation

Hydrogen peroxide is also a powerful *oxidizing agent*; it can add oxygen to other compounds.

If hydrogen peroxide is added to black *lead sulphide*, it turns to *white* lead sulphate, through oxidation.

$$\begin{array}{c} \text{Black} \\ \text{lead} \\ \text{sulphide} \end{array} + \begin{array}{c} \text{Hydrogen} \\ \text{peroxide} \end{array} \longrightarrow \begin{array}{c} \text{White} \\ \text{lead} \\ \text{sulphate} \end{array}$$

Many of the hairdressing processes using hydrogen peroxide require *oxidation*, for example the oxidation of reduced hair keratin in the cold permanent hair set process (Section 10.7).

Concentration of solutions

The concentration of hydrogen peroxide solutions is measured either as *percentage* W/W, or as *volume strength* (*see* Section 9.8).

(*a*) *Percentage* W/W concentration is shown as 3, 6, 9, 12 and 30 per cent. It is determined by different chemical methods of analysis. A 3 per cent W/W solution will contain 3 g of *pure* 100 per cent hydrogen peroxide in 97 g of water, a 30 per cent solution will consist of 30 g *pure* 100 per cent hydrogen peroxide in 70 g of water.

(*b*) *Volume strength.* This means the *number of volumes* of oxygen gas, measured at 0°C and 101 kPa air pressure, produced by fully decomposing *one volume* of the hydrogen peroxide solution. The *volumes* are measured in the *same* units, cm^3, or litres. For example:

> One *cm^3* of 20 volume H$_2$O$_2$ gives 20 *cm^3* of oxygen, or
> one *litre* of 20 volume H$_2$O$_2$ gives 20 *litres* of oxygen, then
> one *volume* of 20 volume H$_2$O$_2$ gives 20 *volumes* of oxygen.

Note: volume of oxygen *increases* with *rise* in temperature and *decrease* in air pressure. Similarly volume of oxygen *decreases* with decrease in *temperature* and *increase* in air pressure. Consequently when *explaining* volume strength, the temperature must be steady at 0°C and the air pressure steady at 101 kPa.

The volume strength of hydrogen peroxide can be *demonstrated* using the apparatus shown in Figure 11.1. Allow 1 cm^3 of hydrogen peroxide solution to drop slowly on to the powdered manganese dioxide in the

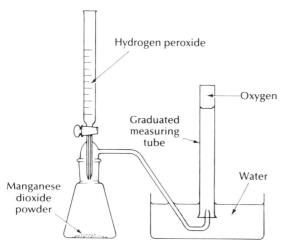

11.1   Apparatus to show decomposition and volume strength of hydrogen peroxide

Percentage strength, W/W (per cent)	VOLUME STRENGTH (volumes)
100	333
30	100
12	40
12	30
6	20
3	10

Table 11.1   Relationship between volume strength and percentage strength hydrogen peroxide

flask. The *volume* of gas collected in the measuring tube is an *approximate* indication of volume strength. More *accurate* measurements need to cool the collected gas to 0°C and volume measured at 101 kPa air pressure.

Table 11.1 compares the percentage strength and volume strength. The solutions are *available* at the following volume strengths, 20 volume and the strongest 100 volume.

High volume strength solutions will have *higher* relative density values than low volume strength solutions. A *hydrometer*, sometimes called a *peroxometer*, with a special scale of volume strength can be used to measure direct volume strength of a solution of hydrogen peroxide.

Dilution of hydrogen peroxide

In order to prepare solutions of *low* volume strength from stock solutions of *high* volume strength, it is necessary to dilute with or add deionized or distilled water. *Tap* water should *not* be used.

The following calculation is performed to determine the amount of water for diluting a certain strength of stock hydrogen peroxide.

$$\frac{Volume\ strength\ required}{stock\ strength} \times 100 = \begin{array}{c}\%\ Stock \\ solution \\ required\end{array}$$

$$\%\ Water = 100 - \%\ Stock\ solution\ required$$

Stock Solution Strength (volume)	Required Volume Strength	Ratio of Parts Stock : Water (: means 'to')
100	60	3 : 2
100	40	2 : 3
100	30	3 : 7
100	20	1 : 4
100	10	1 : 9
40	30	3 : 1
40	20	1 : 1
40	10	1 : 3
20	10	1 : 1

Table 11.2   Dilution table for preparing hydrogen peroxide solution

Example: To make 20 volume strength from 100 volume strength stock

$$\frac{20}{100} \times 100 = 20\% \text{ stock solution}$$

% water to be added $= 100 - 20\%$
$\qquad\qquad\qquad\quad = 80\%$.

Therefore 20 per cent stock is diluted with 80 per cent water or 20 *parts* stock to 80 *parts* water, which is 1 part stock to 4 parts water.

Table 11.2 is a ready-made dilution table.

11.3   HAIR BLEACHING PREPARATIONS

Hair bleaching is a process of changing the *dark* colour of *melanins* to a *lighter* colour, and ultimately a *colourless* state, by means of *oxidation* using different *oxidizing agents*.

The reaction is imperfectly understood. The colour of bleached hair is yellowish blonde due to varying amounts of phaeomelanin.

Bleach components are mixtures consisting of the active *oxidizing agent*, usually hydrogen peroxide, a *mild* acting bleach for delicate natural fibres such as hair, silk and wool. More rapid acting and stronger oxidizing agents include sodium perborate, potassium or ammonium persulphate, also sodium bromate. **Caution:** These oxidizing agents can form *explosive* mixtures with other substances. In view of their more powerful bleaching action they are also called *bleach boosters*.

The second main component in hydrogen peroxide bleach is the alkaline component dilute ammonium hydroxide, ammonium acetate, ammonium carbonate and sodium carbonate. The purpose being to provide an alkaline pH which catalyses the release of oxygen.

Hydrogen peroxide **Alkali** $\xrightarrow{\hspace{2cm}}$ *Water* + *Nascent oxygen*
H_2O_2 $\qquad\qquad H_2O \qquad\qquad O$

The oxygen released is in the form of a very active *nascent* oxygen, consisting of free *atoms*, unlike oxygen of the *air* which is in the form of *molecules*.

(*a*) *Liquid bleach* is a mixture of 20 or 30 volume hydrogen peroxide, made alkaline with ammonium hydroxide to pH 8.

(*b*) *Paste bleach* is a controllable mixture which clings to the hair fibre as a pasty mass. It is a mixture of white magnesium carbonate, an *inert* substance, with 20/30 volume hydrogen peroxide, at a pH 8, from adding dilute ammonium hydroxide or sodium ethanoate (acetate).

(*c*) *Bleach emulsions* are controllable mix-

Eumelanin Black to brown $\xrightarrow[\text{rapidly}]{\text{Oxidation bleaches}}$ *Phaeomelanin* Yellow $\xrightarrow[\text{with difficulty}]{\text{Oxidation bleaches}}$ *Colourless compound* oxy-melanin

tures consisting of non-ionic emulsifying agents, cationic conditions QACs, together with an alkali component. The mixture is mixed with 20 vol. hydrogen peroxide before use.

Factors affecting the bleaching process

The rate or speed of the bleaching reaction is affected by those conditions affecting most chemical reactions (Section 10.9).

1 *Temperature rise* of 10°C doubles the rate of bleaching; this is achieved by accelerating the process with the steamer or infra-red accelerator.
2 *Concentration*: more concentrated solutions of high volume strength act more rapidly than weaker solutions. The normal volume strength is between 20 to 30 volume. High concentrations of bleach boosters have a similar effect.
3 *Solutions* of liquid bleach work more rapidly than *solid* pastes, however they have the practical disadvantage of being difficult to control and drip from the hair surface.
4 *Catalysts*; the main catalytic agent is the alkaline pH, neutral mixtures act extremely slowly.

   The effect of different factors on bleaching rate can be determined as follows.

   Obtain dark hair from the same source, and place small equal quantities in five different test tubes.

1 Control experiment contains *water* and hair sample.
2 Contains 20 volume hydrogen peroxide kept at room temperature, 18° to 20°C.

3 Contains 20 volume hydrogen peroxide *plus* dilute ammonium hydroxide, kept at room temperature, 18° to 20°C.
4 Contains 20 volume hydrogen peroxide plus dilute ammonium hydroxide, kept at 28° to 30°C in a water bath.
5 Contains 40 volume hydrogen peroxide plus dilute ammonium hydroxide, kept at room temperature, 18° to 20°C.

Post-bleaching preparations

The action of excessive bleaching may result in *chemical damage* to the keratin cross-linkage of *cystine* causing their *breakdown* and formation of *cysteic acid*.

$$\underset{\substack{\text{disulphide link}}}{\underset{\text{Cystine}}{-CH_2-S-S-CH_2}} \quad \xrightarrow[]{\substack{\text{Severe}\\ \text{Oxidation}}} \quad + \quad 0 \longrightarrow \underset{\text{Cysteic acid}}{CH_2-SO_3H}$$

Consequently the action of oxidizing agents must be *halted* by means of a *mild* reducing agent namely vitamin C, *ascorbic acid*. This can be achieved by a dual purpose lemon juice rinse which contains citric *acid* to neutralize bleach *alkali*, and the *vitamin C* reducing agent ascorbic acid (*see* below).

Conditioners are components of post-bleaching preparations in the form of cationic QACs.

Brightening agents or *fluorescers* are dye compounds which fluoresce in sunlight or ultraviolet light (Section 13.3). They are also components of brightening shampoos used to overcome *yellowing* seen in bleached hair.

$$\text{Hydrogen peroxide} \quad + \quad \text{Ascorbic Acid} . \xrightarrow{\text{Reduction}} \quad \text{Water} \quad + \quad \text{Dehydroascorbic acid}$$

$$\text{Alkali} \quad + \quad \text{Citric acid} \xrightarrow{\text{Neutralization}} \quad \text{Citrate salt} \quad + \quad \text{Water}$$

Yellowing of bleached hair

Bleached hair has a natural tendency to *yellow* with time; this may be due to several causes.

(*a*) *Photo-tendering* is a process of *oxidation* catalysed by ultra-violet light or sunlight. It causes the loss of strength in the hair fibre and is catalysed by traces of iron and copper metals. In addition, *yellowing* and damage to the epicuticle may occur.

(*b*) *Washing* with alkaline soaps and detergents and frequent exposure to sunlight promotes yellowing.

(*c*) *Other causes* include nicotine from tobacco smoke; lipid oils such as olive oil hair preparations oxidizing to coloured compounds.

11.4   PIGMENTS AND DYES

(*a*) *Pigments* are coloured compounds applied to the *surface* of hair fibre, finger nails or skin, in the form of *solid* or powder deposits, or bonded in a *plastic* medium in a soluble in insoluble form that can be sprayed on hair.

Many coloured pigments are *insoluble*, and those which are applied to *surfaces* are removed by various mechanical means such as rubbing, washing or rinsing. They have poor *colour fastness*, the pigments are not *held* by any special chemical mechanism to the fibre surface.

(*b*) *Dyes* or dyestuffs are mainly *organic* compounds applied to the hair fibre by means of either *solutions* or *suspensions* of the dye in water. The dye is *held* or fixed firmly to the fibre by special chemical mechanisms or by bonds *within* or on the fibre surface.

Dyes have a *fastness* and are not easily removed by rubbing, washing or rinsing. The degree of fastness to *washing* may vary with some hair dyes being called *temporary*, or *permanent*.

Hair *colourants* can alter the natural hair colour in two ways.

(i) *Pigments* forming a temporary *surface* coating.

(ii) *Penetrating* colourants either dyes which enter the hair fibre cortex and form permanent *bonds*, or substances which form *insoluble* pigments within the cortex.

The following is a simple classification of hair and cosmetic colourants.

Pigments
1   Temporary natural vegetable hair colourants.
2   Metallic hair colourants.
3   Plastic bonded hair sprays.
4   Nail enamel.
5   Face powders and lipsticks, mascara and eye cosmetics.

Dyes
1   Vegetable hair dyes.
2   Temporary hair colour rinses, and shampoos.
3   Semi-permanent hair dyes.
4   Oxidation dyes.

11.5   PIGMENTS

Temporary natural vegetable hair colourant

This includes some of the earliest known colourants, for example Chamomile or *Anthemis tinctoria* dried flower heads; it provides a pale yellow surface coating colour to hair. The active component is a flavone compound — *apigenin* or trihydroxyflavone.

Metallic hair colourants

These are two main types:

(*a*) *Metallic* pigments or a deposit of *metal* produced by *reduction* of metal salts such as silver nitrate, or copper sulphate or salts of cobalt and chromium. The *reducing agent* is benzene-triol (pyrogallol). Their effect can be demonstrated by soaking switches of bleached hair in a 2 per cent solution of copper sulphate, and then transferring the hair to a 2 per cent solution of benzene triol (pyrogallol). The hair is rinsed and dried; the colour fastness is determined by washing in a standard soap solution.

(*b*) *Sulphide pigments* are an insoluble deposit of *metal sulphides* produced by the action of soluble sodium sulphide, sodium thiosulphate, or sulphur on soluble metal salts of lead or bismuth.

$$\begin{array}{c} \text{\textit{Soluble}} \\ \text{\textit{lead or}} \\ \text{\textit{bismuth}} \\ \text{\textit{salts}} \end{array} + \begin{array}{c} \text{\textit{Soluble}} \\ \text{\textit{sodium}} \\ \text{\textit{sulphide,}} \\ \text{\textit{thiosulphate}} \\ \text{\textit{or sulphur}} \end{array} \longrightarrow \begin{array}{c} \text{\textit{Insoluble}} \\ \text{\textit{lead or}} \\ \text{\textit{bismuth}} \\ \text{\textit{sulphides}} \end{array}$$

This can be demonstrated by immersing bleached hair samples in a 2 per cent solution of sodium sulphide (**care– keratolytic depilatory**) and transferring the soaked hair to a 2 per cent solution of lead ethanoate (acetate) (**care – poisonous**), followed by rinsing and drying and   testing for colour fastness in standard soap solution.

Hair colour restorers are mainly metallic or metal sulphide type hair colourants. They have several disadvantages in being composed of *poisonous* substances when swallowed acidentally, and are ineffective colourants giving the hair a dull, lustreless appearance.

Several metal salts have harmful effects on other hairdressing processes, notably cold permanent hair setting and bleaching.

Plastic bonded hair sprays

The colour pigment is added to the ingredients of the *plastic setting lotion* (Section 10.4). As the lotion dries on the hair surface, the pigment becomes trapped in the plastic layer. The colour is usually prepared from a mixture of *azo-dyes*, acid and basic dyes similar to temporary hair colour rinses.

11.6   HAIR DYES

Vegetable hair dyes

These include vegetable henna from the Egyptian privet plant, *Lawsonia inermis*, which has the active component *lawsone*, or hydroxy-naphthaquinone, a compound which penetrates the hair fibre giving it a fairly permanent hair colouring.

Walnut shells from the walnut tree, *Juglans regia*, produce the dark brown vegetable dye, the active component *juglone*, or a naphthaquinone compound similar to lawsone.

Both dyes are fast to washing but are slow in penetrating the hair fibre, and have disadvantages in being of variable chemical composition and in producing a range of colour shades modified by acids or alkalis.

Temporary hair colour rinses

These are synthetic organic dyes of *known* chemical composition called *azo dyes*. They are of two main kinds, both of which have very limited colour fastness and are removed by washing the hair.

(*a*) *Acid dyes* or anionic compounds which which are salts of certain acidic compounds, sulphonic and nitrophenolic dyes. The dyes are applied to the hair in 2 per cent solutions of citric or tartaric acids in water.

The acid dye forms a bond with the *amino* group $-NH^+$ of the keratin molecule.

The following are the names of some acid dyes used in fantasy hair colours: Ponceau red, Methyl blue, Naphthol Yellow S, Nigrosine black and Fuchsin.

(*b*) *Basic dyes* are cationic compounds which are applied to hair either alone or with 2 per cent solutions of alkali in water. They form bonds with the keratin molecule carboxylic acid group $-COO^-$. The names of basic dyes include Methylene blue (blue rinse), Methyl violet, Malachite green, Magenta, Rhodamine B and Bismarck brown.

The acid and basic dyes can be demonstrated by immersing samples of bleached hair in 2 per cent solutions of the individual dyes. The samples are rinsed, dried and the colour fastness is determined by washing in standard soap solution.

Colour rinses are extremely dilute solutions of the dye in water. Blue rinse contains *one* part of methylene blue in 100 000 parts of water.

Colour shampoos contain acid dyes or basic dyes in non-ionic detergent mixtures, together with the requisite acid to pH 5.

Semi-permanent hair dyes

This group includes compounds called *nitro-hair dyes*, they are *amino* compounds which have been *nitrated* with nitric acid, their names begin with *nitro-*. Examples include nitro diamino benzene (nitro phenylene diamine), and dinitro amino phenol.

These nitro-dyes are prepared as emulsions with a detergent triethanolamine oleate which forms a semi-permanent colour *shampoo*. This hair colourant lasts up to six or eight shampoos, indicating moderate colour fastness and resistance to removal by washing.

Oxidation permanent hair dyes

Certain colourless *amino-* and *diamino-* compounds can be *oxidized* by oxygen from air or hydrogen peroxide to form *quinone-dümine* compounds.

$$\text{Amino- or diamino-} \atop \text{compounds} \quad + \quad \text{Oxygen} \quad \xrightarrow{\quad\quad} \quad {\text{Quinone-dümine} \atop \text{compounds}}$$

These *quinone-dümine* compounds are the parent substance of this large class of oxidation or permanent hair dyes.

Diamino-benzene (phenylene diamine) penetrates into the cortex and is oxidized to form a double-sized molecule called *indamine*. This large molecule is unable to leave the hair cortex and the pigment indamine is locked-in permanently thus increasing the colour fastness and almost complete resistance to removal by washing.

The following are some other compounds used in addition to diamino-benzenes (phenylenediamines): diamino methyl benzene (diaminotoluenes), amino-nitro phenols, and diaminoanisoles. These substances are present in mixtures prepared as emulsions in triethanolamine oleate soapless detergent bases, *sodium sulphite* is added to prevent the mixture oxidizing during storage. The emulsion is premixed with 20/30 volume hydrogen peroxide before use.

Certain dyestuffs are applied to the hair in a cold solution of either ethanol or ethanol and water; they are called metallized acid dyes. They produce a permanent coloration of the fibre.

When certain *phenols*, such as phenol benzene-triol (pyrogallol) or benzene-diol (resorcinol) are added to the amino- or diamino- compound and *oxidized*, they form a range of coloured dyes called *indophenols*; these are double-sized molecules unable to leave the hair fibre.

$$\text{Soluble} \atop \text{phenols} \quad + \quad {\text{Soluble} \atop {\text{amino-} \atop {\text{or} \atop {\text{diamino-} \atop \text{compounds}}}}} \quad + \quad \text{Oxygen} \quad \xrightarrow{\quad\quad} \quad {\text{Insoluble} \atop {\text{indophenol} \atop {\text{dyes} \atop {\text{(double-size} \atop \text{molecule)}}}}}$$

Precaution

The diamino- and amino- ingredients of oxidation dyes, particularly the *diamino-benzenes* (phenylenediamines) and diaminotoluenes are highly poisonous and can penetrate the body by *absorption* through the skin or by mouth. They may cause dermatitis/

$$\text{Soluble diamino-benzene} \atop \text{(phenylenediamine)} \quad + \quad \xrightarrow[\text{(hydrogen peroxide)}]{\text{Oxygen}} \quad {\text{Insoluble Indamine dyes} \atop \text{(double sized molecule)}}$$

eczema in certain people; this must be pre-tested for a *skin test*. Operatives must wear protective gloves. The use of 2:4 diamino-toluene in hair dyes is banned in the U.S.A.

Laboratory tests on rats, bacteria and certain insects show that some components of permanent and semi-permanent hair dyes can cause changes in cell nucleus structure.

Factors affecting oxidation permanent dyeing

The factors, which affect chemical reactions, also affect the permanent dyeing process for hair (*see* Section 10.9).
1 *Temperature* rise of 10°C doubles the rate of dyeing, consequently acceleration is achieved by the temperature provided by the steamer and infra-red accelerator.
2 *Catalysis* of the reaction is by the alkaline pH 9 provided by ammonium hydroxide components of the dye base emulsion.
3 *Emulsions* facilitate the application of the reactants to the hair fibre.
Post-dyeing preparations include acid conditioner rinses to neutralize residual alkali and the reducing agent vitamin C (ascorbic acid) to remove excess oxidizing agents.

Dye reducers

As permanent hair dyes are applied by *oxidation*, they can also be removed by the reverse reaction of *reduction* by *strong* reducing agents, namely sodium methanal (formaldehyde), sulphoxylate, $NaHSO_2.HCHO.2H_2O$, or sodium dithionite, $Na_2S_2O_4$.

Note, vitamin C (ascorbic acid) is too *weak* a reducing agent for dye removal purposes.

Table 11.3 compares the main hair colourants.

11.7   PHYSICS

Colour and light dispersion

A beam of light from a *lamp* source is allowed to pass through either a solid glass *prism* or a hollow glass prism containing poisonous carbon disulphide (**highly flammable**). The light is seen to be bent or *refracted* towards

Table 11.3   Summary of hair colourants

| | *Pigments : Coat fibre surface* | | |
	Vegetable	*Metallic*	*Plastic bonded*
Components	Chamomile, flavones	Metals, and metal sulphides	Azo dyes in plastic setting lotion
Fastness to wash	Nil	Nil to variable	Nil (*see* temporary)
Attachment to fibre	Surface attraction	Surface attraction	Surface coating of plastic
Advantage	Cheap. Easy to use	Easy to use	Contrasting colour easily applied and removed
Disadvantage	Doubtful colouring function	Poisonous	Nil

the base of the prism and is then separated into its component colours by *disperson* displayed on a screen.

The component colours of white light form the colour *spectrum*, the colours are arranged as follows from red, the *least* refracted and with the *longest wavelength*, to violet, the *most* refracted, with the *shortest wavelength*.

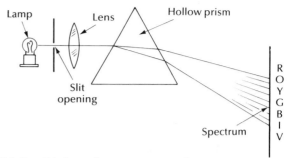

11.2   Light colour spectrum formation

White light	**Dispersion** $\longrightarrow$	*Spectrum colours (roygbiv)*	Red Orange Yellow Green Blue Indigo Violet

Between each colour are gradually merging *shades* of colour. White light can be reformed again from the spectrum by either allowing the spectrum to pass through another inverted prism of a different *kind* of glass, or be reflected from a row of small plane mirros.

Light sources

The colour spectrum of *sunlight* has a different composition when compared to the colour spectrum of light from an electric filament lamp, fluorescent tube lamp (Section 6.7), or from candle, gas or oil light sources.

(*a*) *Electric filament lamp* light is richer in *red* and *yellow* and deficient in blue and green compared to sunlight.

(*b*) *Cold white fluorescent lamp* light is deficient in red and yellow, and richer in *blue* and *green* compared to sunlight.

(*c*) *Warm white fluorescent lamp* light is almost similar to sunlight having increased red and yellow colour content compared to cold white fluorescent lamps.

Dyes: Penetrate fibre surface

Vegetable	*Temporary*	*Semi-permanent*	*Permanent*
Juglone, Lawsone, Naphthaquinone	Azo dyes, acidic and basic	Nitrodiamines and aminophenols	Diamines and aminophenol
Fast	Nil	Fast	Very fast
Penetration and air oxidation. Larger molecule formed.	Links to keratin $-COOH$ and $-NH_2$ groups.	Penetration and air oxidation. Larger molecule formed.	Penetration H_2O_2 oxidation. Larger molecule formed.
Few	Contrasting colour easily applied and removed.	Near natural colour. Easy to use.	Near natural colour, and fashion colours
Uneven dyeing and variable chemical	Nil	Poisonous, and dermatitis. Skin testing needed	Poinsonous, and dermatitis. Skin testing needed.

Colour of objects

1 **White** objects *reflect all* the colours of the light spectrum.
2 **Black** objects *absorb all* the colours of the light spectrum.
3 **Red** objects *absorb* all spectrum light colours except *red* which is *reflected*.
4 **Colour** of object is due to the spectrum light colour which is *reflected*.

Coloured light mixing

Red, green and *blue* coloured *lights* are called *primary* colours; these coloured lights can be produced by passing white light through a *colour filter*; this is a sheet of gelatine coloured with a dye. The three primary coloured lights together give *white*.

Red + green + blue ⟶ *White light*

The *secondary* light colours, obtained by mixing or overlapping *two primary* coloured lights, are as follows:

Primary light colours	Resulting secondary light colour
Red + Green	Yellow
Red + Blue	Magenta
Blue + Green	Peacock blue / Cyan

The mixing together or overlapping of certain primary and secondary coloured lights can produce white light as follows:

Primary light colour	Secondary light colour	
Red	Cyan /Peacock Blue	
Green	Magenta	White light
Blue	Yellow	

Colour of objects in coloured light

The *composition* of light depends on its source; consequently the *appearance* of hair

		Colour of light source	
Hair Colour	*White sunlight*	*Red light (Filament lamp gives reddish light)*	*Blue light (cold fluorescent lamp gives blueish light)*
White hair	White	Red	Blue
Black hair	Black	Black	Black
Red hair	Red	Red	Black
Blued hair	Blue	Black	Blue

Table 11.4   Effect of light quality or colour on natural hair colour

or an object is affected by the colour of the light shining upon the hair or object.

Different coloured objects can be viewed in a dark room under different light colours. Table 11.4 summarizes the resulting *appearance* of different hair colours in different coloured lights. Note: the electric filament *reddish* light *darkens* the blue and *brightens* the red, whilst the cold fluorescent blueish light *darkens* the reds and *brightens* the blue.

From Table 11.4 it is seen that, during the dyeing of hair, it is essential to view the resulting *shade* in natural daylight or employ artificial lighting nearest to dayling such as from *warm* light fluorescent lamps.

Coloured pigment mixing

Objects and hair have colour due to *pigments* which *absorb* and *reflect* certain light colours. Black melanin will *absorb* all light colours, whilst red phaeomelanin absorbs all colours but red which is *reflected*.

Dyes applied to hair are *mixtures* of coloured *pigments*. For example, *brown*, one of the most typical of hair colourants, is a mixture of red (magenta), blue (cyan) and yellow in varying proportions.

The mixing of coloured pigments is as important in painting as it is in hair colouring.

For example, a red coloured dye pigment added to the normal yellow phaeomelanin of blonde hair could result in an orange colour.

Red + *Yellow* *Orange*
dye phaeomelanin ⟶ resultant colour

The selection of hair dye pigment is therefore a specialized area for the hair colourist.

11.8   CHEMISTRY

Benzene and methyl-benzene (toluene)

Benzene and *methylbenzene* (toluene) are two *liquid* hydrocarbons obtained from the distillation of *coal tar*.

Benzene and methyl-benzene (toluene) are both flammable liquids and poisonous when inhaled, and can also enter the body by skin absorption, or by mouth. They have the chemical formula C_6H_6 benzene, and $C_6H_5CH_3$ methyl benzene (toluene), as shown in Figure 11.3. These two organic compounds are the *parent* compounds of many hairdressing colourants.

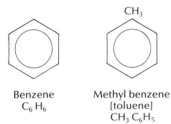

11.3   Benzene and methyl benzene (toluene) molecules

Phenols

These are compounds which have a *hydroxyl* or -OH group attached to benzene or methyl benzene (toluene) as shown in Figure 11.4.

Phenol is known as *carbolic acid* and is a solid and very hygroscopic. Solutions of phenols with soap are called *phenolic disinfectants*, 'Lysol', 'Jeyes fluid', etc. Other phenols include benzenediol *resorcinol*, *naphthols* and *hydroquinone*.

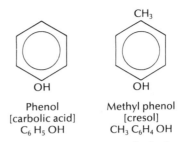

11.4   Phenol and methyl phenol (cresol) molecules

Phenols with *two* -OH hydroxyl groups are oxidized by air or hydrogen peroxide into *quinones*, important dyestuffs.

Amines

This group of compounds has the *amine* or -NH_2 group joined to benzene or methyl benzene (toluene), to form *aminobenzene* (aniline) shown in Figure 11.5. If *two* amine groups are present the compounds are called *diamines*, as in *diaminobenzene* (phenylenediamine).

Most amines form *imines* when oxidized with air or hydrogen peroxide; these are also important in permanent hair dyes.

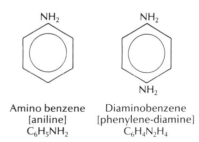

11.5   Aminobenzene (aniline) and diaminobenzene (phenylene-diamine) molecules

Ortho, meta and para

There are *three* different compounds of diamino-benzene (phenylene diamine), each named as follows:

Diamino-benzenes
(phenylene-diamine)

Ortho-diamino benzene
(Ortho-phenylene-diamine)
Melts at 102°C

Meta-diamino-benzene
(meta-phenylene-diamine)
Melts at 63°C

Para-diamino-benzene
(Para-phenylene-diamine)
Melts at 147°C

The ortho, meta and para compounds *differ* in certain *physical* properties by having *different* melting points; they also undergo *different chemical* reactions and produce *different* dye colours.

Their molecules have different structures as shown in Figure 11.6.

As can be seen from Figure 11.6, the *difference* between the diamine compounds is due to the *position* of the second amine group. Most oxidation permanent dyes are made from *para*-diamine compounds.

Nitro compounds

Nitric acid, HNO_3, is a strong *liquid* acid which *burns* the skin and its vapour is harmful to the eyes, lungs and skin which stains a yellow colour. Strong nitric acid readily turns benzene, phenols and diamine compounds into nitro- compounds with $-NO_2$ groups added.

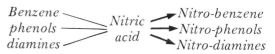

Many nitro-compounds are the parent compounds of dyestuffs used in semi-permanent hair colourants, for example, para nitro-diamino-benzene (para nitro phenylene diamine) and nitro amino phenol.

Coloured dye compounds

The azo dyes have two nitrogen atoms in the azo group $-N\equiv N-$, many other coloured dye compounds used in hair colourants also have amino $-NH_2$, hydroxyl -OH and nitro $-NO_2$ groups.

11.9   QUESTIONS

1 Explain the terms oxidation and reduction. Give two examples in each case of the use of these terms in hairdressing practice.
2 What is meant by hair bleaching? Describe the composition of hair bleaches. What are the causes of yellowing of bleached hair?
3 Explain why black hair appears black to the human eye. Describe the composition of a *metallic* and an *oxidation* hair colourant that can produce a black colour.

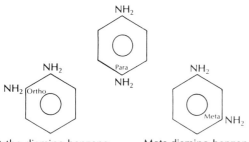

11.6   The ortho, meta, and para forms of diamono benzene (phenylene-diamine)

4 Describe the methods by which *different* hair colourants are held by the hair fibre.

5 Write short notes on the following substances indicating their uses in hairdressing: (*a*) para diamino benzene (para phenylene diamine); (*b*) nitro-diaminobenzene (nitro phenylene diamine); (*c*) azo dyes; (*d*) Juglone; (*e*) Apigenin.

6 Describe what important factors affect the dyeing and permanent hair colouring process.

Describe the structure and mode of operation of equipment used to accelerate these processes.

7 Explain the terms *volume strength* and *stabilizers* with reference to hydrogen peroxide.

How is 30 volume strength hydrogen peroxide prepared from a 100 volume strength stock solution?

8 Explain the importance of an artifical light source when colour matching dyed hair with shade cards.

11.10   MULTIPLE CHOICE QUESTIONS

1 If one part of 40 volume hydrogen peroxide is diluted with 3 parts of water, how much oxygen will be released from 1 cm^3 of the diluted solution?
(*a*) 4 cm^3
(*b*) 10 cm^3
(*c*) 14 cm^3
(*d*) 40 cm^3

2 The stabilizer used in hydrogen peroxide is:
(*a*) ethanol (ethyl alcohol)
(*b*) sodium ethanoate (acetate)
(*c*) ammonium carbonate
(*d*) aqueous ammonia.

3 Which of the following will produce a dark brownish black substance when mixed with a solution of copper(II) sulphate in progressive metal dyeing?
(*a*) aqueous ammonia
(*b*) hydrogen peroxide
(*c*) sodium sulphide
(*d*) lead ethanoate (acetate).

4 The natural colouring material when present in the hair fibre is found in the:
(*a*) cuticle
(*b*) cortex
(*c*) matrix
(*d*) medulla.

5 The important chemical group found in most permanent hair dyes is called:
(*a*) disulphide
(*b*) diamine
(*c*) dioxide
(*d*) dimethyl.

6 Permanent organic hair colourants are chemically called:
(*a*) reduction dyes
(*b*) para dyes
(*c*) oxidation dyes
(*d*) ortho dyes.

12 Hair Drying and Dressing

12.1 CONDITIONS NEEDED FOR DRYING

Hair which is completely *saturated*, or soaked with water, will *feel* wet when it contains 35 per cent of its dry weight of water. If 100 g of hair is dry, it will weigh 135 g when it is saturated with water. This water is held by the *matrix* between the cortex cells of the fibre; as it is absorbed it gives out heat by an *exothermic* reaction.

$$Dry\ hair\ +\ Water \longrightarrow \frac{Saturated}{hair} + \frac{Exothermic}{heat}$$

This explains why wet hair does not feel cold or chilly to the scalp.

Evaporation of water takes place from a surface at *all* temperatures. The *molecules* near the water surface escape from it by evaporation.

(*a*) *Temperature* increase causes the molecules of water to vibrate and move more rapidly out of the liquid; temperature *decrease* slows down the escape of molecules.

(*b*) *Moving air* or wind above the water surface draws away escaping molecules.

(*c*) *Humid air* above the water surface will have a *high concentration* of water molecules in the air and prevent escape of water molecules by evaporation. Removal by wind and replacement by *less* humid air will lower the concentration and allow water molecules to evaporate.

(*d*) *Surface area* or amount of surface *exposed* affects evaporation. A *large* exposed surface evaporates water more rapidly than a *small* exposed surface. *Covering* the head with a cap prevents evaporation since the air inside the cap becomes *saturated* with water vapour.

Energy is needed for water molecules to leave the liquid, this energy is withdrawn from the water causing the water temperature to *drop* and in turn draw heat energy from the *warm skin* nearby. This results in body cooling or chilling, due to the *cooling effect of evaporation*.

Dry hair

Due to its *hygroscopic* property hair has a changing or *variable* water content depending on the surrounding conditions of the air or the water treatments it receives.

Dryness of hair is of *short* duration following the drying process under a salon dryer. The *dry* hair absorbs water vapour from the air until it is in a state of *equilibrium* with the surrounding air moisture.

Dry appearance as a *disorder* is mainly due to hair damage by alkali, ethanol, cold wave lotion, or processing which damages the *epicuticle* or removes the natural *sebum* surface coating.

The various conditions which affect evaporation can be demonstrated as follows.

Surface area
Cut pieces of blotting paper of *different* sizes and place in the *same* amount of water in different beakers and expose together to room air under the same conditions. The water rises by *capillarity* through the pores between the blotting paper fibres. The *control* experiment is a beaker containing only water.

Temperature and moving air
Paint three large metal discs of equal size with cold water. Direct a stream of 'cold' air from a hand hair-dryer on to one plate, and direct a stream of 'hot' air from a hair-dryer on to another plate. Leave the *control* plate exposed to room air without any drying from a hair-dryer. Compare the rate at which the last drop of water evaporates from each plate.

Air humidity
Equal size blotting paper strips are placed in *equal* amounts of water in two similar beakers. One is placed beneath a glass bell jar cover, and the *control* placed alongside in room air.

Wet hair natural drying

Water *droplets* gather on the surface of hair which has a natural film of *sebum*. By *shaking* the hair the water droplets are detached from the hair fibre surface, because the sebum lowers the *surface tension* of the water. This

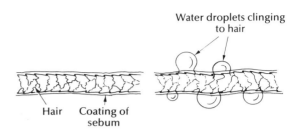

Water droplets clinging to hair

Hair   Coating of sebum

12.1   Hair waterproofing

method of drying the wet *coat* is used by mammals, in addition to the water *dripping* from the hair surface by gravity. The natural *waterproofing* of the fibres is maintained by grooming, and by *preening* of feathers in birds by means of *preen* oil.

Shaking separates the individual hair fibres. Hair then dries by the *natural* evaporation of water aided by wind and the sun.

Towel drying

Wet hair is *rapidly* dried by the *blotting* action of dry towels, the water rising between the tiny spaces between the towel fibres by *capillarity*. Saturated hair is *weakened* by the action of water and wet hair should not be *rubbed* by friction between a towel. Rubbing will *strain* the hair fibres.

Blow drying

This involves heated moving air directed *either* at *separated* hair with a large surface area held apart by a comb or brush, or tightly wound strands on *rollers* of small surface area.

12.2   HAIR-DRYING EQUIPMENT

The different hair-dryers operate by producing *moving air* in salon and hand-held blower dryers, together with *heat* or by heat alone in *infra-red* dryers.
Precaution: The heat of drying must not exceed a temperature of $50°C$ to avoid heat *damage* to the hair and skin *burns*. The

operator must be alert to *over-heating* during the drying process.

Radiant heat or infra-red dryers

Heat rays are also called *infra-red* rays (*see* Section 13.2) and are produced by all hot bodies. The infra-red *lamp* is the same as a filament lamp with a silvered internal reflector surface which reflects the visible light and invisible heat rays. The lamps have dark red glass to reduce the light intensity.

The heat can be directed from *one* hand-held infra-red lamp, or from a *cluster* of up to five infra-red lamps supported on a stand. Heat travels from the lamp to the head by *radiation*. The lamps have the advantage in being focussed on to a head region and promoting *even* drying, and are silent in operation.

Forced convection or blower dryers (Figure 12.2)

1 *Heater elements* are made of high resistance nichrome wire elements supported on *mica* sheet frame or on *porcelain* supports. The heater wattage varies between 500 and 1200 W for hand-held *blower* hair-dryers and 500 to 2000 W for a *hood* hair-dryer.

A bimetal *thermostat* maintains the temperature of the emerging hot air below 50°C. A protective *guard* covers the air outlet.

2 The *electric motor* is connected to a *fan* which drives air *over* the heater element. Air is drawn into the dryer by way of a *grill* by suction.

Precaution: The grill air inlet of a hand-held hair-dryer must *not* become blocked by hair being drawn in through the air inlet. Long hair can become caught in the dryer motor.

The hair-dryer motor is a fractional horsepower motor with a low rating of 50 W. Many dryers have two-speed motors.

3 *Control switches* may be of a simple 'cold/

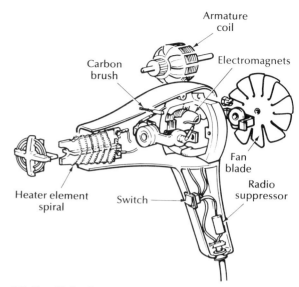

12.2   Hair-dryer, exploded view

hot/off' type or a *variable* heat control from 'low/medium/high'.

(*a*) *Hand-held* hair-dryers have two-way switches with 'hot' switch supplying current to the heater, and 'cold' switch cutting off the heater current.

(*b*) *Hood hair-dryers* have a temperature hand control. In its simplest form this is a *three-heat* switch or *variable resistance* controlling the current supply to the heater element (Figure 12.3).

(i) *Low heat* setting, the electricity flows through *two* resistances in *series* allowing a *low* current to reach the heater element.

(ii) *Medium heat* setting, the electricity flows through *one* resistance allowing a *greater* current to flow to the element.

(iii) *High heat* setting, the electricity flows through *two* resistances in *parallel*, allowing a much *greater* current to flow to the heater element.

(iv) *Off* setting, no electricity flows in resistances.

Precaution: The switch must *not* be operated or touched with **wet** hands, neither should the dryer be used near to water pipes or in a bathroom.

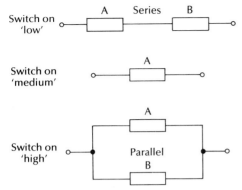

12.3   Three heat switch circuit

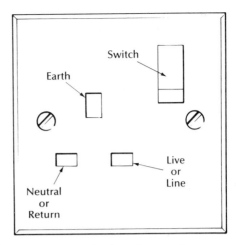

12.4   Electrical socket outlet

The *thermostat* is an automatic cutout switch which operates when the air is too hot. It is placed in the dryer circuit *after* the main appliance control switch.

12.3   SALON SOCKET OUTLETS (Figure 12.4)

All salon electrical appliances, with the exception of clocks, and storage heaters, are connected to a plug-in *electrical socket outlet*. The standard ring-main socket outlet in the U.K. has three *square-pin* openings to receive the three square-pins of the appliance *plug*.

(a) *Number.* The socket outlets can be *single, double* or arranged in a *panel* of four.

(b) *Switch.* The socket outlet can be fitted with a switch or is switchless.

(c) *Neon indicator lights* can be fitted to a switched or switchless socket and indicate when the outlet is *live* and the current on.

(d) *Safety shutters* are fitted inside the switch which only open when the large earth pin is pushed into the socket.

Precautions

1 Never touch the socket outlet with *WET* hands.
2 *Switch off* the socket, or *draw out* the plug when appliance is not in use.
3 Never draw out plugs by pulling on the flex.
4 Electricians should check that the **live**

earth and **neutral** openings are in the correct position in the socket outlet.

Clocks, storage heaters, telephones are some appliances connected by *plugless connection* outlets in a salon; these appliances are *permanently connected* to the main supply.
5 **Adaptors** should not be connected to a socket outlet. *More* sockets should be installed by electricians.
6 *Cracked* or damaged socket outlets must be replaced immediately by an electrician.

12.4   APPLIANCE PLUGS

Each salon appliance must be fitted with its *own* plug. Plugs which connect with ring main socket outlets in the U.K. have three square pins. Round-pin plugs are almost obsolete in U.K. hairdressing salons.

Two-pin plugs are used for connection to shaver socket outlets in bathrooms. Certain double-insulated appliances may connect by a two-pin plug without an earth pin.

Cartridge fuses (*see* Section 4.7)

These are fitted inside all fused square-pin ring main plugs in the U.K. The correct fuse must be fitted according to the following:

$$Fuse\ size\ =\ \frac{Appliance\ wattage}{250}$$

The wattage of an appliance is marked on the *maker's plate* on the appliance. For example, a 1000 W hairdryer requires the following sized cartridge fuse in the plug: $1000 \div 250 = 4$ ampere fuse. The nearest size is a 5 ampere cartridge fuse.

Fuses will *blow* in the plug if:

(*a*) the appliance is faulty.

(*b*) the fuse fitted is too small an amperage, e.g. 2 amperes fitted where a 5 amp is required.

Plug screw terminals (Figure 12.5)

The plug screw *terminals* are marked L (live), N (neutral) and E (earth), the cartridge fuse is close to the L (live) terminal. The ends of the appliance *flex* are connected strictly as shown in Section 12.5.

Plug pins

These are made of brass and are good conductors of electricity. *Safety* plugs are partly *sleeved* with a moulded *nylon* protective insulator sleeve on the live and neutral pins.

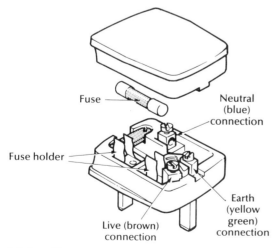

12.5   Plug terminals

Plug tops

These must be complete and any cracked or broken tops must be discarded and replaced by a new plug.

Heating of plugs

If plugs become *hot*, check the terminal screw connections to the flex ends are *tight*. If it continues to heat up, the plug is *overloaded* (Section 4.7) and must be checked by an electrician.

12.5   APPLIANCES FLEXES

The salon circuit has stiff cables carrying the current to the socket outlet. Every salon appliance will be fitted with its own *correct sized* flex. *Earthed* appliances are fitted with a *three-core* flex, whilst double insulated appliance shavers and clippers, have a *two-core* flex.

Flexes are flexible compared to stiff cables.

Flex size

This depends on the rating or wattage of the appliance and the current used in amperes. It is calculated as for fuse size:

$$\frac{Wattage}{Appliance}\ \div\ 250\ =\ \frac{Flex\ size\ in\ amperes}{or\ mm^2}$$

The flex core is measured in square millimetres, mm^2. Table 12.1 summarizes flex sizes, amperage and wattage. If an incorrect flex is fitted to an appliance it will *overheat* through *overloading* and cause *fire* (Section 4.7).

Flex length

The flex must be of a suitable length to reach the socket outlet, it should *not trail* over the floor or be hidden under floor covering.

Appliance and rating		Maximum amperes	Flex size in mm^2
Lamps, radios	720 W	3	0.5
Small one-bar fires, hair-dryers	1440/1.4 kW	6	0.75
Two-bar fires, kettles, large dryers	2400/2.4 kW	10	1.0
Large appliances	3120/3.1 kW	13	1.25
Three-bar fires	3600/3.6 kW	15	1.5

Table 12.1   Flex and cartridge fuse size for different electrical appliances

Frayed flex

This is dangerous and insulation is worn leading to electric shock, frayed flex must be replaced immediately.

Flex core colours

Since January 1971, all U.K. made electrical flex has *coloured insulation* around the *three* wires. The *live wire* is covered in *BROWN* insulation, the *neutral* wire in *BLUE* insulation, and the *earth* wire is covered in *green and yellow* striped insulation.

Wiring a plug (Figure 12.6)

(*a*)   Remove about 50 mm of the flex outer covering and clamp the unstripped flex in the plug *cord grip*.

(*b*) Run the *brown* wire to reach the L (live) pin terminal, and the *blue* wire to the N pin, and *green/yellow* striped wire to reach the E (earth) pin.

(*c*) Remove about 10 mm of the coloured insulation from each core. Twist the bare wires **clockwise** to tighten them.

(*d*) Wind the wires around the pin terminals *clockwise*, or insert into the pin terminal hole. Screw *tightly* in postion, slack screwed wires will overheat.

(*e*) Check there are no *stray* strands of wire and no *bare* wires touching.

(*f*) Check the correct sized cartridge fuse is fitted.

(*g*) Replace plug top and screw down.

Precaution: *Never* pull a flex to withdraw a plug from a socket.

12.6   EARTHING OF A SALON APPLIANCE

All salon appliances apart from double insulated appliances must be *earthed*. Earthing is an electrical *safety device* for removing electricity rapidly by allowing it to flow from the

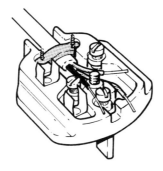
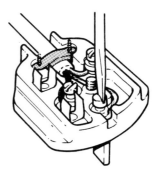

12.6   Wiring a three-pin plug

appliance into the earth through a thick copper *earth wire* (Figures 12.7 and 12.8).

(*a*) The *live* (brown insulated) wire carries electric current **to** the appliance *from* the socket outlet: it usually passes by way of the appliance *switch*, which breaks the circuit in the *live* wire.

(*b*) The *return* or *neutral* (blue insulated wire) *returns* the electric current to the socket outlet, after the *electrical energy* has been changed into *heat* or *mechanical* energy in the appliance.

(*c*) The *earth* (green/yellow, striped insulation) wire is always connected to the metal *frame* or *case* of the appliance. It is given the symbol ⏚

When the appliance is *faulty*, the live or neutral wires may break and *touch* the metal case or frame. If this happens the current immediately *escapes* safely along the earth wire to the socket outlet and down to earth.

The ring main circuit cable has an *earth wire* either bare or covered with *green* insulation. This earth wire, being thick and of a *low* resistance, offers a *quicker* escape route than by the neutral return wire.

The earth wire *end* of a salon circuit is firmly connected to a copper *earth plate*, or to a metal main supply *water pipe*, which reaches the salon buried in earth. *Plastic* water pipes cannot be used since they are *nonconductors* of electricity.

(*d*) If an appliance becomes *live* or faulty, the *fuse* may blow in the plug top and in the main *fuse box*.

Earth test for appliances (Figure 12.9)

If an electric appliance is *not* properly earthed it will be dangerous to use and can cause electric shock.

The appliance can be *tested* by connecting the *earth pin* of the appliance plug with a *lamp* and dry battery. The appliances *must not be connected* to the main when the test is done.

Connect the *test* terminal to any *metal* part

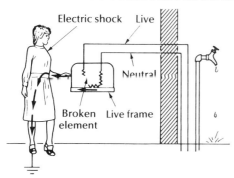

12.7   A non-earthed live electrical appliance

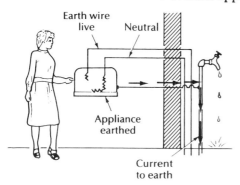

12.8   An earthed electrical appliance

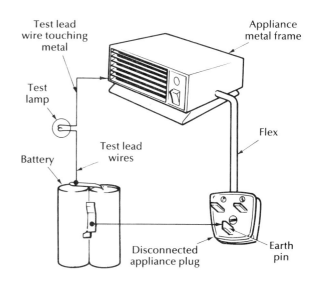

12.9   Earth testing an electrical appliance

of the appliance case, or frame. If the lamp glows *brightly* the appliance is earthed correctly, if the lamp *glows* or *fails* to light up the earthing is faulty and must be repaired.

The lamp should *not* light if the test terminal is connected to the plug's live or neutral pins – if it does, the appliance must not be used.

Precaution

Always check the following:

(*a*) electric appliance is correctly fitted with a *three*-core flex with an earth wire;

(*b*) plug tops have the earth wire correctly connected to the *earth pin*;

(*c*) the *salon wiring system* is correctly earthed;

(*d*) salon *socket outlets* are correctly wired;

(*e*) *water and gas pipes* should be out of reach of equipment, clients and operators;

(*f*) *floors* must be *dry* and *insulated* with rubber mats;

(*g*) switches must *break* the *live* wire.

12.7   ELECTRIC SHOCK

Electric shock occurs when the human body *completes* a mains electric circuit. It can happen in *three* main ways, whichever way it occurs the effect can be *FATAL*.

(*a*) *Touching the live and neutral wires or terminals*; this can occur when changing an electric lamp *without* switching off the current, or touching a *live* socket outlet with wet hands. The current passes *around* the body.

(*b*) *Touching a* **live** *wire or terminal*: this can happen on touching one *live* outlet, appliance or wire that has become exposed by fraying. The current passes through the body and into earth.

(*c*) *Touching a live wire or terminal and an earthed water pipe*. Touching a live terminal, socket, wire or live appliance with a wet hand whilst touching a water tap or pipe, causes the current to pass through the body to earth.

Prevention of electric shock

1 **Turn off the mains** before changing an electric lamp, or examining an appliance.
2 **Check earth connections** to plug and appliance, see that flex is not frayed.
3 **Check plug fuse** is correct size.
4 **Second-hand appliances** must be checked by electricians.
5 **Service salon appliances** regularly. *See* Section 22.2 for effects and treatment of electric shock.

12.8   SUMMARY OF ELECTRICAL PRECAUTIONS

1 **Broken and cracked** switches, plugs, socket outlets and appliances must be *repaired* and not used.
2 **Frayed flexes** must be replaced.
3 **Wet hands** should *never* touch appliances, flexes, sockets or plugs.
4 **Switch off current, or unplug**, after using appliances and before changing lamps.
5 **Sockets must never be overloaded** or adaptors used.
6 **Fuses** must be of correct size for appliance rating.
7 **Appliances must be earthed** correctly with a three-core flex.
8 **Pulling plugs by flex is prohibited** and dangerous.
9 **Trailing flexes** cause tripping accidents.
10 **Service appliances and check main circuits professionally.**
11 **Smoking and overheated appliances**, plugs, flexes and sockets are faulty and dangerous and must be repaired professionally.

12.9   DRESSING PREPARATIONS

Dressing preparations applied to hair after drying have several functions all of which are related to maintaining *hair condition* (Section 9.6). The following are functions related to dressing preparations.

1 *Setting* agents by means of gums, or plastic polymers in lotions or sprays.
2 *Conditioning* agents of various composition which rectify *damage* to hair by bleaching, colouring and permanent waving.

   (*a*) *acid conditioners*, contain citric, ethanoic (acetic) and tartaric acids.

   (*b*) *cationic conditioners*, QACs which are anti-static and give the hair a softer 'handle' or feel.

   (*c*) *protein and amino-acid conditioners* which are mixtures of peptides and amino-acids obtained from different animal proteins by *hydrolysis* and called *protein hydrolysates*. These amino acids *attach* themselves to the carboxylic acid -COOH and amino-NH$_2$ groups of keratin.
3 *Oil conditioners* affect the hair surface lustre and apparent smoothness in forming a thin film of surface oil. The oils used are lipid, hydrocarbon, and water-repelling *silicone* oils.

   Lanolin is a component to replace the natural sebum of degreased hair.

   Control dressing preparations help to *repel* moisture and preserve a hair set, and give the hair the lustre associated with hair in good condition.

   The following are formulations for different dressing preparations, all of which are prepared using ingredients of high purity B.P. and observing strict hygiene in preparation.

Control preparations

Hair or control creams
These are of two main kinds, oil in water, O/W or low oil; and water in oil, W/O, or high oil *emulsions*. Their function is to waterproof, lubricate, provide lustre, hold temporary set, and be attractively perfumed.

   (*a*) *Hair control cream*, O/W, are mixtures of emulsifying wax 10 per cent, almond *or* liquid paraffin oil 15 per cent, lanolin 1 per cent, and 74 per cent pure water. All ingre-

dients are heated together to 75°C and stirred vigorously until cool. Preservative and perfume are added when cool.

   (*b*) *Hair control cream*, W/O, are mixtures of emulsifying wax 10 per cent, almond *or* liquid paraffin oils 45 per cent, and 45 per cent pure water. Procedure is the same as for making an O/W hair control cream.

Brilliantines
These are preparations which are without any water content, and are mainly lipid or hydrocarbon oils alone or in mixtures. Their main function is to provide lustre, and hold temporary set, and be attractively perfumed.

   (*a*) *Liquid brilliantine*: these are liquid preparations at room temperature consisting of 95 per cent almond *or* liquid paraffin oils, mixed with 5 per cent of perfume essence.

   (*b*) *Solid brilliantine*: these are low melting point solid mixtures at room temperature consisting of 70 per cent almond *or* liquid paraffin oils, soft white paraffin 20 per cent, and spermaceti whale wax 10 per cent. The ingredients are melted together at 70°C. Oil soluble colour and perfume essense is added to the mixture before it solidifies.

Conditioner dressings
Conditioner dressings function to waterproof, reduce static surface electricity, improve feel, and *medicate* by the cationic detergent QAC antiseptic component. The hair fibre pH is rectified by the *acid* component. *Protein hydrolysates* may also be incorporated as substitutes for *lecithin*, a fat-like component of egg yolk, or cholesterol, another waxy component of egg yolk and blood.

   The conditioner creams are mainly of two types for *normal*, and for *dry* hair.

Normal conditioner
This is a mixture of emulsifying wax 15 per cent, almond *or* liquid paraffin oils 10 per cent, citric acid 1 per cent, propanetriol (glycerine) 5 per cent, water 69 per cent. All the ingredients are heated together to 75°C and

vigorously stirred until cool when preservative and perfume essence is added.

Lecithin, cholesterol, proteins or protein hydrolysate can be added to the total extent of 1 per cent, before heating.

Dry hair conditioner
This is a less oily preparation of emulsifying wax 1 5 per cent, almond or liquid paraffin oils 5 per cent, lanolin 2 per cent, with lecithin cholesterol, or protein hydrolysate to 1 per cent, water 77 per cent. Procedure is the same as for normal conditioner.

Medicated antistatic conditioner
These are preparations which use *cetrimide emulsifying waxes*, which are emulsifying waxes containing 10 per cent of quaternary ammonium compound or cationic detergent. The same formulations are used as for normal and dry hair conditioners substituting cetrimide emulsifying wax Q.A., B.P.

12.10 CHEMISTRY

Hydrolysis (*see* Section 8.6)

This is the process of *chemical decomposition* by means of *water*. The process is *catalysed* or speeded up by acids, alkalis, and biological *enzymes* called *hydrolases*.

Food components, proteins, lipids and carbohydrates undergo hydrolysis during digestion (*see* Section 15.4).

	Hydrolysis	
Proteins	⟶	*Amino acids*
Lipids	⟶	*Fatty acids and propanetriol (glycerine)*
Carbohydrates	⟶	*Monosaccharides*

(*a*) *Lipid components* of hairdressing preparations can undergo hydrolysis by action of microbes and form sour-smelling or *rancid* mixtures. To prevent this rancidity developing *preservatives* e.g. methanal (formalde-

hyde) are added to lipid emulsion preparations.

(*b*) *Protein hydrolysates* are the mixtures of peptides and amino acids produced by hydrolysis of different protein materials such as egg *albumen*, skin and *meat collagen* or vegetable protein. *Meat* extracts, soups and gravies are also rich in amino acids and peptides or protein hydrolysates.

Amino acid components of conditioner preparations form weak *salt-linkages* between the -COOH carboxylic and -NH$_2$ amino groups of hair keratin.

(*c*) *Saponification*, or soap-making is a process of hydrolysis of lipids with alkali.

12.11 PHYSICS

Magnetism

Certain materials have the property to *attract* iron, this property is called *magnetism* and is seen in natural iron ore lodestone, and in certain steels, and cobalt and nickel metals.

Magnets have certain properties.

(*a*) They have magnetic force concentrated at two points called the *magnetic poles*.

(*b*) A *suspended* magnet will always come to rest in a north—wouth position. The *north magnetic pole* points north, and *south magnetic pole* points south.

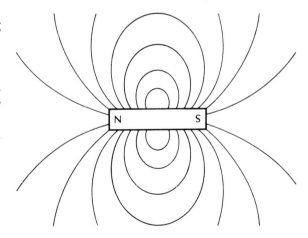

12.10   Magnetic field of a magnet

(*c*) Like magnetic poles *repel*, e.g. N repels N, and S repels S. Unlike poles attract one another. N attracts S, and S attracts N. This *attraction* and *repulsion* is similar to that shown between *electrostatic charges*.

(*d*) Around the magnet is the *force* of a *magnetic field*. This field of force is important in electric motors.

Electromagnetism

When an *electric current* flows through a conductor wire it produces a *magnetic field* around the wire. This is the important *magnetic effect* of a current.

An *electromagnet* can be made by wrapping cotton *insulated* copper wire around an iron nail and connecting it to a switch and battery as in Figure 12.11. The *electromagnet* has magnetic poles formed as shown in Figure 12.12. The type of pole formed depends on the *direction* of current flow.

The electromagnet is a *temporary* magnet; when the current is switched off the *induced magnetism* is lost.

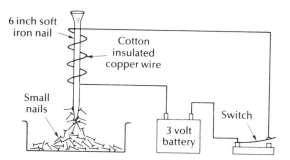

12.11   Simple electromagnet

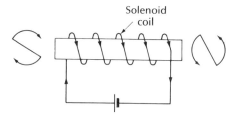

12.12   Magnetic poles of a solenoid coil

The electric motor (Figure 12.13)

The electric motor changes the energy of an electric current into mechanical energy or *motion*.

$$\text{Electric current energy} \xrightarrow{\text{Motor}} \text{Mechanical energy motion}$$

This mechanical energy is used by the hairdressers to do *work* in moving air in hairdryers, or in other appliances, e.g. vacuum cleaners.

(*a*) *Armature coil*. This is a rectangular *coil of wire* mounted on a spindle.

(*b*) *Commutator and brushes*. The commutator consists of two cylindrical-shaped brass conductors, which contact with spring-loaded *brushes* made of conducting *graphite* carbon.

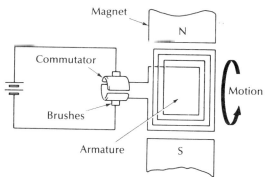

12.13   The electric motor

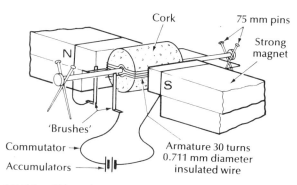

12.14   Electric motor model

(*c*) *Permanent magnets*. The north and south poles of a strong permanent magnet enclose the armature coil.

Direct current from a battery passes into the armature coil by way of the commutators and brushes. This current produces a *magnetic field*, the unlike poles being repelled by the permanent magnet. This produces a *turning force* which *spins* the armature.

A simple motor can be made from cotton insulated copper wire, pins, cork, and two permanent bar magnets as shown in Figure 12.14.

Precautions

With continual use the *brushes* of an electric motor gradually wear down. When this occurs sparks may be seen around the motor commutator of a hairdryer. Frequent servicing will ensure that brushes are replaced before sparking can occur.

Dynamo generator (Figure 12.15)

A dynamo generator operates in *reverse* to an electric motor. *Motion* or mechanical energy provided by different means, wind, water or steam, is changed into *electrical* energy by spinning the armature between strong magnets, the *electric current* produced being collected from the commutator by the brushes. The figure shows the structure of an a.c. generator with *two* slip ring commutators.

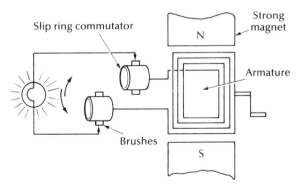

12.15   Alternating current generator

12.12   QUESTIONS

1 Explain the term *evaporation*.
   What main conditions are required for the rapid drying of hair?
2 Describe the typical salon hair dryer, and explain how hot moving air is produced in the equipment.
   What device operates to prevent overheating?
3 Describe each of the following protective devices for users of salon electrical appliances: (*a*) guards; (*b*) fuse link; (*c*) double insulation; (*d*) earthing.
4 If a salon appliance is rated 1000 W at 240 V, describe the type and size flex needed and the fuse link size for the plug.
5 Why does an electric plug have 3 pins? Give the function of each.
6 Give a list of safety precautions to be understood by salon operatives handling electrical appliances.
7 Discuss the various uses of cationic detergent or quaternary ammonium compounds in hairdressing preparations.
   Describe the effect of this substance on the hair fibre.
8 Briefly describe the method of preparation of a hair control cream.
   Indicate how these preparations vary in composition.
9 Explain the terms *chemical* and *physical* damage to hair, and describe how they can occur and to some extent be corrected.

12.13   MULTIPLE CHOICE QUESTIONS

1 Perfume essence should be added to a cosmetic preparation at one of the following temperatures:
   (*a*) 25°C
   (*b*) 50° C
   (*c*) 75° C
   (*d*) 100° C
2 Which one of the following values, shown on a salon electric appliance nameplate,

indicates the appliance's power consumption?
(a) 230–240 V
(b) 50 Hz
(c) 750 W
(d) 3 A.

3 What is the colour of the wire insulation that must be connected to the largest pin in a standard three pin fused plug top?
(a) brown/yellow
(b) brown/blue
(c) green/yellow
(d) red/black.

4 How many 3 kW electric fires can be safely connected to a multi-way adaptor to a 13A electric wall socket?
(a) one
(b) two
(c) three
(d) four.

5 A gentleman's hair dressing consits of 75% liquid paraffin and 25% castor oil, with a trace of colour. This preparation would be called a:
(a) solid brilliantine
(b) spirit brilliantine
(c) cream brilliantine
(d) liquid brilliantine.

6 The effective parts of a three heat switch for controlling heat on a hairdryer are called:
(a) transistors
(b) fuses
(c) resistances
(d) armatures.

13 Treatments

13.1 RADIANT ENERGY

Different scalp and hair *treatments* are sometimes employed in the salon using *different* forms of *radiant energy*, each of which have different *physiological* and *therapeutic* effects on the skin and hair tissues.

Radiant energy is *energy* in the form of rays or waves, which are produced by the movement of *electrons*. Since these rays are produced by movement of electrons, they are also called *electromagnetic* rays.

> **Movement**
>
> *Electromagnetic*
> *Electron* ⟶ *or*
> *radiant energy*

The radiant energy or electromagnetic rays differ from each other in *wave-length*; this is usually measured in units called *metres* and *Nanometres*.

Table 13.1 includes all members of the radiant energy or electromagnetic *spectrum*, grouped according to wavelength from *radio* waves of the greatest wavelength (measured partly in metres — long and short wave radio) down to the shortest wavelength of X-rays and cosmic rays. The methods of *producing* the radiant energy are also shown.

All these forms of radiant energy are able to *travel* from the *source* through the *air* to reach a *surface*; where they are *absorbed* to different extents.

The *penetrating* properties of the electromagnetic rays with reference to the human body are summarized in Table 13.2. *NOTE* that certain ultra violet, X-rays, gamma and cosmic rays are harmful to living tissues in *large* doses.

13.2 INFRA-RED RAY TREATMENTS

Infra-red rays can be *detected* in the dark area next to the *red* of the visible light spectrum. Heat rays can be detected by sensitive *thermoscopes* or *thermistors*.

Infra-red rays are produced by all *hot bodies*; human bodies, heaters, hot water pipes and the sun.

Type of Radiant energy	Wave-length	Production
Radio, and high frequency	Very long	Electrons *oscillating* in wire *coils*, similar to alternating current
Infra-red	Long	Electrons *vibrating* in hot objects
Visible light	Medium	Electrons *vibrating* in *white hot* objects
Ultra-violet	Medium	Electrons *vibrating* or *moving* in *white hot* objects; lamps and discharge tubes
X-ray	Short	*Moving* electrons hitting metal plates
X-rays Gamma rays	Short	*Moving* electrons thrown out of radioactive elements uranium, radium
Cosmic-rays	Very short	*Fast moving* electrons from outer space falling on the earth

Table 13.1   Radiant energy types wavelength and methods of production

Electromagnetic Ray	Penetration in human body
Radio, high frequency	Do not penetrate. Abosrbed only by *metal*.
Infra-red rays	Slight penetration, 0.01 cm
Visible light	Pass through *transparent* tissue of eye
Ultra-violet rays	Penetrate through to blood vessels beneath skin epidermis — some living tissue harmed
X-rays	Penetrate through all body tissues — some tissue destroyed
Gamma and cosmic rays	Penetrate easily through body destroying all living tissues

Table 13.2   Premature effects of electro-magnetic rays on human body

Heat reaches or *travels* towards the human body by either infra-red *radiation* from different sources, or *conduction* from hot water in washing, hot towels, or from warm steam from a steamer.

Equipment and sources

Sources of infra-red rays are of two kinds:

(*a*) **Non-luminous sources** include electrically heated nichrome *elements* wrapped around a fireclay support, or embedded in fireclay and painted black or dark red. The element is backed by a highly polished *reflector*. Infra-red rays are reflected, refracted and absorbed in the same way as visible light rays. The infra-red rays from non-luminous sources are mainly *long wave* infra-red.

(*b*) **Luminous sources** include the electric filament lamp up to 300 W in rating. The lamp may have a silvered reflector interior surface and be painted a dark colour and called infra-red lamps. The nichrome heater element may be contained in a tube of *silica* in other infra-red lamps.

The infra-red rays from luminous sources are mainly *short wave* infra-red.

Sunlight is an important source of short wave infra-red rays; its radiation is 80 per cent infra-red.

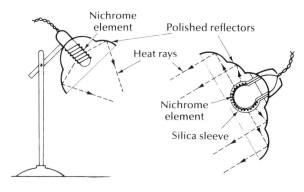

13.1   Infra-red ray lamps

Pure infra-red source

The non-luminous source of infra-red rays gives 100 per cent infra-red radition. Other sources, including ultra-violet ray apparatus give *mixed* radiation and variable amounts of infra-red radiation ranging from 80 per cent in some sun-lamps to 40 per cent in electric filament lamps.

Effects of infra-red radiation

Infra-red rays penetrate the skin by only a short distance up to 0.01 cm; the *short wave* infra-red is *more* penetrating than the long wave radiation. Infra-red rays supply HEAT to the skin tissue; this has the following effects.

(*a*) *Reddening* or *erythema* of the skin due to dilation of skin blood capillaries. The skin may develop a lasting red colour from the destruction of red blood cells through over-exposure to heat rays;

(*b*) *muscles* of the hair and skin relax;

(*c*) *sweating* occurs.

(*d*) *chemical changes* or metabolism in the skin and hair papilla cells occur more rapidly and more food and oxygen is brought to the cells, and wastes are rapidly removed, with increased blood supply. This has also been described for hairdressing processes.

Precautions

1 *Hair* is damaged at temperatures above 50°C.
2 *Burns* to the skin may occur and elements must be protected by *guards*.
3 *Headache* and faintness may occur when back of the head is irradiated.
4 *Eye care*. Continual users of infra-red apparatus must wear protective dark glasses, since over-exposure may cause eye damage.
5 *Electric shock* must be prevented by correct earthing of apparatus, guards, keeping away from water puddles, pipes and gas pipes.

Note: *Electromedical treatments* in any form by electrotherapy, actinotherapy, or any other means, should not be given to a person in a salon without approval of a physician or surgeon. Persons suffering from heart disease, blood disorders, or who have skin sensitivity may be affected by any salon electromedical treatment.

Inverse square law

Radiant energy in all forms whether as infra-red or visible light rays are governed by this law which states: *intensity* of radiation is *inversely* variable as the *square of the distance* from the ray source. In other words the *closer* to the ray source the more intense the radiation.

Figure 13.2 shows how at a distance of 30 cm the *nine* square centimetres must get only one-ninth of the radiation as at 10 cm. If it is to receive the same dose the *time* of exposure must be increased.

Great care and experience is needed to determine the *distance* from the source and *time* of exposure. The source should *never* be positioned close to the person. Expert advice of physiotherapists or manufacturers manuals

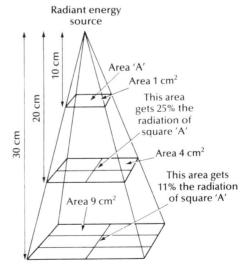

13.2 **The inverse-square law for radiant treatment**

should be followed. *Test doses* are needed also to determine the sensitivity of the person, and the lamp strength.

13.3 ULTRA-VIOLET RAY TREATMENT

The use of infra-red and ultra-violet ray treatments is also called *actinotherapy*.

Ultra-violet rays can be detected by means of substances, for example whiteners and brighteners, which *fluoresce* when irradiated with ultra-violet rays. If a washing powder containing whitener is held in the dark area next to the violet of the visible light *spectrum,* in a darkened room, it will fluoresce. Other chemical substances show *fluorescence*, including finger nails, teeth and *ringworm*. The soils clinging to hair are disclosed by ultra-violet rays (Section 9.1).

Ultra-violet ray *sources* include white hot heat sources from filament, and discharge fluorescent *lamps*, and *arc* lights or lamps of television studios.

Types of ultra-violet rays

There are three main kinds of ultra-violet

radiation differing in wave-length, called UV'A' or long wave, UV'B' medium wave, and UV'C' short wave ultra-violet rays. The different types of ultra-violet rays have the following different properties summarized as in Table 13.3.

Equipment and sources (Figure 13.3)

1 *Sunlight* consists of 7 per cent ultra-violet radiation, the remaining radiant energy is infra-red 80 per cent, and visible light 13 per cent. The sunlight ultra-violet is 95 per cent UV'A', 5 per cent UV'B' and is *without* the harmful UV'C'.

2 *Mercury vapour lamps*, also called Kromayer and Woods lamps, are strong sources of ultra-violet rays; they are tubes of *quartz* with *electrodes* at each end; the tubes are empty of air and contain mercury vapour, and a little liquid mercury. When the electricity is switched on, the electrons are conducted by the mercury vapour in a pale blue coloured arc.

3 *Carbon arc lamps* consist of two carbon rods arranged horizontally with their tips almost touching. When the current flows the rods are drawn apart and electrons pass

Property	Ultra-violet 'A'	Type Ultra-violet 'B'	Ultra-violet C
Wavelength	Long. Close to violet in visible spectrum	Medium	Short. Close to X-rays.
Effect on living tissue and cells	Beneficial	Beneficial	HARMFUL DESTROYS LIFE
Tanning pigmentation	Slight	Causes maximum pigmentation or sun tanning	Slight
Reddening or erythema	Some	Maximum erythema or reddening	Some
Vitamin D manufacture	None	Maximum amount produced	None
Window glass	Pass through easily	Unable to pass through	Unable to pass through

Table 13.3 Comparison of the three main kinds of ultra-violet rays

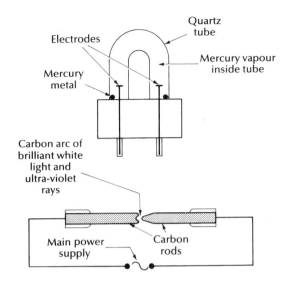

Source	Ultra-violet ray (%)		Infra-red ray(%)	Visible light(%)
Sunlight	7	UV'A' 95 UV'B' 5 UV'C' NIL	80	13
Carbon arc lamp	5	UV'A' 90 UV'B' 10 UV'C' NIL	85	10
Mercury vapour lamp	28	UV'A' 37 UV'B' 48 UV'C' 19	52	20

Table 13.4 Composition of radiation from different sources

13.3 Ultra-violet ray sources

across the gap. A brilliant white light with a certain ultra-violet content is produced. The temperature of the arc light is 3500–4000°C.

4 *Fluorescent tube lamps* similar to those solaria equipment.
5 *Combined* apparatus has infra-red and ultra-violet ray sources in *sun-lamps*, with carbon arc, mercury vapour, fluorescent tube and luminous infra-red source (Figure 13.4).

Table 13.4 summarizes the composition of the radiant energy from different sources.

Effects of ultra-violet radiation

1 **Skin reddening**, sunburn, or *erythema* occurs mainly by means of UV'B'; excessive exposure will lead to blistering of the skin. The *tanning* of skin is due to the change of the amino acid *tyrosine* into the dark pigment *melanin*; this change is catalysed by UV'B'. The skin surface layers *thicken* to produce protection from further exposure.
2 **Vitamin-D** (cholecalciferol) is formed by the action of UV'B' on dehydro-cholesterol in the skin.
3 **Blood circulation** is increased to skin and hair papilla, and wastes are removed rapidly.
4 **Micro-organisms**, mainly bacteria, are destroyed by UV'C' from the mercury vapour lamp, but *not* by sunlight, fluorescent tube lamps or arc lamps. Salon sterilizer cabinets contain a mercury vapour lamp.
5 **Hair** exposed for long periods to sunlight

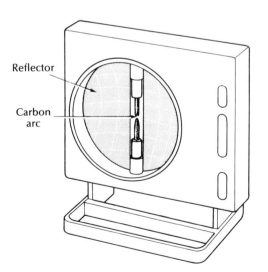

13.4 Combined infra-red and ultra-violet ray lamp

and ultra-violet ray sources experiences physical damage mainly from heat, and may also damage the epicuticle and affect the keratin molecule structure causing loss of fibre strength.

Precautions

Because of the partly *harmful* nature of ultra-violet radiation any treatment to the scalp must be approved or given under medical supervision for the following reasons.

1 *Sensitivity.* Certain people may show skin reactions, dermatitis or eczema rashes due to taking certain drugs, using certain cosmetics or perfumes, hair colourants, and certain foods, for example, eggs or strawberries. Dermatitis and eczema sufferers must not have this treatment.
2 *Skin tumours* or cancers and premature skin ageing are caused by excessive exposure to sunlight.
3 *Eye damage.* Excessive exposure to ultra-violet radiation damages the eye surface layer or *conjunctiva*. This is prevented by wearing dark glasses or *protective goggles.*
4 *Burns, electric shock* are dangers which must be guarded against by protective measures described in Section 13.2.
5 *Ozone.* Ozone, O_3, is a form of oxygen, it is produced when ultra-violet rays pass through air (20 per cent oxygen), and is recognized by its characteristic *smell* associated with ultra-violet treatment.

It is *poisonous* in large doses and a powerful disinfectant able to destroy bacteria. A concentration of one part ozone in a million parts of air can affect the eyes, nose, throat, airways and lungs. Once the smell of ozone becomes strong it should be removed by good *ventilation*.

Preparations

1 *Calamine lotion* is a 15 per cent *suspension* of insoluble zinc carbonate (calamine) and 5 per cent zinc oxide in a solution of 5 per cent propanetriol (glycerine) and pure distilled water or rose water. A trace of pink coloration is provided by a dye or iron oxide. It is applied to sunburnt skin to overcome soreness and acts as an astringent.
2 *Sunscreen* preparations are oils, lotions, aerosol sprays or creams which provide a protective barrier against ultra-violet radiation which causes sunburn, erythema and tanning. Various chemical preparations are used including *menthyl salicylate, para-amino benzoic acid, menthyl anthranilate* or *tannic acid* present in a concentration of 1 to 10 per cent of the preparation.

A typical *suncreen cream* consists of an emulsion of 3 per cent pure liquid paraffin, 10 per cent sunscreen compound, 10 per cent emulsifying wax B.P., and 5 per cent propanetriol with 70 per cent pure water. The ingredients can be heated together to $70-75°C$ and removed from heat and stirred vigorously until cool. Preservative and perfume are added to the cooled mixture.

Hair sprays can also be prepared with sunscreen component to protect the hair from chemical and physical damage caused by ultra-violet radiation.

13.4 MASSAGE TREATMENT

Scalp massage is a recognized important salon treatment for healthy hair growth. *Manual* massage by means of the finger-tips is a means of transmitting *pressure* to *loosen* the tight scalp.

Equipment

Electrically operated *vibrators* or *massagers*, also called *audio-vibrators*, consist of an *electromagnet* (Section 12.10) (Figure 13.5).

A *solenoid coil* of insulated wire surrounds a *core* composed of either a bundle of iron plates or rods. A current interrupter or 'make and break' device switches the current on and off rapidly. When the current flows, the core becomes *magnetized* and attracts an iron *diaphragm*. The current stops flowing and the core loses its magnetism and the diaphragm returns to its former position by spring action. The diaphragm *vibrates* rapidly accompanied by a buzzing sound, by means of the rapid 'make and break' action of the interrupter.

Attached to the diaphragm are *applicator heads* made of soft rubber or plastic.

The electric *shaver* and *clipper* are of a similar construction with a *pivoted* or rocking diaphragm which moves cutters by backward and forward sliding motion, through attraction of the diaphragm between the two poles of the horseshoe electromagnet (Section 8.1).

A small *heater* is incorporated into certain dual purpose vibrators and hair clippers.

Effects of massage

1 **Heat** energy is produced from mechanical energy of manual or vibrator massage; this results in reddening of the scalp or erythema. *Friction* is the force resisting the motion of the fingertips or applicator head; this is overcome by using massage oils, *lotions* or creams as lubricants.
2 **Muscles** in the scalp relax with increasing temperature and vibration.
3 **Sensory nerves** of the scalp are stimulated.
4 **Scaly skin** is abraded and dislodged from the scalp surface.

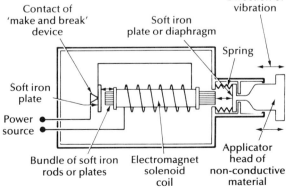

13.5   A simple vibrator massager

5 **Sweat glands** are stimulated.
6 **Sebum** secretion is increased.

Precautions

1 *Skin lesions*, cuts and small harmless growths, warts etc., should not be disturbed by massage.
2 *Eyes* should be protected from accidental entry of massage preparations.
3 *Equipment* must be protected and earthed to prevent electric shock, and should not be operated near to water, water or gas pipes.

Preparations

The following are essentially massage *lubricants*, which also provide a pleasant perfume.

1 *Friction massage lotions* are coloured or colourless *solutions* of 78 per cent toilet spirit or ethanol (ethyl alcohol), or propanol (propyl alcohol) with 20 per cent pure distilled water and 2 per cent added perfume essence. Similar lotions include the different *toilet waters*, Eau-de-Cologne, and lavender water with a slightly more, 4 per cent perfume component.
2 *Massage oils* consist of almond oil to which 2–5 per cent of perfume essence is added. The oil is warmed in a water bath, and massaged into the previously warmed scalp.
3 *Massage creams* are emulsions of oil in water O/W preparations and consist of 10 per cent emulsifying wax B.P., 20 per cent pure liquid paraffin, 5 per cent propanetriol (glycerine) and 65 per cent pure distilled water. The ingredients are heated together to 70–75°C and withdrawn from heat and vigorously stirred until cool, when perfume and preservative are added.

13.5   HIGH FREQUENCY TREATMENT

High frequency treatment is a form of *electro-therapy* or treatment using electricity.

Radio or *high frequency* electromagnetic

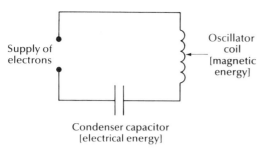

13.6   The oscillator circuit in high frequency

rays are produced by making electrons go to and fro, backward and forward, in an *oscillator circuit*.

(*a*) *Oscillator circuit*. The oscillator circuit consists of *oscillator coil* connected to two plates of a *condenser* or capacitor, which are connected in turn to a supply of *electrons* from the mains or a battery. The condenser (capacitor) provides *electrical* energy and the oscillator coil *magnetic* energy. The *current* will consist of *changing* magnetic and electrical energies (Figure 13.6).

(*b*) *Oscillation frequency*. The current in the oscillator circuit is made to swing backwards and forwards very rapidly in *one second*. Each *complete swing*, from start back to start, is called a *cycle* or *hertz*, Hz. The number per second is called the *frequency*. In a *high frequency* current this can be from 10 000 Hz or 10 kHz (kilohertz) to 100 000 Hz or 100 kHz. As the current oscillates at this very rapid frequency it also produces the radio or high frequency *rays*.

(*c*) *Resonator circuit*. This *second* circuit consists of a coil called the *resonator* coil which collects the high frequency current and rays by *induction*. This coil is in *tune* or *resonates* at the same frequency as the oscillator circuit (Figure 13.7).

Equipment

The salon *high frequency machine* is small and portable and of variable construction, consisting of the basic *oscillator* and *resonator* circuits (Figure 13.8).

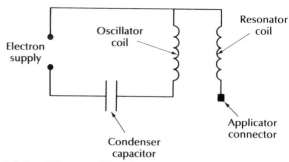

13.7   The combined oscillator and resonator circuits in high frequency

The high frequency current and rays from the *resonator* coil pass to the person receiving treatment by glass *vacuum tubes* or *electrodes* applied to the scalp. The *intensity* of the current is controlled by adjusting the 'make and break' or current interrupter device.

Effects of high frequency treatment

The main effect of the high frequency current and rays in the scalp tissues is the production of *HEAT* energy *within* the tissues. This heating of the tissues is called *diathermy*. This current does *not* cause electrolysis, or affect nerves or contract muscles.

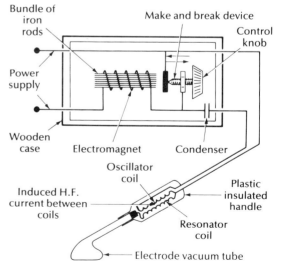

13.8   The high frequency current apparatus

A *high* temperature is achieved in the process of hair removal by high frequency diathermy. The frequency used is much *higher* than for salon scalp high frequency treatment.

(a) *Surgical diathermy* destroys tissues as in hair removal.

(b) *Medical diathermy* gives beneficial warmth to tissues as in scalp treatment. The benefits are summarized as follows:

1 *Acceleration* of tissue chemical changes or metabolism.
2 *Increased blood supply* to hair follicle with improved food and oxygen *supply* and waste *removal*.
3 *Increased secretion of sweat*.
4 *Muscles* of the hair and scalp become relaxed.
5 *Nerves* are rested producing a feeling of well-being.

Precautions

1 *Certain individuals* should not be given this treatment, particularly those suffering or experiencing intestinal ulcers, menstruation, pregnancy, blood disorders, skin disorders and tumours, and paralysis with loss of nerve sensation.
2 *Metals* absorb and *concentrate* the high frequency current and rays leading to burns. Jewellery and hearing aids must not be worn, and people with heart pacemakers and metal implants should not have the treatment. Radios may be damaged if used near to the machine.
3 *Electric shock* must be prevented by taking the usual precautions of placing a rubber mat under the feet and keeping the treatment area *dry* and away from water and gas pipes.
4 *Fainting and dizziness* may be experienced and the treatment discontinued.
5 *Burns* should not occur if the treatment is given correctly. Burns arise from the use of too intense a current.
6 *Ozone* is formed partly due to sparking and by the discharge inside the vacuum tube which forms ultra-violet radiation.
7 *Flammable* lotions containing ethanol or propanol should not be applied to the scalp before treatment.

13.6 STEAM VAPOUR AND OZONE TREATMENT

Water containing different *essential oils* (Section 13.12) is heated to boiling in an apparatus similar to a *steamer* (Section 11.1), the steam vapour with air and *volatile* essential oils passes a small mercury vapour lamp.

The ultra-violet radiation from the lamp forms a small amount of *ozone* by changing oxygen present in the air:

$$\text{Oxygen (air)} \xrightarrow{\text{Ultraviolet ray}} \text{Ozone}$$

In addition, the ultra-violet radiation *ionizes* the air to form *positive* and *negative ions*.

Effects
The effects claimed for this skin treatment include:

(a) *disinfection* by ozone;
(b) *heating* effect from steam;
(c) *neutralization* of surface electrostatic charges by positive ions in the vapour;
(d) *essential oils* provide a pleasant perfume and have an antiseptic action.

13.7 VACUUM TREATMENT

This involves the use of *low pressure* produced by motor-driven *rotary vacuum pumps*. A perfect vacuum is not achieved, and pressures measured are below 80 kPa, less than normal air pressure.

The effects are mainly in the localized lifting of the skin surface layers into the suction cups, allowing free flow of blood in these tissues.

13.8   FARADIC TREATMENT

Faradic types of current are *low frequency* uneven *alternating* currents operating at about 50 Hz. They are produced by faradic *induction coils* consisting of a *primary* coil with its 'make and break' device similar to the vibrator (Figure 13.6). The *induced* current is produced in the *secondary* coil as in Figure 13.9.

The alternating current *cycle* consists of two *phases*:

(*a*) one of *short* duration and *high* intensity.

(*b*) one of *long* duration and *low* intensity. This current travels readily through muscle tissue but with difficulty through fat tissue and skin.

The treatment is applied by an *active* electrode in the form of a disc-shaped pad, the indifferent *electrode* completes the circuit and consists of a lint-covered pad.

Effects of Faradic treatment

This treatment is mainly applied to the body in beauty therapy.
1 **Nerves** are *stimulated.*
2 **Muscles** are made to *contract* and relax, or tone improved.
3 **Blood supply** to muscles and skin is increased by *vasodilation.*

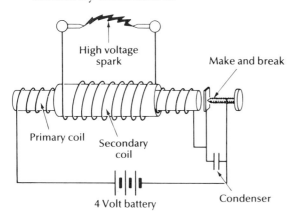

13.9   The faradic induction coil

Precautions

1 *Individuals* with any unusual health conditions should seek medical advice before undergoing this treatment.
2 *Skin* must be free from lesions, damage, cuts or abrasions.
3 *Length* of treatment must be indicated on medical advice.
4 *Chemical* products are not formed by electrolysis since the current is continuously alternating, but care should be taken that burns do not occur.
5 *Safety* precautions for usage of electrical equipment; away from water, damp, and water and gas pipes, should always be observed.
6 *Metal* jewellery, watches must be removed before treatment.

13.9   GALVANIC TREATMENT

This is the passage of a *direct current* at *low voltage* (10–36 V) through the body tissues. The tissue chemical salts undergo electrolysis to produce **acid** products near the positive electrode or anode, and **alkaline** products near the negative electrode or cathode. These different products are claimed to have certain stimulating effects on the skin tissues (*see* Section 8.2).

13.10   NAIL MANICURE PREPARATIONS

Finger nails and the cuticle fold or *eponychium* are both formed of the substance *keratin*, and consequently the chemical substances which affect hair *also* affect the keratin of finger nails, the cuticle, and horny layer of skin of the hands. The hairdresser should protect the hands and nails from discoloration or chemical damage caused by hairdressing preparations. *Protection* can be provided by wearing plastic or rubber *gloves*
1 **Hand creams** are *emollients*, softening agents, which serve to replace moisture lost

from the skin horny layers and also replace the *sebum*, removed by detergent action of shampoos, with *lanolin*.

They consist of oil in water, O/W, emulsions consisting of 3 per cent lanolin, 6 per cent almond oil, 6 per cent propanetriol (glycerine), 5 per cent protein hydrolysate and 10 per cent emulsifying wax in 70 per cent pure distilled water. The ingredients are heated together to $70-75°C$, withdrawn from heat and stirred vigorously until cool. Preservative and perfume being added to the cool cream.

Dry skin hand creams may be prepared from 15–20 per cent cationic quaternary cetrimide emulsifying wax, and contain less propanetriol (glycerine).

2 **Barrier creams** are skin waterproofing preparations to provide protection for skin frequently immersed in water and detergent shampooing solutions.

Emulsions are prepared using 10 per cent cetrimide emulsifying wax, 15 per cent silicone oils (water-repelling ingredient), 5 per cent lanolin and 70 per cent water. The ingredients are heated together to $70-75°C$ and stirred down vigorously. Preservative perfume and colour being added to the cool cream.

3 **Nail cuticle** preparations include: *cuticle removers*, a 2 per cent solution of sodium or potassium hydroxide (**Care – caustic**) in 18 per cent propanetriol (glycerine) and 80 per cent water. The alkali softens the cuticle keratin in a similar manner to a hair depilatory.

Cuticle cream or *oil* is applied by massage after rinsing all traces of the cuticle remover. The *cream* consists of an emulsion composed of 10 per cent cetrimide emulsifying wax, 10 per cent almond oil, 5 per cent protein hydrolysate, and 5 per cent propanetriol (glycerine) in 70 per cent water.

Cuticle oil is a mixture of almond oil and liquid paraffin, or almond oil alone.

4 **Nail preparations**

(*a*) *Buffing cream* is a paste prepared by heating to $70°C$, 2 per cent emulsifying wax, 95 per cent hexadecanol (cetyl) alcohol, with the finest grade abrasive powder, e.g. French chalk, talc, or tin oxide.

(*b*) *Nail whitener* is a mixture of 30 per cent white pigment titanium dioxide added to 70 per cent pure white soft paraffin. It is applied to the under surface of the nail free edge.

(*c*) *Nail enamel* in its simplest transparent form is a 3 per cent solution of white shellac in clear toilet spirit ethanol. It is easily removed by detergents.

Permanent nail enamel consists of 3–5 per cent resins or film formers such as dimethyl hydantoin methanal (formaldehyde), nitrocellulose, or photographic film negative cellulose. The film former is dissolved in a *solvent* such as methylbutyl (amyl) ethanoate (acetate), ethyl ethanoate, or butyl ethanoate, together with propanone (acetone), all of which are highly *flammable* liquids.

Plasticizers, similar to those used in hair sprays, isopropyl myristate and propanetriol (glycerine) are added to improve the resin flexibility.

Coloured nail enamels have added *pigments* of varying composition, and may also include *opacifiers* to give a pearly appearance.

(*d*) *Nail enamel removers* are solutions of the *solvents* used in nail enamel preparation, together with almond oil to prevent degreasing of the nail.

(*e*) *Nail oil* is warm almond oil applied directly to the nail or by immersion of the nails in a warm bath of the oil.

(*f*) *Nail massage cream* has the same composition as cuticle massage cream.

Foot cream

This preparation is an *emollient* softening and soothing agent and is an emulsion of 15 per cent emulsifying wax, 10 per cent soft white paraffin and 70 per cent water. The ingredients are heated together to $70-75°C$ and vigorously stirred until cool. When 5 per cent oil of wintergreen or *methyl hydroxy benzoate (salicylate)* is added, this warms and reddens the skin of the foot.

13.11   CHEMISTRY

Alcohols are an important group of organic compounds containing the elements *carbon*, *hydrogen* and *oxygen* and possess a functional *hydroxyl* group —OH. The names of alcohols end in -OL. Some of the alcohols are *flammable* liquids, and others are waxy solids; they all find use in hairdressing and cosmetic *preparations*.

Table 13.5 summarizes the main alcohols together with their appearance and uses in hairdressing.

Denatured or methylated spirit

Pure *ethanol* (ethyl alcohol) is rendered unfit for human consumption or *denatured* by adding various *poisonous* substances to it, namely methanol (methyl alcohol), *blue* or *red* dye, and unpleasant tasting pyridine or naphtha. The product is called *methylated spirits*.

Toilet or industrial methylated spirit is clear, uncoloured and denatured for use in the preparation of cosmetic and hairdressing preparations. Industrial methylated spirit, IMS, can only be obtained by means of a U.K. Customs & Excise *requisition*.

Esters

Esters are 'salts' formed when an alcohol reacts with an organic acid

$$\text{Organic alcohol} + \text{Organic acid} \longrightarrow \text{Ester} + \text{Water}$$

For example ethanol (ethyl alcohol) and ethanoic acid (acetic acid) form ethyl ethanoate (acetate).

Ethanol (ethyl alcohol) + *Ethanoic (acetic) acid* → *Ethyl ethanoate (ethyl acetate)* + *Water*

Alcohol	Appearance	Uses
Methanol (methyl alcohol)	Flammable and *POISONOUS* liquid in *small* quantities	*Denatures* ethanol and perfumes making them poisonous
Ethanol (ethyl alcohol)	Flammable and *POISONOUS* liquid in *large* quantities	Beers, wines and spirits. *Solvent* for lacquer, essences, perfume oils. Antiseptic, astringent.
Propanol (propyl alcohol)	Colourless liquid	Antiseptic. Solvent and mirror cleaner, scalp lotion.
Hexadecanol (cetyl alcohol) — whale wax	White waxy solid melting point 47°C	Cosmetic creams, soaps, and soapless detergent manufacture
Octadecanol (stearyl alcohol) — beef fat wax	White waxy solid	Cosmetic creams. Soap and soapless detergent manufacture.
Dodecanol (lauryl alcohol) — coconut wax	Pale yellow liquid	Soapless detergent manufacture
Propanetriol (glycerine)	Sweet syrupy liquid — very hygroscopic	Cosmetics, soaps and many hairdressing preparations

Table 13.5   Different alcohols and their appearance and uses in hairdressing

Ester	Appearance	Uses
Ethyl ethanoate (acetate)	Pleasant smelling liquid — — flammable	Solvent for perfume essences and nail enamel resins
Methyl butyl ethanoate (amyl acetate)	Liquid smelling of pear drops — flammable	Solvent for perfume essences and nail enamel resins
Dimethyl benzene dicarboxylate (dimethyl phthalate)	Oily liquid with slight odour	Plasticizer for hair spray resin and nail enamel resin
Glyceryl monostereate	White waxy solid, melting point 58°C	Cosmetic cream
Isopropyl tetradecanoate (myristate)	Colourless oily liquid	Oily component of cosmetic preparations
Methyl hydroxybenzoate (salicylate)	Oily liquid	Oil of wintergreen

Table 13.6 Different esters with their appearance and uses in hairdressing

An important property of esters is a very *pleasant smell*. The *lipids* are also esters of propanetriol and fatty acids.

Table 13.6 summarizes some of the more important esters used in hairdressing.

Other organic compounds

Methanal (Formaldehyde): this is a *gas* with an irritating smell which can affect the eyes and respiratory system. It is sold as a 40 per cent solution in water, used mainly as a salon disinfectant (5 per cent solution) and in salon sterilizing cabinets. Also an important raw material for making formaldehyde *resins*.

Propanone (acetone) as a flammable solvent for lacquer and resins.

Phenols are compounds with the functional -OH hydroxyl group, but differ from alcohols in being *acidic*, and are strong disinfectants and components of hair colorants. Some important phenols include *phenol* (carbolic acid), *methylphenols* (cresols), *benzene triol* (pyrogallol), and *benezene diol* (resorcinol).

13.12 PERFUMES

Perfumes are *mixtures* of pleasant scented chemical substances *added* to a wide range of hairdressing and cosmetic preparations or *alone* in handkerchief scents and toilet waters.

Perfumes are composed of the following main components;

(*a*) *essential oils*, pleasant smelling mixtures of substances extracted mainly from *flowering* plant material;

(*b*) *isolates* or single substances extracted or isolated from essential oils;

(*c*) *animal extracts*, musk, civet, castoreum and ambergris;

(*d*) *synthetic compounds* manufactured in the laboratory as esters, aldehydes, ketones.

Essential oils

These are *volatile* oils produced by glands in flowering and conifer plants. The oils are named as follows, essential oil of lemon, or essential oil of cedar. *Fixed* non-volatile oils are named as follows, almond oil, or cedarwood oil.

Table 13.7 summarizes the parts of a plant which produce the essential oils.

Methods of extraction of essential oils
1 *Steam distillation* involves blowing steam through a hot or boiling *suspension* of plant

Plant part	Essential oil
Flowers	Oils of: lavender, rose, orange blossom jasmine, tuberose, violet and geranium
Fruits	Oils of: lemon, orange, bergamot, lime
Wood	Oils of: sandalwood, pine, cedar
Bark	Oil of cinnamon
Leaves	Oils of: thyme, bay, rosemary, citronella, or lemongrass, and lavender
Seed	Oil of almond (flavouring)

Table 13.7   Sources of essential oils in plants

material in water, followed by condensing the volatile essential oils in a condenser. The essential oil separates above the water as an *otto*, whilst the water becomes saturated with the essential oil to provide a *water*. For example rose petals, steam distilled, give *otto of rose*, and *rose water*. Oils of lavender, rosemary, peppermint, eucalyptus, witch hazel and lemon grass - citronella are produced in this way.

2 *Enfleurage* involves the extraction of essential oils liable to damage by heat. Petals of tuberose and jasmine are spread over pure *lard* smeared on glass sheets. The essential oils are absorbed by the lard to form a *pomade*. The pomade can be used as such or the essential oils can be extracted with *ethanol*, lard being insoluble in this solvent.

3 *Maceration* is the extraction of essential oils using warm $70°C$ lipid oils and fats. Ethanol is then used to extract the oils from the cooled lipids.

4 *Crushing or expression* is used to extract essential oils from fruit skins and rinds and is used mainly for orange, lime and bergamot.

5 *Solvent extraction* uses the highly flammable petroleum solvent called petrol ether. This solvent extracts essential oils and *waxes*. The solvent is distilled or evaporated to leave the residue called a *concrete* mixture of essential oils and waxes. This concrete can then be extracted with warm ethanol to produce an *absolute* consisting only of essential oils.

Essential oil composition
Essential oils are *mixtures* of terpene hydrocarbons and *other* substances, for example oil of lemon has sixty different component compounds, but the major component is the terpene called *limonene*.

Oil of rose is mainly an *alcohol*, 60 per cent phenethyl alcohol, with 40 per cent terpenes citrionellol, geraniol and nerol.

Oil of geranium is mainly terpenes 75 per cent, citronellol geraniol and terpineol, with less than 20 per cent phenethyl *alcohol*.

Plant material
e.g. ROSE PETALS

Steam distillation   Solvent extraction
                            Petrol | ether

ROSE OTTO

ROSE WATER   ROSE   OIL
                  CONCRETE   =   OF   +   WAXES
                                  ROSE

                  ETHANOL | extraction

                  ROSE   OIL OF
                  ABSOLUTE   =   ROSE

Isolates

Isolates are pure single substances *extracted* from the essential oil *mixture* and include pure 100 per cent *terpineol* from pine turpentine oil, 100 per cent *geraniol* from oil of cirtronella.

Essential oil → Phenethyl alcohol isolate
→ Terpineol isolate
→ Geraniol isolate

Animal products

These include glandular secretions castoreum (beavers), musk (deer), and civet (civet cats), and ambergris, a substance from the whale intestine.

These substances, when present in a *compounded* handkerchief perfume, serve to fix and prolong the odour by *slowing* down the rate of evaporation of the *volatile* components.

Synthetic components

These include many hundreds of pleasant smelling compounds including *synthetic* or artificial musks, terpenes geraniol, citronellol, etc. and *esters*.

Perfume preparations

Handkerchief perfume
Perfumers *blend* essential oils, isolates, synthetics and animal components on the basis of odour reaction as it affects the perfumer's *olfactory receptors* in the nose. Odour cannot be *measured* other than by this simple natural method. The ingredients selected and their quantity depend entirely on the perfumer.

Handkerchief perfumes are *solutions* of 10–20% of perfume *concentrate* or *essence* in 90–80% ethanol or methanol, the usual solvent. The perfume is either available in small bottles or as an *aerosol* when it is mixed with either chlorofluorocarbons or *flammable* liquefied hydrocarbons.

Toilet waters or colognes
These are either solutions 2–5% of essential oils or perfume essences in ethanol. The following are typical formulations, in which the small quantities are measured with a 5 cm³ pipette.

(*a*) *Lavender toilet water* consists of oil of lavender 3%, bergamot 2%, rose 0.1%, cloves 0.1%, in 95% toilet spirit or industrial methylated spirits.

(*b*) *Eau-de-Cologne* consists of oil of bergamot 1%, neroli 0.5%, lemon 0.5%, rosemary 0.2%, orange 0.2%, and a denaturant diethyl phthalate 1%, in 97% toilet spirit.

Cream perfumes
These are emulsions containing 5–10% perfume prepared from 15% emulsifying wax B.P., spermaceti wax 5%, propanetriol (glycerine) 5%, and pure ewater to 70%. The ingredients are heated together to 70–75°C and removed from heat and stirred vigorously. Perfume essense is added amounting to 5% or 10% to the cool mixture, together with perservative.

Pomades
These are perfumed mixtures similar to solid brilliantines (Section 12.9). The following can be used as an example of maceration extraction. Dried lavender flowers and leaves 40%, are added to a warm 70°C mixture of soft paraffin 40%, liquid paraffin 10% and emulsifying wax B.P. 10%. The mixture is allowed to cool for 24 hours, then gently warmed and strained free of suspended matter.

Precautions
1 *Flammable* solvent component of bottled and aerosol preparations makes it essential to keep the liquids away from naked flames.
2 *Solvents* ethanol and methanol will readily dissolve French polish if spilt on dressing tables.
3 *Allergy and sensitization* is possible with

certain sensitive skins or when exposed to ultra-violet rays after application.

Medicated preparations

Many essential oil isolates have *antiseptic* properties, consequently oils of bay, cade, rosemary and camomile feature as shampoo medicaments. Oils of peppermint, cinnamon and cloves are internal antiseptics in *mouthwashes* apart from being ingredients of *flavouring* essences. *Menthol* extracted from oil of peppermint has a *cooling* effect on the skin in after-shave preparations.

13.13   QUESTIONS

1 Describe means of producing infra-red radiation in the salon.
 Give two examples of the use of this radiation in hairdressing processes and treatments.
2 Describe one method of producing ultra-violet radiation.
 What precautions must be observed when using this equipment?
 Give one application for the use of this radiation in the salon.
3 Describe the construction of a vibrator massager.
 What precautions should be observed during its use?
 Describe the composition of massage lotions and creams.
4 How is a high frequency current and radiation produced?
 Explain the effects of this current on skin tissue.
 Describe the precautions which must be observed in using high frequency apparatus.
5 Describe the composition of a perfume, naming the sources of the main components.
 What are toilet waters, absolutes and concretes?
6 Write short notes on each of the following: (*a*) toilet spirit; (*b*) nail enamel; (*c*) barrier creams.

7 Describe the main components of sunlight and its effect on skin and hair.

13.14   MULTIPLE CHOICE QUESTIONS

1 When the glass electrode of the high frequency machine is applied to the skin the action of the discharging current produces an antiseptic substance called:
 (*a*) iodine
 (*b*) bromine
 (*c*) oxygen
 (*d*) ozone.
2 The eyes must be protected by special dark glasses from the harmful effects of one of the following treatments in the salon:
 (*a*) infra-red ray
 (*b*) ultra-violet ray
 (*c*) high frequency
 (*d*) longwave diathermy.
3 Infra-red radiation is produced inside the salon accelerator apparatus hood from one of the following:
 (*a*) quartz mercury vapour lamps
 (*b*) carbon arc lamps
 (*c*) tungsten filament lamps
 (*c*) fluorescent tube lamps.
4 Which of the following amino acids is needed to produce melanin pigment in the hair and skin?
 (*a*) cystine
 (*b*) cysteine
 (*c*) tyrosine
 (*d*) threonine.
5 Which of the following has all the properties to act as an antiseptic, detergent and conditioner?
 (*a*) soap
 (*b*) cetrimide (cetyl trimethyl ammonium (bromide)
 (*c*) ethanol (ethyl alcohol)
 (*d*) lanolin.
6 The solvent for most perfumes and toilet waters is:
 (*a*) propanone (acetone)
 (*b*) methanal (formaldehyde)
 (*c*) ethanol (ethyl alcohol)
 (*d*) ethyl ethanoate (acetate).

Section Three
The Hair, Head and Body

Hairdressers and beauticians are dealing with parts of a living body; therefore any techniques used should not be detrimental to Health. Health and beauty are closely interpreted, and the hairdresser uses skill, expertise and artistic flair to achieve this beauty. The applications of the craft need to be supported by scientific knowledge.

There are several branches of science. We have seen that a knowledge of chemistry helps in the handling and use of chemicals in the salon. Many chemical substances are used in hairdressing processes and they are quite safe if correctly used on clients who are not allergic to the preparations. The chemicals and processes for which they are used are dealt with in Chapters 8–10.

A knowledge of physics helps in the safe use of apparatus in the salon, involving electricity, for example. The apparatus and the scientific principles involved are described in Chapter 4. Anatomy, physiology and hygiene are branches of science also.

Anatomy is the structure of the body and a basic knowledge of this and physiology, the functioning of the body, is helpful in the promotion of health. Hygiene is the science of maintaining health. It involves not only cleanliness but also keeping free from disease and illness. Physical fitness should be accompanied by a healthy mental outlook. Skin and hair both reflect health. Personal cleanliness and salon hygiene play an important part in health and beauty.

The hair, head and body will be discussed in Chapters 14 to 18 and the science of health in Chapters 19 to 22.

14 The Head

14.1 THE ANATOMY OF THE HEAD

Externally, the body is divided into head, trunk and limbs, and is completely covered with skin. As in other mammals the skin is covered with hair.

A suitable hair style is indirectly influenced by the shape of the head and face. A skilful stylist should be able to suggest to a client a suitable style to enhance the shape of the head, which depends on the underlying bone structure.

Bones form the skeleton or framework of the body. The skull is the skeleton of the head and is composed of twenty-two bones, joined together. The joints are called sutures and the edges of the bones are serrated for greater strength and rigidity. Eight bones form the cranium or brain-box and the remainder form the face.

14.2 BONES OF THE CRANIUM

The cranial bones are mostly flat bones which form a box for the brain (Figure 14.1). A

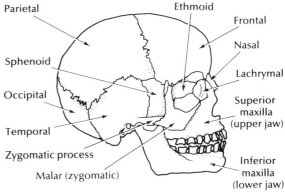

14.1 Skull: side view

single *frontal* bone forms the forehead and upper orbits. In the middle of this bone an indentation, the nasal notch, accommodates the nasal bones of the face. Two *parietal* bones form the roof and upper sides of the skull. Two *temporal* bones form the lower side part in the region of the temples. A single *occipital* bone forms the back of the skull and curves underneath.

The base of the skull is formed by a single *sphenoid* bone which has wings lying between the frontal and temporal bones. The *ethmoid* bone lies between the orbits at the roof of the nose, and forms part of the side walls of the nose.

The brain is housed inside the cranium, and the main nerve cord, the spinal cord, joins the brain through the foramen magnum, a large hole in the occipital bone.

14.3   BONES OF THE FACE

The facial bones tend to have irregular shapes and are mostly paired. Two *nasal* bones form the bridge of the nose and fit into the nasal notch of the frontal bone. Two *lachrymal* bones form part of the orbits at the inner angle of the eye. Two *malar* bones underlie the cheeks. Processes from these join processes from the temporal bones (the zygomatic processes) to form the bony arches of the cheeks.

Two *palate* bones form the roof of the mouth and the floor of the nose. A single *vomer* bone forms part of the bony partition of the nose. Two *turbinate* bones are small scroll-shaped bones in the side walls of the nose.

Two *superior maxillae* are the upper jaw bones containing the upper teeth. They also extend upwards towards the side of the nose and into the floor of the orbit. A single *inferior maxilla* or mandible forms the lower jaw containing the lower teeth. This is the only movable bone in the skull. All other bones of

the skull have serrated edges which lock together to form immovable joints or sutures.

Examples of features of the skull which may influence the choice of hair style are as follows:

The frontal bone may be deep forming a long forehead which may be enhanced by a fringe.

The lower jaw may protrude and need to be balanced by the hair.

The width and shape of the face (oval, round, square) are determined by the bone structure. These features may be balanced by suitable hair styles.

The skull protects the brain and some of the sense organs. It also gives attachment to muscles and ligaments.

14.4   MUSCLES OF THE HEAD AND FACE

Muscles are responsible for movement; those connected to bones are skeletal muscles. They are voluntary muscles, that is, controlled by the will, and they form the red flesh of the body. They are composed of fibres (*see* Chapter 20.12) joined together in bundles. Several bundles join together to form muscles of different shapes according to their position. When stimulated by a nerve impulse, a muscle contracts to bring about movement. The muscles of the head receive their nerve supply chiefly from the fifth and seventh cranial nerves. Some involuntary muscles are present, for example, muscles in the iris of the eye which respond to light intensity to alter the size of the pupil.

The *occipito-frontalis* muscle, overlying the occipital and frontal bones, has anterior fibres (at the front) which raise the eyebrows and wrinkle the forehead (Figure 14.3), and posterior fibres (at the back) which move the scalp.

The *temporal* muscles, at the sides of the head, raise the lower jaw. The *masseter* muscles and the *buccinators*, at the sides of the face, help in mastication. The *pterygoid*

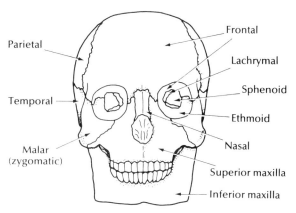

14.2   **Skull: front view**

Parietal

Temporal

Malar (zygomatic)

Frontal

Lachrymal

Sphenoid

Ethmoid

Nasal

Superior maxilla

Inferior maxilla

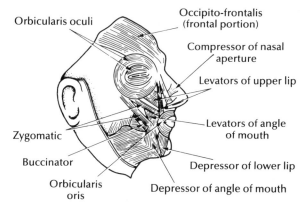

14.3 **Muscles of the scalp and face**

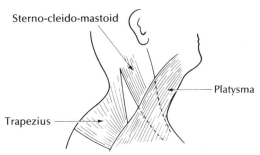

14.4 **Some neck muscles**

muscles are also important in mastication, but lie deeper.

The *orbicularis oris* is the sphincter muscle of the mouth and closes the lips. The muscles of the mouth raise and lower the angles of the mouth and separate the lips.

The *orbicularis oculi* are two circular muscles surrounding the eyes and close the eyes tightly.

Muscles of the nose wrinkle the nose.

Six eyeball muscles at the back of each eyeball move the eyeballs from side to side and up and down.

Most of these muscles are superficial (Figure 14.3) but the temporals, masseters and pterygoids are deeper than the others.

14.5 MUSCLES OF THE NECK

Some of the neck muscles are attached to the bones of the skull, for example, the trapezius and sterno-cleido-mastoid. The *trapezius* muscle, a broad flat muscle on the back of the neck, extends from the occipital bone down to the shoulder girdle. The *sterno-cleido-mastoid* muscle is an oblique muscle at the side of the neck extending from the temporal region to the breast bone.

The *platysma* is a flat muscle under the skin of the neck. It moves the skin in this region (Figure 14.4).

Massage

Massage is a method of influencing body functions by external manipulation of muscles. It strengthens weak muscles and has a soothing effect. In addition, it can improve the texture of the skin by stimulating circulation and glandular secretion in the skin. The scalp is massaged during shampooing. Massage is frequently used in beauty culture with various techniques being applied. (*See* also Section 13.4.)

14.6 NERVES OF THE FACE

Movements of the muscles associated with the head and face are stimulated by nerves coming from the brain (cranial nerves). Of the twelve pairs of cranial nerves (*see* Chapter 17), the fifth and seventh pairs are involved in facial movements (Figure 14.5).

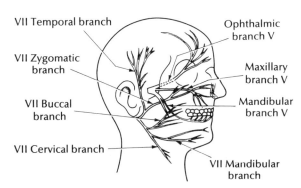

14.5 **Main branches of cranial nerves V and VII**

The fifth nerve, the *trigeminal*, has three main branches:

a *maxillary* branch supplies the upper jaw, part of the nose and cheek, and part of the orbit;

a *mandibular* branch supplies the lower jaw and the muscles of mastication;

an *ophthalmic* branch supplies the upper part of the orbital cavity and also the skin of the nose, forehead and scalp.

The maxillary and ophthalmic branches are sensory, that is, pick up sensations and relay them to the brain. The mandibular branch is a motor nerve stimulating movement, for example, chewing.

The seventh nerve, the *facial*, is responsible for facial expressions. It branches to various muscles:

the *cervical* branch goes to the neck;

the *temporal* branch goes to the forehead and eyebrows;

the *buccal* branch goes to the buccinators and the orbicularis oris;

the *zygomatic* branch goes to the muscles of the nose.

14.7   THE BLOOD VESSELS OF THE HEAD AND FACE

Main arteries

The chief arteries which supply oxygenated blood to the head arise from the common carotid artery on each side of the neck (*see* Figure 14.6). It divides in the neck into an internal and external branch:

the *internal carotid* artery passes through a canal in the temporal bone of the skull to take blood to the brain;

the *external carotid* artery divides to form three superficial branches to the head and face as follows:

the *facial* artery crosses the angle of the mouth and branches into the nose;

the *temporal* artery branches to the side of the head;

the *occipital* artery supplies blood to the back of the head.

Main veins

Blood from the head is drained by the jugular veins on each side. The *internal jugular* vein drains the deep parts of the head, receiving branches from the face and tongue. The *external jugular* veins drain the sides of the face, receiving branches from the temporal and occipital regions (*see* Figure 14.7).

Capillaries

Capillary networks are found in the skin and scalp, bringing nourishment to the skin and hair roots. They also occur in the brain and other organs of the head, enabling oxygen and nutrients to reach every cell (*see* Section 16.5).

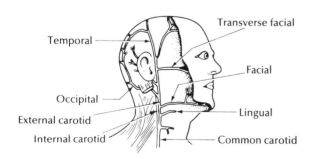

14.6   **Main arteries of right side of head** (*after Gray*)

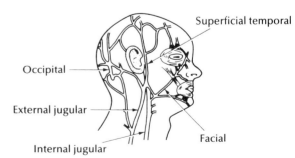

14.7   **Main veins of right side of head and neck** (*after Gray*)

14.8   QUESTIONS

1 Describe the structure and functions of the skull.
2 Name the bones of the cranium and indicate their positions.
  Explain why it is necessary to have immovable joints where these bones meet.
3 Give an account of the facial bones of the skull and indicate how they influence the shape of the face and indirectly the hair style of an individual.
4 (*a*) Name the muscles responsible for facial movements and indicate their positions on a diagram. (*b*) Discuss the importance of massage.
5 Explain how the superficial parts of the head and face (*a*) receive their blood supply and (*b*) have the blood drained from them.
6 Describe the importance of (*a*) the fifth and seventh cranial nerves and (*b*) the external and internal carotid arteries.

14.9   MULTIPLE CHOICE QUESTIONS

1 Which one of the following is the only movable bone in the skull:
  (*a*) malar
  (*b*) mandible
  (*c*) maxilla
  (*d*) ethmoid?

2 How many bones form the skull (excluding ear ossicles):
  (*a*) 2
  (*b*) 8
  (*c*) 14
  (*d*) 22?
3 The muscle which is able to draw the head backwards is called the:
  (*a*) occipitalis
  (*b*) platysma
  (*c*) trapezius
  (*d*) temporalis?
4 The two cranial nerves supplying the face are of the following type:
  (*a*) motor
  (*b*) sensory
  (*c*) mixed
  (*d*) afferent?
5 The internal carotid artery supplies which one of the following:
  (*a*) tongue
  (*b*) neck
  (*c*) brain
  (*d*) ear?
6 Which two cranial nerves supply the face:
  (*a*) 1st and 3rd
  (*b*) 5th and 7th
  (*c*) 9th and 11th
  (*d*) 4th and 12th?

15 The Digestive System and Nutrition

15.1 INTRODUCTION: BODY ORGANIZATION

The human body is a living organism made of millions of tiny cells. Some living organisms are very simple, being composed of only one cell, for example bacteria (*see* Section 19.1). These simple forms of life can feed, grow, respire to obtain energy, excrete waste products, respond to stimuli and reproduce. In a complex body, however, the different functions are performed by special parts designed for the specific purpose. This is known as a division of labour and is highly organized.

Cells of the body are composed of cytoplasm with a dense part called the nucleus. Each cell is bounded by a membrane. The cells take in nutrients grow and divide to form new cells. Numerous chemical changes occur within the cells, such as the use of *fuel* to provide energy. Modifications in size, shape and other characteristics occur so that particular groups of cells are suited to a special function and these groups are known as tissues.

Tissues include four basic groups:
epithelia which form linings and coverings − for example, the skin;
muscular tissues responsible for movement;
nervous tissue for the control of the body;
connective and supporting tissues which link parts together and give support, for example, bone and cartilage.

Organs of the body contain various tissues.

Systems of the body include several organs involved in a particular function, such as dealing with food.

The organization enables the body to function more efficiently. The main systems are digestive, respiratory, circulatory, excretory, nervous, endocrine, reproductive, skeletal and muscular. They will be explained simply to give an understanding of how the whole body works. Microscopic preparations can be examined to identify various cells and tissues. An examination of organs such as a sheep's heart, kidney, lungs, etc. will be helpful in the understanding of mammalian structure.

15.2 THE DIGESTIVE SYSTEM AND NUTRITION

Nourishment is necessary for the health of the body and for healthy skin and hair. It is provided by food nutrients which are needed for several purposes:

(*a*) growth of new cells and tissues, including skin and hair;

(*b*) repair of damaged tissues, for example, cuts or burns on the skin or scalp;

(*c*) production of energy for the activities of the body and for maintaining body temperature;

(*d*) healthy development and maintenance of health.

Nourishment is provided by food. Most foods are complex substances which need to be digested to make them soluble. They can then be absorbed into the bloodstream for distribution to the tissues where they will be utilized. Digestion occurs in the alimentary canal, with the help of enzymes in the digestive juices secreted by glands associated with the canal.

Food nutrients requiring digestion are proteins, the main body-building materials, carbohydrates and lipids, the main energy producers.

Nutrients not requiring digestion are vitamins and mineral salts (already soluble), needed for healthy development and for maintenance of a healthy body. Water is also required and a certain amount of dietary fibre providing indigestible bulk to keep the muscles of the alimentary canal in good working order. Food nutrients requiring digestion are carbohydrates and lipids, the main producers of kinetic and heat energy, and proteins, the main body-builders.

All the necessary nutrients can be acquired from a well-balanced diet.

15.3 CLASSES OF FOOD NUTRIENTS

Proteins

These are complex, organic nutrients required for new growth and also for the repair of damaged tissues. They are present in lean meat, fish, eggs, cheese, milk and in some vegetables and flour. They contain carbon, hydrogen, oxygen and nitrogen, together with varying amounts of sulphur and sometimes phosphorus.

Proteins are composed of units known as *amino acids*. There are about twenty-two known ones of which about ten are essential for the human body to maintain life. Proteins containing most, or all of the essential amino acids, are said to have a high biological value and are usually of animal origin. Those deficient in essential amino acids have a low biological value and are usually of plant origin.

During digestion, proteins are converted back into amino acids, after which selected amino acids can be used to build up new body tissue for growth and repair. *Keratin* is a complex protein present in hair and skin (*see* Section 10.2).

Carbohydrates

These are complex organic nutrients containing carbon, hydrogen and oxygen. They are the chief fuel foods of the body, enabling energy to be obtained. They include starches and sugars and are found in bread, cakes, pastries, potatoes and many other foods.

Monosaccharides or simple sugars are single units, general formula $C_6H_{12}O_6$ and can be readily absorbed. They include glucose or grape sugar and fructose or fruit sugar.

Dissacharides are more complex 'double sugars', general formula $C_{12}=|H_{22}O_{11}$, having one water molecule less than two simple sugar units. They include sucrose or cane sugar and lactose or milk sugar. Another disaccharide, maltose, is produced during the digestion of starch.

Polysaccharides are composed of many units, often millions, and are more condensed than disaccharides. Each unit contains one water molecule less than a monosaccharide, hence the formula $(C_6 H_{10} O_5)_n$, the value of n varying with different examples. They include starch, present in potatoes, cereals, bread and pastries, glycogen, a form of animal starch stored in the human liver and muscle cells, and cellulose, a very complex polysaccharide which is indigestible in humans.

During digestion, carbohydrates are converted to simple sugars. They provide the main source of energy which is liberated by oxidation in the body tissues. The following equation summarizes a complex series of changes essential for the liberation of energy (*see* below).

Lipids (Fats)

These are complex organic nutrients containing carbon, hydrogen and oxygen, but the hydrogen and oxygen are not in the same proportions as in water and carbohydrates. Most lipids are composed of two parts, a fatty carboxylic acid and propanetriol (glycerine), and are converted into these two components by digestion.

Natural fatty foods may be of animal origin, for example, butter, or they may be vegetable oils. Margarine is a synthetic product.

Lipids can be oxidized for energy production, particularly for heat energy. Surplus lipids are used as a food reserve, since they have a high energy value, that is, they yield far more energy than the same weight of carbohydrate or protein. These reserves can be used to provide energy in times of need such as starvation or during slimming. Surplus carbohydrates and proteins can be converted into fatty tissue and deposited beneath the skin and around organs.

Vitamins

These are organic substances co-called because they are vital for the maintenance of health. Several vitamins have been identified and they occur, in small quantities, in many of the foods we eat. They are already soluble in either fat or water, and thus require no digestion. Their absence in the diet leads to disorders known as *vitamin deficiency diseases*. Some of the more important ones, their occurrence and the deficiency effects are briefly shown in Table 15.1.

As long as a mixed diet is taken, the necessary vitamins will be automatically included along with proteins, carbohydrates and fats, and the health of the body will be maintained. Vitamins A, B complex and C are necessary for healthy skin.

Mineral salts

These inorganic nutrients are required for general health. Substances contained in these salts are required for various purposes:

(*a*) iron is needed for the composition of haemoglobin in the blood, without which oxygen cannot be transported;

(*b*) calcium and phosphorus help to make strong bones and teeth;

(*c*) sodium chloride (common salt) is present in all body fluids;

(*d*) iodine is necessary for the secretion of the hormone thyroxine in the thyroid gland.

Glucose	+	*Oxygen*	$\xrightarrow{\text{Oxidation}}$	*Energy*	+	*Water*	+	*Carbon dioxide*
$C_6 H_{12} O_6$	+	$6O_2$		Energy	+	$6H_2O$	+	$6CO_2$

This hormone helps to contol the rate of metabolism (body chemistry) and therefore affects the rate at which hair grows.

Mineral salts are soluble chemicals and thus require no digestion. Like vitamins, they are normally present in a mixed diet.

Water

Water is a necessary constituent of the diet. It is present in many foods as well as drinks. It makes up about 66 per cent of the body weight, being present in the protoplasm of cells. Blood plasma contains water and transports various dissolved substances in the body.

Many chemical changes take place in solution, and water molecules are necessary for the conversion of complex carbohydrates into simple sugars, as shown by the following equation (*see* below).

Water is required for the production of various glandular secretions and also for the excretion of the waste products of metabolism. It also forms the basis of all body fluids.

Drinks, usually containing water, are often taken with meals.

Dietary fibre

A certain amount of indigestible fibrous material is necessary in the diet in order to provide sufficient bulk for the muscles of the alimentary canal to work on. This dietary fibre is present in fresh fruit and vegetables and also in wholemeal bread and bran. Recently there has been more emphasis on the importance of fibre in maintaining health. It is thought to have an important effect with regard to cancer and stress.

15.4   DIGESTION

Before food can be absorbed and utilized by the body, it must be in a soluble state. Digestion converts complex food substances into simple soluble ones by means of enzymes present in the digestive juices. The changes occur as food passes along the alimentary canal.

Alimentary canal

The 'food canal' is a tube, about nine metres long, running through the body from the

$$\begin{array}{ccccc} \textit{Malt sugar} & + & \textit{Water} & \xrightarrow{\text{Digestion}} & \textit{Simple sugars} \\ C_{12}H_{22}O_{11} & & H_2O & & C_6H_{12}O_6 \ + \ C_6H_{12}O_6 \end{array}$$

Name	Occurrence	Deficiency diseases
Vitamin A	Milk, animal fats, green vegetables vegetables	Skin disease, eye disease, lowering of resistance
Vitamin B several members of this group	Most foods, particularly eggs, milk and cereals	Dermatitis, disorders of digestive system, inflammation of nerves, i.e. polyneuritis or beri-beri
Vitamin C	Citrus fruits, blackcurrants, green vegetables	Skin eruptions, anaemia, scurvy
Vitamin D	Animal fats, fish oils, eggs, green vegetables	Rickets
Vitamen E	Wheat germ	Sterility — at least in rats
Vitamin K	Green vegetables	Tendency to bleeding

Table 15.1   Vitamins

mouth to the anus. Its muscular walls can move food along by muscular contractions known as *peristaltic* movement. The canal is lined throughout with a mucous membrane, the secretion of which lubricates the food, assisting its passage along the canal. In man, the parts of the alimentary canal are the buccal cavity (mouth cavity) containing the tongue and teeth, the pharynx, the oesophagus, the stomach, the small intestine consisting of duodenum, jejunum and ileum, and the large intestine consisting of the colon, caecum and appendix and the rectum which ends at the anus. (Figure 15.1).

Digestive juices

Glands associated with the alimentary canal secrete digestive juices which are mixed with the food in the canal. Some glands are situated in the canal lining, for example the gastric glands of the stomach and the intestinal glands of the ileum. Separate glands associated with the canal have special ducts along which their secretions pass into the food tube. These include three pairs of salivary glands, with ducts opening into the mouth cavity, and the pancreas with the pancreatic duct opening

into the duodenum (Figure 15.1). Bile secreted by the liver and stored in the gall bladder, passes along the bile duct into the duodenum. Bile does not contain any digestive enzymes, but is an emulsifying agent, separating lipids into small droplets thus increasing the surface area for enzyme action and making them more digestible (*see* Section 9.7).

15.5   ENZYMES

These are organic protein substances which can bring about chemical changes by acting as catalysts. Enzymes are specific in their action and are sensitive to both the temperature and the medium in which they work. In the digestive juices, there are enzymes acting on proteins, carbohydrates and fats.

Enzymes acting on proteins

Pepsin, present in the gastric juice from the gastric glands of the stomach, converts proteins into proteoses and peptones. *Trypsin*, secreted as trypsinogen in the pancreatic juice, converts peptones into polypeptides in the small intestine. *Enterokinase*, from the intestinal juice, converts trypsinogen into active trypsin. *Peptidases*, present in the intestinal juice, convert polypeptides into amino acids in the small intestine.

Enzymes acting on carbohydrates

Salivary amylase, present in saliva from the salivary glands, converts cooked starch into maltose in the mouth, where the medium is almost neutral. Any saliva swallowed with food can continue its activity in the stomach for a limited period, until the medium becomes too acid. *Amylase*, present in the pancreatic juice, converts starch into maltose in the duodenum. *Sucrase, maltase* and *lactase* in the intestinal juice, convert sucrose, maltose and lactose, respectively, into monosaccharide sugars.

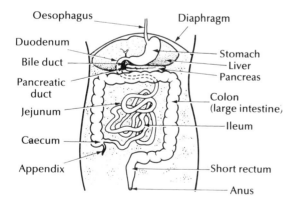

Oesophagus
Diaphragm
Duodenum
Bile duct
Pancreatic duct
Jejunum
Caecum
Appendix
Stomach
Liver
Pancreas
Colon (large intestine)
Ileum
Short rectum
Anus

15.1   The human alimentary canal. Only the abdominal portion is shown. (The liver and pancreas are not parts of the canal; they are merely associated glands.)

Part of Alimentary Canal	Secretions	Enzymes	Changes
Mouth cavity	Saliva from Salivary glands	Salivary Amylase	Cooked starch to maltose
Stomach	Gastric juice from gastric glands	Pepsin	Proteins to proteoses and peptones
Duodenum	Bile from liver	- - -	Emulsification of lipids
	Pancreatic juice from pancreas	Lipase	Emulsified lipids to *fatty carboxylic acids* and *propanetriol*
		Amylase	Starch to maltose
		Trypsin	Peptones to polypeptides
Small intestine	Intestinal juice from intestinal glands	Enterokinase	Activates trypsin
		Peptidases	Polypeptides to *amino acids*
		Lactase	Lactose ⟍
		Maltase	Maltase — To *simple sugars*
		Sucrase	Sucrose ⟋

Table 15.2   Summary of digestion — end-products in bold

Enzymes acting on lipids

Lipase in the pancreatic juice converts lipids into fatty carboxylic acids and propanetriol (glycerine) in the duodenum. The lipids are first emulsified by bile, from the liver, which also neutralizes the acidity of the *chyme*, the liquified food leaving the stomach. The intestinal enzymes require an alkaline medium which is achieved through the presence of bile and pancreatic juice.

15.6   ABSORPTION

The soluble end-products of digestion, namely glucose, amino acids, fatty acids and propanetriol (glycerine), are absorbed into the bloodstream for distribution in the body. The lining of the small intestine is folded into minute finger-like projections called *villi* (Figure 15.2). In each villus are blood capillaries and a central lacteal (lymphatic) vessel. Glucose and amino acids pass directly into the blood via these capillaries. The fatty acids and propanetriol have larger molecules and are absorbed into the lacteal tubes, reaching the bloodstream later from the thoracic duct which empties into the jugular vein in the neck (Section 16.12).

In general, the end-products of lipid digestion have molecules too large to pass through blood capillaries, but some lipids are so finely emulsified that they are absorbed directly into the bloodstream. Some people believe that lipids are absorbed as droplets and digestion occurs in the lacteal.

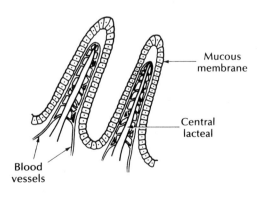

15.2   Villi (longitudinal section)

15.7   DEFAECATION

After food has been digested in the alimentary canal and absorption of nutrients has been completed, a certain amount of indigestible matter remains. This passes into the large intestine and is prepared for evacuation by the body. Most of the water present in it is absorbed making the *faeces* solid but soft. Mucus lubricates the waste to assist its passage to the rectum and anus. Many bacteria are present and also shed cells from the lining of the alimentary canal. Bile pigments colour the faeces, the evacuation of which is termed *defaecation*.

15.8   IMPORTANCE OF A BALANCED DIET

A balanced diet helps to maintain the health and efficiency of the body, and should include all the required nutrients; proteins, carbohydrates, lipids, vitamins and mineral salts. Water is also necessary and a certain amount of indigestible dietary fibre which keeps the muscles of the alimentary canal in working order by providing bulk. Fibrous material is present in fresh fruit and vegetables.

A suitable diet must also supply the daily energy requirements for each individual and there should be a balance between food intake and energy output. Energy is measured in joules and megajoules. Carbohydrates and proteins yield an equivalent number of joules. The yield from lipids is more than double that from the same weight of carbohydrate or protein, and the energy that is liberated is partly heat. A balanced diet should provide about 50 per cent carbohydrate, 32 per cent lipid and 18 per cent protein. If a wide variety of food is eaten, including fresh fruit and vegetables and some dairy produce, the supply of vitamins and mineral salts should be adequate for health. The daily requirement of megajoules sufficient to supply the daily energy requirement would be 9 to 10 for an adult female and 12 to 13 for an adult male.

15.9   THE EXCRETORY SYSTEM

The excretory system deals with the elimination of the waste products of metabolism. The activities of the body result in various types of toxic waste products which must be eliminated in order that the body may continue to function efficiently. Metabolism gives rise to nitrogenous waste, carbon dioxide and water.

Tissue respiration, which releases energy for the functions of the body, produces the waste products, carbon dioxide and water. Carbon dioxide is breathed out from the lungs together with some water vapour (*see* Section 16.5). Some of the carbon dioxide may combine with ammonia in the liver to form carbamide (urea) and this travels to the kidneys.

Protein metabolism results in nitrogenous waste. The breakdown of tissue protein and the conversion of unwanted amino acids to carbamide in the liver both contribute to the carbamide (urea) in the liver both contribute to the formation of the nitrogenous waste which the body eliminates in the form of urine. Water is required for the preparation of urine which is excreted through the kidneys and the bladder. The skin eliminates water and a little carbamide (urea) through sweating (*see* Section 18.5).

15.10   EXCRETORY ORGANS

These deal with the elimination of most of the nitrogenous waste. Two *kidneys* lie in the abdominal cavity with a *ureter* or kidney duct passing from each to the urinary *bladder* at the lower end of the abdomen (Figure 15.3). A passage known as the urethra leads from the bladder to the outside world. Each kidney is composed of two regions, an outer cortex and an inner medulla. Pyramids of kidney tissue in the medulla lead to hollow calyces from which urine reaches the hollow pelvis of the kidney and enters the ureter (Figure 15.4).

Kidney tissue is composed of large numbers

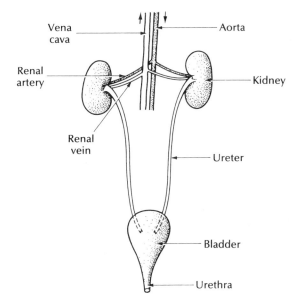

15.3 Excretory organs and the blood supply to the kidneys

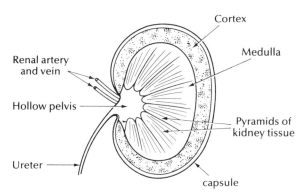

15.4 Vertical section of kidney

of minute tubules or *nephrons* connected to a network of blood capillaries. A nephron starts in the cortex as a cup-shaped Bowman's capsule into which fits a glomerulus or network of blood capillaries. The nephron continues as a convoluted tubule followed by a loop of Henle and then a second convoluted tubule which drains into a collecting duct. From here, urine drips into a calyx, into the kidney pelvis and down the ureter to the bladder.

Formation of urine

Urine is manufactured by the kidney cells. Blood in the glomerulus is under pressure resulting in the filtration of some of the liquid from the blood into the Bowman's capsule. This liquid contains dissolved carbamide (urea), glucose, salts and other substances. The glucose, some of the salts and some water are re-absorbed into the blood as the liquid passes along the nephron which is enveloped in blood capillaries. The kidney cells can secrete some substances into the tubule to add to the urine being formed.

Kidney cells have a selective power enabling them to regulate the amount of water and the concentration of the blood.

Eventually, urine from the collecting ducts reaches the bladder via the ureters. The bladder is extensible and stores urine until it can be expelled, at suitable intervals, through the urethra. When the body is very hot, water is lost through the sweat glands in the skin

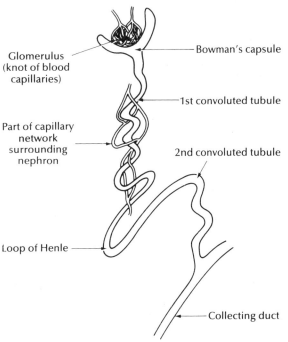

15.5 Structure of nephron

(*see* Section 18.5). There is a balance between the amount of water lost through sweating and the amount excreted in urine.

15.11   QUESTIONS

1 State the requirements necessary for a good diet and briefly describe the importance of each item included.
2 Explain the meaning of each of the following terms, giving one example of each to illustrate your explanation:
  (*a*) cell, (*b*) tissue, (*c*) organ, (*d*) system.
3 (*a*) What would you consider to be a balanced lunch for a busy hairdresser?
  (*b*) Explain the relationship between a good diet and health.
4 Explain how the protein eaten in a ham sandwich is dealt with by the body to enable it to be used for hair growth.
5 Give an account of the part played by the kidney in the excretion of nitrogenous waste from the body.
  How is the skin involved in excretion?
6 Make a labelled diagram of a nephron and explain how it carries out its functions.

15.12   MULTIPLE CHOICE QUESTIONS

1 The food with the highest protein content amongst the following is:
  (*a*) milk
  (*b*) peas
  (*c*) egg
  (*d*) bread?

2 How many different essential amino acids are needed for heathly body growth:
  (*a*) 2 to 4
  (*b*) 8 to 10
  (*c*) 16 to 18
  (*d*) 20 to 22?
3 The daily amount of vitamin C—ascorbic acid in a balanced diet is between twenty and thirty:
  (*a*) micrograms
  (*b*) milligrams
  (*c*) grams
  (*d*) kilograms?
4 Which of the following is needed for healthy teeth and bone formation:
  (*a*) iron
  (*b*) iodine
  (*c*) phosphate
  (*d*) chloride.
5 The process of expelling urine from the body is called:
  (*a*) defaecation
  (*b*) parturition
  (*c*) exfoliation
  (*d*) micturition?
6 Which of the following are normal components of urine in a healthy person:
   (i) haemoglobin   (iv) protein
  (ii) glucose   (v) sodium chloride
  (iii) carbamide (urea) (vi) lipids?
  (*a*) (i) and (ii)
  (*b*) (iii) and (v)
  (*c*) (v) and (vi)
  (*d*) (ii) and (v)?

16 The Respiratory System and Energy

All the activities of the human body, whether it be the work of a hairdresser in the salon, the growth of a client's hair or the general activities in a healthy body, require energy.

Since energy cannot be made, but only changed from one form into another, the body needs to obtain its energy supply from the fuel foods in the diet. The ultimate source of energy is the sun. *Radiant* energy is transformed by plants into chemical energy when carbohydrates and other organic food nutrients are being synthesized.

16.1 RESPIRATION

This is the means by which the potential energy is released, in yet another form, to supply the body's needs. *Kinetic* energy, for work, and *heat* energy, for maintenance of the body temperature, are released during oxidation of fuel foods in the tissues. This is known as tissue respiration, and the oxygen required for it is obtained by breathing and is subsequently distributed to the tissues in the bloodstream.

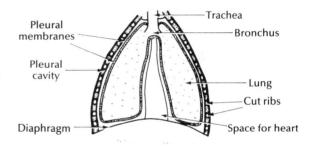

16.1 **The lungs and pleural membranes (the heart is omitted)**

16.2 BREATHING ORGANS AND RESPIRATORY PASSAGES

A pair of *lungs* lie in the thoracic (chest) cavity. Each lung is encased in a double pleural membrane which adheres closely to the lungs and to the inside of the thorax (Figure 16.1). The membrane secretes pleural fluid which helps to reduce friction during breathing movements.

Air is breathed into the lungs from the atmosphere by way of the respiratory passages, starting at the nose and mouth (Figure 16.2).

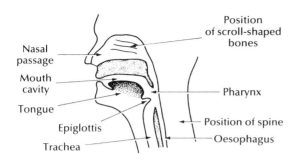

16.2 Section through part of the head and neck to show the respiratory passages

The nostrils lead into the *nasal passages* which are lined with small hairs to filter out dust and dirt that might otherwise reach the lungs. These passages are also lined with a vascular mucous membrane whose secretion also traps dust. The air is warmed and moistened by contact with this membrane. Breathing in through the nostrils enables moist, warm, clean air to reach the lungs and is healthier than breathing in through the mouth. A hairdressing salon needs to be well-ventilated for the comfortable breathing of its occupants. The nasal passages meet the mouth cavity in an area at the back of the mouth known as the *pharynx*. From here, the windpipe or *trachea* passes into the chest alongside the oesophagus (food pipe). The trachea is lined with an epithelium bearing *cilia*, short hairlike processes, which waft in an upward direction thus helping to keep germs out of the lungs. Heavy smoking flattens these cilia, putting them out of action. As well as the risk of cancer, there is an increased liability to chest infections since one of the natural defence mechanisms of the body is removed by smoking.

A small flap of cartilage (gristle), the *epiglottis*, prevents food particles from entering the windpipe, that is 'going down the wrong way'. The airway must remain open and the trachea is therefore supported by rings of cartilage, but these are incomplete where the trachea is in close contact with the oesophagus to avoid damage to the food pipe during peris-

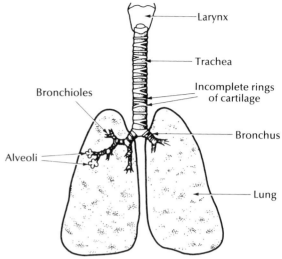

16.3 The larynx, trachea and lungs

talsis. Special cartilages at the beginning of the trachea form the *larynx* which encloses the vocal cords (Figure 16.3). The trachea extends for a few inches before dividing into two bronchi, each of which is sub-divided into bronchioles. These very fine branches eventually end in small air-sacs or *alveoli*, making up the spongy tissue of the lungs.

16.3 MECHANISM OF BREATHING

Breathing occurs unconsciously, but it can be controlled. The respiratory movements cause air to be alternately drawn into the lungs (inspiration) and forced out again (expiration). The movements are brought about by contraction of the diaphragm and the intercostal muscles (those between the ribs). The diaphragm is a dome-shaped muscle forming the floor of the chest. The ribs and intercostal muscles, together with the breast bone and part of the backbone, form the walls of the chest, and the neck seals off the top of the cavity.

During quiet breathing, the diaphragm contracts increasing the size of the chest cavity and creating a vacuum. This causes the inspiration of air, through the respiratory

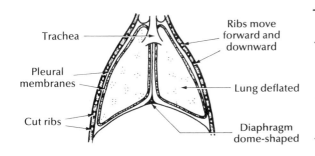

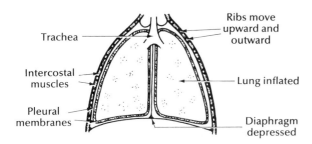

16.4 The mechanism of breathing (*a*) expiration – air breathed out (*b*) inspiration – air breathed in

	Inhaled air (%)	Exhaled air (%)
Oxygen	21	17
Nitrogen	78	78
Carbon dioxide	0.04	4.04
Rare gases	1	1
Water vapour	Variable	Increased

Table 16.1

passages, to the lungs which inflate to fill the vacuum (Figure 16.4). Relaxation of the diaphragm causes expiration, that is, decreases the size of the chest cavity, thus forcing air to be expired.

During deep breathing, the intercostal muscles contract to raise the ribs, thus enabling further expansion of the chest and ventilating the lungs more fully. The muscles relax during expiration.

16.4 CONTROL OF BREATHING

Breathing is controlled both by the nervous system and by chemical influence. Nervous impulses pass from the respiratory centre in the medulla of the brain to the muscles of respiration. The vagus nerve carries these impulses. Chemical control is due to the concentration of carbon dioxide in the blood. This stimulates the respiratory centre in the brain. During exercise, more carbon dioxide is produced, thus increasing the stimulation and resulting in faster breathing. The rate of respiration thus varies according to the metabolic needs of the body.

16.5 EXTERNAL AND INTERNAL RESPIRATION

External respiration, or breathing, results in the alternate inhalation and exhalation of air. The composition of the air, a mixture of gaseous elements and compounds, varies as shown in Table 16.1. A proportion of the oxygen is retained by the body for the subsequent oxidation of fuel. The alveoli of the lungs are in close contact with blood capillaries, thus enabling oxygen to diffuse into the blood for distribution to the tissues (Figure 16.5). At the same time, carbon dioxide passes from the blood into the lungs for expiration. This is known as the interchange of gases.

Internal respiration or tissue respiration occurs when soluble food, such as glucose, is

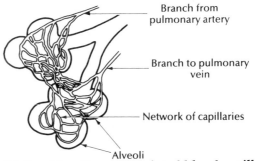

16.5 Alveoli and associated blood capillaries

$$\underset{\text{C}_6\text{H}_{12}\text{O}_6}{\text{Glucose}} \quad + \quad \underset{6\text{O}_2}{\text{Oxygen}} \quad \xrightarrow{\textbf{Oxidation}} \quad \text{Energy} \quad + \quad \underset{6\text{CO}_2}{\text{Carbon dioxide}} \quad + \quad \underset{6\text{H}_2\text{O}}{\text{Water}}$$

oxidized in the tissues to release energy. The process is similar to combustion in many ways: both involve oxygen and the liberation of energy from fuel. However, combustion releases all the energy as heat, whilst most of the energy released in respiration is transferred to chemicals manufactured in the cell, the chief one being adenosine triphosphate (ATP). This provides a sort of 'energy bank' until the energy is required by the cells. ATP can then link up with energy-requiring processes and release its energy in the process. The production of a certain amount of heat energy helps to maintain a constant body temperature. The equation above sums up the complex changes involved in tissue respiration.

The waste products, carbon dioxide and water pass back into the blood plasma, and are returned to the lungs and breathed out. Thus there is an approximate 4 per cent exchange of oxygen for carbon dioxide and an increase in the water vapour content of exhaled air.

The part played by the blood is an important factor in respiration.

16.6   THE CIRCULATORY SYSTEM, BLOOD AND TRANSPORT

The circulatory system is the transport system of the body. Blood is circulated around the body in blood vessels by the pumping action of the heart. Oxygen and other useful substances are distributed, and waste products are taken from the tissues so that they can be eliminated. The blood also protects the body against infection.

Blood

Blood is a liquid tissue. The fluid is a watery solution or plasma containing numerous cells,

both red and white (Figure 16.6). The red cells outnumber the white cells by about five hundred to one, hence the blood appears red.

Red cells or *erythrocytes* are small circular bi-concave discs without a nucleus. They may run together to form rouleaux. Although appearing red in the mass, erythrocytes are yellow, when seen singly, owing to the presence of haemoglobin, an iron compound with an affinity for oxygen. They are manufactured in the bone marrow and live for about three or four months, after which time they die and break up. Their function is to carry oxygen. This combines with haemoglobin to form an unstable compound, oxyhaemoglobin, which readily yields oxygen to the tissues. Blood containing oxygen is said to be oxygenated, but after the oxygen has been released it is said to be de-oxygenated. *White cells* or *leucocytes* are irregular shaped cells with a nucleus and there are different types:

(a) Granulocytes — large cells with granular cytoplasm and a divided nucleus. They are known as polymorphs and can move by amoeboid movement, a flowing action of the cytoplasm. They form the majority of the white cells.

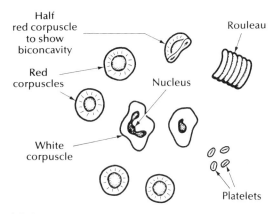

16.6   Human blood cells

(b) *Monocytes* – cells with a large nucleus and cytoplasm with fine granules.

(c) *Lymphocytes* – smaller cells with a single nucleus and clear cytoplasm.

The function of leucocytes is to help to keep the body free from disease in two ways. The granulocytes and monocytes ingest bacteria and other foreign bodies in the blood, thus destroying them. This process is known as *phagocytosis*. They will also ingest damaged tissue, thus helping a wound to heal. The lymphocytes cannot carry out phagocytosis, but they secrete antibodies which counteract the effects of antigens, such as harmful bacterial toxins. Leucocytes increase in number during an infection and are attracted to the site of an infection resulting in inflammation.

Blood platelets or *thrombocytes* are very small cells or fragments of cells in the blood. Their function is to help in the clotting of blood to seal a wound and this helps to prevent bacterial infection.

Normal healthy blood contains plasma proteins including *prothrombin* and *fibrinogen*. An injury starts a chain reaction: injured blood cells liberate thrombokinase; this converts prothrombin (in the presence of calcium salts in the blood). to thrombin; thrombin converts soluble fibrinogen into threads of fibrin which become entangled with blood cells to form a clot.

Blood plasma

This is the aqueous solution which contains the cells. It is composed of water and dissolved substances including the plasma proteins. Two of the proteins, *albumin* and *globulin* cause the blood to be sticky. The function of plasma is to transport numerous dissolved substances. Dissolved food nutrients are distributed to the tissues. Waste products such as carbon dioxide and carbamide (urea) are removed from the tissues and transported, in solution, to the lungs and the kidneys for elimination. Hormones, enzymes

Part of blood	Function
Erythrocytes (red corpuscles)	Transport oxygen as oxyhaemoglobin from lungs to tissues
White corpuscles Granulocytes and Monocytes	Ingest bacteria and foreign bodies by phagocytosis
Lymphocytes	Secrete antibodies
Thrombocytes	Seal wounds by clotting
Plasma	Transports soluble nutrients, excretory products, hormones and enzymes. Buffering. Helps clotting (plasma proteins). Distribution of materials to the tissues, via lymph.

Table 16.2   Summary of functions of the blood

and other substances are distributed by the plasma. Sodium hydrogen carbonate, a salt dissolved in the plasma, acts as a buffer, that is, it prevents sharp changes in the alkalinity of the blood.

16.7   BLOOD GROUPS

People are said to belong to different blood groups according to the presence or absence of inherited chemical factors in the red blood corpuscles. There are two possible factors known as antigens (agglutinogens) A and B, and they may cause agglutination (clumping) of the red cells if introduced into a person whose blood does not already contain them.

Blood may contain either the A factor or the B factor. Some people have both factors present and others have neither. The groups are therefore described as A, B, AB and O. In the plasma of the blood, there are antibodies against a factor which is not present; for example, group A blood has, in its plasma, antibodies against the B factor. In a blood transfusion, it is important not to introduce any antigens which are not already present in the recipient's own blood, otherwise the antibodies will destroy the red corpuscles of the transfused blood. People of blood group O are universal donors since their blood has neither of the antigens present. People of the group AB are universal recipients, that is, they can receive a transfusion from any group since their blood already contains both the factors A and B. In transfusions involving the other groups, it is important to obtain a correct match.

In addition to the A and B factors, another chemical known as the Rhesus factor may be present. Over 80 per cent of individuals have it and are described as Rhesus positive. The remainder are Rhesus negative. This factor is particularly important in some pregnancies. If a Rhesus negative mother is carrying a Rhesus positive foetus, antibodies developed in the mother pass into the foetus and cause jaundice shortly after birth. It is possible that the child may even be stillborn.

16.8 BLOOD DISEASES

The corpuscles of the blood, both red and white may be affected by disease. If the red corpuscles are affected, this will cause oxygen deficiency and symptoms of anaemia will appear. If the white cells are affected, it will reduce the ability of the body to ward off infection. Blood diseases include various types of anaemia, parasitic infections such as malaria, blood cancer (leukaemia) and agranulocytosis.

Formation of blood

Blood corpuscles are manufactured in the bone marrow. Red marrow, which makes red cells, is present in flat bones, such as the sternum, and in the ends of the long bones of the limbs. The red corpuscles live for a few months only and are then destroyed and replaced by new ones. The iron from the worn out cells is used in the manufacture of new corpuscles. Loss of corpuscles through bleeding will therefore lead to iron deficiency. Pregnancy may also lead to iron deficiency.

Factors needed for blood formation include healthy bone marrow, a supply of iron, vitamins and the intrinsic factor produced in the lining of the stomach. Defective blood formation is due to a fault in one or more of these factors, and it occurs in certain diseases and also in lead poisoning.

Anaemia

Anaemia involves a shortage of haemoglobin, needed for the transport of oxygen, and resulting in a lack of energy, general weakness and a tendency to fainting and headaches. The anaemic person is also usually pale.

The shortage of haemoglobin may be due to inadequate red corpuscles or to defective blood manufacture.

Pernicious anaemia is due to a shortage of the intrinsic factor in the stomach which needs to combine with vitamin B_{12}. A shortage of red cells results and some abnormal corpuscles may appear in the blood. Treatment — regular doses of B_{12}.

Aplastic anaemia is due to faulty bone marrow. The marrow may be damaged by irradiation and a shortage of red cells results.

Sickle-cell anaemia is due to an abnormal formation of haemoglobin which causes the red cells to become sickle-shaped and very fragile. This is a hereditary disease.

Haemolytic anaemia occurs when red cells are destroyed at a faster rate than they can be replaced. Malaria leads to this type because the parasite enters the red corpuscles in order to feed on them, thus destroying them. Malaria is transmitted through the bite of an infected female anopheline mosquito. Lead poisoning also damages red cells.

General anaemia often follows chronic infections.

Inadequate red corpuscles

Bleeding causes the loss of red corpuscles

from the body, and anaemia is more common in females than males because of menstruation. In heavy bleeding from a serious wound, a transfusion may be necessary to avoid the fall of blood pressure to a dangerously low level. Continuous slow bleeding leads to a shortage of iron, one of the causes of haemoglobin deficiency.

Inadequate white corpuscles

Agranulocytosis is a shortage of white blood corpuscles (granulocytes) and may occur when suppurating infections have depleted the supply.

Leukaemia is a form of blood cancer resulting in an increase in the number of white corpuscles. These cells, however, are immature and are unable to combat infection. The cause of leukaemia is unknown and there is no known cure.

Faulty clotting mechanism

Haemophilia is an inherited blood disease which affects only males as it is a sex-linked character. Females can be carriers of the disease without suffering from it.

The blood of a haemophiliac is unable to clot because of a missing factor. Even small injuries can result in prolonged bleeding, and internal bleeding frequently occurs, so that haemophiliacs often die in childhood.

16.9 THE HEART

The heart is necessary to keep the blood circulating. It is a hollow muscular pumping organ lying in the thorax between the two lungs (Figure 16.7). It is composed of cardiac muscle (*see* Section 20.12). The heart is divided into four chambers, two thin-walled auricles (atria) at the base and two thick-walled ventricles at the apex. The apex is directed downwards and points slightly to the left. There is no communication between the

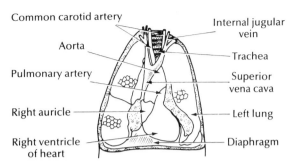

16.7 **Dissection to show heart, great vessels, and lungs *in situ*: certain bones and muscles, etc. have been removed (*after Gray*)**

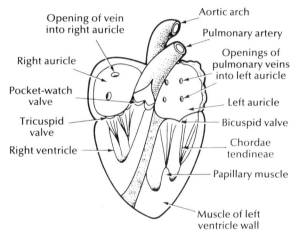

16.8 **Internal structure of the heart**

left and right sides of the heart, but each atrium communicates with the ventricle on the same side (Figure 16.8). Blood flows through these chambers in a definite sequence, always leaving the ventricles by arteries, and entering the atria by veins. The left side of the heart deals with oxygenated blood and the right side with de-oxygenated blood. The ventricles contract simultaneously to distribute blood via the two main arteries. The atria contract simultaneously to drive blood into the ventricles.

Valves of the heart

The flow of blood through this pumping

organ is controlled by valves. Between the atrium and ventricle on the left side is the bicuspic or *mitral* valve, with two cusps anchored by the *chordae tendineae* to papillary muscles. Between the right atrium and ventricle is the *tricuspid* valve with three cusps anchored in a similar way. The two main arteries leaving the heart are controlled by pocket-like *semi-lunar* or pocket watch valves.

16.10   CIRCULATION

Blood must circulate in order to fulfil its functions. Transport of oxygen and nutrients to the tissues is essential. The heart pumps blood alternately to the various sytems of the body and to the lungs in a double circuit (Figure 16.9).

The *systemic* circulation distributes oxygenated blood from the left ventricle of the heart, through the aorta which branches to reach all the body systems, and the blood is then returned, de-oxygenated, to the right atrium in two main veins or venae cavae. Coronary arteries branch from the aorta to supply blood to the muscle of the heart itself. The *pulmonary* circulation takes de-oxygenated blood from the right ventricle of the heart, through the pulmonary artery to the lungs, and then returns oxygenated blood to the left atrium via the four pulmonary veins (Figure 16.10).

16.11   BLOOD VESSELS

Blood is circulated in tubes known as arteries, veins and capillaries. *Arteries* are vessels which carry blood away from the heart for distribution to the tissues and the lungs. They normally carry oxygenated blood with the exception of the pulmonary arteries which carry de-oxygenated blood. Large arteries divide into smaller branches, eventually becoming arterioles. Finally they divide into very fine arterial capillaries. These intermingle with venous capillaries which link up to form veins.

Arteries and arterioles are muscular tubes with a wall composed of three layers:

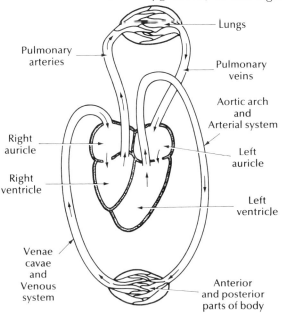

16.9   **Diagrammatic representation of double circuit: direction of flow indicated by arrows**

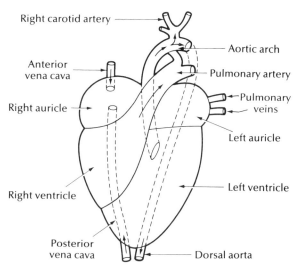

16.10   **The heart and associated blood vessels**

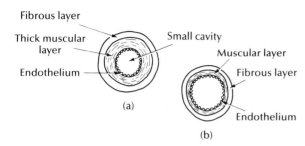

16.11 Artery and vein (transverse section)

1 an outer protective layer of connective tissue;
2 a middle muscular layer with elastic tissue;
3 a smoother inner lining of endotheluim to prevent blood from clotting, (Figure 16.11).

Veins are vessels which carry blood *back* to the heart. They normally carry de-oxygenated blood with the exception of the pulmonary veins which carry oxygenated blood. Veins and venules (smaller branches) have the same three layers as arteries, but the middle muscular layer is much thinner and less elastic than that of an artery. The lining layer has valves to prevent any backward flow of blood (Figure 16.12). This is particularly helpful in the limbs of people whose work involves standing a great deal, as for example, a hairdresser.

Capillaries are very fine branches of arteries and veins forming a network in the tissues of the body. Their thin walls are composed of only a single layer of cells (endotheluim). They enable fluid to escape from the blood to the tissues to transfer nutrients and oxygen to the cells.

16.12   THE LYMPHATIC SYSTEM

This is the part of the circulatory system which transfers useful substances from the blood to the tissues and removes waste products from the tissues.

Some of the blood plasma escapes through the thin walls of blood capillaries and bathes the tissues as tissue fluid. It contains dissolved nutrients and oxygen which has been released from the oxyhaemoglobin carried by red corpuscles. The fluid drains into small lymphatic vessels and is then known as lymph. It contains less protein than blood plasma. The lymphatic vessels start as small hair-like vessels which join up to form tubes similar to veins but with more valves. Eventually, two main ducts are formed, the large thoracic duct on the left side of the body and the smaller right lymphatic duct. The right lymphatic duct drains the upper right side of the body, that is, the right side of the thorax and head and the right arm. The thoracic duct drains the upper left half of the body and also the abdomen and legs.

The lymph re-enters the bloodstream in the neck region but needs to be purified first by passing through lymph glands (nodes). The lymph glands are numerous in the neck, the armpits and the groins and are also in the abdomen. They contain lymphocytes and connective tissue and become swollen during infection. Thus they can prevent infection from reaching the bloodstream. New lymphocytes, which help to fight infection, are also formed here.

The flow of lymph is due partly to suction and partly to pressure.

The special lymph vessels in the villi of the small intestine are known as lacteals.

16.12   Vein (longitudinal section) to show valves

16.13 QUESTIONS

1 Why is respiration necessary?
Explain how air is drawn into and expelled from the lungs.
Why is smoking bad for health?
2 Give an account of the composition of the blood. Explain the part played by the blood in (*a*) transporting materials to keep the skin healthy and (*b*) helping to prevent infection.
3 Describe the structure and functions of (*a*) an artery, (*b*) a vein, (*c*) a capillary.
4 Explain why the lymphatic system is a necessary part of the cardio-vascular system.
5 Make a labelled diagram to show the structure of the heart and the chief blood vessels associated with it.
6 Give an account of anaemia and the factors affecting it.

16.14 MULTIPLE CHOICE QUESTIONS

1 Which people with one of the following blood groups can receive blood by transfusion from any of the four blood groups:
(*a*) A
(*b*) B
(*c*) AB
(*d*) O?

2 Which of the following organs can remove iron from the circulatory system:
(*a*) brain
(*b*) stomach
(*c*) lungs
(*d*) liver?
3 Soluble food is brought to the cells of muscle tissue by means of the:
(*a*) white cells
(*b*) red cells
(*c*) plasma
(*d*) platelets?
4 Which one of the following is suspected of causing damage to the lungs if inhaled over a long period in salon use:
(*a*) talcum powder
(*b*) hair spray
(*c*) hair cuttings
(*d*) steam?
5 The normal rate of breathing per minute for an adult at rest is approximately:
(*a*) 15 to 20
(*b*) 40 to 60
(*c*) 60 to 90
(*d*) 110 to 120?
6 The process of releasing energy from foods is called:
(*a*) digestion
(*b*) respiration
(*c*) breathing
(*d*) assimilation?

17 Body Control

17.1 INTRODUCTION

The activities of the body are controlled in two ways: by the transmission of stimuli through the nervous system and by chemicals through the endocrine system, that is, the ductless glands which secrete hormones.

17.2 THE NERVOUS SYSTEM AND MOVEMENT

The nervous system is a system of communication in the body, through the transmission of stimuli, by means of which the movements of the body are controlled.

Certain body cells are sensitive and receive stimuli. These *receptors* may be scattered, as in the skin which is sensitive to heat, cold and pain, or may be present collectively in organs such as the eye, ear and tongue. The eye is sensitive to light rays, the ear to sound waves and the tongue to taste from solutions.

Other body cells, such as muscle fibres and glandular cells, effect responses to the stimuli and are known as *effectors*.

By conveying impulses (messages) to various parts of the body, the nervous system co-ordinates the responses, that is, brings about reactions to the stimuli. *Co-ordination* ensures that the efforts of the body are not wasted. For example, the juices from digestive glands are secreted only when food is in the alimentary canal, thus preventing these secretions from being wasted.

17.3 NERVOUS TISSUE

Special nerve cells or *neurones* make up nervous tissue. There are different kinds of neurones. Some are associated with the sensitive cells receiving stimuli; these are the *sensory neurones*. Others make connections with the muscles or glands that are going to respond; these are the *motor neurones*. A typical motor neurone is a single nerve cell with a number of short branched projections or dendrons and one long projection or axon leading to a muscle or gland. The axons may be very long, extending perhaps the full length of a limb (Figure 17.1).

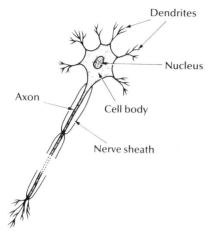

17.1   Motor nerve cell

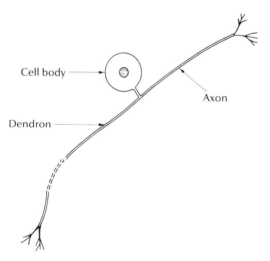

17.2   Sensory neurone

A typical sensory neurone has a long dendron leading into an oval or rounded cell body with an axon leaving the cell (Figure 17.2). Impulses enter neurones via the dendrons and their smaller branches (dendrites), and leave the cell body via the axon.

Medullated nerve fibres are axons covered by an insulating medullary sheath. This is a fatty layer and gives the fibres a white appearance. Collections of axons form the *white matter* of the nervous system and the cell bodies form the *grey matter*.

Nerve cells form the basis of the nervous system which includes:

(*a*) the central nervous system, that is the brain and spinal cord;

(*b*) the peripheral nervous system, that is the nerves arising from the brain and spinal cord;

(*c*) the autonomic or involuntary nervous system.

17.4   THE CENTRAL NERVOUS SYSTEM

This is centrally situated in the head and spine.

The *brain* is a large organ lying in the cranium and composed of grey matter on the surface and white matter inside. It is divided into several parts and is continuous with the spinal cord.

The fore-brain or cerebrum is the largest part and is responsible for conscious activity and all thought processes, memory, reasoning, intelligence and conscience. It has other functions such as initiating voluntary movements. The hairdresser uses this part of the brain to interpret any instructions from a client, to make decisions and to initiate the movements required to carry out the work. This includes the muscles concerned in speech for communication with the client. Co-ordination of movement and maintenance of balance are controlled by the cerebellum. This part also deals with posture reflexes.

The back portion of the brain, which links up with the spinal cord, contains important centres for controlling vital functions such as respiration, heart-beat and temperature control (Figure 17.3).

The *spinal cord* is a cylindrical, hollow cord, tapering towards the end, and situated inside the spine. It is linked to the brain through the foramen magnum, the large hole at the base of the skull, and it serves to connect the brain with other parts of the body. The cord has grey matter on the inside forming a mass in the shape of the letter H in

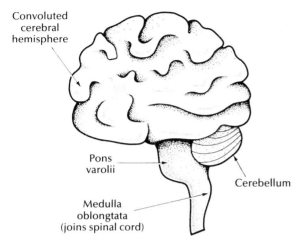

Convoluted cerebral hemisphere

Pons varolii

Cerebellum

Medulla oblongtata (joins spinal cord)

17.3   Side view of brain

section, with nerve fibres or white matter surrounding it. It gives off pairs of spinal nerves.

The functions of the spinal cord are reflex actions, that is automatic responses to stimuli, and also communication with the brain, so that a person is conscious of any automatic response that occurs (Figure 17.4).

17.5   THE PERIPHERAL NERVOUS SYSTEM

This is composed of nerves extending outwards from the central nervous system to the peripheral parts of the body. Nerves arise both from the brain, cranial nerves, and from the spinal cord, spinal nerves. They are composed of nerve fibres which are the axons of *neurones*. Some fibres may carry impulses into the central nervous system from the receptors of the body — these are sensory fibres. Others may carry impulses outwards from the central nervous system to the effectors — these are motor fibres.

A nerve may consist wholly of sensory fibres (sensory nerve), or wholly of motor fibres (motor nerve), or some fibres of each type (mixed nerve).

Cranial nerves

Twelve pairs of cranial nerves arise from the

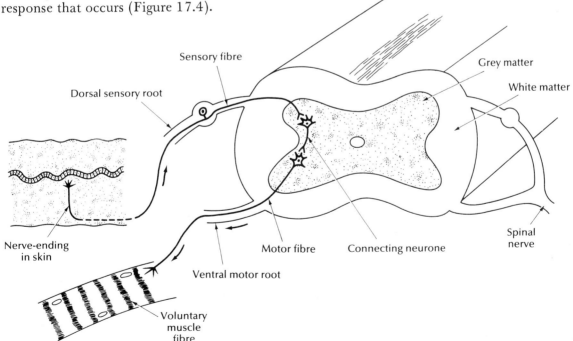

Sensory fibre

Grey matter

White matter

Dorsal sensory root

Nerve-ending in skin

Motor fibre

Connecting neurone

Spinal nerve

Ventral motor root

Voluntary muscle fibre

17.4   Reflex arc

brain connecting it mainly with various parts of the head and neck, although the tenth pair lead into the chest and abdomen. Some are purely sensory, some motor and others mixed. The chief ones which affect the head are the fifth and seventh pairs, while the eleventh pair go to the muscles of the neck (*see* Section 14.6).

Spinal nerves

Thirty-one pairs of spinal nerves arise from the spinal cord and are concerned with reflex actions. Each nerve is formed by the union of a dorsal sensory root and a ventral motor root. All the nerves are therefore mixed, containing both sensory and motor fibres. The cell bodies of the sensory fibres form a swelling known as a gangleon on the root. The nerves pass out between the vertebrae in order to reach the skin and other peripheral parts. Stimuli pass into the cord by the sensory root and leave it by the motor root.

17.6   REFLEX ACTION

A reflex action or automatic response to a stimulus requires no conscious effort. Coughing and sneezing are examples, as well as withdrawing the hand when it touches an object which is very hot. These automatic responses follow a set pattern in five stages:

  (*a*) a group of receptors receive a stimulus;
  (*b*) an impulse travels along the sensory root of a spinal nerve into the spinal cord;
  (*c*) the impulse is relayed to a communicating cell;
  (*d*) an impulse now leaves the cord along the motor root in order to reach the appropriate effectors (muscles or glands);
  (*e*) finally the effectors bring about the response, muscles by contraction and glands by secretion.

These reactions are extremely fast to try to ensure that the body is not harmed.

An example of a reflex action would be the withdrawing of the hand from a hot object.

When a hot object is touched, receptors in the skin, which are sensitive to heat, receive a stimulus. This causes impulses to pass along sensory, dorsal nerve fibres into the spinal cord. Communicating cells relay these impulses to motor fibres in the ventral root. In this way, a stimulus reaches the muscles which will be involved in removing the hand from the hot object (Figure 17.4).

Usually, several reflexes are associated with one stimulus. For instance, the response in the previous example may be accompanied by a cry or by the shedding of tears.

The path taken by the impulses in a reflex action is known as a *reflex arc*.

The nerve cells involved in these reactions do not have any actual contact, but are linked by interlacing processes from the neurones. Special packing tissue or neuroglia holds the cells together and the gap between the interlacing fibres is called a *synapse* (Figure 17.5).

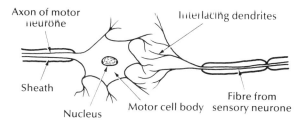

17.5   Synapse

Communication with the brain

Impulses received by the spinal cord are relayed to the brain so that we are conscious of automatic actions taking place. This communication is important because there are times when the brain needs to inhibit a response. For example, although one recoils from a pin prick, one does not recoil when having an injection.

Conditioned reflexes can occur where the response appears to be unrelated to the stimulus. For example, in response to the ringing of a bell, a dog may move towards the kitchen with its mouth 'watering'. This occurs if the dog has been 'conditioned' into associating the bell with food.

17.7 THE AUTONOMIC NERVOUS SYSTEM

The involuntary or autonomic nervous system deals with the automatic control of many of the organs, for example, the beating of the heart, breathing movements and the contraction of muscles in the skin. It is divided into two parts, one for stimulating an action and the other for checking it. An organ has a supply from both parts so that a balance can be achieved. The part which has a stimulating effect is the sympathetic nervous system. Its nerve fibres are linked to ganglia (swellings of nerve tissue) in front of the spine and communicating with the spinal cord by special branches. The part which has a retarding or checking effect is the parasympathetic nervous system. Its nerve fibres accompany some of the cranial and spinal nerves.

By having both parts, the organs can be controlled automatically to suit the needs of the body. This can be likened to the use of the accelerator and brake pedals of a car to achieve varying speeds which suit different road conditions.

17.8 THE ENDOCRINE SYSTEM AND BEHAVIOUR

Glands of internal secretion or ductless glands form the endocrine system. Their secretions enter the bloodstream directly and, in this way, are distributed to the body tissues which they will influence. Endocrine secretions contain *hormones*, chemical substances which influence the behaviour of body cells. Hormones are thus known as chemical messengers. Some of them can influence the texture of skin and the growth of hair. Endocrine glands are situated in various parts of the body, the master gland, the *pituitary*, being on the

underside of the brain. Various hormones from this gland have a widespread effect on the body, some of them influencing the activity of other endocrine glands, hence the term master gland.

The *thyroid gland* in the neck secretes thyroxine, a hormone which controls the rate of metabolism or body chemistry. Thyroxine contains iodine, hence the need to include iodine in the diet. A lack of this hormone causes the hair to become thin and the texture of the skin to become coarse. The *parathyroid glands*, situated close to the thyroid, secrete a hormone which controls the amount of calcium and phosphorus in the blood, two more important mineral substances needed in the diet. The *supra-renal glands* lie in front of the kidneys, secreting steroids and adrenalin. A shortage of the former can affect the pigmentation of the skin. The *islets of Langerhans* situated in the pancreas, secrete the hormone insulin which controls carbohydrate metabolism in the body. A shortage of insulin causes the disease diabetes in which the sufferer needs to control his carbohydrate intake and may also require insulin injections. The *reproductive organs*, the ovaries in the female and the testes in the male, secrete hormones which influence secondary sexual characteristics, that is the features particularly associated with masculinity or femininity, for example the growth of facial hair in men. In addition, the female hormones, oestrogen and progesterone, control the menstrual cycle and the changes associated with pregnancy.

17.9 THE REPRODUCTIVE SYSTEM

In mammals, new individuals are produced by sexual reproduction, involving two parents and the union of special reproductive cells or *gametes*.

The female gametes or *ova* and the male gametes or *spermatazoa* are produced in the reproductive organs, the ovaries of the female and the testes of the male. The union of a single ovum and a single spermatazoon results in a fertilized egg or *zygote*. This grows, by cell division, into an individual and growth continues during childhood and adolescence and stops, after about twenty years, except for a number of special parts such as skin and hair which continue to grow. At *puberty*, there is a gradual transition from childhood to adult life and during this period of adolescence, many changes occur in the body.

The reproductive parts of the body become more active and a person becomes aware of sexual feelings. The secondary sexual characteristics develop under hormonal influence. Testosterone, the male hormone, influences the growth of facial hair, the breaking (deepening) of the voice and the enlargement of the reproductive organs. In the female body the breasts or mammary glands develop (hence the name mammals) and the menstrual cycle begins. At first, it may be slightly irregular, but approximately once a month a mature ovum is released from the ovary. This is termed *ovulation*. Sexual intercourse or *copulation* introduces spermatazoe into the female body. *Fertilization* occurs if one of these sperms fuses with the ovum in the oviduct of the female. The fertilized egg or zygote travels to the womb, becomes embedded and continues development during nine months of *pregnancy* until the birth of a new baby.

If the ovum is not fertilized after ovulation, it dies and another one matures and is released the following month. This continues from puberty until the *menopause* or change of life when the ovary stops releasing ova and a woman can no longer bear children.

Menstruation is a monthly event in the cycle of changes which occur in the female body. Ovulation is stimulated by female hormones which also influence the lining of the womb to thicken in preparation for a possible pregnancy. When ovulation is not followed by fertilization, the thickened lining is not required and so breaks down and leaves the body as the menstrual flow, again under hormonal influence. In the event of pregnancy the hormone progesterone prevents menstrua-tion from occuring and keeps the foetus in the womb.

During the menstrual period of the cycle, personal cleanliness is extremely important. Daily bathing or washing is essential to avoid any unpleasant odours.

Development of the embryo

Once an ovum has been fertilized, it begins to undergo cell division and by the time it is embedded in the womb, it is already an *embryo*, a group of cells developing into an individual. After five weeks it becomes known as a *foetus*, and the nourishment of this developing baby is carried out through the *placenta*, a special organ which develops in the wall of the womb in pregnancy. An *umbilical cord*, containing blood vessels, attaches the foetus to the placenta. Through these blood vessels, food and oxygen are carried into the foetus from the mother, and waste products from the foetus are returned to the mother's bloodstream for removal. The foetus is surrounded by a water sac for protection during the *gestation period*, the development time in the womb. When this is completed, *parturition* or delivery of the new baby is brought about by contractions of the muscular wall of the womb, known as *labour*. After the birth, in which the baby leaves the birth canal head first, the umbilical cord is cut and the placenta is expelled from the mother's body as the after-birth.

Abortion or termination of a pregnancy, causes the death of the foetus and its subsequent expulsion from the body.

A sexual relationship should be a loving relationship so that babies are looked after by caring parents. Promiscuous behaviour can damage health, since it can lead to 'unwanted' pregnancies and mental distress. In addition, there is a very real danger of the spread of sexually transmitted diseases and parasites, such as the crab louse (*see* Section 19.6).

17.10 QUESTIONS

1 Show how the structure of the spinal cord enables it to carry out reflex actions. In your answer, give an example of a reflex action which could occur in the salon and explain how it works.
2 Explain the difference between (*a*) a motor neurone and a sensory neurone and (*b*) a spinal nerve and a cranial nerve.
3 What is meant by an endocrine gland? Give an account of the effects on the body of the secretion from the thyroid and parathyroid glands.
4 Give an account of the effects on the body of the sex hormones in both males and females at the onset of puberty.
5 Explain the difference between the following terms: (*a*) gamete and zygote, (*b*) ovulation and fertilization, (*c*) menstruation and menopause, (*d*) gestation and parturition.

17.11 MULTIPLE CHOICE QUESTIONS

1 The maintenance of balance and an upright posture is the concern of the:
(*a*) cerebellum
(*b*) medulla oblongata
(*c*) cerebral hemispheres
(*d*) spinal cord?

2 Which of the following provides nerves to the forehead and brow:
(*a*) autonomic nerves
(*b*) cranial nerves
(*c*) spinal nerves
(*d*) sympathetic nerves?
3 The point of communication between neighbouring nerve cells, across which the impulse is passed, is called the:
(*a*) nucleus
(*b*) axon
(*c*) synapse
(*d*) dendron?
4 Which of the following is believed to be one of the causes of male pattern baldness:
(*a*) androgens
(*b*) oestrogens
(*c*) thyroxin
(*d*) insulin?
5 The secretion of the testes is believed to be responsible for the growth of hair on the:
(*a*) scalp
(*b*) thyroid
(*c*) pubes
(*d*) axilla?
6 In which part of the female reproductive system are the ova formed:
(*a*) uterus
(*b*) vagina
(*c*) fallopian tube
(*d*) placenta?

18 The Skin and Hair

The mammalian skin, which is a protective epithelium covering the whole body, has hairs growing from it.

The *scalp*, the skin covering the head, fits over an *aponeurosis*, a broad flat sheet of connective tissue, and has terminal hairs which are longer and stronger than those on other parts of the body. A knowledge of the hair and the skin from which it grows is helpful to the hairdresser.

18.1 NOURISHMENT OF THE SKIN AND HAIR

Skin and hair grow as a result of nutrients reaching them through the blood capillaries found in the skin and hair roots. Protein is required for building new cells; the protein keratin is present in hair. Water forms an essential part of the cytoplasm in the cells. Vitamins A, B complex and C all affect the growth of skin, and iodine, a mineral substance, is present in the hormone thyroxine which controls the rate of growth.

18.2 SKIN STRUCTURE

There are two parts to the skin, the epidermis, or outer skin, and the dermis, or true skin, from which the hairs grow.

Epidermis

The outer skin is separated from the dermis by a distinctive wavy outline at the base, the *malpighian* or germinative layer. The pattern of folds in this basal layer is reflected at the surface and is responsible for individual fingerprints. The prominent nuclei of the cells divide to form new cells which are gradually pushed upwards towards the surface. The pigment, melanin, which determines the colour of skin and hair, is present in the malpighian layer. As there are no blood vessels in the epidermis, the new cells being pushed towards the surface gradually die until they become mere scales. Four layers can be distinguished above the malpighian layer as indicated in Figure 18.1.

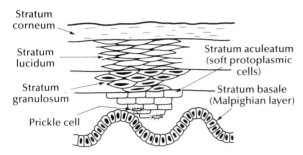

Stratum corneum
Stratum lucidum
Stratum granulosum
Prickle cell
Stratum aculeatum (soft protoplasmic cells)
Stratum basale (Malpighian layer)

18.1 The five layers of the epidermis. The relative thickness of the layers varies

(*a*) The prickle-cell layer, *stratum aculaetum*, contains soft protoplasmic cells, some of which bear tiny outgrowths or prickles.

(*b*) The granular layer, *stratum granulosum*, has nucleated cells with granular protoplasm, but the cells are becoming flatter.

(*c*) The clear layer, *stratum lucidum*, has cells in which the nuclei have died and thus they appear clear.

(*d*) Finally, the outer horny layer, *stratum corneum*, has flat, scale-like cells which have become keratinized (hardened) forming a protective layer at the surface. They prevent the entry of germs and the loss of water. They are constantly shed due to friction and are replaced by the other cells moving upwards from the basal layer.

Dermis

Below the epidermis is the true skin or dermis containing elastic tissue, blood vessels and nerve endings. Hair follicles, containing hairs, and numerous glands are also found in this region. The surface of the dermis has numerous *papillae*, projections which jut up into the epidermis and contain nerve endings and capillary loops. The nerve endings of touch end in rounded bodies or tactile corpuscles, while nerves of pain have delicate branched endings. Coiled sweat glands (sudoriferous glands) in the dermis have ducts leading to the surface and ending in pores. Sebaceous glands accompany the hair follicles to provide the lubricating grease or sebum (Figure 18.2).

Hair and hair follicles

Hairs grow from small pits in the skin known as hair follicles and lined with epidermis. The development of the hair usually starts by part of the epidermis pushing downwards to meet a small portion of dermis which forms a hair papilla. It is from this dermal papilla that the hair grows. Nutrients, required for growth are carried, in the blood, to the blood capillaries in the dermal papilla. A

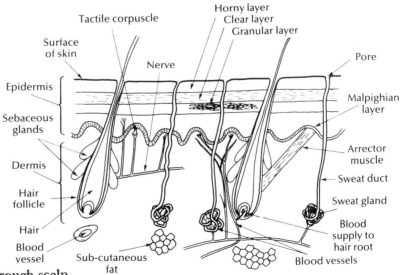

Tactile corpuscle
Surface of skin
Nerve
Horny layer
Clear layer
Granular layer
Pore
Epidermis
Sebaceous glands
Dermis
Hair follicle
Hair
Blood vessel
Sub-cutaneous fat
Malpighian layer
Arrector muscle
Sweat duct
Sweat gland
Blood supply to hair root
Blood vessels

18.2 Section of skin through scalp

thickened layer of epidermal cells form the hair-bulb which fits over the hair papilla (Figure 18.2). The lining of the hair follicle is arranged in two layers, forming an inner and an outer root sheath.

Cell division occurs in the dermal papilla and the new cells pushed into the follicle are cut off from the blood supply and become keratinized. The cells are differentiated into three layers (*see* Section 8.5):

(*a*) the inner medulla or pith;

(*b*) the outer cortex of elongated spindle-shaped cells; and

(*c*) the cuticle of scale-like cells overlapping upwards. The cuticle adhering to the cortex gives the sheen to the hair, and a disturbance of this arrangements, as for example in back-combing, may cause hair to lack lustre.

The medulla may be absent in the fine *lanugo* or *vellus* hairs of the body.

The hair shaft projects from the follicle. The hair root is embedded in the follicle.

The colour of the hair depends on the pigment in the malpighian layer. Absence of pigment makes the hair appear grey or white.

18.3   HAIR GROWTH CYCLE

If a hair grows to a certain length, it then stops growing, becomes loose and falls out. It is replaced by a new hair growing from the same follicle and growth will continue as long as the root remains healthy. Hairs do not grow continuously but alternate between the growing phase or anagen and the resting phase or telogen. The intermediate phase is known as catagen. There are always some follicles resting. At the end of the natural life of each hair, it becomes club-shaped and rises in the follicle. The club-hair is displaced by the new one which grows from the papilla. The new hair may grow past the old hair before it falls out, thus two hairs may appear to be growing from one follicle (Figure 18.3).

18.4   FACTORS AFFECTING HAIR GROWTH AND HEALTH

The rate of hair growth is affected by the age and sex of a person, the diet, glandular secretions, general health and the state of the nerves.

Age and Sex

The rate of growth is faster is women than men and is usually fastest in young people. With age, natural thinning may occur in both sexes, and it is believed that after the age of sixty-five, long hairs do not usually make any further growth. Hairfall or baldness is hereditary. Male pattern baldness may develop even in young men. If baldness starts early in life, its progress is usually rapid and complete, whereas with a later start, progress is usually slower. Excessive exposure to ultra-violet radiation can speed up the process. Female pattern baldness is less frequent and less extensive.

Diet

Malnutrition may affect hair growth. Hair contains keratin, a type of protein, therefore protein deficiency will affect growth. In the case of baldness, however, hair growth cannot be induced by an improved protein diet.

General health and the nervous system

The general health of the body and the state

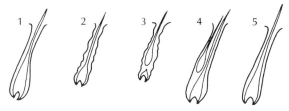

18.3   Hair growth cycle: 1 Hair stops growing; 2 Follicle shrinks, hair becomes club-shaped; 3 New hair starts to grow; 4 Follicle lengthens, new hair grows past the old; 5 Club hair has fallen out

of the nervous system may show their effects on hair growth. Usually hair growth is slower during illness, but quicker during convalescence. Excessive worry or mental work, as well as sudden shocks to the nervous system, may cause exhaustion of the scalp and lack of hair growth.

Alopecia (circular bald patches) is sometimes attributed to nervous factors, though the actual cause is unknown. There is no specific treatment and recovery is usually spontaneous. Alopecia, due to traction, causes hair loss around the scalp margin (*see* Chapter 19) particularly if the hair is fine. Hairfall may also result from diseases of the scalp, some of which are also dealt with in Chapter 19.

Glandular secretions

The endocrine (ductless) glands play a part in influencing hair growth and hair loss. For example, an over-active thyroid gland will result in increased hair growth, but under-activity results in dry skin and some hair loss.

Sebaceous glands

Associated with hair follicles are small flask-shaped sebaceous glands (Figure 18.2). They secrete a lubricating oil known as sebum into the follicle to lubricate the hair and the skin. It keeps the hair glossy and prevents breakage. Overproduction of sebum leads to the hair looking greasy and lank. Regular washing removes the grease together with dust and *micro-organisms*. Lack of sebum leads to dry hair which loses its gloss and tends to be brittle, causing breakage. Special care is needed to maintain healthy hair and skin (*see* Chapter 20).

18.5 TEMPERATURE CONTROL BY THE SKIN

In man, the body temperature is constant at about 37°C (98.4°F). The temperature is kept constant by a delicate balance between heat production and heat loss, helped by the sweat glands and blood vessels in the skin. Heat production occurs by internal combustion and this is increased during exercise.

Heat loss occurs through perspiration, breathing, elimination of waste, conduction, convection and radiation.

The adjustment between heat production and heat loss is controlled by the heat regulation centre in the brain. Sweat glands in the skin assist this regulation by increasing the evaporation of sweat if the body is overheated and reducing it if the body is cool.

Sweat glands (sudoriferous glands) are coiled tubular glands in the dermis. Ducts from these glands pass through the epidermis and open as pores on the skin surface. These glands secrete a watery solution composed of about 98 per cent water and less than 2 per cent dissolved substances including sodium chloride (salt) and a small amount of carbamide (urea). Sweating uses up body heat to evaporate this secretion from the skin surface. Small amounts are not noticeable (insensible perspiration), but we are conscious of larger amounts (sensible perspiration). During exercise, increased heat-production is balanced by increased sweating. During rest, decreased heat-production is balanced by decreased sweating and by contraction of the blood vessels in the skin. Excessive sweating, *hyperidrosis*, is often due to nervous or other disorders.

Blood vessels

Many blood capillaries are found in the dermis. Some capillaries loop into the hair papillae bringing nutrients to the hair roots. Others loop round the sweat glands bringing the waste products which are eliminated in sweat. Blood vessels near the surface may become dilated (vaso-dilation) when the body is over-heated. The skin reddens and *radiation* causes heat to be lost to the air surrounding the skin.

Conduction of heat occurs by the trans-

EPIDERMIS	Horny zone	Protection from bacterial invasion and mechanical damage. Protection from water loss
	Living zone	Growth of new skin cells. Pigmentation giving colour
DERMIS	Elastic connective tissue	Makes skin supple
	Hair follicles	Growth of hairs
	Sebaceous glands	Secretion of sebum for lubrication of skin and and hair
	Arrector muscles	Altering direction of hair at the surface
	Sweat glands	Heat regulation. Slight excretion of carbamide (urea)
	Blood vessels	Transport of nutrients. Heat regulation
	Nerve endings	Sensation of touch, heath, cold and pain
	Sub-cutaneous fat	Insulation. Attachment for muscles

Table 18.1   Summary of functions of the skin

mission of heat to clothing and other objects in contact with the skin. *Convection* causes heat loss by air currents in contact with the skin.

When the body is cool, blood vessels in the skin contract (vasocontraction), thus reducing radiation and conduction since the blood vessels are further away from the surface. The skin appears paler.

Although heat is lost when warm air is breathed out from the lungs and when urine and faeces are eliminated, sweating is the main method of controlling and maintaining a constant body temperature.

Arrector muscles, tiny muscles associated with the hair follicles, can contract when the skin is cold. The contraction generates a small amount of heat, and pulls on the follicles causing goose-pimples on the skin surface. Contraction of these muscles alters the position of the follicle making the hair stand on end in the event of a fright.

An insulating layer of sub-cutaneous fat separates the skin from the underlying muscles.

18.6   QUESTIONS

1 Make a labelled diagram of the skin as seen in section.
 Explain how the skin helps in the regulation of body temperature.

2 Explain the importance of blood capillaries in the skin with reference to (*a*) growth of hairs, (*b*) secretion, (*c*) excretion, and (*d*) control of body temperature.

3 Describe briefly the three stages in the hair growth cycle and give an account of the factors which can affect the growth of hair.

4 The body maintains a balance between heat production and heat loss in order to keep the temperature constant.
 How is heat produced in the body and in what ways can heat be lost?

5 Give an account of the development and growth of hair.
 How is the hair (*a*) nourished and (*b*) lubricated?

18.7 MULTIPLE CHOICE QUESTIONS

1 The name of the muscle which can move the hair in its follicle is the:
(a) auricularis anterior
(b) arrector pili
(c) frontalis
(d) occipitalis?

2 What amount of water is present in the skin and its under-lying tissues:
(a) 12.5%
(b) 25%
(c) 50%
(d) 75%?

3 If a person develops a high body temperature above 40°C this condition is called:
(a) hypothermia
(b) hyperthermia
(c) hyperaemia
(d) erythema?

4 The hair papilla is a part of one of the following layers of the skin:
(a) horny layer
(b) granular layer
(c) dermal layer
(d) basal layer?

5 The hairs which grow on the body surface of the baby and which are shed before its birth are called:
(a) awns
(b) bristles
(c) lanugo
(d) kemp?

6 The monthly rate of growth of hair on the head is about:
(a) 1.25 mm
(b) 10.25 cm
(c) 0.125 mm
(d) 1.25 cm?

Section Four

Diseases, Hygiene, First Aid and Safety

19 Disorders of the Skin and Hair

There is a variety of ways in which disorders of the skin and hair may arise.

Some may be infectious or contagious and there is a danger of these being spread in the salon. Infections are due to the invasion of the body by microscopic organisms such as fungi, bacteria and viruses, and these may spread rapidly. Infestations occur when small animal parasites live on the host's body, obtaining food and shelter from it.

Other disorders are non-infectious and have a physiological cause such as over-active or under-active glands. Some have their origin in the nervous system and others are inherited conditions. The weather and the effects of age may affect the skin and hair also.

In the hairdressing salon chemical and mechanical damage to the hair and skin must be avoided. Harsh treatment and contact with irritant substances can produce dermatitis, damage to the hair shaft and even baldness.

19.1 PATHOGENS AND NON-PATHOGENS

Organisms which cause infections are known as pathogens or pathogenic organisms, and are present in dust, in the atmosphere, on the body and on many articles. There are also some non-pathogenic (harmless) organisms and others which are actually helpful to man, living inside the body (commensals).

Dust and dirt harbour micro-organisms such as bacteria, viruses and fungal spores.

Bacteria

Bacteria are micro-organisms, many of which are pathogenic and could spread in an unhygienic salon. They are minute, unicellular organisms, invisible to the naked eye and difficult to see under the microscrope unless stained. They have no apparent nucleus but the nuclear material is thought to be scattered throughout the cytoplasm. Their shape varies. Cocci are round and appear in pairs, chains or bunches. They are non-motile. Rod-shaped bacteria may be straight (bacilli) or curved (spirilla) and may move by the lashing of thread-like flagella which may be present (Figure 19.1). Spirochaetes are tightly coiled or cork-screw shaped and move by undulating

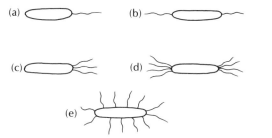

19.1   **Bacteria, showing flagella: (*a*) single flagellum at one end; (*b*) single flagellum at each end; (*c*) several flagella at one end; (*d*) several flagella at each end; (*e*) numerous flagella all over**

or rotary movements. They may also be flagellate. They are measured in micrometres (μm) and their size varies from 0.2μm for some bacilli to 40μm for some spirilla (1μm = 1/1000mm).

Despite their small size, each bacterial cell is a complete and independent unit of life which can carry out the normal functions of living organisms such as nutrition, growth, respiration and reproduction. Nutrition occurs when soluble food enters the cell and growth occurs if the temperature is favourable. The warmth and humidity of a hairdressing salon provides suitable conditions for the growth and multiplication of bacteria. Reproduction occurs by simple transverse fission (Figure 19.2). The cell becomes constricted in the middle, the constriction deepens and finally

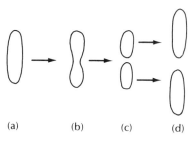

19.2   **Stages in bacterial division: (*a*) bacterium ready to divide; (*b*) constriction appears; (*c*) bacterium separates into two halves; (*d*) each half grows and the cycle is then repeated**

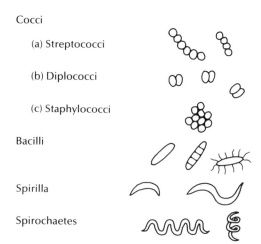

Cocci

  (a) Streptococci

  (b) Diplococci

  (c) Staphylococci

Bacilli

Spirilla

Spirochaetes

19.3   **Classification of bacteria according to shape**

the organism splits into two halves. Each half grows and the cycle is repeated every twenty minutes in good conditions, resulting in a phenomenal number in a few hours. A group which has developed from a single bacterium in this way is known as a colony and is visible to the naked eye. An organism may be recognized by the appearance of its colony.

The different shapes of bacteria are shown in Figure 19.3 and many of these are normal inhabitants of the skin, the scalp, the mouth, nose and throat. They can be spread by hands and dirty nails, and by coughing and sneezing which expels them into the atmosphere. Bacteria breathed in from a polluted atmosphere may cause respiratory infections. Those transferred by touch may enter the hair follicles causing suppurating (pus-forming) infections such as boils, pimples, carbuncles and abcesses. Others may enter cuts and scratches on the scalp, for example scissors and razor cuts or scratches from combs.

Viruses

Viruses are organisms not visible by ordinary microscopic methods, their size being less than 0.2 μm. These are called ultra-microscopic viruses and are responsible for a number of infections such as the common cold, warts, shingles, smallpox and many others. Like bacteria, they may be spherical or rod-shaped, but unlike bacteria, they are always found within living cells and have never been cultivated in cell-free media. They are believed to be composed of a core of nucleic acid covered by a protein shell. Many of them are extremely harmful to the body.

Fungi

Fungi are composed of threads or hyphae which form the body or mycelium of the fungus. Some primitive fungi such as yeast are unicellular. There are some microscopic fungi which are spread by invisible spores present in dust or in the atmosphere. If these spores invade the skin or hair follicles, they can cause diseases such as athlete's food, ringworm and others. The spores germinate in moist, warm conditions, hence a hairdressing salon is an ideal environment for their spread.

19.2   RECOGNITION OF SKIN DISORDERS

The hairdresser has a responsibility to all clients, and should therefore be able to recognize the symptoms of some skin disorders and infections in order to differentiate between the infectious and the non-infectious conditions.

19.3   FUNGAL INFECTIONS

Ringworm (*Tinia tonsurans*) is a fungal infection of which there are different types. Ringworm of the scalp is caused by either *Microsporon*, a small-spored fungus, or *Trichophyton*, a large-spored variety. When the fungal spores enter the follicles, their germination causes damage to the hairs. This results in the formation of circular bald patches. The infected hairs become dull and brittle and

break off. These are highly contagious and can easily be transmitted to combs, curlers, towels, neck strips and gowns. The infection could spread in an unhygienic salon.

Favus or Honeycomb Ringworm is caused by a different *Trichophyton*. It results in cup-shaped discs each pierced by a hair. Pus-producing crusts are formed which have an orange or yellow colour accompanied by a mousy smell and intense irritation. Ringworm is treated by the application of anti-fungal agents to the affected skin areas.

Another form of *Tinea* causes Athlete's foot — *see* Chapter 20.

Trichomatosis is another fungoid condition causing the hair to become matted.

19.4   BACTERIAL INFECTIONS

Impetigo is a bacterial infection (staphylocci) which can be spread not only by direct contact, but also by contact with towels, gowns or other articles that the infected person has used. Blisters develop on the face, particularly around the mouth, nose and eyes. When these dry up, yellowish scabs appear and the affected parts itch. If a client with impetigo seeks a hair-dressing appointment, she should be discreetly advised to wait until the infectious condition has cleared up.

Boils are inflamed spots caused by staphyloccal bacteria gaining entrance to the hair follicles. As the boil develops, more blood circulates to the spot causing an inflamed, painful swelling which comes to a head and bursts. The resulting suppuration causes pus (matter) to be exuded which is very contagious, and hence undesirable in the salon.

Sycosis is inflammation of the hair follicles of the beard, folliculitis. It is due to the entry of cocci or bacilli and is also known as barber's itch.

Conjunctivitis is inflammation of the conjunctiva, the lining of the eyelids. This bacterial infection can be transmitted by towels. Antibiotics are used to treat these bacterial infections.

19.5   VIRAL INFECTIONS

Warts are thought to be caused by the infection of the skin with a virus. Increased cell division occurs in the skin papillae resulting in raised portions of epidermis with a thickened horny layer (a kind of small tumour). The wart usually grows outwards, except on the feet (plantar warts) where it grows inwards and becomes painful. Small flat warts known as plane warts often disappear spontaneously. Verruca is the Latin name for a wart, but the term is commonly used for warts on the feet.

The Common Cold is a virus infection causing a streaming nose and sneezing. A sneeze, a violent expiration, causes viruses to enter the atmosphere, thus spreading the infection when other people breathe in the contaminated air. Tissues are preferable to handkerchieves and should be burned.

Cold sores are caused by a virus, *Herpes simplex*. They occur around the mouth and nostrils and the sores and blisters often accompany another infection. Vitamin C deficiency results in cracks at the corners of the mouth, and these cracks may become infected.

19.6   PARASITIC INFESTATIONS

The skin may become infested with small living creatures or parasites which obtain food and shelter from the host. Organisms infesting the surface of the body are known as ectoparasites, and may spread from one host to another.

Pediculosis is an infestation with pediculi or lice. There are different varieties.

The head louse, *Pediculus capitis*, lives amongst the hairs on the head, and punctures the skin with special mouth parts in order to suck blood from the scalp. The punctures cause irritation and may become infected with bacteria (secondary infection). The female louse, slightly larger than the male, is about 2 mm in length and lays batches of eggs called nits. These white oval-shaped nits are cemented to the hairs by a sticky secretion

from the female. They are laid in the nape of the neck and behind the ears. They hatch in about a week and are fully grown in ten days to three weeks. Multiplication is therefore rapid. The adults cling to the hairs by means of three pairs of clawed legs, so cannot be dislodged by an ordinary comb. Special shampoos can be obtained for the treatment of pediculosis, but the nits require a solvent to dislodge them from the hairs. Lice can be transferred to another person by towels, gowns and hairnets.

The body louse, *Pediculus vestimenti*, attaches itself to clothing near the skin. It is similar to but slightly larger than the head louse. The eggs are laid in the seams or folds of garments and hatch in about two weeks. Like the head louse, the body louse punctures the skin to suck blood, thus causing irritation and the danger of secondary infection. Head lice can live on the body, and body lice on the head if they are accidentally transferred.

The crab louse, *Pthirius pubis*, is smaller than the other two types and has a different shape as the name indicates. It occurs in the pubic region or on other parts of the body where there are short hairs, for example, the armpits. The brown nits are cemented to the hairs as in the headlouse.

Scabies is an infestation sometimes through sexual contact, with the itch-mite or *Acarus scabiei*, now called *Sarcoptes Scabiei*, a small parasite which causes intense irritation. The female mite burrows under the skin where it is thin and wrinkled, for instance, between the fingers and on the skin in front of the wrist. Scratching releases the eggs from the burrows and causes the disease to spread, as well as leading to secondary infection. Treatment is with emulsion of benzyl benzoate. It is also treated at special clinics.

The face mite, *Demodex folliculorum* is sometimes found in blackheads. It has a minute worm-like body and eight very tiny legs and is found where the skin is greasy and sebum tends to accumulate. As the name suggests, it lives in the hair follicles, particularly where an abundance of sebum is produced.

The common flea is a small brown wingless insect, about 40 mm long. It has powerful back legs enabling it to jump from one host to another, therefore it is easy to pick up. The female lays eggs in dust, in cracks in floorboards and in dirty mattresses. The eggs hatch in a few days and the insect is fully developed in about four weeks. It bites humans to suck blood, causing red spots on the skin. The punctures could become infected.

19.7 SYSTEMIC AND GLANDULAR DISORDERS – NON-INFECTIOUS

Several non-infectious disorders may occur due to malfunction of a body system.

Dandruff or *seborrhoea* is a scaly condition due to excessive secretion of sebum from the sebaceous glands. The sebum collects on the scalp as an oily coating which dries to form scales or crusts. Dandruff may be greasy or dry and the superficial horny layers of the skin are shed as scales. Inflammation may occur owing to bacterial infection causing *seborrhoeic dermatitis*. In the treatment of greasy seborrhoea, hair should be shampooed every few days. Excessive shampooing, however, may aggravate dry seborrhoea.

Pityriasis or *fine dandruff* occurs by desquamation, loss of fine scales, on the scalp and beard. If scaling is heavy, the scales adhere to the skin thus restricting the flow of sebum and causing the hair to become dry with no lustre.

Comedones or *blackheads* occur when excessive sebum solidifies in the outlets or pores of the sebaceous glands, thus causing a blockage. The accumulated sebum turns black from oxidation, hence the term blackhead. The sebum needs to be softened by a suitable solvent. This is preferable to manual removal of the blackheads.

Acne vulgaris is a condition which often occurs at puberty when hormones influence body changes and the sebaceous glands increase their activity. The ducts of the sebaceous glands may become blocked with dried grease. Seborrhoea (excessive secretion of sebum) may cause inflammatory spots on the skin, specially on the face and neck. Blackheads are a frequent feature and septic spots are visible. The condition requires medical treatment. Acne usually disappears in adult life.

Eczema is attributed to nerves. Some people have an inherited predisposition to eczema, inflamed scaly patches on the skin accompanied by burning and itching sensations. It may be dry eczema or the moist or weeping variety where there are blisters which exude fluid.

Psoriasis is somewhat similar to eczema, but the patches are covered with silvery scales – usually on the scalp, arms and back.

Alopecia is a condition where circular bald patches appear on the scalp. Possible causes include malnutrition, eye-strain, mental strain, glandular disorders, systemic disorders or inheritance. Also, the increasing use of chemotherapy against cancer cells may cause complete alopecia. As treatment is intermittent or for a limited period, hair growth begins again soon after treatment ceases.

Alopecia areata is the commonest type seen as patches of baldness on the scalp or beard. The hair becomes dry and brittle, and surrounding the edge of the patch are short exclamation mark hairs. This type of alopecia usually disappears and new hairs grow, but it may be some months before normal hair growth occurs. Egg shampoos can be useful.

Hirsuties or *hypertrichosis* is the growth of superfluous hair, possibly caused by glandular disorders. Hair grows in areas where very fine (lanugo) hairs are normally present, or excessive hair growth occurs in normally hairy parts. Superfluous hair can be removed by electrolysis or by depilatories (*see* Section 8.2).

Canities is the greying of hair caused by absence of pigment (*see* Section 11.1).

19.8   HEREDITARY CONDITIONS

Freckles occur where there is an uneven distribution of pigment in the skin. They develop on exposure to sun when the pigment spots expand. Fair-haired and fair-skinned people often have freckles.

Moles are somewhat similar to freckles but they are raised from the skin surface and may be hairy.

Monilethrix is a condition in which the hair becomes moniliform, the shaft having a beaded appearance due to uneven growth.

19.9   DISORDERS CAUSED BY CONTACT WITH IRRITANT SUBSTANCES

Dermatitis or inflammation of the skin has many causes including local irritation due to substances to which a person is hypersensitive. The latter is known as *allergic dermatitis* and may be caused by hypersensitivity to cosmetics, hairdressing preparations, soaps, detergents, perfume and other substances. Some types of clothing may also have irritant effects.

Irritant chemical substances include oxidation dyes, bleaches, permanent waving lotions, hair lacquers, perfume, nail varnish, lipstick and talcum powder. Some man-made fibres irritate the skin. The reaction is due to a constitutional aversion to a particular substance, or idiosyncrasy. One person's constitution may accept contact with a substance which in another person produces an allergic reaction. In the hairdressing salon, hypersensitivity can be determined by patch tests. A little of the particular substance is applied to the client's skin and covered with collodion. It is left on for twenty-four to forty-eight hours (but no longer), and then the skin is examined for any reaction. If the substance proves to be an irritant it should not be used.

Many cosmetics and toiletries are now allergy-tested and known irritants are omitted. The use of moisturisers helps to keep the skin soft, thus reducing the risk of damage to the epidermis and the suceptibility to adverse effects.

Urticaria or nettle-rash appears as an allergic reaction to certain foods.

Twentieth century disease is the name given to total allergy to the majority of substances used in modern living.

Erythema may be caused by contact with some detergents and also by radiotherapy. Red burning patches appear on the skin. Chilblains are a type of erythema (*see* Section 19.11).

19.10   DISORDERS DUE TO HARSH TREATMENT

Alopecia may be caused by traction resulting in hair loss around the scalp margin, particularly if the hair is fine. It may be due to the use of stiff hair brushes, metal curlers, or curlers wound too tightly.

Trichonodosis is a shaft disorder where the hair develops a knotted appearance. It is due to the use of a harsh shampoo, which removes too much sebum, leaving the hair dry, rough and coarse.

Fragilitis artefactus is the splitting of hair due to the application of chemicals.

19.11   EFFECTS OF THE WEATHER

Sunburn

In extremely sunny conditions, the skin may burn, if unprotected, resulting in tenderness and blisters. This is more common in fair-skinned people, whose skin contains less melanin, the pigment which gives some protection against the harmful rays of the sun.

Sun-filter creams, which filter out these hamful rays, are useful in preventing sunburn if applied before exposure (*see* Section 13.3).

Chilblains

In extremely cold weather, inflamed areas may occur, usually on the fingers and toes, which are hot, swollen, painful and itchy. Sometimes the legs are affected also. The condition is often due to poor circulation so that the warmth of the blood does not reach these extremities. The wearing of suitable clothing, gloves and warm boots, for example, is helpful in avoiding chilblains.

19.12   AGEING OF THE SKIN

As one gets older, dryness can result from loss of moisture in the skin. Skin types vary but most people have some dry areas and some oily areas on the skin.

With age, the metabolism of the body tends to slow down. There may be a decrease in the activity of the sebaceous glands and the lack of sebum may cause the skin to lose its suppleness. The skin becomes drier and may flake. The cells may shrink due to water loss and this results in the appearance of lines and wrinkles. The effects of dehydration can be offset by the use of moisturisers. These replace some of the lost moisture so that the cells regain their plumpness, thus helping to smooth out lines and wrinkles. The cells of the dermis tend to lose their elasticity, with age. Nutrient creams may help to restore the elasticity and keep the cells healthy.

Another sign of ageing skin is the appearance of pigment spots which frequently occur on the arms and the backs of the hands. Skin care is important throughout life but particularly as one gets older. As the skin ages, the hair growing from it may also be affected. A lack of sebum will result in dry hair which loses its sheen. The use of moisturing shampoos and conditioners, and the avoidance of harsh chemicals and harsh mechanical treatment is important, particularly if the hair is fine. Hair often loses its pigment with age, becoming grey or silver, but there are many dyes and colorants available if people prefer not to have grey hair. The rate of hair growth is slower in older people and some thinning may occur, so careful styling is important. Regular skin care and hair care will keep older people looking healthy.

19.13   QUESTIONS

1 What is an infection and how is it transmitted?
  Give two examples of infections which could spread in the salon and what steps should be taken to prevent them spreading.
2 Explain what is meant by infestation with parasites. Name two parasites and describe how they can be (*a*) avoided, and (*b*) dealt with.
3 Name three contagious diseases you might meet in the salon.
  How would you recognize them and what action would you take?
4 Give one example of (*a*) a fungal infection of the scalp, (*b*) a staphylococcal skin infection, (*c*) a parasitic infestation of the scalp and (*d*) a viral infection of the skin.
  In each case describe the transmission, the symptoms and the treatment.
5 Give an account of the non-infectious conditions arising in the skin due to (*a*) disorders of the sebaceous glands, and (*b*) the effects of irritant substances on the skin.
6 Describe (*a*) the disorders which can occur in the hair shaft and (*b*) the different forms of alopecia.

19.14   MULTIPLE CHOICE QUESTIONS

1 A part of the human body which is comparatively free from harmful microbes in a healthy person is the:
  (*a*) skin
  (*b*) mouth
  (*c*) nose
  (*d*) heart?
2 Which of the following is a bacterial disease spread by direct contact:

(*a*) scabies
(*b*) influenza
(*c*) ringworm
(*d*) syphilis?

3 Which one of the following can resist high temperatures in sterilization processes and escape destruction:
(*a*) virus bodies
(*b*) bacteria cells
(*c*) bacteria spores
(*d*) yeast spores?

4 The bacterial inflammation of a hair follicle with a pustule and without crust formation or swelling of the surrounding tissue is a disorder called:
(*a*) a carbuncle
(*b*) a boil
(*c*) folliculitis
(*d*) impetigo?

5 Following the use of an oxidation hair dye, a person develops a red itching skin with vesicles breaking down to ooze fluid and form crusts. These signs could indicate:
(*a*) eczema
(*b*) psoriasis
(*c*) nettlerash
(*d*) acne?

6 Scalp ringworm is a disease seen as one of the following component structures when viewed through a microscope:
(*a*) fibres
(*b*) cocci
(*c*) hyphae
(*d*) nits?

20 Personal Hygiene

A hairdresser needs to present a pleasing, healthy, well-groomed image to the clientele. Since the work is exacting and tiring, consideration must be given to various aspects of health, both physical and mental. Posture and deportment are important as well as a clean, neat appearance. Special care is required for the health of the skin and hair, hands and feet, mouth and teeth.

20.1 CARE OF SKIN AND HAIR
(*See* also Sections 9.3 and 12.9.)

Since the skin is inhabited by many types of bacteria, it is important to clean the skin's surface by regular washing with soap and water. Sebum and sweat, together with shed epidermal cells need to be removed, and a daily bath is therefore advisable, or at least a shower or washdown.

A *warm bath* or shower is of the greatest importance for general health and cleanliness. Tepid baths can be stimulating and tone up the muscles. The friction used in drying will stimulate the circulation and thus improve the complexion. Sweat, if allowed to remain on the skin, may produce an unpleasant odour as well as clogging up the pores and interfering with the skin's function.

The condition of the skin and hair often reflect general health and nourishment. Clean, healthy hair, in an attractive style, gives confidence, which will be generated to the client.

Regular shampooing is necessary to remove accumulated sebum, dirt and bacteria. Some people have more active sebaceous glands than others, so hair may be 'greasy' or 'dry'. Sometimes hair is brittle or has suffered damage from various harsh treatments. Different types of shampoos are available to suit these different types of hair. In the treatment of greasy seborrhoea, hair should be shampooed every three or four days. The shampoo emulsifies the grease, which is then washed away together with the dirt particles. Hair which is very dry can be improved by the use of oily conditioners after shampooing.

Brushing and combing the hair are important in the removal of dust and scurf and to ensure that no parasites obtain a foothold. Combing smooths the hair, and brushing stimulates the sebaceous glands thus adding to the sheen. Combs should have blunt teeth which will not scratch the scalp as this would allow bacterial invasion. Brushes should have stiff bristles set separately and not too close together. Both brushes and combs should be kept scrupulously clean.

20.2 CARE OF HANDS AND FINGER NAILS (*see* also Section 13.10)

The hairdresser uses the hands constantly and needs to protect them from invasion by germs and also from damage by chemicals used in the salon. Bacteria multiply rapidly, so frequent washing of the hands is important to reduce the numbers. The skin acts as a barrier to bacteria, but only if it is not broken. Thorough drying of hands is necessary, to prevent chapping, and the use of barrier creams is helpful. Also, hand lotion will help to replace the natural oils which are lost in frequent washing. The wearing of rubber gloves will help to prevent damage to the skin by chemical substances used in hairdressing processes. Nails should be kept short and clean; bacteria breed in the dirt under fingernails and these can be transferred by the hands, thus spreading infection. The nails should be rounded to the shape of the finger ends.

A *nail* grows from a root of soft cells embedded in the epidermis. The nail-plate or body of the nail grows forwards on the nail-bed to which it is attached, except at the free border (Figure 20.1). Blood vessels in the nail-bed account for the pink colour when the nails are healthy. The nail lies in a nail groove within a fold of skin or cuticle. In front of this is the white lunula or half-moon. The side fold of skin is termed the nail-wall. Rough treatment may result in various disorders of both finger nails and toe nails.

Nail disorders

Inflammation may occur if a foreign body, for example a splinter, pierces the tissue associated with the nail. Micro-organisms may be introduced in this way.

Ingrowing nails are more common on the feet than the hands due to pressure from badly-fitting shoes or tight stockings and socks. The nail plate turns in at the edge and pierces the nail groove instead of growing forwards. Inflammation occurs and the condition is very painful.

Thickened nails may result from neglected ingrowing nails or from the use of press-on artificial nails. The nail plate becomes very thick and rough. It loses its healthy pink colour because it is too thick to reflect the colour of the blood underneath.

Ridged nails can develop due to the handling of some chemicals. The hairdresser is advised to wear gloves to avoid skin and nail disorders. Nail lacquers made from synthetic resin plastics give some protection to nails by reducing the water loss.

Ringworm of the nails is a fungal infection which damages the nail. Griseofulvin is used to treat the condition. The drug affects the disease in the nail bed and is retained in the nail growing up with it, a process taking at least six months. The affected nail is eventually snipped off.

20.3 CARE OF THE FEET

The hairdresser spends much of the working day on her feet and therefore special attention is needed to keep feet healthy.

Daily washing is necessary, and the skin

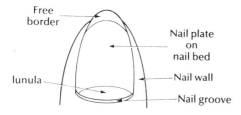

20.1   A nail

should be well dried afterwards. This is particularly important between the toes, since warmth and moisture encourage bacterial and fungal development. Athlete's foot is a fungal infection, ringworm of the foot which occurs between the toes causing the skin to go white and soft. The skin then peels, leaving a painful inflamed area. Anti-fungal powder can be applied or an antibiotic treatment can be used – griseofulvin.

Toe nails must be kept clean and should be cut straight across, to prevent the nail-borders from growing into the flesh instead of along the surface of the toe.

Choice of footwear is important to ensure that corns and collouses are not caused by pressure from badly-fitting shoes. The hairdresser needs to have comfortable feet, so heels should not be too high, for day wear, as this throws the body weight forward and leads to bad posture (*see* Section 20.10). Socks, stockings and tights should be washed daily and these too should fit properly.

The weight of the body is supported by the arches of the feet and these are strengthened by exercise. Obesity can put extra strain on the arches and lead to flat feet (fallen arches). A well-balanced diet is therefore important.

20.4   BALANCED DIET

A balanced diet should provide all the requirements of the body for energy supplies, growth and maintenance of health (*see* Section 15.8). In addition there should be sufficient fuel foods to supply the body's daily needs. Any surplus would lead to obesity with resulting strain on many parts of the body, such as the heart. An overweight hairdresser would soon feel tired after standing for a number of hours.

Diet can also affect the teeth, if these are not properly cared for.

20.5   CARE OF MOUTH AND TEETH

If food is left on the teeth, it may be fermented by bacteria in the mouth and result in tooth decay.

Teeth are outgrowths from the skin covering the jaw, with the crown of the tooth projecting, above the gum, into the mouth cavity. The root, whether single or multiple, is embedded in the jaw bone. A tooth is composed of ivory (dentine) with a hollow centre filled with living pulp. The soft connective tissue of the pulp contains nerve endings and blood vessels through which nutrients reach the tooth when it is growing. The crown of the tooth is protected by a coating of hard enamel (Figure 20.2). Mammals have two sets of teeth, the milk teeth and the permanent set. Tooth decay should be avoided by thorough brushing after meals. Fermentation of food particles in the mouth produces acids which can dissolve the enamel coating of the crown and start the process of decay (dental caries). Sugary foods are particularly harmful. If brushing is not possible after every meal, a crisp apple will help to dislodge particles of food from between the teeth. It has been discovered, however, that this increases the acidity in the mouth and it is better to finish a meal with a piece of cheese instead.

Tooth enamel is strengthened by fluoride which may be incorporated into toothpaste. Some local authorities add fluoride to the water supplies. Brushing the teeth at night

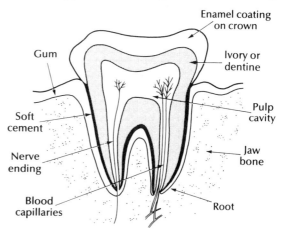

20.2   **Vertical section of molar tooth**

before retiring is important. The strokes should be vertical to clean the spaces between the teeth and also to massage the gums. The brush should be kept sterile by thorough rinsing and allowing it to dry in the air. Formation of plaque on the teeth harbours bacteria and leads to unhealthy gums. Resulting gum disease, gingivitis, may loosen the teeth in their sockets. Special toothbrushes are available to discourage the build-up of plaque.

Dental decay can lead to bad breath (halitosis) which is undesirable, and also allows the bacterial toxins to enter the bloodstream, thus poisoning the system.

Moniliasis or thrush is a fungal infection associated with lack of hygiene. The fungus causes white patches on the tongue and cheek lining. A mouthwash will usually clear it up.

20.6   SUITABLE CLOTHING

In the salon, a clean overall will look neat and will also give protection to the hairdresser against chemicals used in the work. Clothing helps to conserve body heat and so should be made of suitable materials for the conditions in the salon. It should be warm, but light in weight, and should allow free movement, especially of the arms. Clothing should not be constricting so that it does not interfere with the functions of the skin. Dark colours are warmer than light ones since they absorb light rays instead of reflecting them.

Retention of heat and moisture by the fibres of clothing varies. Loosely woven fabrics trap air and also retain moisture which evaporates slowly, thus lessening the danger of a chill.

Clothing materials

Natural fibres of both plant and animal origin are used for clothing, but many modern clothes are made from man-made fibres.

Wool is a natural material obtained from the skin of the sheep. The tubular fibres are loosely woven, thus trapping air between them. It is a poor conductor of heat and retains moisture which evaporates only slowly from it. Woollen garments are therefore warm and are worn usually as outer garments. They are warm next to the skin, but the fibres have serrated edges causing irritation to sensitive skins.

Silk is a natural material made from threads spun by the wilkworm. Like wool, it is a poor conductor of heat, and being soft and smooth, is suitable for underwear and glove linings. Because of its expense, its use has largely been replaced by artificial silk made from plant cellulose.

Cotton and linen are plant fibres and are good conductors of heat. They allow moisture to evaporate quickly from the surface. This makes them less suitable for wear next to the skin, as they could have a chilling effect if the body perspires. They are smooth and hard-wearing and are used for outer, cool summer garments. The flat, twisted cotton fibres are obtained from the seeds of the cotton plant. The branched, cylindrical linen fibres are obtained from flax plants.

Nylon is a man-made fibre. It is a poor conductor of heat and a poor absorber of moisture. It is therefore unsuitable for wear next to the skin. Being smooth and hard-wearing, however, it is suitable for overalls and other outer garments.

Leather comes from animal hides which are tanned or cured to preserve them. Being waterproof, it is used mainly for footwear and gloves. It can be used for jackets and coats, but needs ventilation holes.

Rubber is extracted from the rubber tree as a liquid which sets into a pliable material. Cottons and other durable materials may be impregnated with rubber to make them waterproof. Again, ventilation holes are required.

Fur and fur fabric — are warm because a layer of still air is trapped between the hairs. Fur fabrics are gaining popularity because many people object to animal furs.

20.7   MENTAL HEALTH

A healthy mental outlook on life, the avoidance of stress and the development of social habits which are not detrimental to health are all important. Excesses of food, drink, smoking and sexual activity are all potentially harmful. The development of good habits helps to maintain health.

Stress occurs when extra demands are put on the nervous system. This can be caused by overwork, resulting in tension and lack of concentration. Striking a balance between exercise, rest and recreation enables the body to avoid fatigue. A change of occupation helps one to relax, hence the need for recreation. Rest and sleep restore the body's vitality.

Social habits may sometimes be damaging to health. In recent years, the permissive attitude of society has resulted in an increase in the incidence of sexually transmitted (venereal) diseases and also in unwanted pregnancies and the number of abortions carried out. Sexually transmitted diseases are transmitted by various types of sexual activity. Gonorrhoea is caused by a bacterium, *Gonococcus*, and syphilis by a spirochaete. Inflammation of the urethra (urethritis), the cause of which is unknown, is referred to as non-specific urethritis or N.S.U. Genital warts and genital herpes may be transmitted and also pubic lice (*see* Sections 19.5 and 19.6). Some of these diseases have serious effects on the body functions, as the organisms enter the bloodstream and can damage the heart, the nervous system and other parts.

Promiscuous behaviour increases the danger of venereal disease as well as the possibility of unwanted pregnancies.

Contraception means trying to avoid pregnancy (conception). There are various methods, of which the contraceptive pill is the most widely used. This has a higher success rate than most methods, although no method is 100 per cent 'safe'. The pill contains hormones which inhibit ovulation. Some people prefer the use of devices placed inside the female body. The 'cap' covers the entrance to the womb, whilst intra-uterine devices (I.U.D's) prevent the implantation of a fertilized egg in the uterus. Other devices, such as the sheath or condom, are used by the male to prevent the seminal fluid contacting the ovum. Some men undergo vasectomy, the cutting of the sperm duct, so that semen cannot be passed into the female. Pessaries are chemicals which destroy the sperms. Persons objecting to these methods on religious grounds, can use the rhythm method. This involves avoiding intercourse at the ovulation period of the rhythmic monthly cycle. The so-called 'safe period' would be the first and last week of the four week cycle. The fertile period is the middle of the cycle, from about the eighth to the eighteenth day. This method can be successful if the rhythm is accurately determined, but it can present difficulties because of the normal variations in the monthly cycle.

20.8   SMOKING

The inhalation of smoke is one of the main causes of lung cancer. In addition, a heavy smoker is liable to contract chest infections, such as bronchitis and colds, since the passage of smoke over the lining of the trachea flattens the cilia, the tiny hair-like processes which normally waft germs in an upward direction to be eliminated. If these cilia are permanently flattened by constant smoking, one of the body's natural defence mechanisms is lost.

20.9   DRINKING

Excessive consumption of alcohol or ethanol can be damaging to health. Whereas fats and carbohydrates need to be digested before they can be absorbed, alcohol is quickly absorbed in the stomach or in the upper part of the small intestine. It is used up to provide the body with energy, so that many of the fats and carbohydrates are not used for fuel and are stored as fat. The resulting increase in weight is accompanied by the problems associated with obesity (*see* Section 20.4).

Alcohol also affects the brain, depressing the higher intellectual faculties. This causes reason and judgement to be affected, as well as reactions and movements which become slower and less precise. Initially a person may appear to be stimulated, but this is due to the alcohol depressing that part of the brain which deals with inhibitions — leading to abnormal behaviour. Eventually the effects lead to drowsiness or even stupor until the body has used up all the alcohol consumed.

20.10   POSTURE AND DEPORTMENT

Good posture and good carriage are important since the hairdresser spends so much time standing or moving about the salon.

Posture is maintained by muscles attached to the bony framework or skeleton, thus enabling the body to keep its shape even during movement. Good muscle tone is essential and this is helped by exercise. Lack of exercise leads to flabby muscles, which in turn results in bad deportment.

Good posture should be developed by habit. Although we can consciously 'walk tall', posture is maintained by the autonomic nervous system, hence the importance of developing good habits. The head should be held erect and the spine should be kept straight in both sitting and standing positions. Shoulders, hips and elbows should be kept level (Figure 20.3). Constant unevenness of shoulders and hips may cause curvature of the spine. The body weight should not be thrust forwards, therefore attention to shoes is important. In the sitting position, there should be right angles at the hips and knee joints, and the thighs should be supported.

Bad posture interferes with important processes in the body such as respiration and circulation. Rounded shoulders cause compression of the chest. Abdominal muscles help to keep the internal organs in their correct

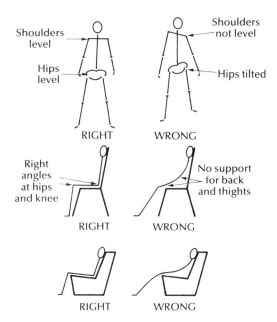

20.3   Correct and incorrect posture

positions, therefore they should have good muscle tone and not be allowed to become flabby.

The skeletal and muscular systems are both important in maintaining health.

20.11   THE SKELETAL SYSTEM

The *skeleton* is the bony framework of the body. Bone is a hard tissue which contains living cells and also important inorganic materials such as calcium salts, notably calcium phosphate.

The *axial* skeleton forms a supporting axis and includes the bones of the head and trunk.

The *appendicular* skeleton includes the bones of the appendages, i.e. the limbs, and the girdles which facilitate the attachment of the limbs to the trunk.

The bones of the skull making up the framework of the cranium and face are described in Chapter 14.

Functions of the skeleton

The skeleton supports the body and contributes to the shape. It protects many of the softer parts of the body.

The brain, an important but delicate organ, is protected by the cranium (*see* Chapter 14). The spinal cord, the main nerve cord, is protected by the backbone (spine or vertebral column). The heart and lungs, the main organs in the chest cavity, are protected by the rib-cage, extending from the back bone to the breast bone.

The skeleton serves as an attachment for muscles, thus enabling movement to take place. The places at which bones can move in relation to each other are known as joints. A variety of movements can occur, according to the type of joint.

Bones store calcium as calcium phosphate. Calcium is necessary not only in bones and teeth but also in the blood.

In flat bones and in the ends of long bones (in the limbs), new red blood corpuscles are manufactured, in the red bone marrow, to replace those which are worn out.

Joints

A joint occurs where two bones meet (articulate). Joints are usually associated with movement but some joints are immovable.

Fibrous or immovable joints occur where no movement is possible. In the skull, for example, the bones are joined together with tough fibrous tissue making fixed joints or sutures (*see* Chapter 14). This arrangement ensures the protection of the brain. The lower jaw is the only movable bone in the skull.

Cartilaginous or slightly movable joints occur where only a slight amount of movement is desirable, and a pad of cartilage (gristle) separates the bone surfaces. For example, the intervertebral joints of the spine have discs of cartilage separating the vertebrae (Figure 20.4). Very little movement is possible at individual joints, but because there are twenty four movable vertebrae the spine is very flexible.

Synovial or freely movable joints permit

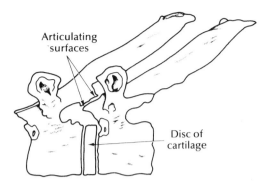

20.4 Two vertebrae, illustrating plane joint

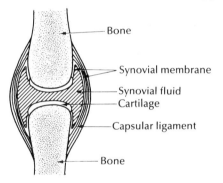

20.5 Synovial joint

great freedom of movement because they are lubricated by a special secretion, the synovial fluid, secreted by the synovial membrane which lines the joint cavity. Ligaments hold the bones together forming a capsule and preventing dislocation during movement. The articulating surfaces are covered with articular cartilage for smooth movement (Figure 20.5). Several varieties of synovial joints enable movement to be angular, rotary or gliding. It can also be a combination of movements. One variation is a *hinge* joint, which allows movement in one plane only, for example the elbow and knee joints. The hairdresser uses the elbow joints a great deal. Angular movements of flexion (bending) and extension (straightening) occur here.

Another variation is a *ball and socket joint* where the rounded end of one bone fits into a socket on another bone. This type is found

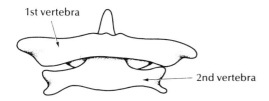

1st vertebra

2nd vertebra

Diagram - pivot joint
allowing head to move from side to side

20.6 Pivot joint — allowing head to move from side to side

at the shoulders and hips and permits angular and rotary movements.

A *pivot joint* is found where the first two vertebrae of the spine meet. The odontoid peg of the axis of vertebra (second) rotates within the ring of the atlas (first) vertebra to allow the head to turn (Figure 20.6).

The spine is important in maintaining erect posture. In the hairdressing salon, the seating should ensure that this is possible for the clients.

20.12   THE MUSCULAR SYSTEM

Muscle is the tissue responsible for movement and is used for both voluntary movements, controlled by the will, and involuntary or automatic movement. There are three types of muscular tissue in the body, responsible for different kinds of movement.

Voluntary or skeletal muscle forms the red flesh of the body. The muscles are under the control of the will and are used in locomotion, normally acting in groups. Voluntary muscle tissue is composed of thread-like fibres (muscle cells) about 4 cm long and 0.1 mm in diameter. They can be recognized microscopically owing to their being striped in alternate light and dark bands (Figure 20.7). Each fibre contains several nuclei and is surrounded by a muscle sheath. Connective tissue joins the fibres together in bundles, and several bundles together form a single muscle. Muscles have different shapes according to their position in the body, being long in the limbs, but broad and flat in the back. Others are strap-shaped as in the neck (*see* Figure 14.3).

Strong tendons which have no 'give' in them attach the muscles to definite points on the skeleton. The more fixed point is the origin and the movable end is the insertion. By contraction, a muscle can become shorter and thicker, thus drawing closer together the two points of attachment. A muscle can bring about movement in one direction only and a different muscle must contract in order to bring about a return to the original position. The contraction of the second muscle brings about the relaxation of the first.

The chief muscles of the head and face, which influence the shape of the face, and indirectly, the hair style, are described in Chapter 14.

Muscle tone

To stay healthy, a muscle needs exercise. Muscular tissue is always in a state of slight contraction or alertness, ready for action. This is known as muscle tone. It means that some of the fibres are alert and ready to respond to a stimulus from the nervous system (*see* Chapter 17). Even when the body is resting in sleep, the stimulus of an alarm bell will cause muscles to respond. The fibres have periods of rest so that they do not become exhausted.

Since a hairdresser, necessarily, has to stand a great deal, exercise such as walking, dancing,

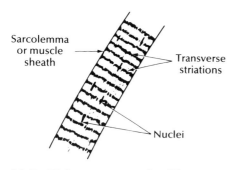

Sarcolemma or muscle sheath

Transverse striations

Nuclei

20.7 Voluntary muscle fibre as seen under the microscope

swimming and tennis helps to maintain physical fitness and improves the circulation.

Involuntary or visceral muscle cannot be controlled by the will and occurs in various internal organs (viscera). It is present in the walls of the stomach and intestines, in the diaphragm and other parts of the body. The arrector muscles of the skin are involuntary.

The involuntary muscle cells or fibres are spindle-shaped and are usually connected together to form sheets. They have a single nucleus, no stripes and no sheath (Figure 20.8). These fibres contract more slowly than skeletal muscle and bring about movement such as peristalsis which pushes food along the alimentary canal.

Although they are not controlled by the will, these muscles require a stimulus from the nervous system — the part which deals with automatic movements (*see* Chapter 17). Exercise stimulates internal movements such as movements of the bowel, thus preventing constipation. If waste matter remains in the bowel, pressure on nerve endings may cause some discomfort.

Cardiac muscle is the special muscle forming the heart wall and is found in the heart only. Cardiac muscle fibres are branched and show irregular markings, both vertical and horizontal. They have no muscle sheath and are bound together by connective tissue (Figure 20.9). This type of muscle is capable of automatic rhythmic contraction throughout life, independent of its nerve supply. However, it is normally controlled by the involuntary nervous system.

Movement

Movement requires energy which is obtained by the oxidation of fuel in the tissue cells (tissue respiration). Oxygen and fuel foods are brought to the muscle by the blood, hence the benefit of improved circulation during exercise. During respiration, most of the energy liberated is transferred to chemicals in the cells and stored until required. The chief

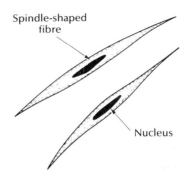

20.8   Involuntary muscle fibre as seen under the microscope

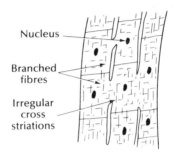

20.9   Cardiac muscle fibre as seen under the microscope

chemical is adenosine triphosphate (A.T.P.) and the stored energy can be released for muscle contraction. During prolonged exercise the increased oxygen required is provided by a speeding up of the heart beat, blood circulation and breathing movements. If the increased circulation does not supply sufficient oxygen, fuel may be broken down anaerobically (without oxygen), forming acid waste products. The accumulation of these waste products in the muscle may cause a state of *muscle fatigue*, when the movements become sluggish. Muscle fatigue must be follwed by a period of rest to restore the tissue to its normal condition. Periods of sleep provide the best form of rest for the body.

20.13   PHYSICAL FITNESS AND THE BENEFITS OF EXERCISE

Healthy exercise, especially in the fresh air, helps to maintain physical fitness, but it should be carried out on a regular basis to be of the most value.

Exercise benefits not only the muscular system by increasing muscle tone, but many other parts of the body also. It stimulates the circulation which is beneficial to all the body systems. More fuel and oxygen are distributed and the waste products of the body are removed more quickly. The rate of respiration is increased and the lungs are ventilated more fully. The increased heat energy produced leads to sweating, thus clearing waste products from the skin and improving the complexion. Exercise usually improves the appetite, and often stimulates peristalsis, thus reducing the risk of constipation. Improved blood circulation results in more oxygen reaching the brain and nervous system and thus alertness is increased.

20.14   QUESTIONS

1 Outline the general principles involved in the care of the hair, giving reasons.
2 Give a brief account of the hygiene care of (a) hands and feet, (b) mouth and teeth, (c) skin.
3 Why is good posture important to health? What part is played by the spine in maintaining good posture?
4 Explain the importance of muscles, bones and joints in the movement of the arm.
5 Describe the different types of muscle tissue. Why is exercise important in maintaining health?

6 Give an account of the main parts of the skeleton. Explain the functions of the skeleton giving one example of each.

20.15   MULTIPLE CHOICE QUESTIONS

1 A sphincter muscle is found in the:
(a) arm
(b) leg
(c) abdomen wall
(d) mouth?
2 Muscles are connected to bones by means of:
(a) ligaments
(b) tendons
(c) fascia
(d) cartilage?
3 Which of the following chemicals collect in a muscle during strenuous exercise and cause fatigue:
(a) glucose
(b) 2-hydroxypropanoic acid (lactic) acid
(c) adenosine triphosphate (ATP)
(d) glycogen?
4 Which of the following nutrients in a diet will serve to harden soft finger nails:
(a) gelatine
(b) iodine
(c) calcium
(d) iron?
5 Which of the following is also called dental decay:
(a) halitosis
(b) caries
(c) gingivitis
(d) pyorrhoea?
6 A finger nail grows at the following rate per month:
(a) 0.3 mm
(b) 3.0 mm
(c) 3 cm
(d) 30 cm?

21 Salon Hygiene

The condition of the hairdressing salon will affect the people in it, both the hairdressers and the clients. If should therefore be clean and comfortable. This involves the standard of cleanliness and also the humidity and temperature of the air, as well as the important safety aspects. In accordance with the Health and Safety at Work Act, 1974, employees have a duty to take care of themselves and of others who may be affected by their acts. Personal care and salon care are essential. An ability to recognize the symptoms of an infectious disease is important so that the right course of action can be taken.

A prospective client showing signs of an infectious disease should be discreetly advised to seek medical help, and return to the salon only when the risk of infection has passed. If a disorder or infestation is discovered when a client is actually being treated in the salon, the hairdresser has a duty to ensure that the infection is not spread. Pediculosis, or ringworm, for example, may be discovered. The hairdresser would finish the work being done but would advise the client, or the parent in charge of a child client, to seek medical attention and not to visit a hairdressing salon until the infection has been cleared up. A discreet approach is necessary to avoid alarming any other clients.

All the articles which have been in contact with an infected person must be disinfected by a suitable method. All hair trimmings must be burned. Clothing and linen should be boiled. Combs, scissors and curlers can be steam-sterilized. In the case of ringworm, articles which cannot be disinfected must be burned.

21.1 STERILIZATION

This is the complete destruction of micro-organisms and their spores. It therefore involves depriving them of one or more of the conditions required for their growth and multiplication. Living organisms need food, moisture, oxygen and a favourable temperature. Many micro-organisms absorb soluble food, so depriving them of moisture will destroy them. High temperatures are usually fatal to bacteria, but some pathogens form spores characterized by a thick protective membrane which makes them resistant to unfavourable conditions. Some spores can remain dormant for years and others can resist boiling water for more than an hour. Sterilization in the salon can be achieved by physical or chemical methods.

Physical sterilization

Since most micro-organisms are killed by high temperatures, heat can be used in various forms.

Dry heat
A naked flame can be used for sterilizing small metal articles, but not sharp instruments which would become blunted.

A hot air oven is useful for destroying bacteria and their spores if articles are heated to 160°C and maintained at this temperature for one hour. Glass containers can be sterilized in this way and also oils, fats and some other chemical substances which are not decomposed at this temperature. Dry heat is less effective than moist heat.

Moist heat
This can be provided by boiling water, steam or steam under pressure. Water boiling at 100°C will destroy all forms of bacteria almost immediately. Some pathogens, however, can resist boiling by forming spores. The living contents of the cell shrink into a small mass covered with a protective membrane. The spore may lie in the centre of the cell, or towards one end or actually at the end (drumstick spores) (Figure 21.1). In this form, they can survive until conditions are favourable for germination, but many can be destroyed by boiling for fifteen to twenty minutes. Some resist for longer periods. Boiling can be used for small articles such as metal combs or curlers as well as towels and personal linen. It is unsuitable for razors as it tends to blunt the delicate cutting edge.

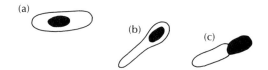

21.1 The positions of bacterial spores: (*a*) central spore; (*b*) spore towards one end; (*c*) spore actually at the end

Steam at 100°C, as it rises from the surface of boiling water, is known as live steam and can be used for sterilizing textiles. If spore-bearing bacteria are present, the exposure to live steam must be repeated several times.

Steam under pressure is carried out in a steam sterilizer or autoclave (like a large pressure cooker). This allows the pressure to build up, resulting in temperatures greater than 100°C. The actual temperature depends upon the pressure:

$$35 \text{ kPa} : 110°C$$
$$70 \text{ kPa} : 115°C$$
$$103 \text{ kPa} : 120°C$$

The usual conditions are 70 kPa/m² pressure for thirty minutes. This rapidly destroys bacteria and their spores owing to the coagulation of the bacterial protoplasm. Certain chemical solutions, rubber gloves and capes can be steam sterilized. This is a very efficient method of sterilization because moist heat has much deeper penetration than dry heat.

Chemical sterilization

Many chemical substances can interfere with the activity of micro-organisms. The substances are named according to the effect that they produce. A disinfectant, germicide or bactericide completely destroys bacteria. An antiseptic or bacteriostat merely inhibits bacterial growth; as soon as the effect wears off, the bacteria become active again. Antiseptics are useful on cuts or burns on the skin as they give the damaged skin a chance to heal before the bacteria become active again.

All disinfectants can be diluted to form

antiseptics, but all antiseptics are not disinfectants.

Hydrogen peroxide H$_2$O$_2$ (*see Section 11.2*)
This is a colourless liquid that will mix with water in all proportions. Solutions of various strengths are used in hairdressing. It decomposes slowly into water and oxygen, but more quickly on heating or in contact with alkalis or with body tissues. The oxygen released during the decomposition combines with bacterial protoplasm, thus destroying it.

Phenolic compounds
Phenol is a colourless cyrstalline solid with a characteristic smell (carbolic). It turns pink on exposure to light or air. A 5 per cent solution of phenol in water is useful for sterilizing brushes, but is bad for plastic materials.

Phenolic compounds are also useful as sanitary fluids for sterilizing drains.

Quarternary ammonium compounds
(*see Section 7.5*)
These are useful as both cleansing agents and antiseptics. They include cetrimide (savlon, cetavlon) and chlorhexidine (hibitane) and are used as creams or lotions.

Methanal (Formaldehyde)
This is a colourless gas. A 40 per cent solution with water is known as formalin. When heated the formalin releases the gas which has the power of sterilization. Methanal is used in some forms of cabinet sterilizers in the salon for sterilizing combs, brushes and curlers (*see* Figure 9.3).

21.2 SALON SURFACES AND DUST (*see also Chapter 7*)

To prevent the spread of infection in the salon the equipment and surroundings must be kept clean and the hairdresser must have high standards of personal hygiene (*see* Chapter 20).

A daily routine is useful in the salon, as well as for personal hygiene.

Floors should have surfaces which do not trap dust and are easy to keep clean, for example linoleum or tiles. Walls and ceilings ideally should have a washable surface, for example, tiles, washable paint or vinyl coverings. Cupboards and shelves should have smooth, hard, washable surfaces, as also should the trolleys and dressing-out tables. Mirrors need cleaning regularly. Basins should be glazed and trapped and need regular flushing. Salon furniture should have plastic or vinyl surfaces which are easily cleaned.

21.3 TOOLS AND EQUIPMENT

Brushes, combs curlers and other equipment must be cleaned and sterilized regularly. Articles dropped on the floor should be sterilized before use. Combs, grips and other articles should never be placed in the mouth, nor should they be used from pockets, where germs are likely to accumulate.

Covered bins are necessary for the placement of hair clippings, cotton wool and other waste. Hair trimmings should be swept up promptly and placed in the bin, not left under the brush in a corner. They are unsightly as well as a hazard. The bins must be emptied regularly and always at the end of the day.

Clean towels and gowns should be provided for each client, as used ones could spread infection. Nylon gowns are quickly washed and dried, but disposable neckstrips are useful.

Clean linen should be stored separately from soiled towels and gowns. The hairdresser should wear a clean overall and have clean hands and nails. Cross infection can occur when bacteria are transferred by dirty hands or equipment. Toilet hygiene is essential. Salon ashtrays should be emptied frequently and the hairdressers should not smoke in the salon.

21.4   WASHBASINS, DRAINS, AND TRAPS

Washbasins and *drains* could be a source of bacteria in the salon, so good drainage is essential. The aim is the removal of waste matter by suitable pipes without allowing air from the sewer and drains to gain access to the interior of the salon. One reason for this is that bacteria are usually present in sewer air.

Washbasins in the salon should have a glazed surface, which does not retain dirt, and should discharge into the open air or to the surface of a gulley. They must be provided with an overflow, as well as a waste outlet, and should have a suitable trap.

A *trap* is a U-shaped bend, in a waste pipe, which retains some water and so prevents any passage of air through it (*see* Sections 7.4 and 7.8). The upper surface of the pipe should dip below the water level so that a water seal is formed. The seal prevents gases from the drain from passing back into the room. The trap should be as simple as possible with a smooth interior surface which will not collect dirt. The water retained in the seal should be completely changed during flushing. Each trap should be provided with a removable screw cap so that the trap can be cleaned if it becomes blocked with hairs and grease. Basins used in the salon can be flushed once a day, with hot soda water to disperse the grease and prevent any blockage arising.

21.5   VENTILATION AND HEATING IN THE SALON

The condition of the air in the salon will affect the occupants and must provide a comfortable atmosphere. Factors influencing the comfort of the individual are the temperature of the air, its humidity, the purity of the atmosphere and the movement of the air. Good ventilation is necessary to replace polluted air with fresh air.

Salon temperature (*see* Chapter 5)

A suitable temperature must be maintained. The body produces heat by tissue respiration and muscular activity but heat is also lost from the body by expiration, radiation, conduction and evaporation of moisture through the sweat glands. A constant body temperature is maintained (*see* Section 18.5) but in cold weather some form of artificial heating will be necessary in the salon and this heating should assist ventilation. In a large salon, central heating by radiators will produce a fairly even temperature. Underfloor heating is good, but expensive to run, and may also prove tiring for the feet of those working in the salon. In smaller salons, if there is no central heating, other types of heaters, including portable ones may be used.

Convector heaters should be sited under windows, since the warm air rises and by mixing with the cooler air near the windows ensures a more even temperature. This also reduces the risk of draughts.

Gas fires are clean and smokeless. Some gas fires do not assist ventilation much, but certain gas radiant-convector heaters have a special ventilation control. Nowadays, small salons sometimes employ portable gas heaters which use butane gas (bottled), and these can be wheeled into different positions.

Infra-red heaters mounted high on a wall provide warmth in a defined area.

Fan heaters circulate warm air and the temperature can be regulated.

The cost of these various methods will be a factor for consideration as the combustion of fuel is expensive; so too is the use of electric current.

Salon humidity (*see* Section 6.4)

Humidity concerns the amount of moisture in the atmosphere and is normally high in a hairdressing salon. The use of hairdryers will add, not only warmth to the salon, but also moisture as this evaporates from the clients' hair.

Dry air irritates the mucous membranes of the body, but if the air is too humid, the body cannot be cooled by evaporation from the sweat glands and discomfort results. Good ventilation helps to remove water vapour from the atmosphere, thus affecting the level of humidity.

Purity of the salon atmosphere (*see* Section 6.2)

The air is a mixture of gases but may contain dust and fumes. The impurities include particles of hair, shed epidermal cells from the skin, lacquer fumes and gases or vapours from the use of chemicals in the salon. The carbon dioxide content is also increased by the breathing of the salon occupants. Dust, dandruff, particles of hair and skin are all sources of bacteria and must be controlled to prevent the spread of infection. Good ventilation will remove impurities.

Movement of air (*see* Section 6.5)

For human comfort, the air in a room must undergo continuous change without creating unpleasant draughts. Some types of heater help to circulate air. Warm air rises from a convector heater and is replaced by colder air moving towards it, thus producing convection currents.

Fresh air

The supply of fresh air in the salon may be natural or artificial, but there must be suitable inlets and outlets for the air. Windows and doors are natural inlets. Natural outlets are usually at a higher level because warm stale air rises. In business establishments, some form of artificial ventilation is often advisable. One of the chief forms is the extraction fan which withdraws impure air from the room by suction. Suitable air inlets must be provided or else air will be drawn in through cracks and under doors and cause unpleasant draughts. The positioning of fans should not be near the inlets, or the fans will draw the air supply from them instead of withdrawing the stale air from the room. The extraction fan will remove impurities, reduce humidity and create movement of air, all factors which affect comfort.

Air conditioning

This involves controlling the temperature of the air as well as the purity, humidity and movement. In an air-conditioned building, air enters and leaves by artificial means (fans) and the fresh air entering is filtered to purify it. It passes through a humidifier to provide a suitable moisture level. The temperature of the air is controlled by the use of heaters and fans. Stale air is constantly extracted by fans as filtered fresh air enters.

21.6 QUESTIONS

1 Describe the ways in which a hairdressing salon could become polluted and explain how these pollutants could affect the health of the occupants.
2 Explain the importance of the following in the salon: smooth washable surfaces; trapped basins; sterilizing cabinets; clean overalls; and neckstrips.
3 Describe a suitable method of heating and ventilating a hairdressing salon, giving reasons for your choice.
4 Discuss the danger of the spread of infection in an unhygienic salon.
5 Suggest a useful daily routine for maintaining hygiene in the salon.

21.7 MULTIPLE CHOICE QUESTIONS

1 Which of the following is a volatile disinfectant used in salon sterilizing cabinets:
(*a*) phenol (carbolic acid)
(*b*) ethanal (acetaldehyde)

(c) methanal (formaldehyde)
(d) essential oil of lavender?

2 Phenols are present in one of the following antiseptics and disinfectants:
(a) lysol
(b) iodine
(c) condys fluid
(d) household bleach?

3 The temperature which effectively destroys most harmful bacteria during the pasteurization process is:
(a) 35–40° C
(b) 65–70° C
(c) 100–120° C
(d) 145–150° C?

4 Curling tongs for the hair can be sterilized by:

(a) rinsing in hot tap water
(b) dipping in antiseptic lotion
(c) heating in a naked flame
(d) wiping with a paper tissue?

5 Which of the following is almost sterile water:
(a) refrigerator drip tray water
(b) boiled tap water
(c) spring water
(d) well water?

6 Which of the following has antiseptic properties but cannot act as a disinfectant:
(a) hot soapy water
(b) chlorine
(c) household bleach
(d) potassium manganate(VII) (permanganate)?

22 Safety in the Salon

The hairdresser should be constantly aware of the safety aspects of all the work and conditions in the salon.

There is hidden danger in the use of electrical appliances, so appropriate safety precautions must be observed at all times. Cuts, burns and scalds could result from careless use of tools, chemicals and hot water. High standards of cleanliness lessen the risk of the spread of infection in the salon. Vigilance in watching for and recognition of infectious diseases also prevents the possible spread of these diseases and maintains the good reputation of the salon.

Cleaning, washing and sterilization procedures should be followed as a matter of routine.

In order to comply with the Health and Safety at Work Act, 1974, fire precautions must be taken, including the provision of fire-fighting appliances in the salon. A first-aid kit must also be available so that first-aid can be given to a client or an employee, should the need arise.

22.1 HEALTH AND SAFETY AT WORK ACT, 1974

A *Code of Practice* approved by the Health and Safety Commission, with the consent of the Secretary of State, giving guidance on the rquirements placed on employers and self-employed persons with respect to the Health and Safety Regulations, came into effect on 1 July, 1982.

In the approved code, it is the duty of an employer to make provision for first aid, and a self-employed person has to ensure that he makes provision for rendering first-aid to himself while he is at work.

An employer shall ensure that equipment and facilities are provided which are *adequate* for enabling first aid to be rendered to employees if they are injured or become ill at work. Employees have a duty to take care of themselves and others who may be affected by their acts. The criteria for deciding what provision is adequate and appropriate include the number of employees, the size of the establishment, its location, and the nature of the undertaking.

Where fewer than fifty employees are at work (for example in a hairdressing salon), the employer has to provide an *appointed person* to take charge of first aid. Where there is known danger from the work processes or from potentially harmful substances (e.g. chemicals in the salon), employers should ensure that first aiders know of the danger and how to take effective action. They should also know of any relevant procedures associated with sending a casualty to hospital. The person appointed by an employer to take charge in the case of serious illness or major injury is also responsible for first-aid equipment.

It is the duty of an employer to *inform his employees of the arrangements* made in connection with first aid, including the location of equipment, facilities and personnel. Employers should ensure that every employee has reasonably speedy access to first aid. A compact establishment might provide centralized arrangements. One or more first aid boxes should be placed in a readily accessible location.

First aid boxes should contain a sufficient quantity of suitable first aid materials and nothing else (*see* Section 22.3). The contents of first aid boxes and kits should be replenished as soon as possible after use in order to ensure that there is always an adequate supply of materials. Frequent checking is essential.

22.2   FIRST AID

First aid is the preliminary treatment given to injured or sick people before expert help arrives. It is based on medical principles and helps to prevent further injury, speed recovery and save life. It is useful for a hairdresser to be able to recognize signs and symptoms and to know the simple treatment for some of the conditions likely to be encountered in the salon.

Fainting and unconsciousness

Fainting is a form of temporary unconsciousness due to a decreased supply of blood to the brain. This, in turn, is due to failure of the heart action. It may be caused by some heart disease or anaemia, but other causes include exhaustion, lack of food, excessive heat, lack of fresh air, emotional shocks (both joyful and sorrowful), and bleeding.

Before fainting, a person usually feels giddy. At this stage, tight clothing at the neck should be loosened and then if the head is gently pressed between the knees, blood rushes to the head and swooning is avoided. If consciousness is lost, however, the person should be kept lying down with the head to one side to ensure a clear airway, and the legs slightly raised on a cushion. Dentures and any small dental plates should be removed to avoid blocking the airway. Tight clothing at the waist should be loosened. There should be an adequate supply of fresh air. If unconsciousness persists, a doctor should be called since, if the brain is deprived of oxygen for more than four minutes, irreversible damage is done to the brain.

Nose bleeding

If the nose starts to bleed, it is normally due to the rupture of small blood capillaries. The person should be kept sitting up with the head back. Cold pads, or ice packs if available, should be applied to the bridge of the nose and the back of the neck, and pressure applied at the bridge of the nose.

Cuts and minor wounds

The aim in treating minor wounds is to stop the bleeding, treat shock and prevent bacterial infection of the wound. *Bleeding* can usually be stopped by using pressure on the wound after first applying a piece of clean material.

Shock symptoms are pallor and coldness, but beads of sweat may stand out on the person's forehead. Sympathy and reassurance should be given and extra warmth provided by blankets and rugs. Warm, sweet drinks, preferably of tea or coffee, help recovery. Milk drinks should be avoided as they may cause vomiting.

To *prevent infection*, minor wounds and cuts should be dabbed with cotton wool dipped in a suitable antiseptic. The wound can then be covered with a dry dressing or with a dressing smeared with antiseptic cream such as cetrimide.

Burns and scalds

These are both caused by heat, a burn by dry heat (including electrical burns), and a scald by moist heat, either very hot water or steam. The treatment is similar for both. The heat must be removed or reduced and the affected area cooled with cold water. If possible, the affected part, for example, a hand, should be immersed in cold water. For scalp burns, which obviously cannot be immersed, a continuous spray of cold water would reduce the heat.

A *burn* should be covered with a dry, sterile dressing and a loose pad of cotton wool. If blisters have formed, they should not be broken.

A *scald* should be covered with a large soft dressing and medical attention should be obtained for the client. Corrosive chemicals can also injure the skin. In this case the area should be bathed with water to dilute the chemical and subsequently treated with a suitable antidote. A check-list of suitable antidotes should be readily available.

Poisons

A poison is a substance which may cause harmful effects on the body, damaging body tissues or even resulting in death. A number of poisonous substances are used in hairdressing, and careful labelling and storage are essential. If, however, a poison is accidentally swallowed, it is important to try and remove it from the body and to give an antidote to prevent harmful effects. Consult the checklist.

The following procedure should be adopted:

(*a*) Send for medical help and give as much information as possible about the nature of the poison. Save any remains for inspection.

(*b*) Examine the person's mouth and lips for signs of burning. If there is no sign of burning, adminster an emetic to remove the poison from the body. An emetic, a substance which produces vomiting, can easily be made by dissolving a tablespoonful of sodium chloride (salt) in a cupful of warm water. The person should be given plenty of warm water to drink to wash out the stomach.

(*c*) If there are signs of burning on the lips, or if the tongue is swollen or blistered, this indicates that a corrosive poison has been swallowed. In this case, an emetic must *not* be given, as the oesophagus and stomach may be injured, and the strain of vomiting could cause further injury. Instead, a suitable antidote should be given. The poison may be acidic or alkaline, and each type requires a different antidote.

(*d*) Find out the nature of the poison.

Acidic poisons require an alkaline antidote. The alkali neutralizes the acid producing a comparatively harmless salt. Suitable alkaline substances are magnesium hydroxide (magnesia) and sodium hydrogen carbonate (bicarbonate of soda). Either of these can be given in water.

Alkaline poisons, such as strong ammonium hydroxide (ammonia) require an acidic antidote, for example, a weak solution of vinegar or lemon juice.

An antidote should be followed by soothing drinks of milk or olive oil. Treatment for shock will usually be necessary also.

Narcotic poisons (drugs) cause drowsiness. In this case, the person must be kept awake otherwise consciousness may be lost. Drinks of strong black coffee should be given and the person should be made to walk about.

Substances in the eye

Foreign bodies or chemicals may enter the eye. A foreign body such as an eyelash or a fragment of hair can be removed with a small camel hair brush. Chemicals which enter the eye should be diluted by washing with plenty of water in an eyebath.

Fits

Three types of fits may be encountered — hysterical and epileptic, both petit mal and grand mal.

Hysterical fits are due to some sort of emotional strain, and the person laughs or screams continuously. Slapping the face usually brings about recovery, and sympathy should be avoided.

Epileptic fits are due to a nervous disorder. There are two conditions. *Petit mal* does not involve loss of consciousness, but the person appears to be day-dreaming. The fit passes off naturally. *Grand mal* usually involves the person falling to the ground with the body twitching and the face distorted. Foaming at the mouth may occur and there may be some incontinence of urine. The first aider should not try to stop the fit, but prevent the person from damaging himself as he thrashes about. Furniture should be moved out of the way. If possible, a gag should be placed between the person's teeth to prevent the tongue being bitten, though this may be difficult. The fit gradually passes off naturally.

Fractures

A fracture is a broken or cracked bone and could result from a client falling in the salon. Fractures may be simple or compound.

A simple fracture is where there is no external wound. A compound fracture is accompanied by an external wound leading to the broken bone, and may even involve the fractured bone protruding through the skin. This could be further complicated by severe bleeding or other injury. The affected part will be painful, tender and swollen and there will be loss of control.

A fracture must be immobilized before the person is moved, unless life is in danger. This can be achieved by bandaging the injured part to a sound part of the body, for example, bandaging a broken arm to the person's side. Where necessary, splints and bandages are used. A splint should go above and below the break and must be well padded. Bandages should be firm, but not so tight as to interfere with the blood circulation. Knots should be tied on the uninjured side. Get someone to call an ambulance.

Electric shock (*see* Sections 12.6 and 12.7)

All electrical appliances in the salon must be properly earthed. With modern equipment, there is little danger of electric shock if the appliances are properly installed and maintained. However, should an appliance develop a fault and a client receive an electric shock, the following procedure should be carried out.

Before touching the client, turn off the current, but if for some reason this is not possible, wear rubber gloves or use some other form of insulating material such as dry woollen cloth. Stand on a dry wooden board or a dry folded coat and pull the client clear of the apparatus. The effects of electric shock may be unconsciousness and cessation of breathing, as well as shock and electrical burns. If breathing has ceased, resuscitation is necessary and when the person starts breathing again, treatment for shock and electrical burns may be given. It is important to summon medical help.

Resuscitation

If breathing has stopped, resuscitation must be started at once to induce breathing to start again.

Mouth-to-mouth resuscitation, known as

the kiss of life, is now widely used and can be given easily and effectively. It is essential to ensure an open airway and ventilate the person's lungs. Lay the person on his back. Gently bend the head well back to avoid any obstruction by the tongue. Take a deep breath, and then exhale, without force, into the person's open mouth, at the same time pinching the nostrils together. Turn your head away while taking another deep breath, thus allowing the casualty's lungs to be emptied. Watch for the breathing movements to re-commence. Repeat these actions until the breathing starts again or until a doctor takes over the responsibility.

If mouth-to-mouth resuscitation cannot be given, because of facial injuries for example, the Holger-Nielsen method can be carried out as follows:

Lay the person downwards with the arms forward and the head resting on the hands. Loosen any tight clothing at the neck and waist. Kneel in front of the casualty's head and spread your hands over the shoulder blades with your thumbs touching. Keeping your arms straight, apply light pressure to a count of three seconds, then slide your hands down to the casualty's elbows on the count of four. To counts of five, six and seven, raise the person's arms and shoulders, rocking back a little. Lay the arms down again to the count of eight and replace your hands on the back ready to repeat these movements. Continue the action until normal breathing is restored or until a doctor takes over the responsibility.

When recovery occurs after resuscitation, the person may vomit or salivate. To prevent the casualty inhaling these substances, he should be placed in the recovery position,

21.2 **Simple trap with water seal**

that is lying on his side with the left leg straight and the right leg flexed. The right arm is flexed also. This position enables the air passages to remain unobstructed.

22.3 FIRST-AID KIT IN THE SALON

In order to comply with the Health and Safety at Work Act, 1974, one or more first aid boxes (kits) should be available in the salon.

It should contain the following:
Burn dressings
A selection of non-adherent dry absorbent dressings in sealed sterile packs;
Cotton wool;
Absorbent lint;
Bandages: 5 or 7.5 cm for the head; 2.5 or 4 cm for fingers; triangular bandage for a sling;
Adhesive dressing strip;
Scissors;
Antiseptic lotion such as cetrimide;
2% boric acid lotion;
2% sodium hydrogen carbonate lotion;
Eye bath;
Pair of dry rubber gloves.

22.4 ACCIDENT PREVENTION

The approved code of practice with respect to the Health and Safety regulations is designed for improving the standards of protection for work people and the general public.

Manufacturers must ensure that their products are safe. Persons who install electrical equipment must ensure its safety.

In the salon, attention to the following details will help to avoid accidents and the necessity for first aid:
Care in the use of scissors and razors;
Use of correct plugs;
Avoidance of trailing flexes and polished floors;
Clear labelling and safe storage of chemicals;
Use of chemicals as directed by the manu-facturers;

Care in the application of lotions and use of aerosol sprays;
Provision of eye masks for clients;
Care in the use of hot water;
Good lighting.

22.5   FIRE PRECAUTIONS
(*see* **Section 6.6**)

Fire hazards

A fire starts when a source of ignition comes into contact with combustible material. The action taken in the first few minutes determines whether the fire remains a nuisance or becomes a disaster.

Before a fire breaks out, know your Fire Procedure, know the risks involved and how to operate your fire equipment.

Flammable materials

Many materials used in the salon are flammable, generally because of the solvent used. This may be *alcohol* as in spirit rinses and shampoos, friction and astringent lotions, setting lotions and hair lacquers.

Propanone (*acetone*) is the solvent for nail varnish remover and also for lacquers and resins. *Petrol* may be present in some wig cleaners. Ethoxyethane (*ether*) is a solvent for oils and fats.

Remember also hairsprays which are in aerosol form, many of which utilize flammable gases as the propellant. Flammable vapours, heavier than air, will travel a considerable distance before ignition by the smallest spark or flame. Exercise the greatest care and ventilate adequately. Containers of flammable liquids should be stored in a metal bin and only enough liquid for the work in hand should be exposed in the salon.

Combustible materials

Many materials will burn, so the salon should be kept tidy and waste materials disposed of regularly. If smoking is permitted, provide sufficient ashtrays. Check thoroughly before closing for the day.

Electrical equipment

Hair dryers and other electrical equipment, correctly installed and properly earthed, should be checked regularly by a competent person.

Legislation

Where persons are employed, hairdressing salons in Britain must register under the Offices, Shops and Railway Premises Act, 1963. The premises must be approved by the Fire Authority for safe exit routes in case of fire, for the provision of suitable fire equipment and for adequate staff training in its use. Seek the advice of the Local Fire Brigade (Fire Prevention Department) on the careful use of materials, suitable types of fire-extinguishing equipment, staff fire training and the proper layout of premises for safety in the event of fire. All such advice is willingly given and free.

Fire equipment

The employer is required, by law, to provide this equipment. Remember the types and know how to use them.

Water is the best medium for free-burning materials such as hair, paper, wood or cloth. A water extinguisher is preferable to buckets of water. *Never* use water on live electrical equipment or flammable liquids.

Other types are carbon dioxide, dry powder, B.C.F. (bromochlorodifluoromethane) and C.T.C. (carbon tetrachloride) extinguishers. *Carbon dioxide* or dry powder types are suitable on all kinds of fire. For fires involving flammable liquids or where live electrical equipment is present, use a carbon dioxide, dry powder or B.C.F. extinguisher. C.T.C. extinguishers are now banned in many countries because of the hazards involved in use. As a liquid, C.T.C. can cause dermatitis. At high temperatures, it gives off a poisonous gas. As a cold vapour, it can affect the liver and the nervous and digestive systems. Maximum ventilation is required and it is not recommended for fighting fires in enclosed spaces.

Clothing on fire

Use a woollen or asbestos blanket when a person's clothing is on fire, laying them down to prevent the flames reaching the head.

Fire procedure

In the event of a fire, raise the alarm and ensure that the Fire Brigade is called. Without delay, tackle the fire with the nearest appropriate type of equipment. Prevent fire spreading by confining the fire. If evacuation of the salon is necessary, instruct clients to leave via escape routes, not to use lifts and not to go back for personal belongings.

22.6 QUESTIONS

1 What sort of accidents occur in the salon and how can they be prevented?
2 (a) Give the three aims in treating cuts and minor wounds.
   (b) What are the symptoms of shock and what treatment would you give to aid recovery?
3 How would you deal with a client who (a) felt faint, (b) actually fainted, (c) had an epileptic fit, (d) suffered a scald when being shampooed, (e) got some perm lotion in the eye?
4 Explain what is meant by 'the recovery position' and discuss its importance.
5 Write a short essay on 'Resuscitation'.
6 Discuss accident prevention in the salon.

22.7 MULTIPLE CHOICE QUESTIONS

1 A slight wound of the skin caused by scissors should be treated by:
   (a) covering with a dry sterile adhesive
   b dressing;
   (b) pressing a finger on it until bleeding stops
   (c) dusting freely with talcum powder
   (d) applying a greasy antiseptic ointment?
2 Which of the following can be given to a patient who is conscious and suffering from shock:
   (a) strong black coffee
   (b) a glass of brandy
   (c) aspirin and plenty of water
   (d) a few sips of fluid?
3 A salon worker spills hot sodium hydroxide solution on her skirt causing burns through to the skin. The suitable first aid treatment would be to:
   (a) leave everything untouched and send to hospital
   (b) sprinkle dry sodium hydrogen carbonate all over the affected area and remove when dry
   (c) remove the clothing, bathe skin with diluted vinegar, and apply a dry dressing
   (d) cut around the affected clothing, leave next to burn, and cover with a light bandage?
4 A person whilst sitting in the salon chair suddenly complains of strangling pains in the upper chest and neck. Their skin is cold and clammy, and they have difficulty in breathing. This could be signs of:
   (a) an attack of asthma
   (b) a heart attack
   (c) indigestion
   (d) an epileptic fit?
5 If the ground floor of a salon is found to be flooded to a depth of half a metre, which of the following would assist you:
   (a) gas service
   (b) water service
   (c) fire service

(d) electricity service?

6 The engine of a client's parked car catches fire outside the salon. Which of the following could be used as the fire extinguisher:

(a) bucket of water
(b) dry powder
(c) vaporizing liquid
(d) soda-acid water?

Indices

CHEMICAL

Page numbers in italics indicate illustrations or figures

Abrasives, 68, 79
Acetic acid (*see* ethanoic acid)
Acetone (*see* propanone)
Acid, 79, 98 *et seq.*
    conditioners, 137 *et seq.*
    dyes, 122 *et seq.*
    hair rinses, 94
    oxides, 57
Acridine orange, 95
Aerosol preparations, 48
After shave lotions, 80
Agar gum, 21
Air, 108
    composition, 56, 57, 58
Alanine, 86, 106, 107
Albinism, 116
Alcohols, 154, *et seq.*
Alkali (*see* bases)
Alkanes, 20 *et seq.*, 67
Alkanoic (fatty) acids, 21
Alkyl aryl sulphonates, 67
Almond oil, 13, 80, 92, 138, 153
Alpha keratin, *87 et seq.*
Ambergris, 155, 157

Amines, 72, 86, 102, 122
Amino acids, 34, 86 *et seq.*, 111, 138, 139
Aminobenzene (aniline), *127*
Amino bonds, 107
Amino phenols, 123
Ammonia (*see* ammonium hydroxide)
Ammonium carbonate, 119
Ammonium ethanoate (acetate), 119
Ammonium hydroxide, 13, 22, 72 *et seq.*, 86, 99, 105, 110, 111, 119
Ammonium thiolethanoate (thioglycollate), 99, 109
Amyl ethanoate (acetate), 155
Analysis, 6, 85
Anhydrous compounds, 14
Aniline (*see* amino benzene)
Animal extracts, 155, 157
Animal lipids (fats and waxes), 21
Anion, 66, 81
Anionic detergents (*see* detergents)

Anthraquinol, 116
Anthraquinone, 116
Antidandruff, 93
Anti-infestive, 93
Antiredeposition, 97
Antistatic, 71, 139
Apigenin, 122
Arginine, 86
Ascorbic acid (Vitamin C), 120, 124
Aspartic acid, 86
Astringent, 81
    lotions, 80
Atom, 5, 33
Azo dyes, 122, 124, 128

Barium compounds, 116
Barrier creams, 153
Bases, 66, 78, 98 *et seq.*, 107
Basic dyes, 122 *et seq.*
Basic oxides, 57
Beeswax, 21
Benzene, *127 et seq.*
Benzene carboxylic acid (benzoic acid), 80, 93

Benzene diamines (phenylene diamines), 123 *et seq.*, *127*
Benzene triol (pyrogallol), 121, 123, 155
Beta keratin, 87 *et seq.*
Bleaching preparations, 57, 119 *et seq.*
Blue rinse (*see* methylene blue)
Bonds or linkages, 20, 33, 62, 86, 87, 102 *et seq.*, *104*, 106, 108, 110, 111
Borax and boron compounds, 91, 99, 107
Brighteners, 119, 120
Brilliantine, 13, 20, 138
Bromates, 51
Buffing cream, 153

Calamine (Zinc carbonate) (*see* Zinc compounds)
Calamine lotion, 148
Calcium carbonate, 99
Calcium hydrogen carbonate (bicarbonate), 62
Calcium hydroxide (lime water), 72, 99
Calcium oxide, 108
Calcium sulphate, 63
Camomile, *122*, 124
Camphor, 93
Candelilla wax, 21
Carbohydrates, 17, 21 *et seq.*
Carbon, 20, *85*
Carbon dioxide, 17, 20, 48, 52, 57, 71 *et seq.*
Carbon monoxide, 48
Carbon tetrachloride (tetra-chloromethane), 21
Carboxylic acids, 21, 86, 102, 139
Carnauba wax, 21
Castoreum (castor), 155
Catalyst, 113, 114, 120
Cationic conditioners, 138
Cationic detergents (*see* detergents)
Cations, 66, 81, 122
Caustic potash (*see* potassium compounds)
Caustic soda (*see* sodium

hydroxide)
Cellulose, 34
Cetrimide (*see* quaternary ammonium compounds)
Cetyl alcohol (*see* hexadecanol)
Chemical changes, 111
Chemical reactions, 113 *et seq.*, 120, 124
Chlorine, 10
Cholesterol, 22
Citric acid (2-hydroxy propane tricarboxylic acid), 15, 80, 94, 99
Citronellol, 156
Civet, 155, 157
Cobalt compounds, 99
Coconut oil, 13, 66
Cohesive set, 104 *et seq.*
Cohesive wave lotion, 110 *et seq.*
Cohesive wave set, 108 *et seq.*, *109*
Colour, 93
Colour rinses, 123 *et seq.*
Colour shampoos, 123 *et seq.*
Combustion, 9, 20 *et seq.*, 51, 57, *58*
Compound, chemical, 5
Concentration, 97 *et seq.*, 113, 117, 120
Conditioning preparations, 94, 95, *et seq.*, 120, 137 *et seq.*
Control creams, 138 *et seq.*
Copper compounds, 14, 85, 99, 121
Covalent bonds, 33
Cream preparations, 92, *93*, 100
Crimping iron, 105, *106*
Cross linkages (*see* bonds)
Cysteic acid, 120
Cysteine, 120
Cystine, 86, 102, 120

Denatured spirit, 154
Deodorants, 48
Depilatories, chemical, 79 *et seq.*, 153
Deposits and stains, 61
Detergents, 66 *et seq.*, 91, 95, 97

Detergents anionic, 66, 71, 92, 97
Detergents cationic, 67, 71, 97, 102, 119
Detergents nonionic, 68, 97, 110, 119
Diamines, 123
Diamino benzenes (*see* benzene diamines)
Dihydroxybutane dioic acid (*see* tartaric acid)
Dimethyl hydantoin methanal (formaldehyde) resin, 35
Disinfectants, 22, 48, 69, 90
Disulphide linkages, 102 *et seq.*, 106, 108
Dodecanoic acid (lauric acid), 66, 67
Dodecanol (lauryl alcohol), 67, 154
Dodecanyl sulphates, 67
Dressing preparations, 105, 137 *et seq.*
Dry powder shampoos, 91
Dust, 61
Dusting powder, 91
Dye reducers, 124
Dyes, 22, 116, 121 *et seq.*, 124, 125

Eau de Cologne, 80
Efflorescence, 14
Elements, chemical, 5, 22
Emollients, 152
Emulsifying agents, 69, 92, 93, 96, 110, 138, 153
Essential oils, 13, 14, 21, 150, 155
Esters, 154 *et seq.*
Ethane, 20
Ethanoic acid (acetic acid), 13, 22, 94, 99, 154
Ethanol (ethyl alcohol), 13, 14, 69, 80, 91, 112, 117, 154
Ethene, 34
Ethyl ethanoate (acetate), 154
Eumelanin, 115
Exothermic, 20, 91, 108, 130

Fats (*see* Lipids)
Fatty acids (*see* Alkanoic acids)

Fatty alcohols (*see also* Alcohols), 21, 154
Fibres, natural and man-made, 84 *et seq.*, 87 *et seq.*, 103
Fire, causes, 51 *et seq.*
Fire extinguishers, 52
Fixatives, 104, 105
Fixed oils, 13, 155
Flavones, 124
Fluorescence, 95, 120
Fluoride, 10
Fluorohydrocarbons (chloro-fluorohydrocarbons), 21, 52
Foam preparations, 97
Foot cream, 153
Formaldehyde (*see* methanal)
Formula, 6
Friction lotions, 149
Fuels, 9, 18, *et seq.*, 51

Gas mains supply, 18 *et seq.*
Geraniol, 156
Glucose, 34
Glutamic acid, 86
Glycerine, glycerol (*see* propane triol)
Granules melanin, 115
Gums, 21, 105

Hair
    acid nature, 122, 139
    basic nature, 122, 139
    bleaching, 119 *et seq.*
    chemical damage, 95, 145
    cleaning, 89 *et seq.*
    cold waving, 108 *et seq.*, *109*
    colour, natural, 115 *et seq.*
    colour restorers, 122 *et seq.*
    colourings, 121 *et seq.*
    composition, 6, 85 *et seq.*
    conditioners, 71, 94, *et seq.*, 131, 137 *et seq.*
    dressing preparations, 137 *et seq.*
    electrical charge, 71
    fibre, 84 *et seq.*
    keratin, 86 *et seq.*, 102, *104*
    overbleaching, 94

permanent waving, 106 *et seq.*
relaxation, 106
removers, 77 *et seq.*
rinses, 93 *et seq.*
set, 102 *et seq.*
shampoo, 91 *et seq.*, 121
straightening, 81, 110 *et seq.*
supercontraction, 81, 87
Hand cream, 152
Hard water, 62 *et seq.*, 66
Henna, 122
Hexadecanoic acid (palmitic acid), 21
Hexadecanol (cetyl alcohol), 21, 22, 154
Hexane, 91
Histidine, 86
Hydrated compounds, 14
Hydrocarbons, 20 *et seq.*, 67, 77
Hydrochloric acid, 82, 99, 112
Hydrogen, 20, 78, *85*, 98, 112 *et seq.*
Hydrogen bonds, 33, 87, 102, 105, 106, 108, 110
Hydrogen peroxide, 51, 108, 116 *et seq.*
Hydrogen sulphide, 85
Hydrolysis, 86, 107, 139 *et seq.*
Hydrophilic groups, 95, 97
Hydrophobic groups, 95, 97
Hydroxy carboxylic acids (*see* citric, lactic, salicylic, tartaric)
Hydroxyl, 128, 154

Indicators, 98, 110
Indophenols, 123
Industrial spirit, 154
Inorganic, 5, 6, 15, 98
Insecticides, 93
Ion exchange, 63
Ionic bonds, 33, 102, 108, 110
Iron compounds, 110
Isolates, 155, 157
Isoleucine, 86
Isopropyl alcohol (*see* Propanol)

Juglone, 122

Karaya gum, 21, 105

Keratin, 34, 85, 86 *et seq.*, 102 *et seq.*, 110
Keratinization, 102 *et seq.*, 115
Keratolytic agents, 80, 110, 122, 153

Lactic acid (hydroxy propanoic acid), 80, 94, 99
Lampblack, 20
Lanette waxes, 22 *et seq.*
Lanolin, 13, 21, 22, 105
Lanthionine link, 106
Lauric acid (*see* dodecanoic acid)
Lauryl alcohol (*see* dodecanol)
Lawsone, 122
Lemon, 156
Leucine, 86
Leucotrichia (white forelock), 116
Lime water (*see* calcium hydroxide)
Limonene, 156
Lipids (oils and fats), 21 *et seq.*, 66, 113, 138
Litmus, 82, 98
Lysine, 86, 106, 107
Lysinoalanine bonds, 107

Maceration, 156
Macromolecules, 6, 33, 86
Magnesium carbonate, 91, 99, 119
Magnesium hydrogen carbonate, 63
Magnesium stearate (octadecanoate), 91
Magnesium sulphate, 63, 110
Marcel heater, *106*
Mascara, 20
Massage preparations, 149
Medicaments, 93, 158
Melanin, 115, 119
Melanocytes, 115 *et seq.*
Menthol, 80, 93
Meta-compounds, 127 *et seq.*
Meta diamino benzene, *128*
Metallic bonds, 33
Metallic dyes, 121 *et seq.*
Metals, 26, 112
Methane, 20
Methanal (formaldehyde), 14, 69, *90*, 93, 105, 113, 155

Methanol (methyl alcohol), 22
Methionine, 86
Methyl benzene (toluene), *127*
Methyl butyl ethanoate (amyl acetate), 155
Methylated spirit (*see* industrial spirit)
Methylene blue, 96, 122
Mineral oils (*see* hydrocarbons)
Mirror cleaning lotion, 82
Mixtures, 6, 95
Molecules, 6, 33, 43
Monoethanolamine, 99
Monoethanolamine dodecanyl (lauryl) sulphate, 67
Monomer, 33, 88
Musk, 155, 157
Myricyl alcohol (*see* tetra-decanol)

Nail, artificial, 153
Nail cuticle preparations, 153
Nail preparations, 153
Nail varnish (lacquer), 121
Nail varnish remover, 153
Nerol, 156
Neutralization, 94, 98 *et seq.*, 110
Nitro-dyes, 99, 123 *et seq.*, 128
Nitrogen, 5, 56, 85, 86
Non-ionic detergents (*see* detergents)

Octadecanoic acid (stearic acid), 21, 99
Octadec-9-enoic acid (oleic acid), 21, 113
Octadecanol (stearyl alcohol), 154
Oils and fats (*see* lipids)
Oleic acid (*see* octadec-9-enoic acid)
Olive oil, 13
Organic compounds, 5, 6, 15, 98, 113
Opacifying agents, 93
Ortho compounds, 127 *et seq.*
Ortho diamino benzene, *128*
Over bleaching, 94
Oxidation, 51, 57, 108, 110,

116, 117
Oxidation dyes, 121 *et seq.*, 123
Oxides, 57 *et seq.*
Oxygen, 17, 51, 57, 85, 119
Ozone, 48, 148, 150

Palm oil, 66
Palmitic acid (*see* hexadecanoic acid)
Para-compounds, 127 *et seq.*
Para diamino benzene, *128*
Paraffin hydrocarbons, 20
Paraffins, soft, hard and liquid, 13, 20, 138, 148
Penetrating dyes, 121 *et seq.*, 125
Peptide bonds, 86, 102
Percentage strength, 82, 97, 117
Perfumes, 83, 110, 155 *et seq.*
Permanent dyes, 123 *et seq.*
Permanent set, 104
Permanent water hardness, 63
Peroxides, 51
Persulphates, 51
pH, 98 *et seq.*, *100*
Phenolic compounds, 22, 69, 123, 127 *et seq.*, 155
Phenols, 155 *et seq.*
Phenylalanine, 86
Pheomelanin, 115
Pigments, 121
Plastic bonded colours, 121, 122
Plasticisers, 153
Plastics, 22, 33, 34, 84
Polymers, 33 *et seq.*, 88, 116
Polypeptide, 86, 102
Polysaccharides, 34
Post-bleaching preparations, 120
Post-dyeing preparations, 124
Potassium compounds, 108
Preservatives, 93, 105
Pre-shave lotion, 80
Proline, 86
Propane, 20
Propanetriol (glycerine), 15, 21 *et seq.*, 66, 80, 117, 148, 153, 154
Propanol (propyl alcohol), 13, 69, 154
Propanone (acetone), 15, 22, 155

Protein hydrolysate, 86, 139
Proteins, 34, 86 *et seq.*
Protofibrils, 85, 87, 88
Pyrogallol (*see* benzene triol)

Quaternary ammonium compounds, 67, 72, 95, 102, 119, 139
Quinols, 116
Quinone diimine, 123
Quinones, 116, 122

Reduction, 113 *et seq.*, 117, 121

Salicylic acid (hydroxy benzene carboxylic acid), 80, 93, 99, 117
Salon cleaning, 61 *et seq.*
Salon fuels, 18 *et seq.*
Salon gas system, 18 *et seq.*
Salts, 98 *et seq.*
Saponification, 66, 72, 139
Scale, 62
Scouring preparations, 68
Sebum, 21, 91, 95
Selenium compounds, 80, 93
Semipermanent dyes, 121 *et seq.*, 123
Serine, 86
Set, 103 *et seq.*
Setting preparations, 104 *et seq.*, 122
Shampoo, 91 *et seq.*, *100*
Shaving preparations, 80
Shellac, 15, 105
Silicones, 95, 153
Silver compounds, 113, 117, 121
Soap, 66 *et seq.*, 68, 72, 80, 91, 92, 100
Soapless detergents, 66 *et seq.*, 68, 72, 91, 92
Sodium
    bromate, 108
    carbonates, 64, 92, 119
    chloride, 81, 93
    dodecanoate (laurate), 66
    dodecanyl (lauryl) sulphate, 92, 93
    hexametaphosphate, 64
    hydroxide, 66, 79, 82, 99

perborate, 108, 110
sulphate, 93
sulphide, 80, 122
sulphite, 110
Soft soap, 66, 72
Soft water, 63
Soils, 61 *et seq.*, 89 *et seq.*
Solvents, 20, 68, 91, 156
Spermaceti, 21, 138
Spirit lotion, 91
Stabilizers, 93, 96 *et seq.*, 110, 117
Starches, 34
Stearic acid (*see* octadecanoic acid)
Stearyl alcohol (*see* octadecanol)
Sulphonated compounds, 66
Sulphur, 72, 85, *86*, 102
Sulphur compounds, 48, 57, 63, 72, 80, 85, 86, 99, 122, 124
Sunburn preparations, 148
Sunscreen compounds, 148
Surfactants (*see* detergents)
Sweeping compounds, 69, 70

Symbols, 5

Talcum powders, 91
Tartaric acid (dihydroxy butanedoic acid), 122
Temporary dyes, 121
Temporary set, 104, 105 *et seq.*
Temporary water hardness, 62
Terpenes, 21, 93, 156 *et seq.*
Terpineol, 156
Tetrachloroethane, 91
Tetradecanol (myricyl alcohol), 21
Thioglycollic acid (*see* thiol-ethanoic acid)
Thiol groups, 108
Thiolethanoic acid (thioglycollic acid), 80, 99, 109, 110
Threonine, 86
Thymol, 93
Titan yellow, 96
Tragacanth gum, 21, 105
Triethanolamine, 69, 72, 91, 99
Triethanolamine dodecanyl (lauryl) sulphate, 67

Tryptophan, 86
Tyrosinase, 116
Tyrosine, 115, 116

Undecylenic acid, 93

Valine, 86
Vegetable oils, 21
Vegetable (plant) dyes, 121
Volatile oils, 13, 155
Volume strength, *117 et seq.*

Washing, 70, 91 *et seq.*, 121
Water, 14, 98
Water distilled, 118, 119
Water hardness, 62, *et seq.*
Water softeners, 63
Waxes, 13, 20, 21 *et seq.*, 79, 138
Wigs, 20, 34, 91, 103

Yellowing hair, 120, 121

Zinc compounds, 91, 99, 112

PHYSICAL

Accelerator, 109
Accidents, 5
Actinotherapy, 146
Adaptors, 133
Adhesion, 62, 89
Adsorption, 62, 89
Air conditioning, 47
Air pressure (*see* pressure, air)
Alternating current (A.C.), 26, *141*, 152
Ampere, 26, 28, 133
Anaeroid barometer, 23
Anode, 78
Area, 7
Armature, *140*
Atmosphere (*see* air)
Atmospheric pressure (*see* pressure, air)

Atom, 5, 33 *et seq.*
Autoclave, 90

Balance, 7
Ball valve, 11, 70
Barometer, *23 et seq.*
Bimetal strip, 40, 41
Blow drying, 131
Boiling, 13
Breaking force, hair, 80
Brush styling, 106
Brushes, generator, 25, *140*
Burette, *12*

Cabinet sterilizer, *90*
Cables, electric, 27, 32
Caliper, 6
Calorie (*see* kilojoule)

Capillarity, 7, 69
Carbon arc lamp, 146, *147*
Cathode, 78
Ceilings, 3, 27, 56
Celsius scale, *42*
Centimetre, 6
Central heating, 38 *et seq.*, *39*
Change of state, 13 *et seq.*
Circuit breakers, 27, 32 *et seq.*
Circuit electrical, 27
Cisterns, 11, 12, 70
Cohesion, 89
Colour, 124
Colour code (electrical), 135 *et seq.*
Colour mixing, 126 *et seq.*
Commutator, 25, 26, *140*, *141*

Concave mirrors and lenses, 82, *83*
Concentration, 97 *et seq.*
Condensation, 9, 13 *et seq.*, *49 et seq.*
Condensers, 14
Conduction, electrical, 27, 28, 33
Conduction, heat, 37 *42*, 106
Conduit, electrical, 28
Continuous phase, 96
Convection, 37, 43 *et seq.*, *44*, *59*, 65, 90
Convector heaters, 38, 39
Convex mirrors and lenses, 82, 83
Cooling effect evaporation, 130
Cortex hair, 84, 88, 102, 109, 115, 121, 130
Costs, gas and electrical, 19, 29
Cuticle, hair, 84, 94, 109

Damp, 4, 49
Daylighting, 53
Density, 107, 111
Depilation, physical, 13, 20
Detergent action, 95, *96*, *97*
Dew point, 9
Diathermy, 78 *et seq.*, 150 *et seq.*
Diffusion, 53, 56, 58, 90, 115
Direct current (D.C.), *25*, 26, 78, 140, 141, 152
Disperse phase, 96
Displacement vessel, 12
Distillation, 6, 13 *et seq.*
Distillation, steam, *13*, 21, 155 *et seq.*
Distributive installation, electrical, 27, *30*
Double insulation, 78, 134
Drainage system, 4, 70, *71*
Draught excluders, 41
Draughts, 50 *et seq.*
Drinking water, 11, 12
Drying, 130 *et seq.*
Dust and dirt, 61 *et seq.*, 89 *et seq.*
Dynamo, 25, *141*

Earth wire and earthing, 28, 106, 133 *et seq.*, 135 *et seq.*, *136*

Effort, 77, 81
Elastic limit, hair, 80
Elasticity, hair, *80 et seq.*, *81*, 87
Electric circuits, *27 et seq.*
Electric costs, 28, 29
Electric current, 25, 33, 43, 141
Electric heaters, 38, 43, 132
Electric motor, 132, *140*
Electric shock, 137, 145, 151
Electrode, 18, 152
Electrolysis, 78 *et seq.*, *79*, 81, 152
Electrolyte, 78
Electromagnetic waves, 43, 143 *et seq.*
Electromagnetism, 25, *140*
Electrons, 26, 33, 71, 113, 143 *et seq.*, 150
Electrostatics, 71, 87, 95, 97, 102
Emulsions, 95, 110, 120
Endocuticle, 84
Energy, 17 *et seq.*, *23 et seq.*, 25, 149
Enfleurage, 156
Epicuticle, 84, 95
Epilation physical, 77 *et seq.*, 150 *et seq.*
Evaporation, 9, 13 *et seq.*, 130 *et seq.*
Exocuticle, 84
Expansion, heat, 41, 42
Extractor fan, 50

Fahrenheit scale, *42*
Faradic treatment, *152 et seq.*
Filament lamps, 43, 125
Filtration, 6, 10, *15*, 16, 48, 91
Fire alarm, 53
Flammable substances, 14, 52
Flexes, 134 *et seq.*
Floors, 3, 41
Flues and chimneys, 19, 48, 50
Fluid, 7, 41
Fluorescence, 55, 90
Fluorescent lamps, *54*, 55, 125, *147*
Forceps, 77
Foundations, 3
Frequency, 25, 78, 90, 149 *et seq.*, 152

Friction, 77, 149
Fuses, 27, 31 *et seq.*, *32*, 133
Fusion (*see* melting)

Galvanic treatment, 152 *et seq.*
Gamma radiation, 144
Gas, 3, 13
Gas costs, 19
Gas heaters, *38*
Gas salon supply, 18 *et seq.*
Glare, 56
Gramme, 7
Greenhouse effect, 54
Gully, 4, 70

Hair
    clippers, 78, 149
    cortex, *84 et seq.*, 115
    cuticle, *84 et seq.*
    dryers, 131 *et seq.*, *132*
    drying, 47, 130 *et seq.*
    elasticity, *80 et seq.*, 87, 95
    form and shape, 102 *et seq.*, 115
    hygrometer, *58*
    medulla, *84 et seq.*
    moisture content, 95
    porosity, 95
    removal, 77 *et seq.*
    stretching, 80
    supercontraction, 81 *et seq.*, 87
    texture, 95, 115, 131
    treatments, 143 *et seq.*
    washing, 47
Head of water, 12, 25
Heat, 18, 36, 51, 78, 144, 145
Heat pumps, 18
Heat sources, 36 *et seq.*, 132, 144
Heat transfer, 37 *et seq.*, 106
Heating appliances, 37 *et seq.*, *38*, 47
Heating controls, 40 *et seq.*
Hertz, 25, 78, 150
High frequency treatment, 149 *et seq.*, *150*
Horse power, 132
Hosing, 70
Hot permanent waving, 106 *et seq.*, *108*

Hot water system salon, 40, 41
  64, et seq.
Humidifiers, 49
Humidity, 48 *et seq.*, 57, 130
Hydrometer, *112*, 118
Hygrometers, *58*
Hygroscopic, 14, 49 *et seq.*,
  80, 95

Image formation mirrors, 82
  et seq.
Incinerator, 70
Induced current, 152
Induction coils, *152*
Infra red appliances, 109, 132,
  144
Infra red radiation, 37, 43, 54,
  109, 132, 144
Inspection chamber, 70, 71
Insulators electrical, 27, 33, 71,
  78, *135*
Insulators heat, 11, 43, 106
Insulators sound, *41*
Inverse square law, *145 et seq.*

Joule, 23, 28
Jumper tap, 11

Kilogramme, 7
Kilohertz, 150
Kilojoule, 23
Kilometre, 6
Kilopascal, 7, 23, 90, 118, 150,
  151
Kilowatt, 28
Kilowatt hour, 28 *et seq.*, 36

Lagging, 11, 41, 65
Lampholder, *55*
Lampshades, *56*
Lamps electric, *54*, 55, 132
Latent heat, 13
Length, 7
Lenses, *83 et seq.*
Levers, *81 et seq.*
Light, 47, 53, 59, 115, 126
Lighting circuits, 29 *et seq.*,
  54 et seq.
Liquids, 5, 13, 109
Litre, 12, 118
Live conductor (positive), 27,

133, 134, *136*
Load, 77, 81
Loading of electrical appliance
  and circuits, 28 *et seq.*,
  31, 52
Lubrication, 77, 80

Macrofibrils, *85 et seq.*, 88
Magnetic effect electric current,
  140
Magnetism, *139*
Magnifiers, *83*
Main electric supply, 27
Manometer gas, 23
Marcel waving iron, *106*
Mass (*see* weight)
Massage vibrator machine,
  148, *149*
Matrix, 130
Matter, 5, 11, 12
Measurement, 7 *et seq.*, *12*
Measuring cylinder, *12*
Mechanical advantage, 78
Medulla hair, 84
Megajoule, 23 *et seq.*
Melting (fusion), 13
Meniscus, 12
Mercury, 7
Mercury vapour lamp, 146,
  147
Meters, 19, 26, 27
Metre, 6
Microfibrils, 85, 88
Microgramme, 7
Micrometer, 7
Microscopes, 84, 115
Milliamperes, 26, 78
Milligramme, 7
Millilitre, 12, 118
Millimetre, 6
Millivolts, 26
Mirrors, 82 *et seq.*, *83*
Motor, 132, *140*

Nanometre, 143
Neutral conductor (negative),
  27, 133, 134, *136*
Neutrons, 33
Nichrome, 26, 43

Ohm, 26

Ohm's law, 26
Opal lamp, 56
Opaque substances, 53
Orthocortex, *84*, 102, 115
Oscillator circuit, *150*
Overflow pipe, 11, 66
Overloading (*see* loading, electri-
  cal)

Paracortex, *84*, 102, 115
Parallel arrangement, *29*, 132
Pascal, 7, 23
Pearl lamps, 56
Peroxometer, 118
Phototendering, 121, 147, 148
Physical changes, 111
Pigments, 126
Pipettes, *12*
Plane mirrors, 82, *83*
Plugs, electric, 31, 133 *et seq.*,
  134
Pomade, 156, 157
Power, electric, 29
Power electric socket outlets,
  26, 31, 32, 34, 52, *133*
Pressure, 7
Pressure, air, 7, 23 *et seq.*, *118*
Pressure, solid, 7, 77
Pressure, water, 7, 12 *et seq.*,
  13
Prism, *83*, 124
Protofibrils, 85, 87, 88
Protons, 33

Radiant energy, 143 *et seq.*
Radiation, 37, 43, 131
Radiators, 38, 39
Radio, 143, 144, 149
Razors, *77 et seq.*
Rectifier, 26, 78
Reflection, 53, 55, *59*, *82*, *83*,
  115
Refraction, 53, *59*, *83 et seq.*,
  115
Refrigeration, 18
Relative density, 112
Relative humidity, 49, 58
Reservoirs, 10
Resistance, 26, 27, 43, 44
Resonator circuit, 150
Ring main electrical circuit, 27

Rising main, 10
Rodding eye, 70, 71
Roller heating, *106*
Roof, *3*, *41*
Rotor, 25
Rubbish disposal, 70

Salon
    damp, 49 *et seq.*
    electricity, 25 *et seq.*, *28*, 135
    energy balance, 17 *et seq.*
    environment, 46 *et seq.*
    gas system, 18 *et seq.*, *19*
    heating, 36 *et seq.*, 48, 50
    humidity, 48, 49
    lighting, 53 *et seq.*, 125
    premises structure, 3 *et seq.*, *4*
    ventilation, 49, 51
    waste system, 70, 71
    water supply, 9 *et seq.*, *64*
Scalp treatments, 143 *et seq.*
Scissors, *78*
Separation, 15, 16
Series arrangement, *29*, 30, 132
Service pipe, 10
Sewage system, 70, 71
Shavers, 78, 149
Shaving mirror, 78
Short circuit, *31*
Shuttered socket outlet, 26, 31, *133*
Soakaway, 2
Soil pipe, 70
Solids, 7, 13, 109
Solubility, 15, 22, 90
Soluble, 15
Solute, 15
Solution, 15 *et seq.*, 90, 114, 120
Spectrum, electromagnetic, 143, *144*
Spectrum, light, 124 *et seq.*, *125*
Spot lighting, 55, 56

Stack pipe, 70, 71
Static electricity, 71, 87, 95, 97, 102
Steam distillation (*see* distillation, steam)
Steamer, 80, 81, *109*, 150
Sterilization, 10
Sterilizing cabinet, *90*
Stone grinding, 77
Stop tap or valve, 10, 19
Strength of solutions, 82 *et seq.*
Sun (solar) energy, 17 *et seq.*, 36, 144, 146
Supercontraction, hair, 81 *et seq.*
Surface area, 7, 130, 131
Surface tension, 7, 95 *et seq.*, 131
Suspensions, 10, 14, 15, 16, 96
Switches, electrical, 33, 34, 132
Synthesis, 6

Taps, draw-off, 11
Temperature, 42 *et seq.*, 113, 120, 130
Therm, 19
Thermometers, 42, *43*
Thermostats, 40, 132, 133
Three heat switch, 132, *133*
Three pin plug, electric, 133, *134*, *135*
Time switch, 27, 40
Towel drying, 131
Transformers, 27
Translucent, 53
Transparent, 53, 115
Traps, sink, *65*
Tungsten filament lamps, 43
Two-pin electric plugs, 133

Ultra-sonic radiation, 90
Ultra-violet radiation, 48, 89, 90, 95, 121, 144, 146 *et seq.*, 150

Ultra-violet treatment, 146, *147*
Under floor heating, 29
Unit of electricity, 23, 28 *et seq.*

Vacuum, 70
Vacuum treatment, 150 *et seq.*
Van der Waal's forces, 89, 102, 111
Ventilation, 3, 5, 14, 19, 40, 47, 49
Volatile, 13
Volt, 26, 27
Voltage, 26
Volume, 11, 111

Walls, *3*, *41*, 56
Washbasin, 65
Washer, tap, 11
Waste pipe, 66, 70
Water closets, 70
Water
    cycle, *9 et seq.*
    freezing, 11, 13
    heaters, 43, *44*, 65
    pressure, 12, *13*
    salon supply, 9 *et seq.*, *11*, 62, 136
    seal, 70
    treatment, 10 *et seq.*
    usage, 11, 12
Watt, 28
Wattage, 29, 31, 55, 132
Wavelength, 125, 133, 143
Weight, 7, 111
Wind, 50, 130
Windows, 3, 41, 53
Wireless waving machine, 107
Wiring of salons, 52
Woods light, 89, 146
Work, 17

X radiation, 143, *144*

BIOLOGICAL

Absorption, 171
Accident prevention, 229
Acid poisons, 227
Acne, 205
Adenosine triphosphate (ATP), 18, 178, 217
Ageing of skin, 207
Agranulocytosis, 181
Air, 175
    conditioning; purity, 223
Albinism, 116
Albumin, 179
Alimentary canal, 169
Alkaline poisons, 227
Allergy, 206
Alopecia, 195, 205, 206
Alveoli, 176, 177
Amino-acids, 167, 171
Amylase, 170
Anaemia – types, 180
Antibodies, 179
Antidote, 227
Antigens (agglutinogens), 179
Antiseptic, 220, 221
Aponeurosis, 192
Appendicular skeleton, 214
Arrector muscles, 196, 217
Arteries, 164, 182
Artificial respiration (resuscitation), 228, 229
Athlete's foot, 211
Atmosphere, 175
Autoclave, 220
Autonomic nervous system, 189
Axial skeleton, 214
Axon, 185, 186

Bacilli, 202, 203
Bacteria, 202, 203
Baldness, 194
Ball and socket joint, 215
Barber's itch, 203
Bath, 209
Bile, 170, 171
Blackheads, 204, 205
Bladder, urinary, 172, 173
Bleeding, 180
Blood, 178, 179,
    diseases, 180,
    groups, 179,
    formation, 180,

vessels, 182,
vessels of heart, skin, 181, 195
Boils, 203
Bone, 214
Bones, of cranium, 161,
    of face, 162
Bowman's capsule, 173
Brain, 186, 187
Breathing, 176, 177,
    control, mechanism, 176, 177
Bronchi, 176
Buccinators, 162
Burns, 227

Cabinet sterilizers, 221
Calcium salts, 168
Canities, 205
Capillaries, 164, 173, 183, 193, 195
Carbamide, 172, 173, 179
Carbohydrates, 167, 170, 172
Carbon, 167, 168
Cardiac muscle, 181, 217
Carotid artery, 164
Catalyst, 170
Cavities, 116, 170, 172, 175
Cells, 166
Cenral nervous system, 186
Cerebellum, 187
Cerebrum, 186
Chest cavity, 175
Chilblains, 207
Chordae tendineae, 181, 182
Chyme, 171
Circulation, 178, 182
Clothes (body) louse, 204
Clothing, 40, 212
Cocci, 201, 202, 203
Cold, common, sores, 204
Colon, 170
Colony, bacterial, 202
Comedones, 205
Conditioned reflex, 188
Conduction, 195
Conjunctivitis, 203
Contraception, 213
Contraction, muscular, 216, 217
Control, of body, 185
Convection, 195
Convector heaters, 222

Co-ordination, 185
Copulation, 190
Cortex, of hair, 194,
    of kidney, 172, 173
Cotton, 212
Crab louse, 204, 213
Cranial nerves, 163, 187, 188
Cranium, 161
Cuticle, hair, 194
    of nails, 210
Cuts, 226

Dandruff, 205
Defaecation, 172
Deficiency diseases, 168, 169
Demodex folliculorum, 204
Dendrites, 186
Dendrons, 185, 186
Deportment, 214
Dermal papilla, 193, 194
Dermatitis, 123, 124, 169, 205, 206
Dermis, 192, 193
Diaphragm, 176, 177
Diet, 172, 211
Dietary fibre, 169, 172
Digestion, 139, 167, 169, 171
Digestive juices, 170, 171,
    system, 167
Diplococci, 202
Disaccharides, 167
Diseases, disorders of skin, 201, 203, 204, 205, 206
Disinfectants, 220, 221
Disinfecting cabinet, 221
Drains, 222
Drinking, 213, 214
Dust, 201, 221

Ectoparasites, 204
Eczema, 205
Effectors, 185, 188
Electric shock, 137, 145, 150, 228
Embryo, 190
Emetic, 227
Endocrines, 189
Energy, 167, 175, 178
Enterokinase, 170, 171
Enzymes, 114, 170, 171
Epidermis, 192, 193

Epiglottis, 176
Epilepsy, 228
Erythema, 145, 147, 206
Erythrocytes, 178, 179
Ethmoid bone, 161
Excretion, 9, 47, 172
Excretory system, 172, 173
Exercise, 216, 218
Expiration, 176, 177
Extraction fans, 223

Face, bones of, 162
Face mite, 204
Facial, artery, 164,
    muscles, nerves, 162, 163
Faeces, 172
Fainting, 226
Fan, extractor, 223
    heater, 222
Fats (lipids), 168, 170-1
Favus, 203
Feet, care of, 210, 211
Fertilization, 190
Fibres, muscle, 216,
    nerve, 186, 187
Fibrinogen, 179
Finger prints, 192
Fire, extinguishers, precautions,
    230
First aid, 226, 227, 228, 229
Fits, 228
Flagella, 201, 202
Flea, 205
Foetus, 190
Follicle, hair, 193, 195
Food nutrients, 167, 168
Footwear, 211
Foramen magnum, 186
Formalin, 221
Fractures, 228
Fragilitis artefactus, 206
Freckles, 206
Frontal bone, 161
Fungi, 203
Fur, 212

Gametes, 189
Gas fires, 222
Gastric glands, juice, 170, 171
Gestation, 190
Gingivitis, 212

Globulin, 179
Glomerulus, 173
Glucose, 167
Glycerine (propanetriol), 168,
    171
Glycogen, 168
Gonorrhoea, 213
Goose pimples, 196
Granulocytes, 178, 179
Grey matter, 186, 187
Growth, factors affecting hair,
    194

Haemoglobin, 178, 180
Haemophilia, 181
Hair, growth cycle, 194
    care of, 209
    structure, 193, 194
Hands, care of, 210
Head, anatomy of, 161
Head louse, 204
Health and Safety at Work Act,
    225, 226
Heart, 181
Heat, energy, 175
    regulation in the skin, 195
Heating in the salon, 222
Henle, loop of, 173
Herpes, 204, 213
Hinge joint, 215
Hirsuties, 205
Holger Nielsen method of
    artificial respiration,
    229
Hormones, 189, 190
Human body, organization, 166
Humidity, 222
Hydrogen peroxide, 221
Hygiene, in the salon, 219,
    personal, 209
Hyperidrosis, 195

Idiosyncrasy, 206
Impetigo, 203
Impulse, 188
Infection, 203, 204
Inferior maxilla, 162
Inflammation, 179, 203, 210
Infra-red heater, 222
Ingrowing nails, 210
Insertion, muscle, 216

Inspiration, 176, 177
Intercostal muscles, 177
Intra-uterine devices, 213
Involuntary muscle, 217
Iodine, 168, 189, 192
Iron, 168, 178, 180
Islets of Langerhans, 189
Itch mite, 204

Jaw, 162
Joints, 215, 216
Joule, 172
Jugular vein, 164

Keratin, 167, 192
Kidney, 172, 173

Labour, 190
Lachrymal bones, 162
Lactase, 170, 171
Lanugo hairs, 194
Larynx, 176
Leather, 212
Leucocytes, 178, 179
Leucotrichia, 116
Leukaemia, 180, 181
Lice, 204
Ligaments, 215
Linen, 212
Lipase, 171
Lipids (fats), 168, 170, 171
Lungs, 175, 176, 177
Lymph, 183
Lymphatic system, 183
Lymphocytes, 179, 183

Malar bone, 162
Malaria, 180
Malpighian layer, 192, 193
Maltase, 170, 171
Maltose, 168, 170, 171
Mandibular nerve, 164
Massage, 163
Masseter muscle, 163
Maxilla, 162
Maxillary nerve, 164
Medulla, of hair, 194
    of kidney, 172
    of brain, 187
Medullary sheath, 186
Melanin, 192, 206

Mental health, 213
Menopause, 190
Menstruation, 190
Methanal, 221
Microbes, 47, 48, 62, 90, 147, 201, 219
Microsporon, 203
Milk, 167
Mineral salts, 168
Mixed nerves, 187, 188
Molecules, 171
Moles, 206
Monilethrix, 206
Moniliasis, 212
Monocytes, 179
Monosaccharides, 167, 170
Motor nerves, 187
Movement, 216, 217
Muscle, 216, 217
Muscles, of face and head, 162
   of neck, 163
Muscle fatigue, 217
Muscle tone, 216
Muscular system, 216

Nails, 210
Nail disorders, 210
Narcotic poisons, 227
Nasal, bones, 162
   passages, 176
Nephron, 173
Nerve fibre, 186, 187
Nerves, 187, 188
Nervous system, 185
Neurones, 185, 186, 187
Nitrogen, 167
Nitrogenous waste, 172
Nits, 204
Non-pathogens, 201
Non-specific urethritis, 213
Nose bleeding, 226
Nucleus, 12, 166
Nutrients, 167, 168
Nutrition, 167
Nylon, 212

Occipital artery, 164
   bone, 161
Occipito-frontalis muscle, 162
Oesophagus, 170
Ocstrogen, 189

Oils and fats, 168
Ophlthalmic nerve, 164
Orbicularis, oculi, oris, 163
Organs, 166
Origin of muscles, 216
Ova, 189, 190
Ovulation, 190
Oxidation, 168, 175, 178, 217
Oxygen, 168, 177, 178
Oxyhaemoglobin, 178, 183

Palate bones, 162
Pancreas, 170
Papillae, 193, 204
Parasites, 204
Parasympathetic nervous system, 189
Parathyroid glands, 189
Parietal bone, 161
Parturition, 190
Pathogens, 201, 220
Pediculi, 204
Pediculosis, 204
Pepsin, 170, 171
Peptidases, 170, 171
Peripheral nerves, 187
Peristalsis, 170
Perspiration, 195
Phagocytosis, 179
Pharynx, 176
Phenolic compounds, 221
Phosphates, 168
Pituitary gland, 189
Pityriasis, 205
Pivot joint, 216
Placenta, 190
Plantar warts, 204
Plasma, blood, 179
Platelets, blood, 179
Platysma, 163
Pleural membrane, 175
Poisons, 227
Polypeptides, 170, 171
Polysaccharides, 168
Pores, 193, 195
Posture, 214
Pregnancy, 189, 190
Progesterone, 189, 190
Proteins, 167, 170, 171, 172
Proteoses, 170, 171
Prothrombin, 179

Psoriasis, 205
Pterygoid muscle, 162
Pothirius pubis, 204
Ptyalin (salivary amylase), 170
Puberty, 190
Pulmonary circulation, 182

Quarternary ammonium compounds, 221

Radiation, 195, 222
Receptors, 185, 188
Recovery position, 229
Reflex, action, arc, 188
Reproductive system, 189, 190
Respiration, 9, 18, 20, 57, 172, 175, 177, 178, 217
Respiratory system, 175
Rest, importance of, 216, 217
Resuscitation, 228, 229
Rhesus factor, 180
Ringworm, honeycomb, 203
   of nails, 210,
   of scalp, 203
Root, of hair, 194
   of tooth, 211
Roughage (dietary fibre), 169, 172, 212, 228
Rubber, 212, gloves, 228

Safety, in the salon, 225
Salivary glands, 170, 171
Salts, mineral, 168
Scabies, 204
Scalds, 227
Scalp, 192, 202, 203
Sebaceous glands, 193, 195
Seborrhoea, 205
Sebum, 193, 195, 209
Sensory nerves, 186, 187
   neurones, 186
Sexually transmitted diseases, 213
Shampooing, 163, 209
Shock, symptoms, 226, 227
Silk, 212
Skeleton, 214, 215
Skeletal muscles, 216
   system, 214
Skin, care of, 209
   structure, 192, 193

Skull, 161, 162
Smoking, 47, 176, 213
Small intestine, 170, 171
Social habits, 213
Sodium chloride, 168
Spermatozoa, 189
Sphenoid bone, 161
Spinal cord, 186, 187, 188, 189
    nerves, 188
Spine, 186, 214, 215, 216
Spirilla, 201
Spirochaetes, 201
Spores, 201, 219, 220
Staphylococci, 202, 203
Starch, 167, 168, 170
Sterilization, 90, 219, 220
Sterno-cleido mastoid muscle,
    163
Stimulus, 185, 187, 188
Stomach, 170, 171, 213
Strata, of skin, 193
Streptococci, 202
Stress, 213
Sub-cutaneous fat, 193, 196
Sudoriferous glands, 193, 195
Sugars, 167, 170
Sunburn, 206
Superior maxillae, 162
Supra-renal glands, 189
Sutures, 162, 215
Sweat glands, 193, 195
Sweating, 9, 47, 172, 195

Sycosis, 203
Sympathetic nervous system,
    189
Synapse, 188
Systemic circulation, 182
Systems of the body, 166

Tactile corpuscles, 193
Teeth, 211, 212
Temperature control, 186, 195
Temporal, artery, 164
    bone, 161,
    muscles, 162
Testes, 189
Testosterone, 190
Thoracic duct, 183
Thrombocytes, 179
Thyroid gland, 189
Tinea, 203
Tissues, 166, 216, 217
Trachea, 176
Trapezius muscle, 163
Traps, 222
Trichomatosis, 203
Trichonodosis, 206
Trichophyton, 203
Trigeminal nerve, 164
Trypsin, 170, 171
Turbinate bones, 162
Twentieth century disease, 206

Unconsciousness, 226

Underfloor heating, 222
Urea (carbamide), 172, 173,
    179
Ureter, 172, 173
Urethra, 173
Urine, 173
Urticaria, (nettle-rash), 206

Valves, of heart, 181, 182
    of veins, 183
Vasectomy, 213
Veins, 164, 183
Ventilation, 222, 223
Verruca, 204
Vertebrae, 215, 216
Villi, 171
Viruses, 202, 204
Vitamins, 147, 168, 169, 180
Voluntary muscles, 216
Vomer bone, 162

Warts, 204
Washbasins, 222
Water, in diet, 169
White forelock, 116
White matter, 186, 187
Windpipe, 176
Wool, 212
Wounds, 226

Zygomatic process, 162
Zygote, 190